THE UNACCEPTABLE FACE

A 21st century story of an itinerant career under apartheid,
European socialism and disparate iterations of capitalism, laced
with corporate politics and skullduggery

by

FLEMMING HEILMANN

TELEMACHUS PRESS

THE UNACCEPTABLE FACE

Cover designed by Telemachus Press, LLC

Cover art:
Copyright © iStockPhoto/518838319/anttohoho

Published by Telemachus Press, LLC
7652 Sawmill Road
Suite 304
Dublin, Ohio 43016
http://www.telemachuspress.com

ISBN: 978-1-948046-41-1 (eBook)
ISBN: 978-1-948046-42-8 (Paperback)
ISBN: 978-1-948046-70-1 (Hardback)

CATEGORY: BIOGRAPHY & AUTOBIOGRAPHY / Political

Version 2019.09.23

To Judy

... always perceptive, ever deft navigator in both calm and roiled waters

Acknowledgements

I have sought and received perceptive advice and great help in writing and editing this story. I am immensely appreciative and grateful. My wife, Judy, has been particularly perceptive, patient and supportive. Steve Himes, Karen Lieberman and MaryAnn Nocco of Telemachus Press could not have been more responsive and professional in meeting my every need. I thank them all.

Prologue

DEMOCRATIC FREE MARKET capitalism has a lot of critics and enemies around the world. It is indeed an imperfect system with which to govern, maintain civic order, or promote economic, technological and social progress to serve a fast-growing global population; but, so far, history has clearly demonstrated that it is the only sustainable system that allows the continuing creation of incremental wealth, which is essential to finance civic order, civilized society and enduring progress in human living standards. The generation of surplus resources is the *sine qua non* for improving the plight of man. The sustainable gains generated via the capitalist system, warts and all, by far outweigh any and all of its flaws and injustices. History has demonstrated just that, repeatedly, over thousands of years. Marxism, socialism, fascism and other totalitarian and tribal systems have all failed mankind, as have all manner of theocracies. All these alternatives have left a measure of destitution, and sometimes anarchy, in their wake.

Almost inevitably, when free market capitalist systems fail, it is because they have been misused or abused by individuals, by civic or religious organizations, by corporations or indeed by governments.

These personal conclusions are far from unique or original, but they are anchored in personal experience and supported by history and by observation in the course of an unusually itinerant childhood, education and working career spanning eight decades, four continents, disparate cultures and concepts of governance. Lessons were learned from life and its realities, sometimes at the edge of fascism and apartheid, at other times under extreme socialism or disparate versions of free market capitalism.

As described in my first book, *Odyssey Uncharted*, published in 2017, I was born of Danish parents in colonial British Malaya in 1936. My father worked there for a Danish plantation company. Geopolitical convulsions, the perils of World War II in South East Asia, time as a refugee in Australia and then teenage years in Denmark and England during post-war recovery provided the backdrop for the views of the world I hold today. My parents, known as PB and Mor (my father's given names were Poul Bent and all Danish moms are called *Mor*), were unswerving examples to me, always exercising a compelling sense of fairness and duty to society. This wide base of experience helped mold the personal opinions and conclusions I hold today.

My schooling spanned Australia, Denmark—where I sank deep, cultural roots—and then England for formative teen years before going on to graduate from Cambridge with a law degree. Personal edification and time-tested perceptions were derived from a kaleidoscopic life and events in colonial Malaya and its post-war communist insurgency, wartime Australia, Nordic socialism in egalitarian Denmark, the raw tribal culture of Swaziland under British rule and South Africa giving birth to the horror of apartheid. During the post-war years I developed an appreciation of America's pivotal role in the rehabilitation of war-torn Europe and in saving many millions from starvation. I saw and came to understand the power and capacity of the mighty US economic engine driving human progress—whether it be economic, technological or social progress.

This story starts at the end of my 1959 voyage from the UK to South Africa, as I disembark to take up my first real job in Johannesburg. That was almost two years after graduating, emerging from the academic cocoon of Cambridge and then undergoing hands-on training in the grimy heartland of industrial Britain. My training with Metal Box Company immersed me in the realities of the blue-collar workman's life. I had been given a one-way passage to Cape Town. Metal Box Company of South Africa Ltd. was the group's largest subsidiary, a public company listed on the Johannesburg Stock Exchange. The new Nationalist government was feeling its oats and getting busy with its mission to write discrimination and racial segregation—apartheid—into the constitution.

The abuse and misuse of the capitalist free market system, wherever and whenever it happens, is heinous, destructive, antisocial, unpardonable and should be uncompromisingly punished. Mostly, alas, the individual perpetrators and leaders of the guilty corporations, government institutions and other entities go unpunished as financial or political settlements are reached—without prosecuting the actual perpetrators, who walk away scot free. Too often, the abusive behavior goes undetected or simply unchallenged. It persists because insufficient action is taken to eradicate it. That is the major contributor to the unacceptable face of capitalism.

My title for the book derives from UK Prime Minister Edward Heath's 1983 characterization—in the House of Commons, no less—of the convicted Tiny Rowland, infamous corporate fraudster, tax evader and con man. Heath pronounced him to be the "unpleasant and unacceptable face of capitalism." Rowland had been found guilty of cheating and gross criminal misconduct under UK laws and those of multiple African states. He was the CEO of Lonrho, a large Anglo-African business conglomerate, who finally got caught with his fraudster's hand in a whole bunch of public and private cookie jars. In this case he got his just deserts, serving time behind bars.

Flemming Heilmann, December 2018

CHAPTERS

THE UNACCEPTABLE FACE

A 21st century story of an itinerant career under apartheid,
European socialism and disparate iterations of capitalism, laced
with corporate politics and skullduggery

Chapter I

Winds of Change

"Cry, the beloved country, for the unborn child that's the inheritor of our fear."
"Cry, the Beloved Country"
by Alan Paton

BEFORE THE TROPIC of Capricorn's sun could lend its orange glow to the grey horizon of the South Atlantic Ocean where it collides with its Indian counterpart, virtually every passenger aboard the Union Castle Line's flagship *Pretoria Castle* was on the promenade deck, straining prematurely for the first glimpse of Table Mountain's fantastic silhouette. The ship's throbbing diesel engines were throttled back to a murmur for the approach to Cape Town's harbor. It took some time before the massive deep purple mesa shape of the mountain slowly emerged, after first manifesting itself as no more than a nondescript irregularity breaking the horizon while dawn broke. To the east, the Cape of Good Hope's jagged rocky spine stretched south to Cape Point, where the two oceans clashed and crashed into the sharp promontory, sending columns of salty white spume soaring hundreds of feet into the air. As the ship drew closer, the dramatic setting of the city was softly illuminated by the pale, post-dawn sunlight. Then the giant backdrop of Table Mountain's perpendicular granite wall rose from the azure sea and the shiny white homes perched on steep slopes of the green foothills reflected the strengthening rays of sunlight. Modest pastel-shaded row houses of the Malay Quarter nestled on the slope right behind the commercial and residential high-rises of the city itself, beyond the harbor and waterfront. Away to the north and west, the immense arc of silver beaches traced the edge of Table Bay, curving their way around to Bloubergstrand, where the iconic view presented the *Fairest Cape of All,* painted by thousands of artists since Jan van Riebeek landed here four hundred years ago. The city's eastern outskirts reach up steep inclines to Lion's Head while the inviting wide beaches of False Bay lie awaiting behind the mountain. The full glory of Cape Town reveals her as the unchallenged queen of this planet's most spectacular coastal cities, topping rivals like Rio de Janeiro, San Francisco, Vancouver, Sydney, Hong Kong and Stockholm.

Excitement bubbled, especially among the younger passengers. For some of them, that morning was to mark the start of a new and very different life on a new continent, a new beginning in a new kind of community of astonishing demographic diversity, under a civic system alien to anything they had previously experienced. For others, it was a homecoming after sojourns "overseas," as South Africans categorize any place north of the Limpopo River or beyond the country's dramatic shorelines. No other country's points of entry could possibly extend a more iconic, dramatic and emotionally evocative welcome than Cape Town's.

~~~~

For me that December 1959 morning was indeed the very beginning of a new life on the southern tip of the vast enigmatic continent that was to become home for seventeen years. It was to bring life-changing experiences in *A Very Strange Society,* so brilliantly described by Alan Drury in his book on earlier 20th century South Africa. Harold Macmillan's winds of change were reaching gale force through the colonies of sub-Saharan Africa to the north, where self-determination and independence were taking hold, while another brisk wind was picking up in South Africa—but here it was blowing in the opposite direction, at a 180-degree variance. Apartheid was on the march.

Change was not new to me. Neither was facing the unknown, nor the need to adapt. Mine had been an itinerant childhood and education, often navigating uncharted waters where risk was encountered and inadequately informed decisions were forced upon me. Born of Danish parents in colonial Malaya (Malaysia today) in 1936, my early years on a rubber plantation at the edge of the jungle were interrupted by Japan's aggression, as they sought control and ownership of East Asia. Their imminent invasion of Malaya caused my father, at the end of 1940, to arrange the evacuation of my mother, brother and myself to an unknown destination in Australia—a decision he made because he did not buy into the British propaganda about "Fortress Singapore" or the invulnerability of Malaya under the protection of the mighty Royal Navy and Royal Air Force. Hence my first uprooting at age five from the bosom of a benign Muslim culture and tranquil life in the complacent colony of His Imperial Majesty King George VI. Being a refugee in Australia meant facing the unknown, yet it was made easy and almost comfortable by the limitless generosity and warmth of welcoming Ozzies, themselves a nation of refugees and immigrants. Adapting to change almost became routine, as I went to four different schools in Melbourne, Bendigo and Geelong in the course of our wartime Australian sojourn.

Repatriated at the end of World War II, I was soon at boarding school in Denmark for the recovery years of 1945–1950, before making yet another move. My parents felt that with their own lives now being transplanted to another Anglophone environment in Swaziland, I would be better off with a British education. After ten incongruous schools involving two hemispheres and different languages, I thrived during four cohesive years at Gresham's School in Norfolk, followed by undergraduate studies in economics and a Cambridge University law degree. However, I simply couldn't afford to apply my legal qualification to preparing to become a barrister—which was my only reason for reading law in the first place—so I opted for a career in industry. I had to make a living PDQ—meaning pretty damned quickly— to avoid being a burden to my parents, who were about to retire after PB's decade as a pioneer citrus farmer in Swaziland. My parents had been 100 percent cleaned out financially by World War II.

So, after seeking an entry level job at a number of British companies, the opportunity to join Metal Box Company as a trainee appealed more than other options did. This preference was prompted not only by the connectedness of the packaging business to global consumers, its social role in distribution and preservation of food and other necessities, but also by the progressive approach of the company's personnel managers to recruiting.

I was the beneficiary of a comprehensive training program over eighteen months, exposing me to the stark realities of industrial life in the grimy heartland of British industry, assigned to stints in half a dozen manufacturing plants in the Midlands and South Wales as well as sales and accounting offices. The contrast with life in the coddled cocoon of Cambridge was salutary—a learning experience of immense impact. After twenty years of experiencing all sorts of horizontal diversity, i.e. of ethnicity, culture, social structure, religion, political systems and dogma, I was now adapting to, and learning from, the vertical diversity of civic systems, social strata and perceived rank in the country's structure and population. My education was importantly extended and enhanced, which I have always considered to be my singularly good fortune.

Given this background, I was uncommonly fortunate, at the tender age of 23, to be embarking on a career with a set of beliefs and values built upon an unusually broad base of personal experience, with an understanding of diversity and strong respect for the benefits derived from man's individualism. Earlier exposure to Denmark's post-war obsession with collectivism under a socialist government had played its part.

I was about to take a front seat in the theater of emerging apartheid. It was relatively early in the National Party's rigorous 47-year rampage to take its vile iron grip on the country and enforce its segregationist credo. The Nationalists had barely a decade earlier displaced the United Party of Jan

Smuts, which then became the official opposition under de Villiers Graff—a feeble and ineffective opponent of the determined Afrikaaners. I was stepping into the confluence of South Africa's highly developed economy led by managers as sophisticated as any around the globe and the evolving police state driven by perverse Calvinism and racial prejudice.

I was also to be introduced to the exceptional enterprise and competence of millions of white South Africans, who had built the continent's most advanced economy and infrastructure, by far—an accomplishment of which the western world was hardly aware. This socio-political confluence was also to expose the enduring audacity and courage of the country's opposition media, the stubborn independence of the judiciary and the determined persistence of truly progressive (with a lower case "p") activists, who doggedly, effectively and constantly alleviated the plight of millions of blacks, particularly in urban areas. These were the heroes of the apartheid era, too readily ignored or forgotten in the politics and unctuous media analysis of the struggle against apartheid, up to and beyond that evil system's final demise with the release of Nelson Mandela a quarter century later.

~~~~

By the time the *Pretoria Castle* had eased into the dock, fond farewells had been bidden, luggage was stacked on deck and ready for disembarkation as excitement peaked. My personal welcome ashore was warmly extended by Andy Page-Wood, the Cape Town sales manager for Metal Box Company of South Africa. He provided generous hospitality and personal guidance outside business hours, opening his home to me during three days of orientation before heading north to Johannesburg, the seat of the company's head office. The orientation encompassed visits to the factories serving the Western Cape's productive agricultural and fishing industries, as well as the city's consumer goods businesses. Cape Town was also the company's base for food technology and bacteriology labs, technical customer services and machinery building. The company's precision engineering unit built equipment used in its own plants and specialty cannery machinery for its customers.

It was December, when a Mediterranean summer climate enveloped western Cape Province, almost cloudless, warm and ventilated by welcome breezes off the Atlantic and Indian oceans. The natural beauty of the Cape was unfurled at its sun-soaked best as we motored into the surrounding countryside; the variety of scenery and the ethnic diversity of the region was highlighted at every turn. Wondrously wide white beaches bordering two peacock blue oceans set against a background of rugged granite and Cape Limestone skylines. Mixed farming on the sandy flatlands between Cape Town's scenic suburbs encircling the base of Table Mountain and the magical wine growing areas alternated between pastures, crops and woodlands. By the roadsides and along the streams and irrigation ditches, wild Calla Lillies, Crane Lillies and Strelitzias bloomed in casual abundance splashing white, orange and red patches onto the lush landscape. The drier spots were adorned with Namaqualand Daisies of every pastel hue. The more arid areas offered a variety of eucalyptus trees and occasional casuarinas. Hedges along the roads and median plantings bursting with lovely heavy white and pink Oleander flowers, their latent toxic qualities nonchalantly ignored.

The planet's most picturesque and verdant vineyard valley stretches eastward from Stellenbosch to Franschhoek, hundreds of immaculate vineyards flanked by towering, craggy grey mountains. Brightly whitewashed Cape Dutch homesteads with characteristic rounded neo-Gothic gables, thick reed-thatched roofs and dark green window shutters and doors, added elegant patches of bright white light across the fertile U-shaped valley. Blue-green groves of conifers took over from the vines at the foothills, stretching up to the precipitous rocky face of the mountains, which coddle the gorgeous vineyard enclave, protecting it from the occasionally harsher elements of the Cape climate. The Franschhoek valley remains an exquisite (in every sense of the word) reminder of the Protestant Dutch and French

Huguenot settlers' distinct imprint on South Africa's history and culture well before the Brits muscled their way into the picture.

Beyond this vineyard paradise, over the range flanking it to the north, endless thousands of acres of immaculately groomed deciduous fruit orchards fed the huge canning industry of the Western Cape, producing pears, peaches, apricots, nectarines and plums. Apart from canned whole fruit or halves, they produced juices, nectars, jams and jellies for domestic as well as export markets around the world. The industry's biggest enterprise was the largely Afrikaans farmers' co-op, Langeberg, but other South African and international companies were also prominent, such as the American Delmonte and Australian H. Jones & Co.

A giant Metal Box South Africa, or MBSA, food can plant was strategically located to serve the canning industry on the outskirts of Paarl, a small town named for an enormous round, silvery rock that looked like a massive fairy tale pearl about 800 feet tall and a mile wide. Three MBSA plants in the Cape Town area drew from the Cape's harlequined population. Blacks of different Bantu tribes—Xhosas, Zulus and a few Ovambos, who had migrated southward, respectively from the distant northeast and South West Africa (the erstwhile German South West Africa protectorate assigned to South Africa's care by the Versailles Treaty after World War I). There were white Anglophones, Afrikaaners and sundry Caucasian immigrants from everywhere. The *Coloureds* (as those of mixed race are known in South Africa) were the major population group including Cape Malays descended from slaves brought in from the East Indies by the early Dutch settlers. The Malays were Muslims and contributed Oriental traditions and a rich culture to the region.

Behind the Cape's glorious beauty and charm lurked hideous practices and consequences of creeping apartheid laws written to define race and institutionalize the segmentation of the past's *de facto* color bar. Designated residential areas for blacks, *Coloureds* (including Indians) and "Europeans," meaning anyone who passed for white. Segregated schools. *Whites Only* signs on public facilities and entrances to parks or beaches—no different from those of America's southern states at the time. Less visible were the rabid promoters of apartheid, who went to shocking extremes in defining the boundaries between racial categories. The emerging politics of the country were soaked in the venom of racism. In the USA, people with any trace of African ancestry are termed African American, black or people of color; but in South Africa a strict distinction was made between the blacks (100% African blood) and *Coloureds*, the latter designation being reserved for those of mixed race. A detectable trace of African or Malay blood classified you as *Coloured*. To distinguish between light-skinned South African *Coloureds* and people registered as European, the authorities could go as far as obscene tests based on the ease with which a comb would pass through someone's hair. There were ghastly stories of *Coloureds* who would go to any lengths of deception or pretense to cross the color bar, even if it meant leaving siblings, parents or even children "on the other side." Basil Warner's play "Try for White," was based on one of them.

"Black" American luminaries of today, such as Barak Obama, Colin Powell, Harry Belafonte, the Gumble brothers, Lester Holt, Susan Rice, Charles Rangel or Eric Holder would in 1958 have been registered as *Coloureds* if they had been in South Africa. Contemporary black South Africans would not consider them black or African in the way they perceive themselves. On the other hand, Morgan Freeman (despite a rumored Caucasian great-great-grandmother), Bill Cosby, Shaquille O'Neal, Magic Johnson or someone like Jesse Owens or Paul Robeson would certainly have cut it as blacks in South Africa.

Blacks and Africans were pure Zulu, Xhosa, Tswana, Sotho, Ovambo or members of dozens of tribes of far northern origins. People of Indian descent were simply Indians, but sometimes lumped in the *Coloured* category for legislative purposes. The majority of them lived in Durban and the surrounding Natal province to the northeast, by the Indian Ocean. *Coloureds* and blacks were themselves quite discriminatory in their perceptions and treatment of each other. For example, the Cape Malays with their Muslim faith and culture from the East Indies, or Indonesia today, looked down their noses at *Coloureds* of African blood.

The various population groups had always concerned themselves with tribal and ethnic distinctions, so this very deliberate segmentation was not exclusively the creation of Afrikaaner apartheid. Discrimination was not alien to any of them. History relates the slaughter of the original population of South Africa, the Khoisan peoples—Hottentots and Bushmen—as the Bantu tribes drove down from territories north of the Limpopo to invade and seize grazing lands to support their growing numbers, leaving a legacy of bitter Khoi hatred of the Zulus and Xhosas in particular. Bloody tribal and clan conflicts had been constant since the dawn of history. The poor Khois and San people, who survived the Bantu onslaught died in thousands from the white man's venereal diseases imported with European settlers. In the eighteenth and nineteenth century, conflicts within the Bantu group led to new alignments, and the formation of new tribal nations, such as the Matabele, Shangaan, Ndebele and Swazi, who in turn ravaged the Tswana and Sotho groups in genocidal wars and territorial land grabs. Well after democracy triumphed over apartheid in 1994, Zulu-Xhosa conflicts roiled the country's politics and caused bloodshed as Chief Buthelezi of the Zulus, for example, crossed swords with the Xhosa-dominated African National Congress over purely tribal issues. Tribal fighting in the dormitory towns, which housed migrant labor on the many mine properties, regularly caused gruesome bloodbaths.

In America, perverse sensitivity to skin pigment—akin to what was happening in South Africa—is encountered among people of color even in the new millennium. When the left leaning activist Harry Belafonte, blessed as he is with fine Hollywood features and skin of golden hue, attacked Condoleezza Rice, suggesting that she was a puppet of the white establishment, she famously snapped back:

"I don't need Harry Belafonte to tell me how to be black."

Prejudice and *de facto* discrimination were for generations typical of British and other colonial territories, but the *Nats* (Nationalists) were now forging ahead with specific legislation for "constitutional reform" under Prime Minister Hendrik Verwoerd. The grandfather of legislated apartheid was Prime Minister D. F. Malan; his successor, Strijdom, removed people of mixed race from the common voter's roll, introducing a separate *Coloureds' Roll.* Meanwhile, north of the Limpopo and all the way to the Sahara, the British government's decolonization policy had been slowly evolving under the Labor Party. Now the Tories were implementing the "liberation." Harold Macmillan made his famous Cape Town speech on February 3rd, 1960, three weeks after he made a similar one in Ghana, which went largely unreported. To the people of Ghana he had said:

> "The wind of change is blowing through this continent. Whether we like it or not, this growth of national consciousness is a political fact. We give you our earnest support and encouragement."

Macmillan's Cape Town version included a significant addition to deal with a very different concept of national consciousness embraced by the Afrikaaners in power:

> "It is our earnest desire to give support and encouragement, but in South Africa there are certain aspects of your policy which make it impossible for us."

The British leader's confrontational words in Cape Town reverberated throughout Africa and the western world, although they were given a frigid reception by his official hosts at the continent's southern tip. The local press, on the other hand, made sure that the country heard him. In the fairest cape of all, the wind was changing too, but there it was turning to the opposite direction and would bring a cold front of tyranny, violence and bigotry with it.

~~~~

My journey into the interior was romantic and almost luxurious. The famous Blue Train, which ran the 900 mile route between Cape Town and Pretoria and Johannesburg, was very comfortably furnished with dark blue, shiny leather benches, chairs and sofas, while its elegant dining car presented eclectic cuisine and excellent wines from the Cape region. There was a comfy observation car, which served its purpose well through the picturesque wine and deciduous fruit country, as the train climbed steep inclines through the narrow passes of the Langeberg towards the scorched scrub (known as *fynbos*) and semi-desert landscapes of the Little and Great Karoos. The Karoo was real Afrikaaner country, sparsely populated by a few sheep and even fewer patches of maize and Boers, barely making a living from the barren land. Somebody once described the Karoo as "miles and miles of bugger-all, surrounded by miles and miles of bugger-all." The veracity of that statement rendered the Blue Train's observation car temporarily redundant.

My economy class ticket provided a good upper bunk in a double cabin with a huge window for hours of extraordinary sightseeing, even under a bright full moon. I was too excited to sleep. As dawn broke, the view stretched across the high-altitude plains of the Orange Free State and then the southwestern Transvaal, where thousands of square miles of cattle ranching and extensive *mealie,* or maize, and other cereal crops stretched to the horizon in every direction. A bright blue sky with summertime's enormous, billowing silver-white cumulonimbus clouds reaching 30,000 feet and more.

The only scheduled stop for passengers' purposes was Kimberly, where the famous "Big Hole" had precipitated history's most frantic diamond rush and discovery of the record-holding Cullinan Diamond at the turn of the century. There were a couple of unexplained ten-minute stops in the middle of nowhere, in total darkness of the wee hours of the morning; but quite sensibly, nobody seemed to care.

Over an hour before arriving in Johannesburg, hub of the Witwatersrand's gold mining industry at an altitude of nearly 6,000 feet, the view from the Blue Train changed from expansive treeless *highveld* farmland to a rather sinister vista of pale yellow mine dumps, small mountains of mined ore, processed and almost entirely robbed of its golden treasure. (That was at a time when the global price of gold bullion was about $35, long before the price increased 40-fold to allow the re-refining of these yellow mountains for profit). Between the dumps there were stands of blue gum trees, hundreds of mass-produced dormitory compounds for black mine labor, interspersed with spartan yellow brick bungalows under corrugated iron roofs to house white mine technicians, management and staff. It looked like a mechanically disturbed moonscape invaded by some primitive form of humanity, ugly in every respect except for its creation of employment and the provision of a living for hundreds of thousands of people drawn from abject poverty in rural areas, where they struggled to sustain life at perilous subsistence level.

Johannesburg and the *Rand* are the core of South Africa's mining, industry, commerce and finance. The Witwatersrand's Afrikaans name, which means white-water ridge, belied the largely Anglophone, heavily Jewish population of Johannesburg and its mining communities along the *Rand*. This forty-mile reef of rock outcrop, stretching from Jo'burg eastward to the town of Welkom, was once Boer farming country of the old *Zuid Afrikaanse Republiek*. The first record-breaking gold deposits were found in the mid-1880s, causing a feverish gold rush and explosion of development and *uitlander* (meaning foreigner) population. This spawned territorial tensions among Afrikaans farmers, while greedy Brits developed their plan to invade from their colonial Cape base to the south. The aim was to overthrow the Afrikaaner republic and take over the territory with its extraordinarily rich mineral resources. The Afrikaaner republic, in time, became the British province of Transvaal, the territory north of the Vaal River which marked the border with the Orange Free State to its south and Southern Rhodesia to the north at the Limpopo River.

~~~~

My parents, who lived in the beautiful northern suburb of Bryanston, were on Jo'burg's Main Station platform to greet me, along with brother John and his wife Inge-Marie. It was a rare, warm and emotional reunion of the whole family. John and his family lived in the slightly less well-heeled suburb of Northcliff, under a rocky bluff surrounded by Jacaranda trees, also to the north of the city. In the background, on the platform well behind the family, was Eddie Enright, the nominal personnel manager of MBSA, who had come to welcome me and bring good wishes from my new employer. His main role in the company was acting as gopher for the chairman and CEO, John Baxter, whom he now represented as he kindly helped with my luggage. It later became clear that Baxter had directed every detail of my reception and orientation program in Cape Town. This was my first experience of John Baxter's personal attention to detail, especially in matters concerning the welfare of the company's people. It was a hallmark of his leadership, which otherwise could be quite authoritarian.

I was to stay with my parents until I "found my feet" in Johannesburg and could make a judgment as to what I could afford to rent. Living with mother and father presented me with unfamiliar luxuries. With the exception of a few vacations spent with them, this was the first time in ten years my old folks were covering my day to day living expenses. It was a decade earlier, in a little hotel room in Norfolk when I was a 14-year-old at boarding school in England, when my father had put me in charge of my own finances, taught me how to use a bank account, steward a capital sum in the form of British "Gilts"—UK government bonds—and independently manage cash flow and my own budget, which meant I was in charge of all expenses including school fees, travel, clothing, etc. The value of the Gilts had been estimated to get me through eight more years of education. World War II had wiped out my parents' savings in Denmark and their current assets in Malaya, so, as a priority, they had focused on financing the best education my brother and I could absorb before attending to their own retirement needs. My dad put me in charge of my own finances at a tender age.

But that's not where the generosity of their welcome ended. *Mor*, as my mother was known, had practically stopped driving a car herself, so her tiny Fiat 500 with 70,000 miles on the clock was bestowed on me. My first car.

Life for the next few months in Bryanston was very comfortable, but in no way lavish. There was a *house boy*, Pearson, from distant Nyasaland (as it was then called) and a local Sotho *garden boy* named Sixpence, who hailed from Basutoland. Both of them lived in quarters at the back of the house. Beds were made, shoes polished and laundry seen to by Pearson, so I had little to do by way of daily chores. *Mor* did virtually all of the cooking, fussed over my father, *Far*, and mothered me as if I were twelve years old. Weekends were spent playing very social tennis and lounging by immaculate swimming pools, usually with John and Inge-Marie, their kids and friends. Rugby had been a big part of my life in England, so I very briefly tried playing for the Old Johnnies Club before giving up the game for good, almost permanently maimed by the cement-like grounds we played on—they were parched and dusty from the cloudless *highveld* winter. The circle of friends grew, thanks to the warm welcome extended by Johannesburg's carefree white society. It was so easy to acquire comfortable habits under those privileged conditions, reminiscent of a British colonial style, but more informal and light-hearted, blessed with a glorious climate and a humming economy affording lots of opportunity, not just to white people, but also endless black migrants from the poverty-stricken homelands. Late summer afternoons at an altitude of six thousand feet brought gigantic towers of muscular cumulonimbus clouds delivering dramatic thunderstorms, but usually at the end of hot sunny days by the pool or on the tennis court. The showers would bring fresh rain-cooled evenings with the Southern Cross rising quickly to adorn a cleared night sky. Then came winter, again, cloudless days of outdoor life and only the occasional overnight ground-frost. Shirt-sleeved lunches in the winter sun. All very seductive and easily taken for granted. If this was a state of careless oblivion, it was of course not sustainable. I knew many relatively wealthy South-African-born people who had never known any life but that of unworried sunshine and wealth; their expectations and view of life often endured.

Sixty percent of Johannesburg's white population was Jewish. Apart from dominating industry, commerce, mining and banking, the Jewish community was inevitably at the cutting edge of cultural, social, philanthropic and progressive civic initiatives—and here "progressive" means characterized by real progress or advance, not just a name for left-leaning ideology. At the core of Jo'burg's high society, anglicized Jews lived in large white-washed Cape-style houses with cathedral ceilings under heavy thatch roofs, or in imposing Italianate villas, or elegant petits chateaux with turrets behind grand gates. Weekend parties playing or watching polo in Witkoppen with the mining house set, or at the Inanda Club with stockbroker's Pimms No. 3 in hand. Top socialites included the Hersov and Mennell clans of the Anglo-Vaal mining dynasty, the Oppenheimers of the dominant Anglo-American mining and industrial conglomerate. The Goodman twins, tall and handsome with RAF moustaches, were top dogs on the polo field, who could afford it by virtue of marrying two golden Albu sisters, whose father, Sir George Albu, had been the top dog mining magnate of Union Corporation. These men's suits were cut immaculately, either by Savile Row tailors in London or their local equivalent, working to the same exacting standards. They wore cream-colored, hand-made silk shirts, cravats or regimental ties, to which few of them were entitled. Suede ankle boots or *veldskoen* over weekends, Donegal or Harris tweed sports coats, fitted at the waist, over jodhpurs. They were all armchair liberals, some showing more willingness to risk real effort for change than others. Helen Suzman, who grew up in this rarefied society, was of course the exception, the obvious and very strong stand-out, who fought a courageous solo battle in Parliament as the only woman, the only representative of the Progressive Party for decades, reviled by the Nationalists, utterly fearless and persistently articulate and outspoken.

From high society to middleclass whites, everyone employed black servants who lived on the property in servants' quarters normally placed right behind the kitchen and laundry. The juxtaposition could be dramatic, as each genotype could share the sights and sounds of the other's domestic life, personal habits and beliefs. House and garden servants were drawn from all the major tribal groups, as blacks from every impoverished corner of the country (some designated *bantustans*) sought employment in the big city—mostly Zulus, Xhosas, Vendas, Shangaans, Tswanas and Sothos. Their languages differed, but fell into two main groups akin to either Zulu/Xhosa or Sotho/Tswana linguistic families. They were a diverse lot, but had one thing in common apart from skin color: *tokolosh*, or tribal superstitions and cures for illness or a faltering love life. These cures and medicines could be quite innovative. Selina, a maid who worked for my parents at some stage, was to her chagrin failing in her romantic relations with a fellow Shangaan. She needed help to regain his interest and fond attention, so after consultation with the equivalent of a witch doctor, she prepared her prescribed potion. Selina boiled up a pot of water, added a handful of gum tree leaves, a segment of rusty link chain, one safety pin and an old padlock, to which an orange liquid was added and then left to simmer for hours. We never knew whether the liquid was ingested, but assumed that the metal components were not. Poor Selina's love life did not immediately recover, but she persisted with the potion until she eventually got her romances back on track—with another Shangaan gentleman.

~~~~

During the early days of 1960 when I did some volunteer work associated with fund raising, I made friends with Arthur Goldreich, who was the captivating, well-respected Chief Interior Architect for OK Bazaars, the country's largest retail chain. His pretty wife, Heather, was a successful oil painter. I met him in the course of my work in consumer market research. Arthur was not only extremely talented, but also handsome, engaging and well connected in Jo'burg's upper crust society. Some of these people were supporters of Helen Suzman's Progressive Party, to which I was attracted. They all sought out Arthur and Heather as guests for parties thrown for their "enlightened and progressive" friends on the *Rand*, as the Witwatersrand was known.

In late 1962, well settled in Jo'burg and quite unbeknownst to me at the time, I had a brush with history at a dinner party in the spacious Goldreich home, Lilliesleaf Farm, in the northern suburb of Rivonia. Arthur and Heather treated their fourteen dinner guests to four courses and nice Cape wines at a long elegantly decked table. It was a quasi-business dinner, with a number of men attending solo, so it took time for the conversation to veer away from the gold price, the stock market and the next Springbok rugby "test" (meaning international match) against the New Zealand All Blacks. The conversation gradually became livelier and, as always at Jo'burg dinners, kept returning to political chatter, often superficial and divested of conviction or passion. There could be no doubt that the group was generally unhappy about the Nationalist regime, yet nobody would stick their neck out too far.

The dining room was large and oval in the style of a rondavel with thick white-washed walls and a high, thatched cathedral ceiling. Tending alertly to every need of the guests were four African men stationed along the dining room walls in crisp white uniforms, little white Nehru hats, white gloves and bright red sashes across their chests. The man serving me and my neighbors at table stood out. He was almost six inches taller than anybody else in the room, with a handsome round face, but otherwise lean and dignified in his bearing. Years later, as details of the evolving struggle—the fight for democracy and independence—emerged, I was to learn that my server that night at Liliesleaf Farm was none other than Nelson Mandela, in hiding. The other "servants" looking after us that night included Secretary General of the ANC, Walter Sisulu, who was also on the run. All of them were sheltered and fed by the Goldreich's and their communist organization, which gave all manner of support to its ally, the ANC. Of course, none of the guests at the time had any inkling of what was going on. Our host Arthur was later identified as a senior international Communist Party leader from Israel, trained in guerilla warfare by the Soviets. He headed the armed wing of the Communist Party in all southern Africa. He was apparently in charge of armament supplies, recruiting, prioritizing sabotage attacks (alongside Mandela) and preparing for broader armed conflict. Everyone living and hiding at Lilliesleaf farm was eventually tracked down and arrested on site by the SA Police, leading to the infamous "Rivonia Trial," which sent Madiba (Mandela's nickname from his Transkei youth) to jail for 27 years.

This all came about in the aftermath of the much earlier "Treason Trial," when the pressures under which Mandela and his cohorts were working escalated in the late 50s, so he was forced to go underground. After frequent moves, operating from all sorts of temporary hiding places, he came upon a better alternative. In October 1961, he found the ideal shelter at Liliesleaf, in the almost rural suburb of Rivonia, which was, of course, Goldreich's up-market home, which could fit with his respectable day job at OK Bazaars as Chief Interior Architect of the group. Arthur had persuaded the founder and chairman of OK Bazaars, Sam Cohen, to hire him as an Israeli-educated architect and, given his creative talents, his story was very credible. His job at OK Bazaars served as the perfect front for his clandestine role. He had hoodwinked the whole world. Until the police eventually tracked them down, Lilliesleaf Farm in the affluent northern suburbs was secretly owned by the Communist Party. It had been an unlikely Communist Party nerve center and safe haven.

They were caught in 1963 and that marked the start of Madiba's 27 years on Robben Island. Arthur's truncated prison sentence was served in downtown Jo'burg's Marshall Square, the police headquarters. At the Rivonia Trial, Madiba, in giving testimony, said:

> "The ANC has never at any period of its history advocated revolutionary change in the economic structure of the country, nor has it, to the best of my recollection, ever condemned capitalist society."

The fact that thirty years later, Madiba, upon his release, broke with his communist brothers in electing to take the path of reconciliation ahead of revenge, and that he chose free market capitalism ahead of a Marxist regime, is an extraordinary testament to his vision, political skills and leadership. The man had been transformed during his 27 years of incarceration, during which he took an advanced law degree, read philosophy, economics and the biography of every significant world leader. However, having once delved into Marxism with revolutionary zeal, his studies and analysis on Robben Island had confirmed a long-held respect for the overarching value and benefits of capitalist systems. He had come a long way from being the revolutionary who embraced armed conflict and violent acts of terror.

Arthur was in Marshall Square with fellow inmate and Communist operator, Harold Wolpe. Arthur already had a beautiful dark beard, which Wolpe then emulated, and they then managed to bribe a prison guard to take delivery of a parcel containing two dark brown hooded cassocks with tasseled white rope for waist ties. Again, with the help of a befriended warder, they escaped into the busy streets dressed as Franciscan monks. The two hirsute Hebrews ambled calmly along the sidewalks of downtown Jo'burg all the way from the police headquarters up to the Central Station, smiling benignly, greeting grateful passers-by while slicing the air with outstretched hands to make signs of the cross.

> "Bless you, my son!" said Harold to a cocky young *totsie* skipping by. "Have faith in Jesus!"

> Arthur prayed for the health and happiness of a portly Zulu mama sitting on a doorstep: "May Christ the Lord be with you, Sister! And may his light shine upon you always!"

Safely aboard a train bound for Mbabane, they fled to Swaziland, where a small plane awaited them for their covert flight to Gaborone in what now is Botswana, and then on to Nyasaland or Tanganyika. Fifty years later, back in Israel, Arthur became a high-profile critic of his country's hawkish

Palestinian policy, particularly regarding West Bank settlements, likening the Israeli occupation and land grabs to South Africa's apartheid and Bantustan policies. According to The *Times* of London Goldreich died there in 2012.

~~~~

It was suddenly the first Monday morning in January 1959; time to report for work at the Metal Box Company of South Africa.

Fifteen miles of easy navigation through the green suburbs in the Fiat 500 placed me in the parking basement at 40 Fox Street in downtown Johannesburg. A granite edifice, which was part of Anglo-American Corporation's huge headquarters complex covering two city blocks. The top two floors of "40 Fox" housed the head office of MBSA, where I was immediately ushered into the office of John W. Baxter, Executive Chairman and Managing Director, or CEO in today's parlance.

Baxter was a large, impressive Englishman, who had attended the famous Christ's Hospital boys' school in London, which many Anglican scholarship students from underprivileged parts of London attended. All pupils wore ankle-length blue, belted habits, yellow socks and black shoes. He had been a decent scholar, but declined opportunities for further education beyond what Americans would call high school. He had chosen to head off to the icy wilderness of Labrador, where he started work as a fur trapper and trader with the Hudson Bay Company. After a few years in the territory where Quebec's endless coniferous forests give way to tundra, he somehow changed course quite radically to end up with a job working for The Metal Box Company of India, the group's fast expanding Asian subsidiary in the late 1930s. The energetic Baxter steadily worked his way up the ranks to become its young managing director and chief executive. His performance in India triggered his promotion to lead the group's largest subsidiary, MBSA, in 1947. Since then, he had more than doubled the size of the enterprise and taken it public on the Johannesburg Stock Exchange.

The company employed over 5,000 people throughout a network of strategically located plants in southern Africa.

Over time, I was to know Baxter as an effective leader, hard-charging executive, with an insatiable appetite for detailed planning and an extraordinary sensitivity to other people's feelings, likes and dislikes. He constantly jotted notes on bits of paper, later feeding them into categorized notebooks. He would later use these notes when arguing his cause; his notes prompted recall of exact words long since spoken, which he could then use to overwhelm his opponents in debate, be they overseers in London, his customers and suppliers or his subordinates. Baxter managed largely by example, leading from the front. He made people around him, of all levels and ranks, feel appreciated and relevant. He was equally persuasive as a teacher, often getting his point across with a hint of humor and mischief in his eyes. He was addicted to making puns, which he would use to defuse tension or the potential for controversy in a situation. On occasion he could lose control of his very short fuse, but not for long because he was very conscious of this personal weakness. For years, he was an invaluable mentor to me. I never learned more about leadership or planning from any other source. His attention to detail did not get in the way of his comprehension of the big picture or his skill in setting priorities.

Here I was on a Monday morning in the big boss's office. All six-foot, four-inches and 250 imposing pounds of him, with jutting chin, aquiline nose and usually an engaging twinkle in his eye. Leaning across his pristine, paper free, custom-built desk, he stretched out his meaty hand to bid me welcome. Baxter had a small writing pad in front of him, with scribbled bullet points, as he checked that everything had gone smoothly in Cape Town, asking which plants and offices I had visited, which managers I had met—having, in fact, written the detailed itinerary himself. Each of my answers prompted a tick or check mark against notes on his pad. In the course of half an hour he paid me the compliment of summarizing, in very broad terms, his five priorities for improvement and growth of the company. His view was that the company should continue to do exactly what it had been doing for the last fifteen years, just better, and more of it. He gave me a job description in one sentence:

> "We need to get better at understanding our customers' real needs," he said before a pause.

> "We are quite good at responding to what they think they want, but that's not always the right way to go. We and our customers need to do better at understanding consumers' preferences and real needs. It is also our job to innovate and help our customers make the best of new technology and new materials. The better they do, the more we can grow. I am told that you can help build that ability by using market research at retail and industrial level. So it's now up to you and Pat Sullivan to do just that. I'll walk you down to the office you'll be sharing with him, and I'll introduce you to your superior, Mr. Sevenoaks."

He eased his big frame out of his chair and started for the office door, but then turned to me again.

> "Heilmann, we'll not necessarily be seeing much of each other these coming months, so I now wish you all the very best, young man. I am pleased you did well in your training with the home company in England, and we're delighted that you have joined us. Mind you, this is a very different world from old England, as you'll see. You'll have to make some adjustments, but it's a good bunch of people we have here … and I mean all five thousand of them," he said with a little chuckle. "Welcome aboard!"

John Baxter had scant understanding of market research or how to go about it. I later heard that Sir Robert Barlow had suggested that the burgeoning domestic market for consumer staples could lead to rapid growth of the existing business, which was heavily based on exports of canned foods, and MBSA's understanding of the market, new technology and materials could be used to help our customers anticipate change. That was why market research had been made part of my training program in the UK.

At the end of a long corridor deeply carpeted in rich burgundy, Baxter ushered me into a sparse room with a polished brown linoleum floor, two standard secretarial desks and a couple of windows facing a deep multi-story courtyard well, which separated the building from Anglo-American's offices. Our office décor stood in sharp contrast to the plush hallway and the senior offices we had walked past. Behind the occupied desk sat Pat Sullivan, who sprang to his feet, greeted the chairman with deference and eyed me cautiously.

> "Sullivan, this is Flemming Heilmann, your new partner in crime. Do show him the ropes and tell him where the pee-house is, and take him to the canteen at lunchtime. I was going to introduce him to Denis Sevenoaks as well, but I see I'm running late, so please fix that for us, will you?"

With that, the Chairman was gone. Pat shook my hand and suggested that I take a seat at the other desk. In the soundless void of the next minute or so, I realized that while the company's chairman had planned every detail of my arrival and introduction in Cape Town, absolutely nothing had been done at this level to anticipate my arrival. There was nothing by way of stationery, pens, or other supplies in my desk drawers, only an iron table lamp with a canvass shade and a telephone on a corner of my desk.

> "Good to meet you, Pat! I've been looking forward to this,"
> I said, breaking the silence.

"I've reeely been looking forward to meeting you, man," he said in his super-clipped South African accent, un-knitting his furrowed brow and relaxing a bit as we took each other in. "It's only coupl'a weeks since I was told you were coming. You know, man, I am not sure how we are both going to fill our bloody days, let alone deserve a pay check. Nobody has clue what consumer research is. So ah've hed nothing to do, even while flying solo! Now, two of us are going to be kicking our heels, unless something reeely chainges. Reeely, man! Bugger-all to do, man. Every now and again, Sevenoaks orsks me to run an errand for his wahfe, which jus' cheeses me off. Yis man, no! I spind a bunch of mah days on the 'phone chetting to mah old pels in the sayles force, because I can quite often hulp them with mah old customers." Pat paused and then asked "You hev any ideas, Flemming?"

Pat had, a couple of years earlier, quit his salesman's job in MBSA, taking himself off to London to get "overseas experience" and had landed a job in market research with Metal Box in the Baker Street office, where I had just spent my last months in London. This was news to me. He had returned to SA almost a year ahead of me under his own steam and, after a vacation, cast around for some months before being hired back by MBSA in anticipation of my arrival. After getting acquainted and swapping notes for an hour or so, Pat suggested we cross the corridor to say hello to Denis Sevenoaks.

Our boss was English, slightly stooped and chinless, both physically and in his approach to life. Brylcreemed black hair slicked back to the right side from his forehead, close set and shifty green eyes behind heavy horn rims. His handshake was sloppy and even his hello was hesitant.

"So you've arrived, have you? Well, we were wondering when you would turn up! Pat will do his best to make you comfortable. Keep me posted on what you are up to, both of you … See you later! I'm off to see Grant Advertising."

One of the girls in the typists' pool quickly came to our office to stock me with stationery, a desk pad, pens and the things you have in the drawers of your office desk. She told me Sevenoaks had just confessed to forgetting that Baxter instructed him to get my work place ready.

Sevenoaks was in charge of the company's miniscule advertising budget. MBSA's top management believed the company served only industrial customers, rather than consumers, so neither Baxter nor the board considered PR a priority, except for Bryan Smither, the urbane banker, who served as non-executive Vice Chairman and handled investor relations deftly, almost single-handedly. Sevenoaks milked the tenuous relationship with Grant Advertising to fill his days with visits to the ad agency and attend every cocktail party or luncheon he could talk his way into. His feather-light workload peaked during the preparation of the company's annual report. Another crescendo was the design and construction of the company's booth at the annual Rand Easter Show, the country's major industrial convention.

Sevenoaks was a trivial stooge. Apart from the warmth of Baxter's initial welcome, that first Monday was a truly inauspicious start for an ambitious young man, hell-bent on building a career. I was quite distraught. When I talked about it that night with my parents at home, clearly reflecting my impatience to *Far*, he poured me a drink, sat me down and basically told me to exhale.

In Danish he told me to take it easy, boy!

"Ta' den med ro, min dreng!"

"Careers, as you know, Flemming, are not delivered overnight unless you dig up gold in your backyard, have a lucky breakthrough to stardom in show business or as a qualifier get to the semi's at Wimbledon. No instant gratification, even with an education like yours! Business careers are built on persistence, hard work, good judgment, good results and a lot of luck ... And you have plenty of time," he said. "That's just as well, boy, because you know so little and have so far to go. Put your nose to the grindstone, get to understand the details of the business and what makes it tick. You may have the time, right now. So use it! And keep your nose clean, boy! Don't underestimate your inexperience and don't take yourself too seriously. Give it what you've got and you'll get your chance. You're only twenty-three!"

I had never had it explained so clearly.

Six weeks into the job, out of the blue, I contracted a serious nephritis, which kept me bedridden in Bryanston for some weeks. This caused me enormous grief as I was so anxious to engage in my job and fretted over the opportunity cost of being absent. On the other hand, being immobilized gave me plenty of time to think, and it prompted me to take stock of my situation. It was clear in my mind that I had landed myself in a very strange society. On balance, I saw South Africa as singularly endowed with resources—climate, productive land, minerals and metals, strategic location, human talent and natural beauty—so I concluded it presented unmatched potential—not just to me, but to the world. It was a good place to be, I reasoned, because the country would become a first world nation as it built on its burgeoning economy and corrected its current political course. Having yet to experience the front lines of apartheid to see how it worked (or did not work), I underestimated the determination of the *verkramte* (Afrikaans for intellectually constricted) Calvinist Afrikaaners. The darkest implications of what was happening socio-politically were still not clear to me, or to the world around me. I also learned that my parents' retirement to Denmark was imminent, and that brother John and his family were also preparing to move on. It would not be so long before I was to be alone in South Africa, and yet I was encouraged, even excited, about my opportunities. As for the plight of the Africans and other non-whites, I could only see that it would improve with the elevation of living standards outpacing economic development, and believed their contribution to the country's economy would be recognized in a dramatic change or reversal of the current political thrust. I wanted to be part of all that progress and change.

While I was convalescing, I received a letter from Marilyn Harter with whom I had developed a close relationship in the months before leaving London. She was one of three girls sharing a flat just around the corner from where I was also sharing digs with young men embarking on disparate careers. One of my roommates had introduced me. All three girls spoke genteel English, shared a taste for landed gentry or "County" fashion, favoring pastel twin sets, strings of pearls and sensible shoes. Each had social aspirations beyond her budget. Penny was well into a relationship with an heir to the Symington port wine dynasty, and Phoebe was recovering from an aborted romance in British colonial Kenya. Marilyn was working as private secretary to an upper crust solicitor in a city law office after she had very quickly dropped out of an extraordinary undergraduate opportunity at Lady Margaret Hall, the coveted women's college at Oxford University. She was very bright and had won an "exhibition" or top scholarship awarded only to the country's most gifted. As we became friends, she told me quiet forthrightly about her "stupid decisions" and how she had flung herself into Oxford's febrile undergraduate social life at the expense of academics.

> "I was just—well, overwhelmed," she explained quite openly, "by the fab social life and all the parties. I was in denial, ignoring the polite warnings of my tutor and supervisors. Little thought was given to the once-in-a-lifetime opportunity I had been given. Everything had been handed to me on a silver platter. I just took it all for granted. No one was there to stand over my shoulder and crack the whip. I was just having so much fun, Flemming. Nobody

reminding me how damned lucky I was. Then all of a sudden
it was too late. I totally buggered up the "prelims" [Oxford's
first examinations to test the efforts of freshmen after about
nine months] and I was suddenly a goner! It was all over! Just
like that."

We had maintained a warm and lighthearted correspondence. She
indicated that she had bought a passage to Cape Town, and would be coming
to see me in about two months' time. It was a possibility we had
contemplated before I left England, which suddenly became a reality. I
certainly did not discourage her, and plans were cemented when my parents
generously invited her to come to stay in Bryanston during her time in
Johannesburg. I looked forward to that, without giving a great deal of
thought to what this could precipitate.

Then, only three months after my disembarkation in Cape Town, a new
and violent phase in the evolution of apartheid and black resistance erupted.

For thirty years the movements of black men had been increasingly
constrained by the authorities' abuse of pass laws; but Verwoerd's
Nationalist government started to use these laws as tools to enshrine stricter
segregation. For the first time he applied the stricter laws to women as well.
The pass laws imposed stifling rules requiring that elaborate ID papers or
"passes" be carried 24/7, with disproportionately heavy penalties for
transgression. The Nats increasingly used the pass laws to harass blacks and
to track down political activists, usually members of the African National
Congress or the more extreme Pan-Africanist Congress. This caused the two
rival organizations to focus on their shared hatred of these laws, fermenting
popular resistance and to spread their political message.

The ANC had planned to launch a carefully coordinated protest against
the pass laws on March 31st, 1960, in Sharpeville and the industrial area of
Vanderbijlpark, some forty miles south of Jo'burg, where coincidently
MBSA had its largest manufacturing complex. However, the rival PAC
leadership decided to launch their own campaign ten days earlier, seeking to

eclipse the ANC by pre-emption. On March 21st, nearly 7,000 blacks surrounded the police station in Sharpeville, a black dormitory township. The protesters deliberately left their pass books at home and offered themselves for arrest. Many were spontaneous and voluntary participants, but the PAC also used intimidation and coercion of bus drivers transporting hordes of morning commuters. Their operatives threatened to beat up the drivers' families back home, distributing pamphlets to passengers as they did so. The crowd remained peaceful for a time as it grew, behaving cheerfully and doing their iconic African jogging and stomping dances to the point of appearing festive. But that didn't last. By ten o'clock, there were about twenty policemen at the station, and then suddenly 130 heavily armed reinforcement officers and armored Saracen cars were called in from neighboring areas as the crowd, now carrying sticks and rocks, swelled to 20,000. The atmosphere grew tense and hostile.

The police linked quickly with the Defense Force, which sent in Harvard Trainers and even Sabre jets to buzz the mob at about a hundred feet, hoping to scatter the crowd. The people simply responded by hurling their various missiles and striking three policemen. Around lunchtime the police attempted a first arrest, and that ignited an explosion of violence as the mob approached the police station fence and the shooting began. The police then panicked as the crowd pressed forward. They opened fire with automatic weapons as sixty-nine people were killed, including women and children, and one hundred eighty were injured. Many were shot from behind as they fled.

The country's black population was outraged, and the uproar among the white opposition was also widespread and vociferous. The following days and weeks saw black riots all over the country, strikes, marches and every manner of demonstration among people of every race and political conviction. On March 30th, the government declared a state of emergency as 18,000 people were rounded up and detained, including white, *Coloured* and Indian anti-apartheid members of an organization called the Congress Alliance. The PAC and ANC were both banned and simply went underground to build their armed resistance movements, named *Poqo* and *Umkhonto we Sizwe* respectively, the latter meaning "Spearhead of the Nation."

The inevitable storm of international outrage eventually led to a United Nations "condemnation" and the Security Council's sterile Resolution 134, which had zero impact on the Nationalist regime for the next thirty years. The resolution voiced the Security Council's "anger" at the policies and actions of the South African government, just as endless other sterile UN resolutions and condemnations have in the following half century. It was only after more than twenty years that sanctions and other more effective means of isolating the apartheid regime had real impact.

The Sharpeville massacre took place at about the time when the American Civil Rights movement was coalescing and getting itself organized to bring about a starkly different direction of change in American society. The Montgomery Bus Boycott had taken its course earlier in 1955-1956; the Greensborough sit-ins in 1960; and Sharpeville happened well before the Civil Rights and Voting Rights Acts of 1964 and 1965 respectively. In 1962 the Russians placed ballistic missiles on Cuban land; JFK set his target to get a man on the moon by the end of the decade; the Beatles recorded *Love Me Do*; and the first James Bond movie, *Dr. No*, was screened.

Meanwhile South Africa and the United States were tragically moving in opposite directions—America was getting things right, directionally. South Africa was shaken. Sharpeville's ghastly impact was memorialized thirty-six years later when Nelson Mandela, on December 10th, 1996, signed into law the new Constitution of South Africa at the very site of the killing.

People reacted in many different ways. My brother John and Inge-Marie hastened their plans to move out of the country. They embarked on a long circuitous journey, which in time led them to Mexico City, where John worked for a family-owned Pepsi bottler. My parents fastened their metaphorical chin straps and charged on for the time being; retirement was fast approaching and my father's view was that he had a job to complete. He knew his responsibilities for shareholders' investment, for his employees and the other stakeholders in UPSA, United Plantations of South Africa. I was myself worried, of course, but not to the point that I felt any need to change course. My naïve reasoning was that the Nationalists' objectives and policies were unsustainable, and their whole philosophy would sooner rather than later be trashed. This big, beautiful, richly blessed country would come around to become the "United States" of Africa. I was going to be part of that.

~~~~

Relations between South Africa and the British Commonwealth countries became seriously strained. One enduring set of relationships centered on rugby. For example, the British rugby establishment maintained a tradition of assembling teams of exceptionally talented players from all of the British Isles and Europe to play in ad hoc matches on tours of the antipodes. The teams were always known as the *Barbarians,* with those selected usually being *"Internationals,"* meaning they played for their respective countries' national teams. In late 1960, Andy Mulligan and his Irish team mate Tony O'Reilly were selected to tour South Africa. Andy had been my closest friend and soulmate at boarding school, Gresham's, in England, and again while we were undergraduates at Cambridge. Rugby was still an amateur sport, but players at this level had their expenses fully paid before, during and for some time after such tours. Andy and Tony had still to settle on some means of making a living when they were not playing rugby. They had registered a little trading agency in Dublin which, they declared with solemnity, would sell anything Irish to anyone around the world, and they would buy anything around the world that they could sell to the Irish. The world for them consisted of rugby crazed Australia, New Zealand, South Africa and perhaps Argentina. In international rugby territory, the two Irish boys were household names and heroes. Andy had morphed into a markedly Irish persona by this time, compared with his accent and demeanor as a schoolboy or undergraduate. Playing for Ireland had clearly facilitated visits to The

Blarney Stone in County Cork, where its magic had honed his storytelling and whole Irish image.

Andy wrote me a long epistle in his neat italic hand on their new business stationary. The fine watermarked paper was immodestly headed *Ireland International* in a large emerald italic font, with a giant green shamrock topping an elongated wavy stem stretching all the way down the left margin. The two directors were named boldly in the same green, top center:

A. J. F. O'REILLY

A. A. MULLIGAN

The letter explained that they wanted to exploit the imminent *Barbarians* tour to build their business base. They would pitch their wealthiest fans, leveraging their great fame in South Africa's rugby-obsessed environment. Their business plan was to build limitless exports of Irish products in South Africa, New Zealand and Australia, and then represent manufacturers of goods from the southern hemisphere throughout rugby-playing Europe.

> "We'll sell anything Irish," he wrote, "Butter, Jamieson's whiskey, Donegal tweed, linen, Waterford crystal, whole golf courses or luxury vacations in Irish castles. Note, dear Flemming, that we have already secured exclusivity on a unique supply of hand-woven Irish linen contraceptives especially designed for Afghani nomads!!! What Tony and I would ask you to do," he continued, "is to set up meetings for us with the country's top retailers and wholesalers, that is their CEOs, so we can sell them on *Ireland International.* We would be so damned indebted to you, Flemming! It would be such a fantastic help."

Enclosed was a list of a dozen luminary CEOs, like Sam Cohen of OK Bazaars, Sidney Press of Edgars Group, Roy Ackerman of Ackermans, the Blochs of Edblo and so on. Andy and Tony were asking me as a newly arrived entry-level market research clerk, to arrange this gathering of retail tycoons, who wielded extraordinary power from the Limpopo to Cape Point. I decided to give it a go.

I had no rugby credentials at a level to impress or attract these people's attention, so I had to leverage the O'Reilly-Mulligan fame with a differentiated invitation. I invited them to join Tony and Andy to share a session of Danish meatballs, cheese, marinated herring, Carlsberg and Aalborg *Akvavit*, at which they would chat with the two stars face-to-face, and get to know them. To my utter astonishment and trepidation, seven or eight of them accepted.

The *Barbarians* played against the Western Transvaal provincial team on a Saturday afternoon at two o'clock. In Potchefstroom, seventy miles west of Johannesburg. To allow time for the after-game social and the drive back to Jo'burg, the invitation was for eight o'clock that evening at my humble abode (I had moved away from my parents in Bryanston by then). The eager guests were there promptly and wasted no time in tucking into the *Akvavit,* chased down with Carlsberg, and even enjoyed the herring along with the other Danish delicacies. Eight-thirty arrived and went without sign of Andy and Tony. Nine o'clock, still no rugby stars. My supplies were beginning to run a little low. By nine-thirty some irate guests had departed with ill-concealed irritation. Ackerman and Press were still hanging in there, draining the Aalborg bottles, when there was a prolonged honking outside. Out of a black chauffeur-driven Bentley tumbled Mulligan and O'Reilly, followed by two pretty blonde *boeremeisies,* Afrikaans farmers' daughters. All four were inebriated. The two aspiring wizards of international trade barely managed to greet my remaining guests, and there was nary a mention of the export/import business. The Irishmen's blurred focus was mainly trained on getting the two Afrikaans girls into horizontal mode. Messrs Ackerman and Press went home drunk. The intended business purpose of the exercise had come to naught. By next morning my two chums' collective memory of the evening had vanished with the morning mist. They had moved on to join their Barbarian teammates, leaving the country for home a few days later. I never heard a peep from either of them. Fortunately, I sensed that my reputation among the retail kings of Africa had been left unscathed. My next contact with O'Reilly was twenty years later, when he was Chairman and CEO of H.J. Heinz in Pittsburgh. Even my treasured friendship with Andy suffered a dent. Andy was shocked when I reminded him of the debacle years later over a nostalgic lunch in DC.

Meanwhile, back at work it was a challenge to address under-employment by trying to be creative. Sharpeville did little to change the routine and modus operandi of the business, certainly at my level. Tucked away in the ivory tower of 40 Fox, Pat and I were seen by those who acknowledged our existence as wasteful overhead. Attempts to engage the sales people with suggestions or ideas for customers were simply seen as unsolicited interference. We eventually took to creating a little sport: Who could design and build the better paper dart, to remain airborne the longest (measured by stopwatch) when launched from the sixth floor into the deep concrete well between our building and Anglo-American's HQ? When commissioned in 1983 to write the company's 50-year history, Anthony Hocking related the story and noted that the value of Heilmann's and Sullivan's effort for the company did eventually improve:

> *"Fortunately the new market research department soon came into its own as Metal Boxers learnt what it could do. Before the well (between 40 Fox and Anglo-American's building) filled up with paper darts, head office moved to more spacious premises at Edura House, where seventy-five whites and twenty-six blacks were accommodated on the upper four floors of the Brand-new building."*

Sir Robert Barlow made another one of his regular visits to South Africa to inspect the new head office, and no doubt also to get a feel for post-Sharpeville South Africa. He suggested John Baxter look at the accelerating trend to plastic packaging, which was in fact threatening certain segments of the company's sales of traditional metal and paper products. One morning

Baxter and Barlow appeared unannounced in our office, where Sir Robert immediately perched in relaxed fashion on the corner of my desk:

> "Both of you have spent time with our market research people in London under David Buist at Baker Street, so I know MBSA is fortunate to have you here as a resource," he said as John Baxter almost winced in discomfort as he stood behind Sir Robert.

I wondered if Sir Robert could possibly have known that we were so badly underutilized.

> "South Africa has to be ready for its winds of change" he said without any acknowledgement of Harold Macmillan's prescient speech. "Plastic packaging is going to cause some new markets to develop, and plastics are going to steal some of our existing customers, so you fellows need to pinpoint the way forward for the company as these trends develop. I am particularly keen to have us find our way into consumer goods, which have traditionally been the domain of glass, paper or board. This country has enormous growth potential, so we have to plot our course, besides riding the growth in canned food exports to under-nourished people around the world."

Barlow then chatted with us for a few minutes about our personal lives and a forthcoming series of cricket "*test matches*" between England and South Africa, which had not yet been subjected to boycott initiatives. He then made a move to leave.

> "Anyway, chaps, that's what Mr. Baxter might be asking of you. We need to move into plastics, and you can help us do so in the right way. So, good luck to you both!"

"There you have it, gentlemen," Baxter chimed in, as he
ushered Barlow out, "straight from the oracle! Think about
it, and I will get back to you on the matter."

Sir Robert took me completely by surprise when he delivered a
conspiratorial wink as he turned to me in the doorway. I never learned what
that signal was meant to convey. A similar unexplained, theatrical wink was
to be experienced under very different circumstances some years later.

Next day John Baxter called me to his office, having sent Sir Robert on
a quick (meticulously planned) photo-safari in Kruger National Park in the
Eastern Transvaal, almost 250 miles away.

"Heilmann, you heard what Sir Robert said yesterday? I want
you to start work at once and have your report ready in six
weeks, before I go to London for the next Overseas
Company board meeting. I need to know what's happening
in our traditional tinplate markets threatened by plastics,
what our role might be in any market segment for plastics
packaging ... and how we should contemplate a market
entry. You have my full authority to spend what it takes to
get this done PDQ. I'll tell Noel Frank, who will be
approving your expenses. You'll need to get access to
customers' plans and ideas, so that means reaching some
pretty senior people around the country, but you will sort
that out, no doubt. Now get on your bicycle, young man!
Good luck, Heilmann! ... and I said six weeks!"

Within minutes of my returning to our office, Pat was also summoned
by Baxter and instructed to segment and analyze the combined canned food
exports of all MBSA's customers, which meant deciduous fruit, citrus,
pineapple and vegetables, along with meat and fish packs, all to be

summarized by product, value and destination. The company had the statistics in-house, as they were regularly used to argue our position in representations to Iscor, the government-owned steel mill which supplied all our domestically sourced tinplate. The chairman's timing was deliberate. He was not about to allow one of us to feel more relevant or needed than the other.

The plastics assignment launched me into a precipitous tour of every major city in southern Africa and literally hundreds of interviews. Cosmetic and pharmaceutical companies, detergent and household cleaner producers, fertilizer manufacturers, users of plastic components like caps and closures for glass and metal containers. New ground was broken as top-level contacts had to be made in companies outside MBSA's historical reach. Travel was scheduled five days a week. Weekends were spent analyzing and organizing information, defining technical terms and researching technologies and raw materials quite foreign to the existing business and, of course, to me. The days of paper dart design were gone. Insufficient time, even for sleep. The report was written and presented as a briefing for Baxter's London trip, which he checked and cross-checked five ways to Sunday. He took off having left no stone unturned.

A week later our fearless leader was home again in Jo'burg for MBSA's own board meeting, immediately after which I was again summoned to his office. The Overseas Company in London, which oversaw international holdings, had briefly studied the plastics market analysis. Aware of Barlow's interest in the matter, its directors had quickly authorized Baxter to devise a business plan. So MBSA's directors then promptly authorized my start-up capital budget, almost certainly without having a clue as to what it would actually take.

"So, Flemming, you might think you have delivered on your assignment, and in fact you have. Well done! But that's just the beginning," Baxter said, chuckling and suddenly using my first name. "You haven't even really started! We have decided to invest modestly in the plastics market segments you have recommended. However, I didn't tell London about your unsolicited implementation plan, which you had the balls to attach as an addendum to the report you gave me ... And, in fact, I haven't shown it to anybody yet. Did anybody ever tell you to be careful what you wish for, young man? What we now need from you is a complete business plan and a reconsidered budget," he said, still chuckling. "You made the recommendations, so you can now deliver on them, too! Ha-ha! Flemming, I called your bluff and can now congratulate you on your first promotion." His demeanor suddenly serious, he continued. "You are now Project Manager, Plastics, for the Metal Box Company of South Africa, reporting directly to me. I'll deal with Sevenoaks."

Aged just 24, I was suddenly a manager responsible for a little start-up designed by myself. I was a bit wobbly at the knees as I made my way down the burgundy-carpeted corridor to my desk.

So now what?

Left to my own devices, I did a decent job in aspects of starting the business from scratch, selecting entry markets, securing access to alien technologies and state-of-the-art equipment from around the world, recruiting and arranging technical training for engineering and operating staff. Target customers were secured to nail down a baseload for the business. A rented manufacturing site was prepared. However, in financial terms, the start-up was unnecessarily expensive, as I failed to control costs sufficiently. Capital invested in manufacturing capacity was excessive. Headquarters bailed me out of cash flow crunches. A stint at business school focused on corporate finance and accounting, might have pre-empted these mistakes. Some early start-up losses could have been avoided, so achieving profitability took longer than it should have. I was reporting directly to John

Baxter, a growth-oriented builder who showed amazing faith and patience. I was conscious of the fact that not everybody on the MBSA board shared Baxter's enthusiasm and faith. Some directors did not think plastics were a field in which to make a competitive return on shareholders' funds. Why mess with the unfamiliar?

The requisite expansion of sales, however, was achieved over time, so the embryonic plastics business was moved from the rented downtown premises to a brand-new custom built 100,000 square foot factory in the industrial suburb of Isando just outside Johannesburg, hard by Jan Smuts Airport. By this time some painful lessons had been learned and some financial disciplines mastered, so the business grew steadily, edging into the black. One problem was that new technology kept causing mistakes and hiccups. The plastics division remained an outlier in terms of the company's core business, its culture, tradition and organizational pecking order.

~~~~

Travelling to Europe and America was part of the job, in order to secure technology, equipment and imported raw materials. Principals of multinational customers and suppliers had to be cultivated. My very first visit to the States, in 1960, cemented a lifelong love affair with America. As a student in the post-World War II years, I had understood and respected the colossal role of the American economic engine—in saving Europe's millions from famine and for financing its economic recovery. New York, of course, overwhelmed me in every way, but it was its people more than anything else, who bowled me over. I spent every free hour exploring the city's distinct segments and cultures. One very long walk from the Sheraton Russell hotel just north of Grand Central all the way to Harlem's 125th Street took me to a number of bars and coffee shops where my accent prompted probing questions and midnight conversations with people of amazing disparity. In Harlem, curiosity rather than any hint of animosity drove all sorts of questions about apartheid. I was myself a curiosity. One local resident questioned me thus:

> "What are real Africans like, man?—those guys out there in the bush, or jungle, or whatever? Do they really wear leopard skins? And put bones through their noses?
> What'a they do all day in the jungle?"
> "Why do they put up with all that segregation shit when they are the three-to-one majority?" asked a black cab driver taking a coffee break. "If they ain't happy, why don' they jus' shut the whole fuckin' place down?"

> "Whach you doin' over there, man? You sell stuff to the blacks? Bet they get screwed! Ha, ha, ha!" He laughed as he patted me on the shoulder, to show he meant no offence.

In an upper East Side bar, where I stopped in for a scotch, an attractive all-American blonde with wide-set blue eyes, a Pepsodent smile and perfect superstructure, just two stools away, asked where my accent was from, and upon learning that I was Danish but the accent was English she expressed her relief:

> "Thank God for that, honey! The way you asked for your *whiskey sohdah*, that crazy suit, cute striped shirt and with that haircut, you just HAD to be British or queer as a goddamned coot!"

Given her looks and friendly demeanor, I invested some time and dollars that long night to ensure the lady gained clarity regarding my sexual orientation.

After a Wall Street meeting with W.R. Grace (then a major producer of polyethylene and other petrochemicals we used in Isando) a peak-hour traffic jam meant a horrific cab ride back to the Sheraton Russell. My conversation with the African-American driver was fun and free-flowing all the way. I asked questions about New York and his life in Alabama; he enquired about every aspect of life in South Africa, its peoples, politics, climate, industry, the white minority government and of course the plight of the black majority under apartheid. He was extremely well informed and intelligently inquisitive, avoiding strong opinions, just nodding his head as I talked. At last back at the hotel, as I paid and gave him his tip, my new friend flashed the most expansive gleaming-white smile:

> "Man, know what?" he asked and paused a moment, " ... to me duh Union of Saahth Africa sounds a helluva a lot like duh State of Alabama ... or Mississippi, or Saahth Carolina ... but you jus' movin' in duh opsit direction." Then with another huge smile, "You have a great time, now. Thanks a lot, man, and take care ... and, sah! Don't ever forget ... us minorities gotta stick together!" He chuckled out loud. "Yeees, man! Us minorities gotta stick together!"

Travelling across the States, through the Midwest to California, the warm, friendly curiosity was consistent. Many critical judgments of the apartheid regime were to the point and based on accurate understanding of the injustices and inhumanity of the regime. Not surprisingly, in Europe it was more common to encounter animosity and ill-informed criticism of South Africa. In the USA, it was only in San Francisco that unctuous but equally ill-informed disapproval was aggressively expressed.

~~~~

Verwoerd's government articulated its apartheid agenda pretty clearly, and the Afrikaner population, along with many poor white Anglophones, were eager to support it, including measures reflecting the Nationalists' loathing of the Brits. Hateful memories of concentration camps, ghastly mistreatment of Afrikaaners before and during the Boer War, bitter accounts of British theft of land in the Dutch Cape Colony and Eastern Cape were kept up front and center in Afrikaans schools, in their media and Dutch Reformed churches. At every opportunity, the great *trek* was enshrined and glorified, segment by segment; episodes and tales of the Boers' bravery and suffering during the *trek* were exaggerated or simply manufactured. Verwoerd seeking to secure a fat majority of votes in all-white elections reduced the voting age to eighteen. This strategy was based on the Afrikaners' higher birthrate and much younger average age than that of Anglophones. He also placed the white population of the South West Africa protectorate (now Namibia) on the South African electoral roll, since the Afrikaans- and German-speaking population there was heavily Nationalist, easily outnumbering English-speakers. He then launched the referendum on whether the country, then known as the *Union of South Africa,* should terminate its membership in the British Commonwealth to become the totally independent Republic of South Africa. This would sever ties to the UK, its dominions and all the ex-British territories. The Nats were determined to rid themselves of "all relics of British imperialism."

The United Party's pathetically passive opposition and the much smaller Progressive Party appealed for a NO vote in the referendum. Only in Natal province was there an Anglophone majority opposed to the Nats, but the country's substantial Jewish population was also solidly opposed to defection. Jews were consistently the leading source of everything progressive in South Africa.

I volunteered to work door to door for Helen Suzman's Progressives in the Afrikaans-speaking Jo'burg suburb of Jeppe, a shabby suburb known for its *Poor Whites*, most of whom worked for South African Railways in menial unskilled jobs. My Afrikaans was always bad, but my understanding was helped by the Afrikaans words shared with Danish or German. My English accent only made things more difficult. At one door I was met by a young blonde girl to whom I posed the referendum's question in Afrikaans: *"Is U ten gunste van 'n Republiek vir die Unie?"* Are you in favor of a republic for the Union? The girl scornfully tossed her head back and scoffed at me, answering with her own question: *"Stem NIE vir die kaffirs???"* Would I vote NO to support the blacks? she asked. *Kaffir was* the commonly used equivalent to the "N" word in the USA or England, derived from the Arabic word for "Infidel."

The whites-only vote was YES by a margin of 52.3 percent to 47.7 percent. Within a year even the currency based on the British system was changed, replacing South African pounds, shillings and pence with the *Rand* (two to the pound), worth 100 cents. Rand in Afrikaans means ridge, as in Witwatersrand.

Despite all this turmoil, the country continued to function and economic growth persisted. The infrastructure generally worked very well, built with substantial investment of British capital over many decades. It was, by far, the most advanced economy on the African continent. With a strong administrative bureaucracy, it continued to serve the country's burgeoning industry and commerce efficiently. The fabulous treasure of natural resources continued to be exploited and exported around the globe, while Anglo-American, de Beers, JCI, Rand Mines, General Mining and a handful of other mining conglomerates dominated international gold and diamond markets. They also had huge positions in world markets for iron ore, anthracite coal and almost every strategic metal from platinum and uranium to copper. As they had for decades, the country's rich agriculture and fisheries helped to feed a hungry world at home and abroad. South African management talent was abundant, while the work ethic was as strong as anywhere in the world. The only missing resource was oil, a fact that became a nervous obsession of the Nationalists.

Cutting edge scientific and medical research blossomed. In Cape Town Christian Barnard was busy developing the world's first heart transplant methodology, which he was soon to apply to global acclaim in Texas. Most importantly, commerce and industry generated and invested endless capital, creating jobs for millions of people—the vast majority of whom were black—providing a living for themselves and their poverty-stricken families in distant rural areas trapped, at best, in subsistence level farming. On the other hand, the conditions under which black labor toiled in most of the mines and in too many of the country's agricultural industries remained, in varying degrees, unacceptable. South Africa's immensely able entrepreneurs, professionals, managers and financiers kept driving the growth of the continent's powerhouse economy, while most of the European population remained in denial of apartheid's vile objectives and inhuman consequences. Many people either swallowed the Nationalist dogma or simply chose to ignore it. Too many simply bought into the Nats' facile propaganda, their disingenuous *Separate but equal* slogan for their concept of two societies within one nation. Verwoerd's Bantustan policy was being put in place step by step with the creation of the "tribal homelands" with carefully chosen tribal leaders as figureheads or puppets.

Marilyn's passage to South Africa turned out to be a one-way ticket. After she and I together had shared my parents' hospitality for a month or two in Bryanston, we became engaged. A modest mid-July winter wedding was staged by my parents, allowing Marilyn's widowed mother to travel from genteel Frinton-on-Sea in Essex, and for a spinster Aunt Muriel to travel down from Salisbury in Southern Rhodesia (today Harare and Zimbabwe, respectively). I committed the ultimate bridegroom's sin of entirely forgetting the wedding rehearsal in Rosebank's Anglican Church on the Friday afternoon before the wedding, when I was rounding off a good week's work at the office. It took an extremely irate call from sister-in-law, Inge-Marie, to alert me to the situation, allowing me to arrive over ninety minutes late, rushing headlong from downtown Jo'burg. Of course, everybody was seriously miffed, but it was Inge-Marie who delivered the severest tongue-lashing, the most dramatic castigation ever. My friend John Lang, a Johannesburg lawyer who had taken me under his wing when I was an intern during my final Cambridge vacation in 1956, handled all the formalities of the nuptials. His wedding present was an anti-nuptial contract, which actually came in handy more than a decade later. There were no more than a score of us in my parents' *highveld* winter garden for the sunny champagne party. Apart from John and Brenda Lang, there were a few of my newfound Jo'burg friends, business associates of PB's, Mor's bridge partners and some neighbors. London friends of Marilyn had given her introductions to some Johannesburgers, who rounded out the guest list. After a short honeymoon in Lourenco Marques, we moved to a very modest apartment, part of a commensurately modest bungalow in Parktown North, just north of the city. I got back to work.

The friendship with John and Brenda soon withered, with social contact becoming irregular and then ceasing all together. Some years later the reason was clear. John had, for several years, been running clandestine financial operations in support of the ANC, and the South African secret police eventually caught up with him. He was linked to some radical American group engaged in funneling money to help finance the arms, sabotage and propaganda activities of the ANC. The Langs somehow evaded arrest and disappeared from the Johannesburg scene. Sadly, it was then discovered that John had dipped into client trust funds held by the law firm. They were at some point forced to leave the country and were said to have continued their efforts in support of the ANC quite openly from London, where they made their new home.

Despite the steady imposition of new apartheid legislation, Johannesburg's cultural initiatives could still reach across the color bar. This was particularly true in the realm of performing arts, especially music. Some months after Sharpeville, a group of exceptional musicians and singers in Soweto teamed up with white civic and cultural leaders in Johannesburg to produce a groundbreaking *township musical*, financed by well-heeled people in the business community. The set and costumes were designed by no other than Arthur Goldreich, with whom I became friends (and who, as already related, later astonished me and the whole country when the dimensions of his moonlight job were revealed). Lilting *Township Jazz*, with its captivating melodies, New Orleans style combining with uniquely African harmonies and rhythm, was the medium for the story of a professional boxer and his tortured life of dingy gyms, drugs, alcohol, crime and sex. *King Kong* was initially produced as a fund-raiser, for which I worked as a volunteer, to provide support for the needy of Soweto, Sophiatown and Alexandra townships. It was staged in a large auditorium in Milner Park, the industrial show grounds and home to the annual Rand Easter Show. The spectacular show was an immediate knockout and spawned several great stars. Tons of money was raised for priority causes in the townships, going directly into the coffers of genuine and effective social service programs, with all expenses covered by generous philanthropists. Since the venue was otherwise idle at that time of the year, the show's sold-out run could be extended for weeks. Ticket sales exploded as the media and word of mouth raved over the talent and quality of artistry, so the businessmen who had bankrolled *King Kong* decided they could kill two birds with a single stone: promote the world class talent of the artists and raise large sums for their favorite township causes. The show was then permitted to move into downtown Jo'burg, to the Coliseum Theatre on Commissioner Street, the city's main drag. It was the largest indoor venue in the Transvaal. Almost every song or number was recorded and sold in neighboring African countries, but, more importantly, in Europe and the USA. Nathan Mdledle starred in the title role. Miriam Makeba's early reputation as a member of the Soweto-based *Manhattan Brothers* jazz group immediately went into orbit as she took the female lead.

Makeba's stellar international career had been launched. Her head-turning beauty, captivating personality and spectacularly powerful voice bowled over every audience and conquered the airwaves. The success of this extraordinary musical drama also propelled Kippie Moketsie to stardom in the burgeoning world of *Township Jazz*. The appreciation of talent and the leadership exhibited by good people in that Johannesburg environment made good things happen for a lot of people. Among the good people was Trevor Huddleston, the beloved Anglican bishop and true activist leader in the opposition to apartheid. Along the way, he had helped many people to remarkably better lives through his focus on their most urgent and serious needs—tens of thousands of African children attending the schools for which he was responsible; scores of township musicians launched by *Huddleston's Jazz Band* in Sophiatown (including Hugh Masekela, whose artistry on trumpet became legendary on a global basis); hundreds of Black activists to whom he brought focus and help in defining prioritized action— they honored him with the nickname *Makhalipile*, the dauntless one.

The King Kong show soon went on tour in Japan, with runs in Tokyo and Osaka. Miriam Makeba achieved international stardom, moved to the USA, blossomed, went through several marriages including her long relationship with Stokely Carmichael, and she inspired American song writers for years. In 2011, she sadly died in relative obscurity, in Italy.

~~~~

My job took me on frequent travels to the urban centers of southern Africa, most frequently on sales and factory visits in the coastal cities. Occasionally, travel by land rather than air would allow opportunity to sense and fall in love with the country's natural beauty and its people. Vacations would add many more such experiences.

Durban, after Cape Town, had the most to offer as a shoreline setting with a diverse demography. The large Indian population, their Hindu temples and markets, brought Asian sounds, sights and welcome scents of spices to parts of the city. Indians were generally engaged in industry, commerce and the services. They were less often employed as unskilled labor. The burly ink-black Zulus reflected the proximity of their homeland just to the north and constituted most of the labor force. Zulu rickshaw men in their traditional warrior garb added color and humor as they pranced and danced around to lure customers. The whites in this province of Natal were predominantly Anglophones and seemed to hanker after the British lifestyle of their forebears. There was a lot to remind them of the old colonial days, particularly the much-favored club life, rigid dress codes, hints of snobbery and overt racial prejudice. The Durban Club was the revered temple of such colonial tradition. The waterfront was a sunny parade of multistory holiday hotels, apartment houses and broad promenades facing predictably perfect sunrises over the beach and ocean surf. The Indian Ocean shores to both north and south were graced by endless miles of kids' paradise beaches, sub-tropical flora and exotic fruits. The winter months of May through October guaranteed vacations of perfect cloudless skies, dry warmth and twinkling temperate sea.

Fifteen miles north of Durban, the shimmering white beach was interrupted by the craggy Umhlanga Rocks outcrop, a favored family vacation spot, where the brand-new high-rise Hotel Beverly Hills had been opened by its young developer Sol Kerzner. I decided to try it out on a business trip and met Sol at the bar. There was a nice correlation between the hotel's name and his Hollywood taste, reflected in his glitzy cream-colored shark skin suit, black shirt and white silk tie. He was very engaging and immediately extended an invitation to join his dinner party that evening for a group of Jo'burgers invited to Umhlanga Rocks as a marketing promotion for his new venture. When I explained that I had a business commitment with Unilever people, he insisted that I would be free to join him by nine o'clock, when his party would only be settling down. He would save me a place for dessert and coffee.

> "For Chrissake, man, yer stuffy old dinner porty will be done before it's bidtarm for those old buggers, at narno'clock. Boring as hill, thay ore! Ah bit your dins isat the Derbin Club, where thay'll all be horf asleep anywaaiy, man. You'll see juss now, I am tilling you! Yor dins will be aver baai aight-thirty, man!

Sol was right. I was back at the hotel in ample time to take a seat at the long table where all his guests were relaxed, chatting over wine and dessert. A place had been saved for me, next to a Johannesburg soap and detergent manufacturer, Aaron Silberman. He had a deep-tanned rugged boxer's face, honest wide-set green eyes and a thick—appropriately silver mane of perfectly kempt, wavy hair.

"So you must be Sol's first paying guest here at The Heavily Bills, Flemming. It's a bit better than his dad's old dump on The Front," chuckled Aaron, referring to the senior Kerzners' two-star family vacation hostelry on the downtown Durban beachfront. "Young Sol will do well out here if he doesn't get too cocky. Beautiful holiday spot, here at Umhlanga, for Jo'burg families with kiddies and great for European tourists. His daddy always overplayed the caution side of the equation, you know ... He wouldn't spenda penny on the place. The old man hates risk. But Sol's different; he has big balls—maybe too big—see what I mean, Flemming?" Another pause for a sip of his pinotage. "But, what are you doing here? You visiting from overseas or something? From old England? How do you like our country?"

I explained I was on business from Johannesburg, where I lived. In answer to persistent questions, I told him I was in the plastic packaging business. This, at once, pricked his interest. He told me about his new liquid detergent product for dishwashers, developed as his answer to Unilever's latest innovation, *Lux Liquid*. Both products were marketed in plastic squeeze bottles.

"It's retailed under the *Tubs* name. I think that's a much better name, don't you, Flemming? More imaginative, eh? *Lux Liquid* could be some sort of stuff for your face, for your complexion or for the shower. *Tubs* tells you up front that it's all about washing up, doesn't it? You should come see me in Jo'burg. I'll show you my plant. We go first class with everything we do … you'll see! Maybe you can do a better job on our bottles than Plastex does—they're not the greatest suppliers," he said, handing me his business card. "Do you have a card, Flemming?"

Aaron paused, looking hard and long at my business card. He then told me how impressed he was with Metal Box and their enlightened position on so many issues. He had been a shareholder since John Baxter had taken MBSA public. After some more chat about this and that, he turned to me.

"Tell me something, if you don't mind my asking. Your card says C. Flemming Heilmann. What does the C. stand for?"

"Aaron, that's actually for my first name. C for Christian," I told him.

He had been so full of non-stop chat all evening, but now suddenly, there was a really long pause. Again he turned towards me, his brow deeply furrowed over a puzzled face.

"You know, man, really—that's a strange bloody name for a nice Jewish boy like you!" Another short pause. "What on earth happened, Flemming?"

Aaron and I became friends and Metal Box Plastics Division sold him a lot of *Tubs* bottles over the years. His little company actually gave Unilever a run for their money in the competitive detergent market.

Sol Kerzner, of course, became rich and famous, almost a household name in the world of casinos, flashy hotels and middle-class resorts. First *Sun City* two hours north of Jo'burg, in what became the ostensibly independent Tswana *homeland* Bophuthatswana, in 1977, under apartheid homelands policy. Later a casino on the Jersey shore in the USA and then the *Atlantis* resort in the Bahamas—his biggest and most vulgar gambling cum vacation resort, insanely overleveraged, was eventually bought out of bankruptcy.

Along the coastline of the Indian Ocean, to Durban's south and west, the boring little towns of East London and Port Elizabeth interrupt almost nine hundred miles of spectacular, unspoiled seaboard. Part of it is aptly named the Garden Route, which stretches all the way from Port Elizabeth to the gorgeous Cape of Good Hope and Cape Town itself. Along this reach of the Cape coast, there are pristine, beautiful little towns and fishing villages, each with its river mouth, like Plettenberg Bay, Knysna and Hermanus separating some of the world's most spectacular beaches, wide and silvery or golden, below giant sea-grassed dunes, all backed by the ranges of the Cape Fold system: the Suurberge, Amatola, Outeniqua and Hottentots-Holland mountains, smoky blue below the azure sky.

Northeast of East London, the majestic emptiness of the craggy Wild Coast separates the Transkei, homeland of the Xhosa tribe and Mandela's clan, from the ocean. This was the land of Madiba's home *kraal* or village, where he was raised as a very young boy. Breathtakingly empty, gleaming beaches onto which the Indian Ocean's heavy surf crashes, generating rip currents that can suck any helpless intruder into a sea full of whales and sharks. Fast-flowing river mouths between towering rocky bluffs falling straight into the ocean from smooth, rounded grazing-green hills.

Just inland and to the north of Durban are the rolling sugarcane farmlands of Natal (now Kwazulu province). Westward lies the warm, welcoming highland country, rising toward the elevated *highveld* plateau beyond the Drakensberg escarpment: softly undulating grassy green hills, clustered reed huts built in circles within the *kraals* of Zulu subsistence farmers; narrow valleys dissected by fickle little brown creeks and bigger, more permanent bush-lined streams. This tranquil, silent countryside, the empty air hanging dead still, belies the violent warrior history of the Zulus. The stillness is barely broken by the distant call of a hadeda ibis flapping his way from a bush to a higher vantage point, the barking of a dog in the hillside *kraal*, or the shy ivory-white smile and *saku bohna, n'kosi!* greeting of a lonely teenage cowherd coaxing his two emaciated cows.

Majestic rounded emerald hills elicit Alan Paton's beloved country for which the whole world still cries. This was also home to the great and revered Chief Albert Luthuli, Zulu tribal leader, Christian missionary, anti-apartheid activist and head of the then non-violent ANC. He won the 1960 Nobel Peace Prize before the ANC espoused guerrilla warfare and overt terrorism and well before the prize was prostituted by yet another iteration of the Nordic leftist catechism. The annual award was still an acclaimed international recognition of substantive, effective achievement in the field of human rights and peace by *the person who shall have done the most for fraternity between nations, the abolition or reduction of standing armies and for the holding and promotion of peace congresses.*

Luthuli's peace prize was awarded in the epoch before Alfred B. Nobel's noble notion was terminally degraded by populist political correctness, before erstwhile terrorists like Yasser Arafat, or inept abstractions like The United Nations Peace Keeping Force were favored by the unctuous Stockholm committee in charge.

Still further inland the colossal escarpment, with the igneous crescent of the magnificent Drakensberg amphitheater leaps heavenward, like a giant retaining wall keeping the *highveld's* plains and the tiny landlocked kingdom of Basutoland (now Lesotho) in place. Further to the north and west, the high-altitude grasslands, or *highveld*, roll to the distant horizon; huge cattle ranches and extensive *mealie* or corn farms of the big sky provinces of Transvaal and Orange Free State, the treasured heartland of the Afrikaner, the traditional farmer.

Given my parents' base in the northernmost corner of Swaziland, UPSA's Ngonini Citrus Plantation became a favored vacation destination, about six hours' drive from Jo'burg.

The trip entailed a dead-east trek across rolling, treeless *highveld* grazing and *mealie* lands. The sunny winter drought dries the long grass to shiny gray and the wind causes it to ripple like silvery waves washing across the open sky landscape. The main tarmac road was broad and ruler straight, disappearing over the crest of the nearest swelling hill, only to reappear as a black ribbon leading to the next more distant hill, finally becoming an ever-thinner thread disappearing into a tiny black spot on the horizon. After a few hours, the *highveld* suddenly gives way at Machadodorp to the East Transvaal escarpment, kloofs and valleys leading down to the *lowveld* bush country, the terrain dropping nearly four thousand feet in the course of only a few miles. This region, now named Mpumalanga, enjoys a warmer, more temperate climate, which allows the bush to flourish densely, the subtropical flora, softwood plantations, banana, avocado or citrus groves to thrive—all set in dramatic topography, a scenic paradise. This indigenous bush country is home to almost all of Africa's fantastic fauna. The region attracted tourists from everywhere, seeking safari experiences in the Kruger National Park and a small number of private game reserves. Licensed game hunting and wonderful river fishing drew international sportsmen.

The northern approach to Swaziland from Johannesburg and Pretoria takes you through this exotic wonderland, the most iconic "African" of all South Africa's disparate regions. The road, which continues east all the way to Lourenco Marques (now Maputo), passes through Nelspruit, a bustling little market town of wide jacaranda-lined dirt streets, then along the Komati River valley to Komatipoort, just miles north of the Swaziland border post. The time it took to reach Ngonini Estate from the Swazi border depended on the condition of dirt roads, which developed corrugated ruts in the dry winter season and muddy quagmires during summer's heavy rains. The other variant was the alertness and sobriety of the somnolent Swazi "guard" at the boundary gate.

In a fertile valley resembling those of inland Natal, Ngonini Estate's wide tiers of orange grove and smaller acreages of lemon, lime and grapefruit were spread along the banks of the Lomati River. Along the very edge of the river, banana palms would waft peacefully in the slightest breeze created by convection currents over the cool rushing water. The citrus was gravity irrigated, thanks to the Lomati's dependable flow and the ingenious combination of a weir, miles of canal, multiple pumping stations and a power-generating turbine station where it terminated miles downriver and about 400 feet above it. All contrived by my father, PB, and his technical advisors.

The plantation's tidy village development housed several hundreds of Swazi families and provided them basic schooling for the first time, medical attention and a living standard, which was light-years removed from the subsistence-driven struggle of the people scattered in the surrounding hills. A general store offered supplies otherwise only available in Pigg's Peak, a tiny village fifteen miles away, up in the hills to the south. Large corrugated asbestos structures served as fruit sorting and packing halls, where millions of cases of oranges and other fruit were prepared for their journey to distant markets around the world under the *Outspan* label of South Africa's citrus agency. Management's housing was built atop a crescent shaped hill, along a red dirt road, with lush gardens offering a magnificent vista of the valley, backed by a smoke-blue skyline of hills on the distant Transvaal boundary. Tennis courts and a swimming pool were among the amenities next to a whitewashed *rondavel* clubhouse, which also offered ping-pong, a card room and a small bar under its traditional open thatched roof. It was the social center where the staff and their families relaxed at weekend *braaivleis* or BBQ parties. Ten years earlier and pre-PB, all of this had been indigenous Swazi bush, home to a few cattle and even fewer Swazis, but lots of birds, snakes, various types of antelope and their feared predators. From this isolated outpost of Danish enterprise, Ngonini Estate managed to compete successfully with the established giant citrus producers of Brazil, California, Florida, Israel and Spain. Little did we then know that this whole development initiative was doomed by HIV/AIDS to closure fifty years later. The pandemic caused labor, training and medical costs to soar, rendering the whole business hopelessly uncompetitive. An average of three or more workers had to be trained and held in reserve for every single work station on the estate. Employees were dying like flies early in the new millennium. I have always been relieved that my father, PB, had been long retired in Denmark and then re-settled in Connecticut before this came about.

Other family vacations, or holidays, as they are called in British English, took us to quivering hot tropical beaches in Xai Xai on the Mozambique coast, way north of Lourenco Marques; to the Cape's spectacular surf beaches in Plettenberg Bay, backed by the Outeniqua Mountains; or game watching in the Kruger National Park. Many a reachable white man's paradise within reach in every direction, for those of us so privileged.

By the mid-60s, Macmillan's winds of change were gusting at increasing velocity throughout Africa. They reached gale force just north of the Limpopo. As the struggles for independence escalated and Britain withdrew from her colonial possessions, the UK government aimed to establish majority rule in Southern Rhodesia, which of course meant a black government. White Rhodesians did not generally agree with that notion, so Ian Smith's ruling Rhodesian Front party grappled fiercely with Whitehall in a losing political battle. A Unilateral Declaration of Independence was crafted and actually presented, in the most pointed way possible, to Parliament in London on November 11th, 1965, at eleven o'clock in the morning. It was the moment at which Britons would commemorate their heroes lost in mortal battles to protect Britain's freedom and that of the rest of the planet, for that matter. Rhodesians meant to remind the world of their sacrifice and role in support of exactly that struggle in two world wars. There were agitated and eloquent protests from Whitehall, other Commonwealth countries and, of course, the ever-vocal United Nations pontificating in distant Manhattan. All to no avail, except that Rhodesia was soon forced to join South Africa as an ex-member of the British Commonwealth of Nations. South of the Limpopo, the Nationalist government relished these developments, as did many white South Africans. The halls of government in Cape Town and Pretoria rang with Nationalist rhetoric, ever supportive of the Rhodesian rebels.

South Africa's steady march to apartheid madness and the plight of her non-white population rightly caught the attention of the western world.

What was not always so right was the way in which the world responded. All sorts of anxious NGOs, international and UN-related agencies sent people to the country and its neighbors Bechuanaland, Basutoland and Swaziland. Oxfam and Amnesty International were the most active of them. With a few brilliant exceptions they were not focused on the priorities and thus generally ineffective. Their emissaries were often ill-informed and ill-prepared. Too many of their agents were simply on boondoggles from the northern hemisphere, or on feel-good missions, posing for holy pictures. One pale Englishman, Roy Manley, with struggling flaxen whiskers reminiscent of the Miller's in Chaucer's tale, was offered transit lodging in our Bryanston home, en route to teach Basutoland's inadequately fed youth about "nutritional priorities"—as if they had the luxury of choice! He took a lecherous interest in almost any female within striking distance. Our nanny Victoria's nubile daughter, visiting "mama" from the family's distant Shangaan *kraal,* didn't escape his eye. Even Marilyn, I detected, was at the receiving end of his tactile attention, which did not seem totally abhorrent to her. My confidence in the true objective of his Basuto mission was hardly boosted when his suitcase accidentally sprang open as he was departing, spilling dozens of Durex condom tri-packs onto the floor of our entrance hall. I had no reason to believe that family planning was part of his mission's curriculum. It was, however, an omen of things to come: in the new millennium, Oxfam's reputation and self-righteous PR efforts had to battle through extensive and revolting reports of widespread abuse, sexual exploitation and selling of access to youth and young children in underdeveloped countries, where their "aid workers" had unfettered access to their prey. Among NGOs even the best of western intentions were, in too many cases, dissipated by naïve, uncoordinated activity driven by misdirected feel-good agendas.

Chapter II

Material Transition

"The path of civilization is paved with tin cans."
-Elbert Hubbard

AS MBSA'S PLASTICS Division grew and eventually reached sustainable profitability, I was, at age 29, moved to Head Office as General Sales Manager for the whole company, which meant re-integrating with the mainstream metal packaging business—steel and aluminum cans, boxes and tubes for myriad consumer goods. In turn, this required even more travel, visiting the operations and offices of customers including agricultural and fish processing companies, often far off the beaten track. It was a testing time in terms of some personal relationships in the company. I was reporting to the Sales Director, Ed Loughlin, a sharp, but hyperactive American board member, who had little idea about managing people because he had spent his life working solo, as the sales representative of US Steel Corporation for all of Africa south of the Sahara. His range of contacts in the business world seemed limitless in Southern Africa. Athletic of build, he dressed meticulously in the American button-down IBM style of the times, standing tall in his Brooks Brothers suit and narrow brimmed felt hat. Narrow set eyes, a high brow and receding hairline, with a small tight mouth over a slightly receding chin. Ed was also a bit of a Jekyll & Hyde character, quite charming and amusing, but suddenly vicious when he felt threatened or insecure. He communicated upwards particularly well, and the mesmerized John Baxter was his only superior in the pecking order. He had a loaded rolodex and a winning ability to engage people. Ed could open doors through which conventional Metal Box executives could never have walked. However, he was allergic to planning, had no clue about business strategy, finance or leading a team. My challenge was to build some structure, develop marketing strategy and introduce some planning into MBSA's sales effort without treading on my boss's toes. Not easy!

The Western Cape's prolific deciduous fruit growing valleys of Robertson and Langeberg were reached from Cape Town within a two-hour drive. The job called for direct interaction with many Afrikaans customers in an unfamiliar business environment. The company's largest customer was an Afrikaans farmers' co-operative, which covered a score of canning facilities processing every kind of peach, apricot, apple and pear in the deciduous fruit spectrum, along with jams, juices and nectars and many different vegetables—all of which ended up in billions of our cans and then helped feed people all around the world. Langeberg Ko-Op's CEO was predictably a very Afrikaans Dr. Geert Moolman, who would not readily engage you in English. His black middle-parted, slickly combed hair sat atop shaven temples and neck. He did not enjoy people like me addressing him in English. My very first call on *"Meneer Doktor"*—Mr. Doctor—did not go very well. His office looked like a Secret Police interrogation cell: brown polished *slasto* (local slate) floor and cream painted walls with chocolate brown trim, a large empty desk upon which there was nothing but a leather-framed blotting pad and a stainless steel table lamp standing sentinel. The man himself sat in a hard, armless steel chair. There was a single visitor's chair, which I guessed he had taken from the staff canteen, placed against the wall, ten feet from his desk. After my perfunctory greeting in Afrikaans, I stood awkwardly, facing him and clasping my document folder as he leaned forward, glaring at me. I broke the silence by proceeding to address him in English. I talked of production plans for the coming canning season. His staccato response was in his own preferred tongue as he stared me down, bespectacled under heavy black eyebrows drawn into a scowl. I gathered that he was telling me that the country was meant to be bilingual. Some of his Afrikaans was recognizable to me, quite a few words being close to Danish or German. The exchange didn't last long. Dr. Moolman gruffly acknowledged my courtesy call and closed out the brief meeting in heavily accented English:

> "Misterrr Hailman, pleess addrrress me in Afrrrikornss next
> tarm yoo kom," he admonished me. "Aw will eefen giff yoo
> a better cheerrr to set on eef yoo do thet! *Tot siens, meneer!"*
> he said, bidding me an abrupt farewell.

My Afrikaans did not improve enough in time for the next scheduled visit to Langeberg, so I sent another senior manager, who could pay our respects in the correct lingo. It took a couple of years before I could haltingly exchange a few ideas with Dr. Moolman, but he did give me credit for trying.

Our meat can business meant customer calls in Gaberones, the center of all things commercial and political in Bechuanaland. No language problems there, but accommodations and living conditions were about as sophisticated as an outback sheep station in the arid Northern Territory of Australia. The Tswanas, like their ancestors going back a thousand years, are herdsmen and hunters rather than farmers. White South Africans added organized ranching and huge cattle herds to the country's beef production. There was also a developing platinum mining industry, which would eventually assume global scale. It was immediately evident that the inherited British colonial schooling system was intact and effective and, as a result, the literacy rate among the blacks tended to be a lot higher than in South Africa. Over half the territory is Kalahari Desert, and the balance is high plateau savannah and dry scrubland. The economy, based on beef and mining, was growing rapidly. The country was renamed Botswana when it gained independence in 1965 under the able leadership of Seretse Khama, who was educated in South Africa and then England, where he acquired his then controversial English wife, Ruth Williams, a clerk with Lloyds of London. The Queen later awarded him a knighthood for his effective leadership and good work in his home country, where he rightly emphasized education and training at all levels as his priority.

The cattle-slaughtering and meat processing industry had its very own culture. A very competent and enterprising Cyril Hurwitz from Johannesburg had built a huge business that contributed crucial employment and revenue in support of the country's development. It also provided a source of low cost, high protein canned food for millions of people around the globe. But it was not pretty. Gruesome, bloody scenarios in the slaughterhouses, nauseating smells in the processing and canning plants where operators went about the production of products such as soups, corned beef, minced meat, sausages and stews consumed by the poor and the hungry in every part of the world, all in cans of every shape and size destined for retail outlets or further industrial processing in Asia and Europe. It was difficult to acknowledge that this unsavory scene was clinically clean and that operations were maintained at internationally acclaimed hygiene levels, way above the legislated minimum.

The most fascinating and dramatic of all these food processing and cannery destinations was Walvis Bay on the Atlantic coast of South West Africa (now Namibia). The territory was a German colony before the obscenely botched 1919 Treaty of Versailles after The Great War. The British, legitimized by Versailles, confiscated South West Africa from the defeated *Reich* and put it under the "protection" of the Commonwealth dominion next door, the Union of South Africa—exactly as UK Prime Minister Lloyd George wanted it. This was but one reflection of the avaricious ineptitude of Lloyd George, America's pontificating Woodrow Wilson and France's "le Tigre" Clemenceau—victorious allied leaders at the infamous post-war conference. Woodrow Wilson did nothing to avert the Treaty's territorial land grabs. Today we can attribute the insanely greedy and ill-informed carving up of the Middle East and Africa after World War I to this bunch of self-serving, land grabbing politicians. The 21ˢᵗ century's

Middle Eastern mess is in large part the legacy of this communal land grab, memorialized by the flawed treaty it delivered.

South West Africa is a huge, parched wilderness, stretching from the Orange River mouth in the south to the Kunene River on the Angolan border to the north. Most of the coastline marked the western edge of the Namib desert, which stretched inland to the bush country and mountainous core of the country at its center, where Windhoek housed the protectorate's capital and the majority of white Namibians. It was a very empty territory where the Ovambo tribe, derived from central and east African Bantu peoples, dominate the sparse population in the north while the indigenous Khoisans (a collective name for the original Khoi and San peoples), or Bushmen or Hottentot pygmies eked out a hunter-gatherer's subsistence, living in the Kalahari and Namib deserts, always seeming to get the short end of the stick in every encounter with blacks or white people.

The diminutive Khoi and the San peoples were once known collectively as Hottentots, but this nomenclature is no longer considered politically correct, perhaps because the old name reflects the unusual configuration of their hair-growth, in tightly knitted knots dispersed across their yellow scalps sometimes referred to as peppercorns. These diminutive, peace-loving, yellow-skinned people, once sole inhabitants of all South Africa's territories, were brutally decimated by the arrival of the white man and his venereal diseases and smallpox or driven from their territories into no-man's-land. At the very same time, the more bellicose Bantu tribes, not just the Zulus and Xhosas (but also others including the Tswanas, Sothos, Ndebele, Shonas, Shangaans, etc.), driving south from equatorial Africa, did their equally brutal, genocidal part as they grabbed territory for their herds and killed off the Khoisan population. Meanwhile, popular myth as well as revisionist historians and anthropologists claimed that the whites "stole" South Africa from the blacks. Mainstream western historians do not seem to have deemed this genocidal history sexy enough to immortalize. They have, however, been happy to memorialize the struggle between the blacks (particularly the Zulus) and the whites, which followed sometime after the displacement and slaughter of the Khoisans. The revised history of the white man's land-larceny is an easier fit with today's infallible doctrines.

Namibia's spellbinding allure is rooted in a variety of the planet's more captivating fairy tale landscapes. There is the Namib Desert itself, where under the usually cloudless baby-blue sky, golden pink dunes surge, perfectly smoothly, to sharp curlicue escarpments or ridges, several hundred feet high, before plunging just as smoothly down the other side into shadowy grey-blue valleys of mystery. The dunes then rise again into the pulsating desert sunlight, to repeat their variations of this enchanting pattern, as they swirl their winding way across the desert floor to nowhere. Their silent silky smoothness conceal the work of desert airstreams, which relentlessly shift the landscape from hour to hour, yet this creeping movement is not to be perceived by the human eye. The distant white horizon shimmers, often causing a Fata Morgana dancing in the blinding, relentless sun. Between the dunes lie areas of rippling corrugations in the firm, flat desert floor, telling one that stronger winds have previously been in play. When the wind is not at work, the fairytale scene is dramatized by colossal silence, now and again enhanced by the softest rush of a gentle, grainy breeze. The daylight magic is quickly transformed into blue and silver lunar wizardry as night descends and the moon rises above the towering dunes or the spiky skyline of the mountains at the desert's periphery.

Inland and northward are the contrasting landscapes of the parched bush of Ovamboland, Tsumeb and the Etosha Pan, teeming with game of every kind, far to the north. In fact, some of the world's very best game watching is to be experienced in the northern reaches of Namibia, including the long Caprivi Strip forming the northeastern boundary with Angola and Botswana. The forbidding dryness and arid landscapes present such dramatic contrasts to the flooded Okavango swamp, for example, in the weeks and months after the rainfall brings life to fauna and flora throughout this unique natural history paradise. In the mountains at the heart of the country is Windhoek, where German and Afrikaans were more often spoken than English by the white urban population.

The bleak little town of Walvis Bay, totally divested of anything green outside concrete planters along the barren streets, was devoted exclusively to exploiting the incredibly rich but fragile pelagic pilchard fishery off South West Africa's Skeleton Coast, which stretches many hundreds of miles from Sandwich Bay to the Kunene River. The shoreline is a maritime graveyard, a particularly treacherous coastline named for its skeletal waste of whale and seal bones, along with the wrecks of hundreds of ships that have foundered there over the centuries. This coastal area endures a wicked climate caused by persistent hot winds blowing from desert to the sea and a curious upwelling of the cold waters of the Benguela Current, which produce thick fog upon meeting the heated desert airstream. It is not surprising that very few souls populate the region. A century earlier the last of the *Strandlopers* (their Afrikaans name, meaning "beach runners"), who were derived from the nomad San people of Namibia, either perished or left to join their inland cousins.

Similar to mackerel, the pilchard is a herring-like fish that populates the Atlantic waters cooled by the Benguela Current flowing north from the frigid Antarctic, along the southwestern coast of Africa. These fish live off certain plankton which feed and breed at specific water temperatures found at a given depth in the Benguela Current. The fishing industry processes its catch into either fishmeal, used widely as a component of animal feeds and fertilizers, or into canned pilchard prepared according to different recipes to suit a wide array of regional and ethnic consumer tastes around the world. Canned pilchard products, along with corned beef, were the world's most valued low-cost, high-protein foods. Most well-fed westerners don't even know of these products, which help to feed literally hundreds of millions of poverty-stricken people, particularly in South and East Asia, and the slums of Europe. Only one similar fishery off the northern part of Chile's 4,250-mile coastline, cooled by the Humboldt current from the Antarctic—the Benguela current's Pacific equivalent—comes close to rivaling Walvis Bay's bounteous production. The weakness of this pivotal Namibian industry is its vulnerability to changing oceanic flow patterns caused by irregular variations in the Benguela Current's cold waters. If the relevant plankton-laden layer of cold water should descend to depths beyond the pilchards' reach, the fishery simply dies: no plankton, no pilchard! In the late 1970s, exactly this happened, causing the industry and this invaluable food source to collapse for years. Politics could also intervene. In the years when South African products were boycotted, a year or two after the Sharpeville massacre, Walvis Bay lost major markets for canned pilchard in the Philippines and Indonesia, which slowed the otherwise thriving industry. New markets were soon found, however, and traditional UK and Eastern European markets expanded, so the volume of fish processing quickly recovered.

Through the 60s and early 70s, however, Walvis Bay was going gangbusters and reveled in its own wild culture. The community was a Cannery Row unto itself, consisting of the most colorful characters imaginable, rivaling any of John Steinbeck's Monterey counterparts. The tiny singlepurpose town was sandwiched between the shifting, shining sand dunes of the Namib on one side and the tempestuous, often vicious South Atlantic on the other. If it were not for the pilchard, no man, no tree and no dry-land mammal had any business to be there. Just birds, reptiles, fish and shipwrecks. Stretching half a mile along the shoreline north of the large manmade harbor was a row of fish canning and fishmeal processing plants. Supplying the needed cans was MBSA's single-purpose plant, a major capital investment that housed state-of-the-art, specialized machinery to serve the pilchard canning factories. It produced a variety of shallow oval containers and round cylindrical cans of multiple specifications for an even wider variety of processed pilchard recipes using olive oil, tomato sauce, brine, mustard and different curries—to suit consumer tastes from Huddersfield to Hong Kong, from Potsdam to Penang. The plant was surrounded by double corrugated metal walls, built thirty feet high to protect the sensitive equipment inside from desert storms, which would propel clouds of sand horizontally at fifty or more miles per hour.

All of the town's residential area was south of the harbor, quite deliberately upwind from the foul stink of fish being processed into meal.

Fortunately, the prevailing south wind did indeed prevail. Bare concrete roads and sidewalks in the village were stark and unadorned, except for occasional painted oil barrels in which ambitious plantings usually withered in the wind-driven sand and salt. It was a bustling town, where everybody had a specific reason and strong motivation to be there. The only quiet time of day was either side of the noon hour, when many would get essential sleep. The fishing fleet would be out from sundown 'til sunrise, returning to unload the catch in time for the fishermen's mid-morning breakfast, which always followed a stop at the quayside bar on the way home. The stores kept in step with the drinking hours of the six bars in town, which meant they were open from sunrise until 10 o'clock in the morning, when the last fishermen went home for their morning repast. Opening time was 6:00 PM, and business would be conducted until the last drinker stopped drinking. Before dawn, at about 5:30 AM, the barmen had dozens of double shots of KWV brandy neatly lined up on the counter, ready for the returning crews.

The social life of administrative employees and management of the fishing and processing companies was lively and liquid. The party circuit over weekends was highly organized and predictable. Everybody took turns hosting everybody else, prompting great, eclectic gatherings with nary a hint of social rank or corporate status. Visitors from out of town were particularly welcome and quickly swept into the parties. New faces meant new opportunities for fun and games. The few single women of Walvis and the more flirtatious wives would extend a particularly warm welcome to male visitors. The parties were wild, carefree and easygoing in this permissive society. What happened in Walvis stayed in Walvis. Only very rarely did this philosophy lead to enduring complications. On the other hand, if at any moment the safety and efficiency of the industry, or the welfare of its people were in play, conventional civic norms and discipline would immediately reassert themselves, and it was all business. People understood exactly why they were there, in combat against nature's many challenges in this outlandish outpost. There was keen competition between rival enterprises, but the town's collective responsibilities and teamwork always remained paramount.

Several thousands of Ovambos from the distant hinterland found employment on Walvis Bay's cannery row and means to support destitute families left at home in the bush. They worked and lived under conditions incomparable with those of black miners on the Rand, enjoying clean accommodations, free tribal foods and more than adequate medical care. In MBSA's case, their food was enhanced with nutritional supplements and vitamins.

Twenty miles north of Walvis Bay, along a dead-straight, well paved coastal road was the tiny town of Swakopmund. A nineteenth century German colonial village, it had long been a singular seaside resort for well-to-do merchants and officials from Windhoek. People would make the trek from the territory's capital two hundred miles to the west, over the craggy Auras Mountains, before descending 2,500 feet to cross one hundred miles of Namib dunes and sand flats to reach Swakopmund. The roads were frequently blocked by the shifting desert, making traffic somewhat unpredictable all year round. Swakopmund, however, was a popular destination for dinner or a party away from the fishy stink of the fishmeal plants when the prevailing south wind blew from a less friendly direction. Bars and restaurants reflected their Teutonic heritage. A couple of old German jewelers made a living by applying their skills to the territory's abundant diamonds, opals, rubies and semi-precious stones, such as *tiger's eye*. Their trade employed an early version of mail-order retailing, incoming orders sent from jewelry wholesalers around the globe. One or two of the beautiful 19th century quasi-gothic villas attracted occasional Walvis Bay fishermen seeking comfort from certain *frauleins* of the night, who clearly hailed neither from Hamburg's Reeperbahn nor Windhoek's modest red-light district. The constraints and boundaries of apartheid were blurred along the Skeleton Coast. Swakopmund was an incongruous confluence of early twentieth century German culture, Nationalist government racism and all sorts of enterprising commerce, set in an extraordinary wilderness of sand and cruel sea.

Reaching MBSA's plant in Walvis Bay entailed a routine Springbok 727 flight between Johannesburg and Windhoek, but traveling to and from Walvis Bay from Windhoek was always an adventure. The alternatives were light aircraft or sturdy four-wheel drive trucks. The former took about an hour, weather permitting, and would provide dramatic views of mountains and desert en route. Towering thunder storms over the mountains often disrupted late afternoon or evening flights, as massive cumulonimbus cloud formations would reach as high as 45,000 feet way beyond the boundaries of light aircraft flights, even in the best of weather. If you were flying in a small plane, the storms could toss you around the sky like flotsam in a tsunami.

On one trip to Walvis, we were caught off guard by such a very sudden storm, in a small single engine Cessna; the storm's merciless peripheral convection currents drove the little plane almost straight up through 13,000 feet to an altitude where oxygen became short, despite the pilot's white knuckles desperately jamming the joy-stick full forward, as if for a nose dive. After a terrifying minute or two, as we gasped for air with heart in mouth, the plane burst free of the storm's iron grip, escaping into normal airspace and a precipitous dive before the pilot could ease the joy-stick back, bringing the elevators back to horizontal.

The land option took at least seven hours of rough riding, through the mountain range, down the Kuiseb River gorge into the Namib, and then across the sands and between dunes on a road that was not always there. Sudden thunderstorms could upset the best laid travel plans—very quickly. An unexpected cloudburst behind you, up the Kuiseb gorge, could send a 20-foot wall of water down the narrow canyon to sweep you away.

Leisure trips into the Namib would sometimes display the weirdest array of fantastical desert flora, the occasional insect-eating plants and slithering reptiles. The dunes offered sporting locals many choices between sightseeing in conventional four-wheel drives, camping, dune-boarding and all-terrain motor adventures. To the east, where the desert gave way to the distant mountains, an assortment of antelope, scavengers and a variety of carnivorous felines added excitement. A huge, but very shallow saltwater lagoon called Sandwich Harbor was just ten miles down the coast south of Walvis. It was loaded with just the right varieties of algae, marine critters and plant life to afford sanctuary and nourishment to literally hundreds of thousands of flamingos. The exotic birds would create swooping clouds of pink in the sky, or miles of pulsating slashes of shocking pink across the lagoon's turquoise shallows. Every kind of seagull, tern and the occasional albatross danced in the sky. The ocean's shoreline, all the way up to the Kunene River, hosted a million sand runners and different migrant bird species.

The human population was no less colorful. The fishermen numbered among them defrocked clergymen, released jailbirds, retired schoolteachers, a failed jazz trombonist and a solitary blacklisted stockbroker. Some of the operations managers were equally unconventional characters, as were several of the leading entrepreneurs who had built the great fishing industry of Namibia and the western Cape Province. The industrial fishery of South West Africa was established in the early 1950s by investors from the older and strongest fishing companies of the Cape. The leaders were industrial dynasties, including the Ovenstone family of Cape Town and the du Preezs of Kaap Kunene. Among them were characters like Jeck Ovenstone and Aapie du Preez. Aapie was a wildly gregarious Afrikaaner, who loved a party and never called a spade anything but a fucking shovel. He was a brilliant chef, so a senior business lunch with the Kaap Kunene Company would mean sitting at a marble counter overlooking Aapie's state-of-the-art kitchen located to one side of his Cape Town office, sipping great goblets of Nederburg Riesling and chatting as he displayed his culinary skills. He was simply trying to soften you up in order to strike a deadly deal for his annual fish can supply contract.

Aapie once asked us, wives included, to visit his game farm deep into Ovamboland's bush, a couple of hundred miles northwest of Windhoek. A small twin-engine Piper got six of us overhead of the du Preez camp to find a crude grass airstrip cleared in the bush. The strip had also been carefully cleared of giraffes, zebra, impala or wildebeest, and streams of toilet paper fluttered from the stunted treetops to indicate the wind direction for landing—no wind sock for Aapie. For two days guests were treated to his spectacular game-spotting jeep rides, endless anecdotes, crates of Pinotage, Riesling and chef du Preez's culinary magic. The open jeeps were equipped with comfortable bench seats mounted on elevated platforms for optimal viewing. Each seat had a device to hold your beverage, served in wine glasses irrespective of specification (his was always Nederburg Riesling, except for his very first drink on the dawn ride, when it would be *du Preez's Afrikaanse Koffie*—steaming and heavily laced with KWV's best brandy, no sugar, no cream. Aapie would blow a strange sort of hunting horn at about 5 AM, well before dawn, to ensure we were ready for the sunrise cruise. By mid-morning, an enormous brunch and buckets of Buck's Fizz (Mimosas to Americans) or Nederburg Riesling would welcome us back to camp. Again an eclectic feast of sub-tropical fruits, omelets, grilled tomatoes, crisp bacon, venison steaks and *boerewors* (Afrikaans for farmers' sausage). By noon, everybody was ripe for an extended siesta, to recover and be sharp for the late afternoon game-spotting cruise. This was the time to see the widest variety of Africa's fauna assemble to enjoy their evening drink at the edge of any body of water. As the yellow late-afternoon sun prepared for its gorgeous soft landing on the bushland horizon, its orb expanded and turned ever deeper orange before its final plunge from sight. No high-end safari camp for coddled western tourists skimming the surface of Africa in ten days could match Aapie's earthy hospitality.

By contrast, the Ovenstone clan was headed by a Ralph Lauren type silver-haired anglophone named Jeck. He was urbane and socially sophisticated with a racy style about him, yet equally gregarious and generous in his own style of hospitality, which was up-market Anglo-Saxon. House parties at his lovely Cape Dutch villa, high up in Constantia in the shadow of Table Mountain, or at their vacation home set on steep rocks with grand views of the pristine beach and lagoon at Hermanus on the Cape's Indian Ocean coastline. Game fishing and sunset cruises aboard beautifully appointed motor yachts, just as you might expect to find them in St. Tropez or Cap d'Antibes. Game watching with the Ovenstones was enjoyed in the lap of luxury at their private game lodge on thousands of acres at the edge of Kruger Park in the eastern Transvaal, complete with hard top landing strip and real wind socks, finished off with the company logo—a heraldic fantasy with a piscine motif.

The pilchard industry's marketing and distribution was looked after by a cooperative organization, encompassing all the canned fish and fishmeal producers, initiated and headed by the extremely energetic and intense Abe Shapiro. He was a first-generation Lithuanian immigrant, from a Jewish refugee family that had escaped the vicious pogroms in the eastern Baltics. Abe sold astronomic numbers of tons of canned pilchard to multinational food companies, wholesalers, governments, UN agencies and NGOs in every corner of the earth and he directed Walvis Bay's fishmeal production to agricultural industries and development agencies on all seven continents. Abe was a tubby man, about five foot four, with the figure of a new potato on toothpicks. He could sell coal to any colliery in Newcastle, the Ruhr or West Virginia.

The greatest business priority and objective for MBSA at that particular time was to convert the sub-continent's Coca Cola business to marketing their carbonated soft drinks in metal cans. The brand totally dominated the market, with Pepsi's small share running a very weak second. South African Breweries had significantly expanded volume in each of their bottled beer brands by gaining incremental sales in cans, yet Coke would not learn from the market indicators, nor budge. Coke claimed their capital was sunk into glass bottles, bottling lines and pallets designed specifically for the traditional Coca Cola glass packaging, which prohibited a switch. Their bottlers would not agree to the change either, they claimed. This situation was the motivation behind my weekly call on Coke's CEO for Southern Africa, headquartered in the fashionable suburb Rosebank, just north of the city.

Ian Wilson and his staff were given endless presentations pointing to the metal can's marketing advantages, including African consumers' preferences and compelling economics enjoyed around the world. Ian just wouldn't budge. Golf, dinners, sporting events and trips to Swazi casinos, private game reserves—all to no avail.

Meanwhile the mercurial Ed Loughlin had long since befriended an ebullient and very influential fellow American named Hack Wilson. Handsome, tall, sartorially sharp in Californian style and very well connected, Hack had cut a broad swath through business circles as he built a headline-grabbing career in South Africa. His very first project was the launch of Pepsi Cola in competition with the long-established Coca-Cola in the early 1950s. Where Pepsi failed to make much progress against Coke, Hack personally raced ahead. It did him no harm that he had married Stella, attractive heiress to the omnipotent OK Bazaars retail empire founded and still led by her father, Sam Cohen. The retailer was the Walmart of sub-Saharan Africa at that time. As a director of SA Breweries, Hack Wilson introduced American marketing moxie and strategies to the conservative brewing monopoly. He was an energetic and highly visible extrovert, the epitome of an American sales executive, who could create headlines on command and could work a crowded room like a seasoned senator from New York.

Hack at some point asked about my family background, seeking an explanation for a Dane having such a German surname. I explained that Heilmann was not an uncommon name in Germany, but in Denmark there was only one Heilmann clan, which had migrated from the Krefeld area in far western Germany some four hundred years ago. He knew my brother John, but had apparently never asked him this question. Hack then told me how and why his parents had made a name change.

"Heilmann's a pretty simple one, but in my old *meshpokhe*, which means family or clan in Yiddish, we had a really unpronounceable *mittel*-European name starting with a W and ending in *–ski*, it was as long as a wet weekend,

Flemming. A goddamned hassle for all sorts of reasons," he laughed, "so we took a good Anglo-Saxon tag, which is of course quite user-friendly, and it doesn't have all the baggage attached. I'm a member of all sorts of clubs, which I couldn't have joined if they didn't think I was a *goy*."

Ed and Hack were regular golf partners. Between them they conjured up a creative, high-risk scheme to force change and a breakthrough for our cans in the carbonated soft drink market. The project was nothing short of Machiavellian. Wilson, in cahoots with Bryan Smither, a fellow SA Breweries director, persuaded the beer company to invest in a separate soft drink business with a dedicated canning facility for a brand-new family of fruit-flavored carbonated beverages, which were to be marketed exclusively in cans. Loughlin's teenage daughter contributed the name—very hip for that era. The soda drinks would all be under the *Groovy* logo and label with different colorful graphics for each flavor. MBSA's American technology licensor, Continental Can Company in New York, was enlisted under tight secrecy to produce the printed tinplate for shipment all the way to our Vanderbijlpark factory, where the cans would be manufactured, only on night shifts and with a minimum of people involved. Hack's US friends from his Pepsi days helped formulate a range of syrup bases for the different fruit-flavored sodas. At SA Breweries' Isando plant, the new canning line was explained away as incremental capacity needed to market a new, secret brand of lager to be brewed under license from a Bavarian brewery. Their top marketing manager worked with a specially appointed advertising agency, removed from their beer business. Ed and Hack had an eager conspirator in Sam Cohen of OK Bazaars, who would orchestrate the distribution, retail merchandizing and market launch of the product. My own role was to coordinate the production planning, brief the specially selected production supervisors and work with my SA Breweries colleague to do the compliance and administrative work for the new product—all outside the normal MBSA routines and system. This called for a bogus story to explain the nature of this new mystery customer to those employees who needed to be involved. As launch-day approached, the inventory of filled *Groovy* cans was to be held under lock and key at our Vanderbijlpark warehouse, ready to go to OK Bazaars' stores across the Witwatersrand region—in Johannesburg, Germiston, Boksburg, Springs and Benoni. The *Groovy* range of drinks had been conceived, produced and then sprung on the market in only nine months, a fitting gestation period for the new baby. Not even our full board of directors could be told of the capital committed to the costly project, as money would be squandered if the surprise element were blown. I continued my sterile weekly calls on Ian Wilson at Coke, still negated at every turn. It was high drama. Mighty Coca Cola was about to be ambushed. Loughlin was so excited his skin could hardly contain the man. Gunpowder, treason and plot!

On a Friday evening after the end of the regular business day, with fourteen days to go before *Groovy's* retail launch, the phone rang in my office.

"Ian Wilson here!" A three second pause. "Flemming, get your arse over here this very minute! What the fuck do you guys think you are up to? You're out of your minds."

I knew exactly what had happened, and shuddered at the thought. There had been a leak.

"Good grief! What's wrong, Ian? Whatever the hell it is, how can I possibly help at this time of day, on a Friday night?"

"I don't care if it's Christmas Eve!" bellowed Ian, "just come right here to Rosebank! As for your fucking weekend, you can forget it ... and the next few bloody weekends, unless you kill this dirty, nefarious and totally unacceptable intervention by Metal Box and your conniving friends at SA Breweries."

The tail end of the Friday night commuter traffic made the three miles on Jan Smuts Avenue a long and anxious ride. It was obvious that a lot about the Groovy project had leaked, but how much, and what? Coca Cola's offices were as empty as those I had left at MBSA. Ian, a handsome man, in his early forties with a chronic five o'clock shadow, thick black eye brows, always Savile Row suited, usually very smooth and quietly spoken, was puce in the face, tapping a pencil on his empty desk top as I reached his office. His pale blue eyes, like those of an angry Alaskan Husky, flashed lightning, his lips parted in a snarl. He was sweating profusely.

"Why the fuck didn't you tell me, Flemming?"

"Tell you what?"

"You know what the hell I'm talking about, man—you've stabbed me in the back, you have violated the trust we shared, Flemming—you have just prostituted yourself, man! More seriously, Metal Box has betrayed Coca Cola. Unless you call this thing off at once, you guys are going to pay for this from here to Timbuktu and around the bloody world, man! Unless you halt, or at least delay the launch of *Groovy*, there'll be hell to pay for Metal Box here in this country and anywhere else we do business with your group. Do I make myself clear, Flemming?" A brief pause and then, "Metal Box has to put the launch on hold for at least a month. Give me time to fly in sufficient canned Coke from London or Stuttgart or even the States! I simply cannot have someone else's soda on the market in cans ahead of us. Don't you get that?" Another menacing pause followed by, "Why, oh why didn't you tell me, you arsehole? You have just cut yourselves out from making Coca Cola the biggest customer you will ever have in the whole of Africa." Yet another pause before Ian pronounced us "stupid fucking idiots!"

I tried to explain the obvious. We as suppliers of branded consumer goods packaging, just like advertising agencies, always had to respect the confidentiality of our customers' marketing plans and other secrets. How could we possibly do business otherwise?

> "The commitment to keeping a confidence is, of course, a very cornerstone of our business, Ian. You, of all people understand that. You would obviously expect no less of us if we were supplying you and were party to your confidential marketing strategy and product launch plans. You know we wouldn't go blabbing in the market place, leaking your secrets, Ian, to your competitors or anyone else. Our rules protect any and all of our customers, big or small—that has to be so obvious."

> "C'mon, man! Grow up! We were going to be your biggest customer on the whole bloody continent, Africa's biggest user of cans—don't you get that?" he barked. "You should have protected your own position, man—and mine—by warning me, instead of fucking around with an amateur fly-by-night project like *Groovy*. You'll now end up missing the boat with canned soft drinks. We'll make our own bloody cans! Or get American Can or Crown Cork in here from the States. That's what's going to happen if you don't give me this break. Do I make myself clear, Flemming?"

Ian was spitting venom by now.

"Look here, Ian," I pleaded. "You know there's no way we are going to break a commitment made to a bona fide customer, irrespective of size, and we will be proceeding along our tried and trusted practices, whatever that entails. You have to respect our discretion and integrity, and you know it! And it isn't as if I had not spent the last two years trying to persuade you to make this very move, for heaven's sake." I paused and drew breath. "What would be your position, Ian, if your wife's gynecologist were to be unprofessional enough to gossip about her medical issues with your friends over cocktails at a party? You would have his balls for breakfast, wouldn't you, and you would have him run out of town, out of his profession! It's a straightforward matter of professional conduct and practice. I've sat here in this very chair in front of your bloody desk every week, giving you the facts, explaining the economics, imploring you to get real and catch up with the rest of the world. It's not as if I hadn't busted a gut to make you see the light. No, Ian, with all due respect, this situation is of your own making, not mine, and not Metal Box's."

Ian, perhaps sensing that he had hit a stone wall, turned away, got up from his desk, picked up his slim leather Gucci briefcase and walked out of his office without saying another word, turning the lights off on his way. I followed him through the darkened hallway, but he had disappeared before I could reach the elevator lobby. When the elevator returned, an African office cleaner with bucket and mop stepped out and glanced at me with a distraught look.

"Dee beeg boss iss gone home verry, verry ungrry about sumfin'. Pliss, not me *n'kosi*! Goot naaight, *n'kosi*!"

Ian was right: I had a highly disturbed weekend of frantic communication ahead of me. Baxter, Loughlin, Smither and I conferred endlessly with Hack Wilson and Sam Cohen, and our own people who were in the loop. Hack never stopped chuckling. He was having fun, the time of his Pepsi Cola life.

Coca Cola's muscle power is not to be underestimated, nor their ability to use it. They chartered a brace of Boeing 707 freighters to carry countless thousands of cases of canned Coke from their British operations on multiple round trips between London and Jan Smuts Airport over the next two weeks, with the empty planes deadheading northbound each time, at enormous cost. They used their retailing clout, actually beating *Groovy* to some supermarket shelves in Pretoria and one or two selected Jo'burg retail outlets by two days, as the MBSA/Groovy stealth team tried unsuccessfully to accelerate planned distribution.

So the battle was on.

Upstart *Groovy* had its moment of glory and was in due course distributed to the Cape Province and Durban markets, lasting about three years before the brand withered on the vine and then died, crushed under the Coca Cola Company's steam roller.

Groovy's battle was lost, but the great, pivotal breakthrough for canned soft drinks and soda products had been accomplished. Coke eventually engaged us in a five-year can supply contract and never again mentioned the threat of in-house can manufacturing or encouraging the American companies. Ian Wilson even came around to giving me a grudging acknowledgement that MBSA had played by the rules. SA Breweries moved the Groovy canning line into the giant brew house, putting it to work, producing their true and trusted Castle Lager and Lion Ale, favorites of all consumers, of every skin color. Canned beer even gained share against the bottled product in the slipstream of this marketing adventure.

Ian rose fast through the international Coca Cola ranks, soon running a major chunk of Coke's world outside the USA. He was extremely close to Paul Austin, then Chairman and CEO of Coca Cola Company. In 1979

Austin and Wilson prematurely celebrated Ian's succession to the throne in Atlanta over champagne with their wives in Austin's penthouse apartment. In fact, Ian missed becoming Chairman and CEO by a whisker because he had allied himself with the outgoing leader, who had, in fact, lost the support and confidence of Coca Cola's *éminence grise*, Robert Woodruff, all-powerful ex-Chairman—as well as President Don Keough and the board. Instead, Roberto Goizueta succeeded Austin, who soon after fell victim to Alzheimer's. Ian left the Coca Cola Company almost immediately, to take control of some food businesses in California and Hawaii. A few years later he ended up in jail for fraud, misrepresenting the financial results of a public company in order to goose the price of its stock. It was a steep and dramatic slide from the ivory tower into the slammer. At least the system in this case punished an abuser of our capitalist system based, as it surely is, on trust.

~~~~

Home and family life was a roller-coaster experience. PB and *Mor* had retired to a small forestry property in Denmark. Marriage had brought the life-changing joy of three children between 1960 and 1964, two boys and a girl, who in their early school days attracted a lot of love and fatherly attention whenever weekends and vacations allowed. With time, however, Marilyn perceived me as being "married to Metal Box," and that was perhaps not entirely without justification, depending on one's view of balance between work and family life. The job was very demanding, involved a lot of travel, and as an ambitious young manager, I just loved doing what I was doing and wanted to do it well. The job, however, was not the sole force at play in an increasingly fragile marriage. Life beyond the home and immediate family was to some degree affected by Marilyn's own preferences. She was uncomfortable, if not disinterested in, entertaining at home. She was perhaps intellectually bored in the materialistic and somewhat superficial social environment of white Johannesburg. She showed signs of a strange ennui, swinging between intellectual snobbery and mental laziness. Her daily agenda was hardly demanding. The material needs of the children and the homemaking as she perceived it were largely managed by sweet Victoria, the Shangaan nanny-cum-cook.

We had divergent views and aspirations as to what home and family meant and should be. Once transport to and from school was looked after, a white mother's day in Johannesburg was no more and no less than what she made of it. Our respective priorities in the home, socially or pertaining to the extended family, were miles apart. My love of, perhaps obsessive devotion to, deep-rooted Danish traditions, mores and extended family may have been part of the problem. If family life and home to her was what she grew up with in Frinton-on-Sea or rural Dedham in Suffolk, it was little wonder that tensions and frustrations grew. When I expressed criticism as the relationship crumbled, I was labeled a "barrack room lawyer." On the other hand, it took many months of insomniac nights, contemplating the agony of separating from the kids, the horror of telling them I was leaving them, before I finally decided to move to an apartment five miles down the road, in early 1970. I knew I was going to hurt them, inflicting lifelong wounds. Marilyn refused divorce for three years before she finally gave in and moved home to England with the three children in the spring of 1973. Christian and Nick went to Gresham's in Norfolk, where I had very happily spent my last four years of boarding school, and Claire ended up at the Godolphin School in Salisbury.

I had met wonderful Judy only six months after I had moved away from the family. That was the genesis of a long and brilliant marriage, which has only become more brilliant over the decades. My children would spend their summer vacations in South Africa with us in the Bryanston home they knew so well, although it had been remodeled. We had married in September 1973.

Back in August of 1970, I tagged two weeks of bachelor's vacation on the French Riviera onto one of my trips to Metal Box HQ in England. I was in St. Tropez when I learned that my wonderful secretary, Mrs. B, had undergone serious surgery and would not be back in the office for some weeks after my return to Jo'burg. Upon getting back, I immediately called to check in with Bryan Smither, and when I told him of my predicament, he said he had an ideal temporary fill-in for Mrs. B.

> "Flemming, this young lady has just returned from a lengthy sojourn in London, where she earned her keep as a typist or secretary. I think she would jump at the chance of a temporary job while she looks for the right long-term position. She's a friend of Cindy's (Bryan's daughter)—they shared a flat in London. You ought to have a chat with her, and I'll have her call you, if you like." Before hanging up Bryan chuckled and warned me, "Be careful, Flemming. Judy Tucker is a very beautiful girl!"

Miss Tucker did call, we did have a chat and, yes, she was a very beautiful girl. Between jobs in London she had been studying antique furniture at the Courtauld Institute after graduating from acclaimed Rhodes University with a B. Soc. Sci. degree. I hired her, and that was the beginning of the long and very happy story which has not ended. On Mrs. B's return, Judy went to work for the chairman of J Walter Thompson, SA. Miss Tucker became Mrs. Heilmann almost three years later. Judy quit working for the advertising company and became a busy home maker and volunteer for African Self Help, an organization that secured access to nourishing food, clothing, groceries as well as health and child care for blacks in the township.

~~~~

Late in the 60s, as General Sales Manager, I was appointed to the board of MBSA, while still reporting to Ed Loughlin, so there was an uncomfortable awkwardness of having one executive board member technically reporting to another. However, that did not last more than a few months because in 1970 I was given a new job as Assistant Managing Director, basically number three in the company's pecking order. Baxter was signaling that a changing of the guard was at hand. Number two, Managing Director Lewis Beaumont, was a chartered accountant—a CPA in America—who ran finance and the administrative functions of the company. Technical and manufacturing aspects of the business were in the capable hands of a relatively young physicist, Pat Seddon, who inherited a world class manufacturing operation, built with unswerving faith in American technology and practices acquired from our US licensor, Continental Can Company and other US companies he befriended on frequent visits to the States. This division of labor allowed me to step into a gap and do some needed work in the area of strategic planning and preparing a restructuring of management for growth. Relevant technology change was accelerating and so were the demographics in MBSA's markets—domestic and those of our exporting customers.

Tragically and very suddenly Lewis Beaumont died of a massive heart attack late in 1970. The MBSA Board, with the blessing of a new Metal Box group chairman and CEO, Alex Page in London, appointed me Managing Director and CEO. At the same time, John Baxter announced that he would become a non-executive Chairman, as he phased himself out and announced he would soon be leaving the board of directors. Bryan Smither, my early mentor in undergraduate days, would succeed him. Events had run away with John Baxter's carefully prepared plans; change was accelerated. The company was to be set on a new course under a very much younger team, quickly nicknamed *The Young Turks* by employees across the country. The team did not mind the innuendo. The nickname accurately suggested that an energetic and somewhat radical force was going to work for positive change, just as the young Levantine Turks had done at the end of the Ottoman Empire.

John Baxter's departure had a huge impact on me and, of course, the whole company. Over nearly a quarter century his drive and leadership had powered the enterprise into the top-ten list of South African public companies, which meant it was among the very largest on the African continent, and he had made it the crown jewel of the global Metal Box group. The performance of the business and its role in the economy of southern

Africa had caught the attention of the international packaging industry. Behind the empire-building Robert Barlow, who by now had been knighted, Baxter's business record had gained a reputation, which opened doors for the South African company throughout Europe and in the States. He was an insistent user and promoter of some very effective management tools, especially those pertaining to leadership aspects of the profession. I learned more from John than from any other source. His use of the first-person singular was ever modest; he was quick to acknowledge and praise the work of others. His self-discipline on the job and attention to detail were extraordinary. His sensitivity to the whims, needs and fortunes—good and bad—of individual people was unique. Baxter was physically impressive and individualistic in style, a style that called on a wide vocabulary, was laced with mischievous humor and incessant puns; he was nothing short of charismatic. He had perceptive commercial vision and was quick to develop tactics in its support. Very occasionally he would fail to execute effectively because he was such a control freak; his micro-management could be an obstruction. John had a short fuse, an explosive temper that was usually ignited by carelessness or what he perceived as conceit or arrogance in others. He had a great way with words, which he employed to command attention in any discussion, whether at board level or one on one. Sir Robert Barlow on one of his many visits to Jo'burg gave Baxter a copy of Roget's *Thesaurus*, and wrote on the flysheet:

> *To John Baxter,*
> *With affection and respect.*
> *May you never be at a loss for a kind word.*
> *Robert Barlow, July '62*

Baxter on one occasion blew me to bits for suggesting that he was guilty of nepotism in securing special treatment for a young employee, John Loughlin, Ed's son. Johnny, who had only recently joined the company as a trainee sales clerk, had out of the blue been selected for a cushy overseas training jaunt to the UK, Europe and America, the relevance or purpose of which was less than clear. Baxter was not amused.

> "Now you just listen here, my fine-feathered friend!" he bellowed, leaning across his desk, poking his forefinger into my face. "If I hear another word of that, you will regret it until the very day you drop. That boy's father has served this company better, and has done more for it than you could hope to do in a month of Sundays. Who the hell do you think you are, boy?" he asked after snatching his breath back. "It takes a lot of time and effort to make friends—it takes no bloody talent to lose them! Now get out of my office, young whippersnapper, and think about that! Nepotism, my arse! You probably don't even know how to spell the bloody word, let alone define it in this context! Get outta here!"

Chastised thus, I took the matter no further

When I first got to work under Ed Loughlin as General Sales Manager, our relationship got off to a rocky start—mainly because we had very different views about managing people—in this case a sales force of about fifty people throughout the country. Over time, however, it became a valued friendship as we learned to appreciate each other's strengths and talents while adapting to each other's weaknesses. When traveling together we discovered we shared a fun-loving approach.

In 1973 a worldwide shortage of tinplate arose, and MBSA lost its European suppliers on whom we depended for more than half our needs— the domestic state-owned monopoly, Iscor, had neither the capacity nor the technology to meet all our requirements. The parent company in the UK had usurped us, taking our place in relations with British, German and French steel mills. MBSA was left without adequate supply lines. So Ed, with experience from his US Steel Company days, and I made for Tokyo to engage Mitsui, Mitsubishi and Marubeni, the giant trading companies that acted as marketers for all the Japanese steel mills, to secure adequate supplies.

This entailed traveling all over the country, including Fukuoka in the distant southwestern end of the Japanese archipelago. I got separated from Ed on this jam-packed flight on a 707 with three seats on each side of the aisle. I found myself between two older Japanese businessmen, one of whom, by the window, spoke unusually good English and was unusually engaging and curious. He quizzed me on my whole life story, pressing for every detail. When I told him of my family's displacement by the Japanese invasion of Malaya in 1941, he winced and fell silent. After a few moments he asked,

> "Do I understand, sir, that your family had to flee from your home in Malaya?"

I merely nodded, but this prompted the elderly gentleman to struggle to his feet, hard against the window behind him, and then bow deeply:

> "Sir, I am ashamed, and so is my country. I am very sorry."

Taking an overnight train to Sapporo in the far north presented us with an unusual challenge. Well before the train was due to leave, we discovered that the restaurant car could not provide ice for our regular sundowner, Johnny Walker Black Label—always part of our luggage because even Suntory's best attempt at scotch was not palatable in 1973—so we had to be a little creative. Ed engaged the maître d' of a small eatery alongside the platform.

> "Solly, sah, no ice for whiskey, velly solly!"

Ed drew on his thespian talents, clutched his brow, leaning forward as he grimaced.

> "I have this terrible migraine, terrible pain, only whiskey with much ice can help me on long night time journey to Sapporo. You must help me, please help!"

The maître D's jaw dropped. He was clearly concerned. Close to tears, he gesticulated.

"Wait two minute. You need herrup, I see you need herrup!
I come back two minute."

Ed's new friend disappeared into the back of the restaurant, but true to his word, he was back in two minutes with a block of ice, a twelve-inch cube, wrapped in a large dish cloth. He bowed politely as he presented Ed with the precious package.

"Pliss accept gift. Many good wish for het pain. Go now quick to train leaving!"

Safely aboard in our sleeper compartment, the challenge endured. How to reduce one cubic foot of ice to chunks in dimensions compatible with of our plastic 6-oz drinking cups. Our solution was to take a pillow slip from one of the bunks, drop the ice block inside and bash it against the steel frame of the door leading to the next rail car. By the time the block was smashed into useable fragments and shards of ice, we had attracted the attention of a conductor wearing a black cap reminiscent of Tojo himself and half a dozen curious fellow passengers peering out of their compartments—their faces expressing varying degrees of disapproval or scorn over the antics of these two crazy *gaijins*. The conductor's ire was unmistakable in the delivery of his admonishment in staccato Japanese as we sheepishly withdrew to our compartment and prepared our well-earned sundowner. We doubly enjoyed our double Johnny Walkers on the rocks.

There was nothing parochial about Ed, who had spent a good part of his life travelling outside America for US Steel, living in Belgium and briefly in London, where he covered Europe and all of Africa before joining MBSA in Johannesburg. He was, however, a conservative Irish American Catholic with no curiosity, let alone appetite, for the exotic in culinary matters. When a senior Mitsui general manager arranged a grand, traditional farewell dinner at a quasi-Geisha establishment (a beautiful girl in Geisha costume to serve each guest exclusively), Ed was confronted with the inescapable obligation to address raw fish and other unprocessed delicacies. We were inevitably seated next to each other, so Ed made good use of this happenstance. He employed two evasive moves to escape the situation, both of which required that he cause a distraction of sorts: He would point to some decorative wall hanging behind our host and ask a question about it; then, while all eyes were thus turned, he would shovel offending pieces of raw tuna or salmon into the well under the very low dinner table, where *gaijins* could comfortably place their feet instead of sitting cross-legged. Or, he would point to the *obi* worn by a Geisha on her way out of the room, asking how it was tied. With our hosts' attention diverted, he pushed some other unprocessed food morsel onto my plate.

Ed got away with it. Back home in South Africa, he would enjoy munching *biltong* as much as millions of South Africans would—it is sliced, but completely uncooked sun-dried red meat—usually venison of some sort!

MBSA's performance and market valuation after twenty-five years of John Baxter's very personal leadership spoke to his effectiveness. The country and its people shared in the fruits of South Africa's bountiful food industry's development. MBSA had contributed to the creation of several hundred thousand work places across the food processing, consumer goods, marketing and distribution arenas. Like many other industries, it had generated jobs, education, training and trade skills for people who had known nothing but living in abject poverty. The potential of the country's agricultural resources had been enhanced by technology and research brought to the party; exports were facilitated, new and better consumer goods had added to the standard of living for all who bought essentials, whether in OK Bazaars or in a remote Transkei general store. The world would have been a much better place for having many more John Baxters. He was a small but real part of the wealth creation benefiting South Africa and her millions of needy people. He saw that as his main reward, and he shrank from attempts to give him public recognition of his achievements.

When he finally handed the reins to me, he presented me with the copy of the Thesaurus he had received from Sir Robert. It was a touching private gesture of encouragement and support, and it was typical of the man. He left very big shoes to fill, as the saying goes.

At the time of this transition the country's leading business magazine, *Management*, wrote of Metal Box South Africa:

> *The company is in good hands, but the wrench from somewhat diffident management paternalism (pre-occupied more, perhaps, with manufacturing than marketing developments) is not complete.*
>
> *However, the new look MBSA seems more suited for what is needed to play container-making under today's conditions than the highly centralized machine Baxter built. That he should have recognized the need for change, and helped the men he picked to succeed him achieve it (sink or swim), says much for someone so long accustomed to holding all the power in his own hands.*

The *Young Turks'* nickname was only inappropriate if it conjured up visions of wild young men in turbans wielding long knives. The emerging leadership team was indeed young. One man was 29, one was 40 and the rest in their mid-thirties. The group was six in number. Three of us formed the core: Nigel Gilson, who was among the very first regional or business unit managers of the new decentralized era, Peter Campbell as head of accounting and finance—and me. Gilson, an intelligent, energetic and gregarious fellow with a winning sense of humor was a natural communicator and leader; Campbell, deeply religious and less urbane, set about addressing the wider horizons of business with a keen intellect and professional dedication, sleeves rolled up. Peter helped me obtain a better grasp of finance, accounting and an understanding of the financial implications of differing management approaches and new ideas. These innovations introduced participative decision making, greater delegation and decentralized, market-oriented profit centers. Middle managers were given authority and held accountable. Headquarters and central staff were vigorously evaluated and pared on the basis that if the operating guys didn't see cost/benefit values of a central function, the staff managers were eliminated or redeployed to an operating unit that was prepared to pay for their services. *Management* magazine reported:

> *Heilmann says there's no policy limiting us to rigid metal or plastic containers. For decades they said, "This is our [production] capacity. Let us use it well and just fill it. But now we're moving toward the Unilever or Colgate approach, in which you not only see a market need and create a product to satisfy it, but you actually generate new markets. [We have] a campaign currently under way in every supermarket to promote new packaging ideas, especially for convenience foods."*

The new team also accelerated education, training and advancement of black and *Coloured* employees to the maximum extent allowed under the emerging apartheid legislation. This improved productivity as it improved wages, enhanced communications and introduced better working conditions. The country's sociopolitical and legislated constraints of that era were tested. Highly participative management practices were the cornerstone of the new modus operandi. The level of autonomy from the British parent company, so carefully developed and nurtured by Baxter, left the Young Turks free to innovate without hint of interest, let alone interference, from London. In the early days of the new era all they were concerned with was our profitability, which had great impact on their own reported performance.

Metal Box in the UK had also changed. Towards the end of Sir Robert Barlow's mostly brilliant if patriarchal leadership, fresh blood and new eyes had been brought to the parent board by way of non-executive directors drawn from British industry, commerce and banking. Alex Page took over leadership of the group in 1970. Baxter's retirement from the *Metal Box Overseas Company* board, however, left a vacuum of operating experience in its oversight of international operations. It was a vacuum *The Young Turks* stepped into deftly. The South African company set itself up for growth and selective diversification.

The MBSA team soon enjoyed overt support from the UK parent company, its main board and particularly from the new chairman and CEO, Alex Page. My own relationship with Page quickly grew remarkably close, to an extent that it raised eyebrows in the *Overseas Company*. Alex was nearly twenty years my senior, a Cambridge engineering graduate of sharp intellect. He was a relaxed, fun-loving fellow. MBSA was racing ahead in terms of size, scope and return on shareholders' funds. This de facto reporting relationship as head of the South African business evolved quietly and strengthened. The reality was that in practice I reported directly to Alex rather than the *Overseas Company* board. It was an effective relationship with easy and open communication, in contrast to the bureaucracy and second guessing of the *Overseas Company* with its water fountain politics and personal agendas. They were in effect circumvented. This strange situation was partly facilitated by the fact that the *Overseas Company* managers were almost all retired Colonial Service officers with minimal business acumen and very modest management talent. They divided what was once the British Empire between them as *Territorial Officers* reporting on Metal Box's subsidiary companies in Asia, Africa and a couple of Mediterranean countries. They commuted from their stockbrokers' Tudor homes in Surrey, wearing pinstriped suits, starched white cut-away detachable collars, club ties and bowler hats. Come rain or shine, they carried tightly rolled black umbrellas and polished black brief cases containing their lunch, the *Times* or Daily Telegraph and copies of *The Tatler* or *Country Life*. When they were through with their paperwork, they practiced golf putting on the office carpet. None of them were university graduates, but most had at some stage served as officers in the armed forces or colonial service. They conformed tightly to a little world of their own, in bubbles of particularly British sub-culture, distanced from the realities of industry and commerce. The *Brolly Brigade*, as we called them, presented a stark contrast to the impressive talent of Metal Box Company's domestic operating management in the UK and the managers actually running the operations abroad. They survived only as groupies acting in cahoots, using well-honed political skills learned in the services. They were, however, formally in charge of corporate governance and finance outside the UK and could thus be dangerous. Unfettered bureaucracy is a predictable breeder of vicious office politics. The *Brolly Brigade* was tight and worked carefully to protect their jobs and corporate comforts, sniping at each other only when in competition for promotion.

In South Africa, MBSA's new structure and sharper focus triggered the early retirement of a few executive directors, along with some senior and middle managers, some of whom had served the company for two or more decades. Fixed cost and overheads as a percentage of growing revenues were reduced. Labor productivity was enhanced by progressive training practices and sharpened management focus using an informal version of John Gamble's 1970 *Management by Objectives*, which was a popular approach at the time. Results improved steadily and were reflected in the company's share price. MBSA's market capitalization by the mid-70s exceeded that of the parent Metal Box Company, the global group listed on the London Stock Exchange.

Growth was accelerated by an explosion in demand for carbonated beverage cans, aerosol cans and by buy-outs of several of the large canners' in-house manufacture (self-manufacture) of cans. Plastic packaging was growing. Several small mergers and acquisitions were successfully accomplished. Improved productivity allowed the level of employment to be held almost steady as revenue increased and the scale of operations grew.

Meanwhile, apartheid's advance and its implications did not, of course, escape the world's attention.

Little wonder!

Chapter III

The British Inquisition

"…put down a motion on the Order Paper to give a Select Committee of the House locus standi to enquire into this question."

Harold Wilson, MP, to Prime Minister Edward Heath concerning British companies' employment practices in South Africa. Hansard, House of Commons, Westminster March 27th, 1973. (Locus standi is the parliamentary term for authority to file legal charges. Hansard is the British equivalent of the US Congressional Record).

IN THE EUROPEAN spring of 1973, the Manchester Guardian accused a list of one hundred British-controlled companies in South Africa of abusing and underpaying blacks employed in the country's mining, industrial, commercial and agricultural sectors. The journalistic initiative was led by Adam Rafael, a young investigative reporter, who has since become a well known, decidedly left leaning, anchor and commentator on BBC's TV roster and in the print media, writing for The Guardian, The Observer and the Economist of today. In his opening salvo Rafael wrote with fervor that:

"An investigation of 100 companies found only three—Shell, ICI and Unilever—who were paying all employees above the minimum for an African family to avoid malnutrition."

The article went on to claim that other companies were paying *"substantiated numbers well below the poverty datum line,"* which was defined as the minimum amount needed to support a family of five. The list included high profile names such as British Leyland—of Land Rover fame, Tate & Lyle, Courtaulds, Slater Walker, General Electric, Chloride Electrical—and Metal Box South Africa.

> *"Metal Box,"* the paper continued, *"employs more than 5,500 Africans, at least 30% of whom are paid below the poverty datum line. C. F. Heilmann, the managing director (CEO), said that the company was paying 40% above the Government's wage determination for the industry. He also claimed that no employee was being paid below the poverty datum line."*

Rafael, the product of an elite British *public school* (as the elite private boarding schools are known in the English nomenclature), Charterhouse, and Oriel College at Oxford University, received national acclaim and awards for his work on labor conditions in South Africa. He described visits to Natal sugar plantations where he saw children suffering from *Kwashiorkor*, a serious disease caused by malnutrition, and he cited reports that employers treated their people like machines:

> *In fact, machines are better looked after. Workers were in rags and said they could not buy clothes.*
> *If these chaps earn too much, you know, they just take a holiday, an employer said.*

The truth was that blatant injustices were indeed far too common in South Africa, most of them inflicted on unskilled rural workers as opposed to urbanized blacks, who were employed in the service sector or manufacturing industries like MBSA's. Serious abuse was widespread in the mining and agricultural sectors, but Adam Raphael had generalized wildly and went way beyond the facts in his accusations directed at many of the British industrial companies he named. He wrote with heavy bias at best, and with venomous mendacity about selected targets, no doubt hoping to get away with it. Obviously, and quite rightly, the article stirred up the mother of all political hornets' nests. Edward Heath was British Prime Minister at the time, when James Callaghan, the shadow foreign secretary called for investigation by the full Select Committee on Industry & Trade (of The House of Commons). The matter was, in fact, referred to a sub-committee extant.

The most despicable element in Rafael's reporting on MBSA was the fact that he knew better. Yet he smeared us with lies and falsehoods, despite his visit to our Vanderbijpark factory complex at my invitation, where he was given carte blanche access to anything he wanted, so he could check any local or company-wide accounts he might find relevant, and was encouraged to talk to any employee he might choose to engage. Back in London, Alex Page had him to lunch and invited him to ask any question, see any accounts or reports of his choosing. Raphael was strangely reluctant to avail himself of the opportunities proffered.

There was an active exchange in the House of Commons. Harold Wilson and Michael Foot, a left wing Labour member who later led the Party, were joined by a female Member of Parliament or MP (recorded by Hansard as a Miss Lestor) in calling for the inquisition. On the floor of the House, Miss Lestor accused the Tory government of condoning apartheid:

... investment in South Africa means investment in apartheid.

Prime Minister Heath readily agreed that any abuse was absolutely unacceptable and should be exposed, but he also pointed to the benefits of British investment, respected and regularly practiced British employment standards and their positive influence on labor and social issues in South Africa. It is to be noted that it was also Edward Heath who characterized Tiny Roland, head of the then infamous Lonrho conglomerate, as *the unpleasant and unacceptable face of capitalism* when he was finally exposed and convicted of fraud, tax evasion and corruption in multiple African countries and the UK. Roland was duly punished, harshly.

It was the once and future Prime Minister Wilson, who specifically demanded that the sub-committee be given *locus standi* (the right to file legal charges) and permission to dig deeply into the matter. This House of Commons enquiry was to be the forum in which the responsible executives of Metal Box, along with those of 27 other selected companies (out of the list of 100), then appeared to give evidence on their workers' employment conditions in South Africa. All one hundred companies had already submitted written responses to a detailed questionnaire.

In May 1973 it was our turn. On the third day of the House of Commons hearings, Alex Page, Jim Gilbertson and I made up the Metal Box team. Gilbertson, who had in prior years headed MBSA's Durban operation before moving home to England, had just become chairman of the *Overseas Company*. It was my job to present the South African position and to document all the supporting facts.

The sub-committee was chaired by Bill Rodgers, another Labour Party MP. In the hearing chamber we faced eleven interrogators, five Labour MPs and six Tories, deployed around a grand horseshoe table. Note that while it was a Tory government, the committee was chaired by a Labour MP. We sat *en face,* at our own little table for three, placed centrally opposite the U-shaped committee table. Alex was in the middle, between Jim and me. Headlines of major newspapers had for the previous two days shouted that some companies had come out of this process very badly, shamed if not savaged by the hearings, and it was immediately clear that several of the MPs relished the prospect of nailing us, or at least mauling Metal Box viciously. They smelled blood in the water, and the Labour members in particular were seeking headlines, preferably with a confession that we paid morally unjustifiable wages, imposed indefensible working conditions and made obscene profits on the backs of our 5,500 black employees. Behind us, the public galleries were chock-a-block with spectators and media people loaded for bear. I felt an extraordinary, unfamiliar confidence welling up within me as we got down to the business of confronting false and vicious claims—a confidence that could only be felt when armed with unimpeachable facts and deep pride in our practices, which were clearly progressive, humane and way ahead of the game. The tensely insistent interrogation, loaded with animus, lasted just under an hour. The next day, *The Manchester Guardian* quoted me:

> *There are no laws on the books [in South Africa] inhibiting the progress of rates of pay. I think the figures we have put before you illustrate how the statuary minimum [pay rate] has been left far, far behind by the rates we actually pay.*

I had referred to a schedule included in our written response to the questionnaire issued by the enquiring committee. It illustrated how MBSA's minimum rate over my three-and-a-half-year tenure as CEO had increased by 116.66 percent, and how our current minimum rate was 95 percent over and above the legal minimum. MBSA had never been paying employees at— let alone below—the poverty datum line since it was conceived. In addition, the committee learned that we paid and held in escrow an incremental monthly vacation allowance, which was paid out when the employee took his or her annual paid leave of two or three weeks, depending on seniority. The Labour Party hotheads were visibly surprised, if not a little frustrated, to be thus thwarted. They looked skyward at the vaulted ceiling of the chamber as they learned of our expenditure on subsidized, nutritionally balanced meals of meat, veggies, *mealie-meal* or maize porridge and gravy for all employees, thus providing meals for a price reflecting only fifty percent of cost. The committee as a whole nodded their reluctant approval of our 200-Rand 25-year service awards (US $250 at the time)—in the form of Rolex watches, to qualifying employees irrespective of race, and the 350-Rand awards to all 40-year employees, who could make their own choice of gift or cash. At the time, the SA Rand was worth US $1.25. These details had not been addressed by the slanted questionnaires issued by the committee.

Answers to several questions already given in response to the questionnaire prompted astonished faces, which clearly demonstrated that at least a quarter of the MPs had not even read our submission provided weeks before the hearings. They, and a good portion of the British public, had relied entirely on *The Manchester Guardian* and Adam Rafael—disingenuous at the very best.

Alex Page and I told the committee of our expansive training programs and our personnel practices at a brand-new beverage can plant at Rosslyn in the Transvaal, where newly taught skills had facilitated the advance of aspiring blacks to supervisory positions of unprecedented responsibility and remuneration. Committee members again squirmed as we told them of the universal access to qualified nursing and medical attention at all MBSA plants and the provision of subsidized medical help when outside treatment was called for.

Jim Gilbertson didn't open his mouth once at any stage of the proceedings—quite appropriately, in my opinion, as I regarded him to be only an ex officio passenger on the board of MBSA.

It was quite obvious that Metal Box and MBSA had been vindicated in no uncertain terms. Complete exoneration. The Labour Party's most outré activists, who had been misleading their constituents and fellow MPs in the House of Commons with crass falsehoods about MBSA, were exposed and embarrassed, but sadly unpunished. *The Manchester Guardian* had been exposed as grossly inaccurate, biased and guilty of generalizations totally divested of facts in major segments of Raphael's reporting—such as those pertaining to his accusations against me and MBSA. I caught Adam Raphael's eye in the gallery as we were dismissed and marched out of the chamber. He gave me a wry smile and a jumbo wink of his left eye, which I have yet to interpret or understand. I just found it obnoxious. What the hell was he signaling? On only one other occasion was I at the receiving end of such an enigmatic wink. That was Sir Robert Barlow's wink as he left the market research office when I was a junior clerk, but that time I sensed it was friendly signal of some sort. I had no idea what Raphael meant to convey.

A celebratory martini with Alex and Jim was relished over an al fresco lunch on the terrace of *Les Ambassadeur's* on Park Lane that sunny May afternoon. We had never quarreled with the investigation per se, or its honest quest for decent employment practices in South Africa; but there was joy in our vindication, given the media's dishonesty and false accusations. Adam Raphael's report on the hearings never made reference to his earlier misrepresentations of our practices; nary a confession, and no apology, of course. However, to his credit he did note that:

> *By the end of 1973, no less than 43 non-Europeans [employed by Metal Box South Africa] will have received 40-year awards; and 374 will have received 25-year awards. 3,100 non-Europeans have served the company more than five years.*

The Company was only founded in Cape Town in the early 1930s, about forty years earlier, when the single manufacturing location employed less than 200 people. The lion's share of the company's expansion only started well after World War II, post 1945! The arithmetic and percentages pertaining to MBSA's employee retention performance was now clear for all to see. Even with this *post factum* acknowledgment from Raphael's report on our proceedings, I feel bilious to this day when I see or hear him on BBC America's panels. Despite his lies about us and multiple other companies, and simply ignoring his odorous overstatements, the UK's media establishment used the 1973 British Press Awards to select him to be honored as *Journalist of the Year* for this South African story. But that was no real surprise then, and it wouldn't be today.

Back in Johannesburg, the parliamentary hearings were followed meticulously by the press, word by every uttered word. Great gobs of Hansard transcript, hot off the press, were being telexed to The *Rand Daily Mail.* The paper quoted Alex's answer to repeated questions from MPs as to whether he was happy with the present channels of communication with black workers:

We have publicly stated through Mr. Heilmann that we would welcome the establishment of proper black trade unions and we would do all we could do to promote them as soon as possible.

The *Rand Daily Mail* went on to quote Heilmann on the subject:

"At present the only official and legal communication between management and factory workers is through departmentally elected works committees, which the company has had in South Africa for more than 20 years. I personally believe that there are black labor organizations, that they do exist. I have voiced the opinion that the way forward is for the law to admit that they exist and to allow for their recognition, and the recognition of their leaders.

At the time, South African law recognized only white, *Coloured* and Indian unions. Black trade unions were merely tolerated as "unofficial," and therefore excluded from government-approved industrial bargaining procedures. I did not broadcast that I personally knew, visited and had open discussions with de facto black labor leaders in several of our ten MBSA plants as well as the officially recognized black union leaders in our sister companies in Southern Rhodesia (now Zimbabwe) and Mocambique. Throughout the country MBSA's evidence in the House of Commons was considered newsworthy, even revolutionary in some quarters. The government could not have liked what they heard, but I experienced no direct hint of disapproval. For my own part, I had been cautious enough to say that, on the subject of unions, I was speaking from personal conviction without necessarily representing the views of all members of the MBSA board and management team. Some of my colleagues felt I had gone too far. I was led to believe that, beyond the group of *Young Turks,* some managers and other stakeholders had expressed opinions among themselves:

- *He's going much too fast.*

- *He's ahead of the game by a long shot, way ahead of the right time.*

Others, less discretely said:

- *Heilmann's off his bloody rocker! He thinks he's back in Denmark or something!*
- *Maybe he should never have left his lefty friends in Cambridge?*
- *Does he think he's Albert Luthuli? Is he looking for the Peace Prize?*
- *He has read too much Alan Paton.*

Face to face, however, nobody challenged me specifically; they used more cautious language. The Board never once put an obstacle in the way of management's policies; we did stay within the letter of the prevailing law. However, two non-executive directors, both Nationalists, cautioned that we should not put ourselves "out on a limb." One of them, Ian Fleming, was among his party's rare Anglophones. It would be less than fair to say he was a token Anglo, as he openly held some strong pro-Nationalist views. Yet he was always careful, in Nationalist circles of his hometown Pretoria, to emphasize the importance of "our crucial relations with the Englishmen." Ian was at times a useful conduit to Iscor, as he was a director of that state-owned steel monopoly, from whom we procured tinplate. Iscor was seen by the government as one of its tools in nudging the economy one way or the other, even trying to manipulate the inflation rate via control of the price of steel. Another Anglophone director repeatedly pointed out that to promote enduring progressive policies, we needed to enlist Nationalist allies, not alienate those who could help us. The other Nat on the board was Dawie Malan, an intelligent, quietly spoken and well-connected actuary, from Pretoria's Afrikaans mandarin community, who would only occasionally show emotion when arguing for the government's policies. Pretoria was so different from Johannesburg, being the executive capital of the country (Cape Town was home to the legislature). Despite Sir Herbert Baker's dominating neo-classical Union Buildings (the actual site of the government's executive seat) reflecting its British colonial history, Pretoria was distilled Afrikaanerland. It was a physically attractive city with its wide streets, fabulous jacaranda blooms and lovely gardens. It had a provincial feel to it.

Only a few miles from Pretoria, the huge red brick Voortrekker Monument stood as the massive, ugly temple of Calvinistic, racist Afrikaanerdom. When, decades later, elements of the African National Congress party called for the demolition and removal of this icon of apartheid, Nelson Mandela denied them, arguing that one cannot rewrite history or remediate it by removing the evidence left in its trail. Madiba (Mandela's nickname) declared the Voortrekker Monument should always stand there to remind us of apartheid and ensure that its horrors would never be forgotten or repeated. He emphasized the imperative of learning from history, rather than hiding from it. This decision almost matched the wisdom of two other historically pivotal decisions made by Mandela when he was still molding and defining the democratic constitution of the new South Africa in the early 1990s: He chose reconciliation over revenge, and he chose the free market capitalist system over the Marxism being advocated by his cohort in the ANC. Most of his senior collaborators during the struggle for democracy were Communists—some educated in Moscow, others at the London School of Economics.

Alex Page openly supported my view that if black unions were not recognized, they would simply be driven underground or forced to operate in ways which would pre-empt any attempt to negotiate with them or influence their thinking. Under the circumstances at the time, however, one could officially only work with the legally available tools, which in the mid-1970s meant "works committees." They varied from plant to plant, ranging from the most sophisticated in the Cape region where the *Coloured* labor force dominated and the committees were vehicles for deep discussion (if not negotiations) to the pineapple can plant in East London, where the labor force was mainly Xhosa—straight out of the Transkei *kraals* and totally illiterate. In the latter category, management often appointed *indunas*, black leaders in their own communities with some level of education, who could help management bridge communication gaps caused by multiple black and white languages in use. They could also explain unfamiliar Xhosa customs, taboos and tribal behavior patterns to European supervisors as well as migrant Zulu or Tswana workers; the *indunas* helped explain some of the white man's rules and ideas which were alien to the Xhosas. They also helped resolve inter-tribal confrontations within the black labor force.

MBSA's evidence in the House of Commons had included my contention that the greatest obstacle to black advancement was illiteracy. In MBSA's Durban plant, a start had been made in addressing this crucial issue: *Operation Upgrade* had been launched to establish literacy classes where Zulus (who had never used script of any form) learned to read and write both English and Zulu—there was no illiteracy problem with the many Indian employees. At the brand-new Rosslyn plant north of Pretoria, the approach was much more radical. Nigel Gilson, in charge of the company's Central Region, insisted that plant management only hire blacks—mainly Tswanas or Shangaans in this area—who could already read and write, and only whites who were prepared to work with blacks along groundbreaking principles calling for promotion on merit and integration in the supervisory ranks.

Meanwhile, the company's management challenges were far from confined to sociopolitical issues. In 1974, a tip-off from the marketplace informed us that one of our top customers, South African Breweries (our ally in the Groovy project), had been approached by American Can Company to start in-house manufacture of beer cans, utilizing brand new technology and quite different production equipment. They were reportedly about to commit a major capital investment to a joint venture with the Americans, who were invading the market so jealously guarded by MBSA. The business at stake was a huge chunk of our total revenue. This prompted a frantic global scramble involving face-to-face consultations in the UK, our technology licensors Continental Can in the USA and with Japanese associates to prepare a counterproposal for presentation to South African Breweries. In the course of only ten days, financials, a business plan, intricate technical and manufacturing issues, along with crucial supply lines were organized into a defined project, which was presented in an emergency meeting of our full board. A team led by Nigel Gilson, Peter Campbell and technical director Pat Seddon then went to bat with SAB's leadership. Bryan Smither and I were not on the front line. We were trying to keep our powder dry for a last-ditch stand, in case it came to that. Over the following weeks of frantic meetings, it was demonstrated to the satisfaction of the customer that our scale, technical moxie on the ground and country-wide deployment of production facilities would, in the long run, serve their multiple breweries better than an in-house facility at a single SAB location. It was a close call, but American Can Company was finally beaten off and sent packing. They had made the mistake of sending in parochial junior managers from the States to negotiate with the worldly top brass of South African Breweries, an enormous brewing enterprise. MBSA had all its top executives involved and a common board member in Bryan Smither to represent our case in the customer's boardroom (Hack Wilson had by this time left South Africa for California).

~~~~

By the mid-70s, the relationship with our British overseers had become strained by a series of financial challenges and corporate politics. MBSA's growth and profitability made it the focus of the parent board of Metal Box, which over the years had recruited strong non-executive directors from British industry circles and the City. Executive board members were, for the first time, challenged by outside experience, views and talent. MBSA was becoming a standard for performance within the group, as its market cap rose. This prompted comparisons with other parts of the group— comparisons which were not universally welcomed by the *Brolly Brigade* in the *Overseas Company,* who got the wobbles under the unfamiliar scrutiny.

A member of the brigade, Dennis Allport, had in fact assumed a very senior domestic role heading up the UK food and beverage can business. From his new perch, he made a move aimed specifically at discrediting

MBSA's capital utilization and productivity. He maliciously suggested that our capital invested in production capacity was excessive, underutilized and therefore sloppy. The reality in South Africa was that demand for canning fruit, vegetable, fish and to an extent, beverages was highly seasonal—all very concentrated in a peak demand within a twelve-week period from early January through March. So, to meet customers' concentrated peak demands, quantities of cans were produced in off-season periods to be held in inventory; but even so, some installed capacity just had to be sub-optimally utilized during off-season periods. Customers in the fruit canning business made their can size and specification decisions based on what the unforeseeable crops called for. Flexibility and available capacity during the peak season were prerequisite to serving customers' unpredictable requirements. Their raw materials were highly perishable, and had to be promptly canned and processed. If MBSA did not meet their needs, somebody else would. Or, the largest customers could make their own cans in partnership with our competitors, as we had seen with South African Breweries contemplated partnership with American Can, and at H. Jones & Co., who made their own cans.

Allport's mischief was to accuse MBSA of undisciplined capital expenditure and financial irresponsibility. Our response was to invite the Brits to send their very best productivity and planning expert to South Africa, where our production records, capital expenditures and accounts were open for analysis. All relevant plants could be evaluated in situ and even our customers could be interviewed for an appraisal of our performance in meeting market requirements. Alex Page accepted the invitation, and his expert emissary was a truly competent and pragmatic veteran from Acton, Metal Box Company's global food packaging nerve center. Doug Hadland spent six weeks with MBSA, touring the relevant plants and visiting dozens of customers. On his return home, he reportedly delivered a glowing appraisal of what he had seen and heard in South Africa. The conclusion, according to the rumors reaching Johannesburg, was that market share would be lost to in-house can manufacturing by customers or to inter-

national competitors, if the seasonal demands of each market segment were
not satisfied exactly as per MBSA's strategy. The South African company's
strategy, he concluded, also permitted uncommonly healthy pricing and
margins. Customers had told him that they liked the status quo because it
saved them from tying up major chunks of their own capital, but if MBSA
did not invest adequately, they indeed would. The appraisal and the report
itself, however, were never heard of again in Johannesburg. Hadland's report
had been buried. My repeated requests for a copy of the findings only caused
the line to go dead. Water fountain politics, however, continued to thrive in
the halls of the *Overseas Company* on Baker Street, and indeed later in Reading,
the city on the Thames to which Metal Box moved its HQ. The incident was
a vivid example of an unacceptable face of corporate politics.

One of the consequences of MBSA's evolving relationship with the
parent board was the circumvention of the *Overseas Company* through
accelerated visits to South Africa by parent company executives and some
non-executive directors. Representatives of Continental Can Company and
their family of technology licensees were including South Africa in their
itineraries. In the mid-70s, the chairman and CEO of Continental Can in
New York, Robert S. Hatfield, and his wife Bobbie, toured MBSA's
operations and took a quick look at the wild life scene in the Eastern
Transvaal en route. It was a typically American-paced tour, at the end of
which my personal relationship with Bob had firmed up in a very positive
way. The Hatfields were flown around the country, saw six key plants out of
the fifteen on the sub-continent and met multinational and other customers
in the largest cities. A chatty farewell at Jan Smuts Airport prompted a
conversation that was to have consequences.

> "Well, young man, you have quite an operation going down
> here. We Americans tend not to understand how
> sophisticated some of you Africans can be," quipped Bob.
> "You certainly make better use of Continental's technology
> than your British friends. I guess that's because you don't

always think you have to mess with it and reinvent the wheel! I've seen you put our equipment and practices right to work the way we do. You don't screw around with them. And Continental Can does a lot better with the stock we hold here than we do with all the dollars we have committed with the Brits. Do those guys ever bother you, Flemming?"

Music to my ears, but I just shrugged and grinned, not uttering a word in response.

"I wish more Americans could see what we have seen this week," Bob continued. "Most of us have absolutely no idea of the South African realities. We have college kids at home, sleeping in tents on their campus, telling us to divest. Now, what I have seen here on our tour tells me that most American and European corporations at work here are providing a relatively decent living, training and fringe benefits unheard of in the rest of Africa. I guess you have a good few immigrants from the north, too. Without you guys operating and investing here, I know they'd be back there somewhere in the bush, scratching the dirt to grow a few sticks of corn, while their kids go hungry and lack any form of schooling. You've obviously got to change one hell of a lot in this country, as a matter of urgency—that's for sure— but I can't see that we Americans and Europeans would be helping anybody by pulling our dollars and jeopardizing half a million jobs."

Bob and Bobbie had captured hearts at every level as they talked to all and sundry, asking incisive questions as they travelled from Walvis Bay and Cape Town to Johannesburg and Durban. One Ovambo machine-minder with whom Bob had been chatting in the Walvis Bay plant asked me quietly:

"Iss dat baas dee King of Ameriika?"

The Hatfields returned home from their first African experience with warm feelings for this very strange society. Bob's departing words at Jan Smuts airport told us that.

> "Good job, young man! Keep doing the good work," Bob said, "you have some unusual challenges—problems which we do not come across in the same way back home. But don't get me wrong, we have our own race problems and are moving too slowly. We are, however, moving in the right direction, which your government certainly is not. As I see it, the South African business community is playing the greatest role in creating employment and a measure of upward mobility—even alleviating some damage caused by your government's flawed policies. The country really needs enterprises like Metal Box and the other multinationals and good local companies like SAB and OK Bazaars all doing a great job. I wish some of our American companies operating here would play a more active role alongside you. Jobs to create and build a black middle class, like any other country …" Bob paused for a few moments. "But, Flemming, should South Africa ever wear thin on you, or should you ever tire of the Brits, give me a call. You might want to consider the States figuring in your future." Bob chuckled, giving me a pat on the back as they made their way to the plane. "But don't ever tell anybody I said that!"

The British Metal Box non-executive directors came south to see for themselves. To comprehend the context of what was being done, to educate themselves on South Africa's problems and indeed take in its fantastic potential. Visiting heads of Continental Can's European licensees were surprised by the quality of South Africa's industrial management, and stunned at the sophistication of the country's infrastructure, medical science, research and services and the magnitude of her natural resources. However, they were often naïve in their comprehension of what it would take to resolve the country's problems, most of them coming from democratic welfare states at home. Alex Page, however, was the most regular and informed visitor, and by far the most incisive when it came to South Africa's many complex issues.

~~~~

President Balthazar Vorster of the South African Republic, enjoying his mid-term power, steadily advanced the Nationalist's apartheid policies. He had abolished the *Coloureds'* voters roll, but he was cunning enough to respect the international PR value of caution. He managed a strategy of pseudo-détente with other African nations, even to the extent of allowing black diplomats from the north to live in residential areas otherwise designated white in Pretoria and Cape Town. He infuriated his party's extremists when he authorized the participation of several Maoris on New Zealand's rugby team touring South Africa. Ironically, the New Zealand team's nick name was, and still is, *The All Blacks.* Under diplomatic pressure from Henry Kissinger, Vorster leaned on Prime Minister Ian Smith of Southern Rhodesia to accept that minority rule, with such a tiny white population, was not sustainable. One has to wonder what Vorster and Kissinger privately said to each other about minority rule south of the Limpopo? Just how big did the white minority have to be, to sustain apartheid? The ratio of blacks to Europeans in Southern Rhodesia was about three times steeper than South Africa's. The omniscient Kissinger, King of all Pontificators, probably never got into that.

~~~~

When Bryan Smither succeeded Baxter as chairman of MBSA in 1971, Alex Page had told him that his board should be aware that the parent company "would probably want Heilmann to move to the UK in about five years' time, as part of my succession planning for the Metal Box group." Bryan was asked to let me know that.

Starting in 1973, Alex would inevitably initiate conversations with me, in Jo'burg or in the UK, about my future in the context of the Metal Box group. I was newly married to Judy, my beloved seventh-generation-South-African bride. Alex would expressly discuss a "return home" to the UK.

> "You are going to be starting a new family, and you have to think ahead. At thirty-seven you've already had this job for over three years, and although you've done us proud, I don't think it's good for any CEO to stay in one spot for more than seven or eight years. We could certainly use you back home. And I have to start thinking about my own age, my own succession planning. Flemming, I think you ought to envisage moving back to the UK two years from now, to straighten out the *Overseas Company*, while keeping a very close eye on South Africa." Alex then went on to explain, "I want to set up a horse race between you and Allport! Hey, what d'you think of that?" We both laughed out loud before he continued. "We need to see how the two of you handle things, and who should take over from me in a few more years from now, certainly before this decade is out. You would immediately join the main parent board where the directors can get to know you. We all agree that my successor should be chosen from our own ranks." Alex paused yet again, then looked into my eyes, flashing his wide ivory grin. "What do you say to an arrangement like that, Flemming?"

Taken completely by surprise, I struggled to contain my excitement, hardly able to believe what I was hearing. It was almost as if Alex were writing my ticket for me.

> "Good grief, Alex. That would just suit me down to the ground. I couldn't think of a more exciting challenge than taking on the *Overseas Company*, where I know we could make a lot of progress and generate enormous growth. And I like the horse race idea! I know Judy would be happy at the prospect, despite her family and deep roots in this country— she's no happier than I am with the direction in which things are going and is anything but blind to the problematic future here. As you know, she's spent some happy times in the UK."

Apparently a course had been set for us. However, with the passage of the next couple of years that was to become a very dangerous and stupid assumption.

This conversation was repeated in quite specific terms several times, including one occasion at Alex's country house, Merton Place in Surrey, where I would often spend a Saturday or Sunday during regular visits to the Metal Box headquarters. Alex even issued a warning about the higher cost of living in the UK, in comparison with Jo'burg's affordable, easy life and creature comforts.

> "You and Judy are going to make babies at some stage, and it's a lot more expensive to run a nice home and give kids a decent education in the UK. You'd have to make some adjustments, as you probably realize. Our dear leader Harold Wilson has told his cabinet—damn them all!—that he wants a lid put on senior management salaries and perks. Even I am unable to be properly paid, old chap! I mean compared

to the Germans and the Frogs—let alone the Americans! The Labour Party is making it as difficult as possible for British industry to attract talent to keep the UK competitive. British talent keeps leaving us for the Continent or the States—they're killing us, Flemming. But I'm pleased you still like the plan."

In fact, the corporate compensation issue became a Labour Party cause célèbre, lasting well into James Callaghan's regime as he took over as prime minister. The socialists passed several bills, which drove British management talent, business start-ups and even well-established companies to move to the European continent and the USA. A serious brain drain ensued. All this at a time when the UK's deficit spending created a crisis and the economy was in dire straits. Public finances were floundering, Denis Healey was seeking a loan from the IMF and the US was to give the UK a standby loan facility.

One Jo'burg morning in July 1975, at the height of the Highveld winter, the *Sunday Times* carried a banner headline: *"ALL BLACK TRADE UNIONS BANNED OUTRIGHT."*

In the article's opening paragraph, it was reported that any employer or its representative caught communicating with black union leadership would automatically spend eight years in the slammer. The Nationalists had an obsessive fear of all trade unions, but especially the non-European labor organizations, fearing that the ANC would use them as propaganda platforms and vehicles for organized subversion. The Nats had decided to make good on their threat to disrupt, if not bury, organized black labor.

By this time, MBSA employed around 6,000 people, of whom more than 5,000 were black, Indian or *Coloured*. While my personal views on non-white trade unions may have been at variance with many of my peers in business, the CEOs of listed multinational subsidiaries were generally much closer to Metal Box's position. However, very few of them employed as many blacks as MBSA did. Without consulting my management colleagues or Bryan Smither, I quickly called half a dozen of the multinational cohort—those with whom I felt we could most usefully be allied. There was general agreement to meet and discuss how best the damage from this legislation might be communicated to the domestic and international public and particularly to government leaders. The resulting discussion was all sweetness and light, with an expressed agreement that the group work together and speak as one.

> "Absolutely right! On the nail! The public must be alerted and warned, and the outside world must know what's happening here. We are right behind you, Flemming!" one of them said as they responded almost in unison.

There seemed to be a shared commitment to act, and I thought I was being given an encouraging pat on the back. That soon proved to be another of my naïve assumptions. It was a consistent group, declaring they were right behind me—but unfortunately that's exactly where they stayed publicly, in silence. I became a lone voice in terms of expressing myself in public, with some measure of caution and diplomacy, I thought. However, my position drew the ire of the authorities while the media lapped up what I had to say, quoting me in the business section of the papers. After a period of my being given spasmodic publicity, my office phone lines developed unusual clicks and echoes during random conversations.

This radical legislation was fiercely attacked by the country's ever courageous English-speaking media, but business leaders were generally reluctant to oppose it overtly. All political factions got involved in a debate. Overseas, western media gave it full attention for a 24-hour burst of ill-informed comment and sensational reporting. The Afrikaans-speaking community supported the legislation with few exceptions, such as Anton Rupert, head of the Rembrandt Group's cigarette and distilled spirits empire, which some years later expanded into luxury goods with brands like Dunhill and Cartier. While Rupert was a declared Nationalist, he would from time to time be a lone Afrikaans voice for restraint and moderation. He was also a rare internationalist among Afrikaaners. After all, he was a global player working hard to sell Rothmans cigarettes, brandy and aftershave lotion all over the world.

Within a few months, I received two or three letters from unhappy shareholders, addressed to me personally as CEO. They liked neither my views on black trade unions nor my calls for their recognition. Statements made by Alex Page and me after the House of Commons hearings (cited in the South African media) were recalled with disapproval. They accused me of jeopardizing the value of their MBSA stock. With a bit of reluctant help from company secretary Jock McMurchie, who had opened the letters, I kept this to myself. I sensed the possibility of a very difficult fiduciary problem for me personally. Although I had spoken in a personal capacity, not as CEO, and not as a representative of management or the board, my opinions did not necessarily serve the best interests of all shareholders. A dip in the MBSA stock price could cause a very awkward situation. The issue could also spark a divisive debate in the ranks of MBSA's management.

In most countries, including South Africa under Roman Dutch law, it is the fiduciary duty of a public company CEO to represent and act in the interests of all shareholders—not just one segment, unless that segment has unchallenged control. South African shareholders in MBSA were a very significant minority at only a fraction under 50 percent. Chairman Bryan Smither and Alex both suggested I back off my public pronouncements in the expectation that the furor would simmer down, which in fact it more or less did. However, the Nationalist legislation had its intended impact: black labor lost a platform for negotiation, protest and the expression of frustration. It also had the predictable effect of driving the labor organizations underground, out of reach, where the communists and left-wing radicals could exert their influence unfettered and unchallenged. MBSA beefed up its emphasis on effective works councils making the best of their value as legal communication conduits to internally elected black labor leaders.

In 1975, Mother Nature brought a crisis to the pelagic fishing industry along the coast of South West Africa. The temperature layers at various depths of the Benguela Current in the South Atlantic changed radically. This caused the specific layer of water carrying the plankton upon which the pilchard fishery fed, to descend to a depth where it was out of the pilchards' reach. The fish lost access to their food. The pilchard population virtually vanished in a matter of weeks, removing ninety percent of the raw material on which the fish canning and fishmeal industries of Walvis Bay were based. The place came to a standstill, vast capital investments in fishing vessels, harbor infrastructure, factories and equipment were rendered sterile. A significant chunk of MBSA's turnover, cash flow and income evaporated. This misfortune sent one or two of our senior management off on a global exploration for other places to apply the company's industry-specific expertise, technology and equipment. Chile's endless coastline was explored for opportunities to pursue in that country's thriving fishing industry. The company's historical growth rate decelerated and results temporarily plateaued.

Other problems arose and had to be managed. Iscor, the state-owned steel monopoly struck technical problems in producing certain specifications of cold rolled steel and tinplate, causing MBSA's imports to explode and the cash committed to inventories rose steeply as supply lines lengthened. At the same time, government-imposed controls put a lid on MBSA's can prices. Severely squeezed, the company struggled through a year or so of heavy pressure on profitability, and particularly cash flow, as debt was incurred at levels previously avoided in the business. It was new territory for the *Young Turks*. Growth had been accomplished at a healthy clip under the team's regime, with net income growing by 290 percent in the period 1970-1976. Cash flow worries were new to us. Countermeasures were initiated. New growth was found through acquisitions within the packaging industry as well as other manufacturing and engineering fields, where MBSA's expertise and human resources were relevant. Management worked with engaged and competent non-executive directors led by Bryan Smither, doors were opened and insights into unfamiliar industries were gained. Selective acquisitions were made in metal fabrication, engineering, machinery and specialist services.

For a year or so, growth at MBSA had taken a pause, but gradually got back on track and continued to develop.

Chapter IV

The *Brolly Brigade* and Betrayal

"There comes a time when silence is betrayal."
- Martin Luther King, Jr

THE OVERSEAS COMPANY and the parent had been alerted to a potential plan for a cash injection via a rights issue of MBSA stock, which meant that the parent company would have to take up its share and maintain their percentage holding in MBSA or cede control. Opposition to the idea in the UK caused delay, which forced MBSA to undertake some sub-optimal short-term financing. Eventually, the rights issue became a near-imperative. This drew indignant howls of protest from Reading, where the parent company was itself struggling with stagnation under the Labour Party's restrictive policies, elevated debt, cash flow problems and a weak share price. An agitated Alex Page chastised his *Overseas Company* directors led by Jim Gilbertson, a little unfairly, given the fact that they had barely been involved or consulted on MBSA issues discussed directly with Johannesburg along the way. In a peevish letter to Gilbertson he wrote:

> *Everything of even a minor nature, when it occurs in South Africa, seems to become a crisis. We have to make decisions, I believe, far too quickly without always all the necessary documentation and consultation … this is now just the latest case. I would remind you of the general*

consensus of the [parent] Board that they would not take kindly to having to make further emergency decisions in South Africa without very good cause.

Alex continued:

Why is the South African company always managing from crisis to crisis? Why is Reading never kept informed of developments on a running basis? The South Africans should not be allowed to treat their parent as a cash cushion!

Dennis Allport was reported to be applauding Alex's outburst from the sidelines.

The truth of the matter was that MBSA's detailed monthly reports had flowed to England over the preceding months and years, meticulously feeding the *Overseas Company* and the parent board with every financial detail and all major initiatives. This included the raising of working capital in local South African funds in order to immunize the parent from contributions and dilution of their position. (MBSA paid healthy dividends on the parent's holdings, technical licensing fees—largely wasted, as MBSA relied mainly on its Continental Can technology license and a corporate "consultancy fee.") These reports seemed to have escaped the attention of the *Overseas Company* chairman, Jim Gilbertson, who sat on both the parent's and MBSA's boards. Bryan Smither, to whom Peter Campbell and I deferred in corporate financial matters, took the Brits to task in no uncertain terms, bringing his keen intellect and financial expertise to bear. Bryan took Page through his repeated warnings and explanations sent in the course of the previous year or so, pointing to the absence of response or counterproposal from the Brits. His decades of Baring Bros. and Barclays Bank experience exposed the fact that the whiners in Reading were out of their depth. The sole exception was an independent director, Philip Walker, Executive Chairman of Sun Life. As a conscientious board member he had grasped the subsidiary's financial issues and was apparently a vocal supporter of MBSA's position. The whole incident exposed Reading's chain of command as dysfunctional.

> "The dogs will bark," Bryan said back in Johannesburg. "But the caravan moves on. We'll stick to good business sense and logic, Flemming, and they'll come 'round."

Bryan was right. The Brits nervously announced they would follow their rights in full measure, desperate not to lose a single percentage point of their invaluable South African holding. Preparations for the rights issue moved right ahead. The parent knew which side of their bread was buttered.

This incident was not atypical of the *Overseas Company*'s management, or indeed the parent board's capacity when it came to international issues. Territorial jealousies and corporate politics caused the group to squander global opportunities. It was symptomatic of the *Brolly Brigade's* incompetence. The group had no integrated international strategy, no coordinated approach to its many multinational customers like Coca Cola, Unilever or Shell—all significant to the business wherever Metal Box operated. No global strategy for competing with better coordinated competitors such as Crown Cork & Seal or American Can. No cross-border exploitation of the group's huge purchasing power—Metal Box was the British Commonwealth's largest purchaser of sheet steel outside the auto industry. Human capital remained underutilized, as inter-company cross-pollination of specialist talent was only rarely considered at levels below chief executive of a subsidiary (Alex, in all fairness was starting to recognize and address this). Outside times of severe crisis, the Metal Box group's global financial resources were rarely managed optimally.

In April 1975, Alex paid one of his regular visits to MBSA. Sitting in an armchair by the coffee table in my office, in the presence of Bryan Smither, he again told me that I should start preparing my family and the South African management team for my "return home." He cited a 1973 conversation in which I had indicated my eager agreement to have the second half of my career with Metal Box in England.

> "This way, Flemming, you will be in a horse race with Dennis Allport to succeed me. You will have time to get used to the way things are done in the UK, understand our unions, our politics—and our home company management can see that you're not a bad chap, and that they can work with you. The idea is that a three-legged corporate structure will be established, with Allport running the UK packaging business, you running the rest of the world and Bob King in charge of our research and diversified holdings in the UK and internationally. That new structure has to be in place for a couple of years before I go on to become Non-Executive Chairman. That way my successor can finally be selected with some experience under our belts. But it's really between Dennis and you."

Bryan had obviously been briefed and was privy to Alex's thinking.

Judy and I were enthusiastic as we developed our domestic planning. There was much to consider, with some potentially negative changes in day to day lifestyle, a tighter economic situation because of the higher cost of living in England. Judy would be leaving her home country of seven generations. But the overarching sensation was that of excitement, and, for me, the exhilaration of taking on a new and bigger challenge for which I felt qualified. It was good to have some clarity after the anticipation triggered by Alex when he shared his plans with me over two years earlier. However, three months went by with nothing being said or done to further the matter or follow up on Alex's specifically defined plans.

Tempus fugit, I thought. 1975 was running out.

On the next business trip to Reading, this time with Judy and infant son Per, we spent a Saturday at Merton Place with Alex and his current girlfriend called Pippa—he was long divorced and had several romantic relationships of noteworthy longevity while I knew him. I was helping him chalk the lines on his lawn tennis court. Out of the blue, he suddenly made reference to an incident at a dinner party he had given for Peter Campbell and me, with a dozen top UK-based executives, earlier in the week at the Company's West End apartment. During drinks before dinner Dennis Allport had over-indulged, as was his wont, and at the table he used some really foul language in disparaging a couple of his English colleagues who, as a direct consequence, left the party very early. Now Alex wanted me to know that he had spoken to Dennis about it. In response, I said that I had shared my own opinions on the episode with Peter. Later, relaxing after an hour or two of chores in the garden, Alex once again repeated his succession scenario, as communicated earlier in Johannesburg, with no change in timing or the roles of Allport, Bob King or myself. Gingerly, I then asked what Jim Gilbertson would do after I took over his role as chairman of the *Overseas Company*? Alex brushed off the question.

"Oh, don't worry, old boy! There's plenty for Jim to do elsewhere in the Company, I've appointed Derek Huffam and Mac McAllum as senior parent board directors to formalize the plan and make the whole thing evolve. I'll arrange for you to chat with them both this coming week."

"Well, Alex," I countered, "since we're on this subject, some attention also needs to be given to Van Willis's job, since you have specifically called upon me to keep close tabs on MBSA after I make the move. Van has the title of Deputy Chairman of *Overseas*, and on paper he is Territorial Officer for Africa. It's obvious that I can't have him intervening in my relationship vis-a-vis the next CEO in South Africa. He could potentially get between me and my successor—not so, Alex?"

"I don't recall that Van has any such title. We don't need a deputy chair of *Overseas*! And Van has enough to do in the other African territories," Alex replied, showing signs of irritation.

"But Alex, you must have known that his title as Territorial Officer for Africa has been made only too clear to us all, and in Johannesburg these past couple of years he's been handing out his business card, as if it were candy for kids in Soweto, declaring that he is *Deputy Chairman, Metal Box Overseas Ltd.*" I was beginning to fear I had touched on some sensitivities. "May I ask if any of this stuff has been discussed with these fellows in the *Overseas Company* or with your colleagues on the parent board? Who else is in on your plan, apart from Derek and Mac—and me?"

"Flemming, you'll sort all that out with the two of them next week. I'll set up the meetings first thing Monday."

The promised conversations left me comfortable and gullibly sanguine. Derek and Mac seemed to have a clear understanding of Alex's plans exactly as he had presented them to me—and to Bryan Smither, for that matter. Huffam said that they would handle Gilbertson. He seemed more worried that Judy and I might find the cost of living and educating children in England difficult to stomach. However, I did make sure to indicate that I had confidential records of all my conversations with Alex over the previous years, in the form of memos to file, safely tucked away in the vaults back in Johannesburg. Upon hearing that, Mac, who as a lawyer and chartered accountant was corporate secretary, visibly flinched as he lost color in his cheeks. I dismissed the observation without further thought.

That comfort level plummeted quickly a couple of days later when I took a phone call at the Hyde Park Hotel just as Judy, Per and I were leaving for Heathrow to fly home. Jim Gilbertson, whose office I had left in Reading just a few hours earlier, was completely atwitter. An avalanche of agitated verbiage tumbled out of him.

"It's imperative that I clarify something before you leave here," he bellowed, audibly gulping for air. "Under no circumstances, Flemming, should you let your conversations with Page, Huffam or McAllum lead you to think that anything here in Reading is cut and dried." He gasped again for air. "And you must understand that your future with Metal Box can only be defined and managed by one person, and that's me. I am Chairman of *Overseas*—and that's an executive role that I intend to play in mapping your future. I, and only I, will tell you who is to succeed me. The whole process of planning management succession as it pertains to me, or indeed to Alex himself, is to evolve in the full parent board. And it will do so with me in charge of defining your future and the associated timing. I will be confirming this in writing, but it is absolutely vital you understand the situation, the realities of this issue—here and now! Is that understood, Flemming?"

"Okay, Jim," I said without further comment, "I do understand very clearly what you're saying, and I'll certainly take it under consideration," giving him no time to continue before I quickly said, "must fly! We're off to Heathrow. Bye, for now."

I quickly hung up.

It took only a nanosecond to comprehend exactly what was happening. I truly did understand the situation from that moment on, and I did immediately take it under consideration. I was badly shaken, shocked and suddenly very worried about the key people and the modus operandi at the top of the Metal Box group. I told Judy we would now be developing plan B, and we made a good start on the 12-hour flight home to Jo'burg.

Apparently, all hell had broken loose in the hallways of the Reading HQ. Gilbertson, and therefore Willis, had, somehow for the first time, learned what Alex was planning. That was seriously at variance with their own schemes plotted carefully for the five or six years remaining before their retirement at age 63. They had formed some sort of coalition-in-crisis with my designated competitor Dennis Allport, who was no better disposed to Alex Page's plan than were Gilbertson and Willis.

The proverbial shit had hit the fan—big time.

A week or two later, Gilbertson wrote me a very formal offer (with copies to four parent board directors), which stretched the time sequence of Alex's plan by three full years, and presented me with a job description about as illuminating as an autumnal fog on the River Thames Estuary. He explicitly set the scene so as to isolate me from the succession process and preserve his own and Van Willis's plans for their rank, income and maximum pension base for their remaining years. To buy time, I simply promised a response once clarity could be achieved regarding South Africa's exchange control regulations pertaining to my departure. I needed to know what funds I could extricate from the Republic of South Africa. I also had to confirm the portability of my MBSA pension benefits earned over the previous seventeen years. This was, of course, stuff and rubbish because I had no assets that mattered in the context of exchange control rules governing the amount of money one could take out of the country. The government had imposed a limit of 38,000 Rand per adult leaving the country, which meant 76,000 Rand between us. Even after collecting the cash value of my MBSA pension, my net worth was below that limit. I had just settled a divorce with a one-time, upfront payment funded by a sizable mortgage on the home, and Judy didn't have a penny to her name.

Alex had finally realized that a nasty storm was brewing; after all, it was one of his own making. He sent McAllum on a three-day trip to see me in Jo'burg, allowing him to review my understanding of the whole sequence of communications between me and Alex, knowing that I had documented everything in memos to file written at the time. Poor Mac writhed in discomfort as I took him through every step-in detail, openly referring to my typed memos going back to the very first conversation in 1973. He developed a serious case of the wobbles.

Mac had made few comments and asked very few questions during the hours in my office, as I recounted meetings and conversations, including those shared with Bryan Smither. Finally, he sat back and looked me in the eye.

"My goodness! I must say, Flemming, all of that does appear to be rather conclusive. I will report back to Alex accordingly," said Mac. "Do you think Mrs. B could get me on tonight's BA flight back to London? There seems to be little point in my hanging around until Friday."

I wondered what he had planned to do for three whole days with me in the office. But within the hour, Mac sheepishly took his leave and left the office to collect his luggage at the hotel before being driven to Jan Smuts Airport. In the hallway, Peter Campbell, ever curious, looked puzzled as he saw me escort Mac to the elevator, but asked no questions. My colleagues knew something was up and probably exchanged speculative thoughts, but they were discrete enough to avoid comment or question.

In Reading, in early October 1976, the Metal Box group's worldwide forecasts and strategies were being prepared for so called "integration" and presentation as a global corporate plan. My personal plan was that I would deliver my promised response to Gilbertson's obnoxious letter in a face-to-face session with Alex Page, who had of course received a copy. Meanwhile, I told them both that we could work to clarify outstanding issues and put them to bed at that time. I thought they actually believed I would buy into their malodorous scheme.

It was quite obvious to me that my future in Metal Box, within the framework so deliberately communicated to me by Alex, was not going to happen. The international executive recruiting shops in London, Brussels, Lausanne and New York were alerted. The call was made to the prescient Bob Hatfield at Continental Group's headquarters in New York. (The corporate name had been changed, to reflect the diversification of the business beyond the dominant can business, into the insurance and energy sectors). Bob did not need reminding of his open invitation to call him, extended upon departing Johannesburg after his South African visit. With a chuckle, he asked if I had already tired of the Brits? He was told I was far from bored with South Africa, but the Brits had indeed prompted a need to change course, so Judy and I were planning to make some adjustments. South Africa was not a preferred base for building a new career. Nor was it necessarily an ideal place to raise a family. That did not seem to surprise him.

> "Thank you for calling, Flemming. I am pleased to hear from you," and after chatting about this and that, including my situation, Bob said "I think you can expect a call from the president of our Continental Can Company within a week or so, just to talk about the future. Tell me, young man, does Alex know you have plans beyond Metal box?"

> "No sir! But he will soon. I'll be talking with him in Reading in a couple of weeks' time."

> "Okay, Flemming, then we'll take this thing a step at a time."

Meanwhile, interviews were set up with Chesebrough Ponds in Brussels, from where they ran their European, African and Middle Eastern operations; meetings were arranged with ITT and W.R. Grace in London and New York.

ITT could have been an interesting career possibility because of the conglomerate's array of industrial and service enterprises around the world, accumulated under Harold Geneen working with Felix Rohatyn, his renowned Lazard banker. Interviews with ITT involved weird psychological tests administered by shrinks—all part of the Geneen management philosophy, but new to me. The talks with ITT in New York became quite serious, and also served as cover for a covert visit with Continental Can Company, which I made at the invitation of its president, Warren Hayford, who called me, as Hatfield had predicted.

The quick trip with Judy was taken to New York for talks with Hatfield and to meet Hayford. In Connecticut, we were given red carpet treatment. We met senior managers, whom Warren had gathered for a party, which served as our introduction to the culture of American college football—a tailgating picnic ahead of the Army vs. Colgate game at West Point. Hatfield and Hayford were warmly encouraging us to think about joining them, but explained that they would not offer me anything specific until I had expressly resigned from Metal Box: They were not in the business of poaching from their licensees. Playing it safe, in case things did not pan out with Continental, I used the trip to engage in several more interviews with executives at ITT's headquarters on Park Avenue. They were in the market for senior operations managers with international industrial experience.

Come October, during a very brief visit to *Mor* and *Far* in Denmark before the planning meetings in Reading, I called Bryan Smither to engineer a face to face conversation with him. He was fortunately in London on banking matters, so we met for a drink in comfort and privacy at the Baring Brothers' apartment on Eaton Place, in the heart of opulent Belgravia on a Sunday evening. My deliberate plan was to tell him of my resignation before my date with Alex first thing the next morning in Reading. A civilized, at times emotional, conversation with the urbane Bryan lasted more than an hour over a couple of generous scotches. I had put a lot of myself into seventeen years with MBSA, and had sunk deep roots in South Africa, so the situation could not be entirely divested of emotion. He knew me well and was more than understanding; he had long since diagnosed and sympathized with my frustration. Bryan and I had over the years developed a valued relationship of mutual trust and respect. He had anticipated that something would have to give, sooner rather than later.

We quickly agreed that after seeing Alex I would fly to Cambridge, Mass., where Nigel Gilson was attending the Harvard Executive Management Program, to give him the news that he would be taking my place. My succession plan for MBSA had for some time been virtually clarified with Bryan and indeed with Alex, ever since he first mentioned his plans for my return to the UK. Nigel was the designated successor, just ahead of the very competent CFO Peter Campbell. Both of them had been on the board for some time.

Alex must surely have anticipated that I would have problems with Gilbertson's attempt to dupe me (presumably with Page's blessing), but appeared absolutely flabbergasted to hear my decision, dumbfounded to a point of naïveté, given the tortuous unfolding of the situation at hand. He shifted restlessly in his chair, drawing heavily on a morning cigar as he spoke. With hints of impatience in his voice, he attributed my decision to a "personal intolerance and your vendetta with Allport." He carefully avoided any discussion of our previous conversations over the years.

> "Damn it, Flemming, I know you have a problem with Allport, and you are not the only one. But you have made him into your *casus belli*. You must just learn that it's an imperfect world, and things can't always go exactly the way you want them to, at your personally chosen pace. Patience is a necessary virtue, old boy. And you're too bloody impatient." Alex sighed heavily. "But I should have seen this coming, I suppose." Then, after a long silence, he asked, "Where are you going, Flemming? I assume you're leaving South Africa, but I would hope you're not just switching

horses and going to some competitor, joining the opposition? You and I should remain friends."

I had planned to say as little as was necessary. I wanted to keep this guy guessing. I was angry enough to take pleasure in his visible discomfort—*schadenfreude*, justified or not!

> "I think it's a little late in the day, Alex, to debate my capacity for patience. And, if you'll forgive me for saying so, I trusted your word and I religiously respected the confidentiality of our conversations over the last three years. I have a pretty high threshold when it comes to frustration, but I also have a career to look after—not to mention a certain level of pride."

Fortunately, Alex made no attempt to identify the opposition to which he had referred. He could have been referring to Crown Cork, Continental, American Can or one of the European companies—Schmalbach in Germany or Thomassen & Drijver in the Netherlands. Continental's name, per se, never came up. He was told that while I was considering possibilities in various industries, nothing was yet put to bed, so I was not in a position to discuss the matter. Since there was no particular rush, Bryan Smither and I had agreed that the handover would happen in about three months' time, after the year end, giving Nigel time to complete the Harvard program and allow me to help him in getting to know the ropes during a short but civilized transition. Alex said he was genuinely sorry that it had come to this point, but made no more of the occasion on that Monday morning. From my side there was no compulsion to explain or debate—just a wish to get the process behind me. Alex, of course, knew the facts, and did not want to go there.

That left only the practical details to be addressed, including Alex's knee jerk concern about communicating to the South African management, shareholders and media. I told him that the issue had, in fact, already been addressed. Handwritten letters to my closest colleagues and friends and twenty other senior managers were locked up in my desk at the office. I could not resist telling Alex that Mrs. B. in Johannesburg was extremely well briefed, as she had typed every memo to file I had dictated during the decade we worked together. She had the key and would distribute the letters before the morning was out; a press announcement I had prepared before leaving for Europe would be handed to Ed Loughlin for immediate release—there is only an hour or two time difference between the UK and South Africa. Alex was palpably astonished at the finality of the situation with which I had confronted him. He was back on his heels, so he did not hesitate one moment before endorsing my immediate departure to Boston, where I would brief Nigel Gilson and make appropriate plans before returning on the next available flight.

With the critical conversation taking little more than half an hour, my instinct was to get the hell out of the Reading office and let the news brake in whichever way Chairman Page chose to communicate it. I could only imagine that running into Huffam, McAllum or members of the *Brolly Brigade* would be awkward and to be avoided. I left Page's office and headed straight for my rental car in the basement garage and then to London.

Telling Nigel the news was the only enjoyable part of the whole melodrama. He drove in from his business school digs in Soldiers Field Park to meet me at Logan Airport. We spent quite a few hours reviewing the new situation, talking about the MBSA management team and options for a transition after his return to Johannesburg. We did also find time to enjoy Nigel's excitement and have a scotch or two to celebrate his imminent elevation. After less than eight hours stateside, British Airways again had me at 35,000 feet—this time headed eastward. Throughout the exercise, in personal as well as more public settings, only one reason for my resignation was communicated and acknowledged: It was always a variation of the brief statement released to the press back in Jo'burg.

After seventeen years in South Africa and seven as Metal Box South Africa's Managing Director and CEO, Flemming Heilmann at age forty-one has decided to explore new horizons in Europe or the United States.

There was some speculation, private and in the media, as to destination, but never the slightest hint of a squabble with the Brits or personal views on South African social or political affairs.

A week later, after the corporate planning meetings in Reading, Alex gave a farewell dinner party for me, attended by some twenty-five of his top men, at the company's West End townhouse on Chandos Street, hard by the BBC's formidable headquarters at The Langham. The *Brolly Brigade* was there in force, along with some valued and respected friends from the parent company. It was an awkward evening, but not because Alex was less than gracious in any way. Bryan was still in London, so his presence certainly had a very civilizing effect. It was once again Allport's express lane passage to inebriation that caused embarrassment and chilled the atmosphere. Once the port decanter was on its way around the table at the end of dinner, he wasted no time in getting to the topic of my departure, presenting the view from his particular perch.

"To each his own, I suppose! It IS a free world isn't it, Heilmann? I bet you've landed some sort of cushy, overpaid job with a Yankee outfit—their authorities don't seem to give a shit about overpaying their executives." Allport veered off the subject of my departure. "The Americans don't have the Labour Party's obsessions over salaries, perks and sensible incentives. Actually, I wish we could take a more American view of the matter here in England." Then turning again to me, he said "Anyway, old boy, I accept that for a mercenary like you, it's only the money and the limelight that

counts. I know every man has his price, so good fucking luck
to you, Heilmann!"

I did not let the silence in the room linger.

"Sorry Dennis, did I hear you say that every man has his
PRIDE?" I asked. "Or maybe you said every man has his
PRICE? Either way, thank you very much for those kind
words!"

Bryan cracked a smile and rolled his eyes heavenward. Alex grimaced in
his chair at the head of the table and turned ninety degrees away from
Allport's side of the table as he took another big puff at his cigar. Allport,
delivering a totally irrelevant and rambling soliloquy on "America's standard
business attire and ghastly lack of sartorial taste," made sure the conversation
at the dinner table did not come to a complete halt.

After the news had broken officially, and we were back in Johannesburg,
it was a matter of only a week or so before a letter from Connecticut was
delivered by courier, quite explicitly offering me the top marketing and
development job at Continental Can's Rowayton headquarters, replete with
detailed employment conditions and benefits. I would report to Warren
Hayford, the head of the world's biggest can-making operation. Most
analysts had declared Continental Can the preeminent packaging company
in the world. A very short but unreservedly positive response was
immediately telexed back to Hayford, who had signed the letter. Once Nigel
had returned from Harvard, passing the baton was easy. Being good friends
and kindred spirits ensured that. The management team was a pragmatic and
tight-knit group, which adapted quickly, and a low key but heartwarming
series of farewells around South Africa, South West, Mozambique and
Rhodesia commenced. There were gratifying gestures from shop floor
employees in the Durban plant—Zulus and Indians, and Coloured works
committee members in Cape Town. In late December 1976, Bryan Smither

gave a large farewell dinner party at Johannesburg Country Club—predictably low key, but elegant and classy. He presented me with a beautiful early nineteenth century Sterling silver claret jug from Scotland. I felt as if I had won the British Open.

Judy, 18-month-old Per and I were on our way to the United States within weeks.

A chapter was closing. Parting with South Africa quite naturally prompted emotions, reflection and self-appraisal at the time, and the conundrum lives on, to this very day. Life is not a rehearsal: There could be no reruns, no rewrite of this seventeen-year history, nor any part of it. Those years were set in an extremely complex and traumatic socio-political environment. The norms of that time, in South Africa or the United States and around the world, were very different from today's. South Africa had embarked on its apartheid trajectory before I chose to launch a career there; no diktat, no lack of options had forced my hand. It was my very own choice. The question was, had the choice been a good one—social and family life, aside? Had I made the best of the choices presented by my education? Had I optimally used the privileged springboard I had been given, from which to dive into a career? Had I made the best of my opportunities to contribute positively to social progress in this very strange society? How had I done in terms of what I set out to do when I left the UK for Cape Town? I had certainly not traveled to South Africa to be some sort of socio-political missionary? The main objective had been to build a career in a responsible way, working for an enterprise that made a positive contribution to society, to the community at large. But, had I personally made a positive difference in a country that was, in fact, regressing on many social, political and human rights fronts?

What would I have done differently if I had the luxury of the second chance that life precludes? These were the key questions, and they were not entirely futile. Taking stock of one's life every now and again can but have a salutary effect. The process, if it is truly honest, discourages rationalization of mistakes made, knowingly or by accident. The process can also help to rethink priorities and test long held beliefs—especially at age 40-ish. I read somewhere that people who can't change their minds can rarely cause enduring change for the better in the world around them.

I concluded there was no major cause for regret over the choice of South Africa as my stage; nor had MBSA been a bad scene in which to play a role, however small, in the troubled affairs of the land. I had always thought that this incredibly endowed country had the potential for becoming an African USA. In economic terms that potential had only grown and strengthened in those seventeen years, despite all the negative impact of apartheid. Human rights had been criminally trampled upon, and yet apartheid had not prevented huge material gains and a degree of social progress for tens of millions of South Africans, black and white. In this specific context, capital investment, both foreign and domestic, and commercial enterprise had trumped politics and ideology. Without that economic driver, the plight of the non-white victims of apartheid would have been immeasurably worse by the mid-70s. Thousands upon thousands of otherwise uneducated blacks received informal as well as formal education and training from employers, putting them on track to becoming contributing citizens of a middle class with upward mobility. Many learned pragmatic skills, from accounting to mechanical adroitness in industry, commerce and agriculture. The positive impact of economic development on the lives of the neediest outweighed every other force for good that played on the South African scene.

But it was far from enough. The non-white population was being disenfranchised and suppressed.

One could but wonder at the quality and effect of the opposition mounted by many blacks and a significant segment of the white South African minority during this period of escalating bigotry and discrimination. It was courageous but not enough to change the course set by the Nationalist Party. It is impossible to overstate the human and material value created by international and domestic companies in the betterment of black people's daily lives, their standard of living. This was not understood on American and European campuses where they were screaming for divestment and total, unplanned withdrawal. Via the western media, Archbishop Desmond Tutu, in magenta bib and with Thespian vigor, reached overseas audiences, impulsively calling for non-selective, across-the-board divestiture with a bizarre pronouncement cited around the globe:

> *"The divestment movement makes it clear that our black people are suffering for a purpose."*

It got him a Nobel Peace Prize, but caused no significant change—positive or negative.

On the other hand, informed and genuine intervention, such as the American-derived Sullivan Principles mandating decent, practicable employment conditions, surely worked for progress.

But it was not enough.

Informed and courageous South Africans on the ground, both black and white, did make a positive difference. Inestimable support, comfort and succor were provided to suppressed people by domestic activists, volunteer groups, progressive politicians and the domestic English-speaking press. The stubbornly independent judiciary slowed the Nats down, sometimes halting them in their tracks. The Jewish population, in particular, led from the front. Organizations such as the Black Sash, African Self Help (for which Judy worked in Soweto) and the student councils of Anglophone universities were outstanding. Witwatersrand University's student body was particularly effective. One of the earliest and most successful indigenous organizations working to stem the tide of social destruction under apartheid was SACHED, the South African Committee for Higher Education, which was founded in 1959 to combat the impact of the Government's imposition of apartheid in all universities. The Nationalists' *Extension of the University Education Act*, as it was known, banned non-white students from the established universities and led to a handful of all-black institutions, ensuring unacceptable academic standards. SACHED worked initially with London

University to create a bursary system to send many hundreds of blacks to the UK to earn degrees. When high school standards fell to a point that prevented even the brightest from qualifying for entry to British institutions, SACHED successfully introduced the very earliest distance learning programs to address this problem. Under the radar of publicity, funding was quietly contributed by numerous British and American charities and corporations. Avoiding publicity generally meant escaping the attention of the Nationalist government, which in turn allowed their programs to achieve maximum effect. It was a forerunner to other sound international intervention in South Africa. In 1988, Ford Motor Company founded TEASA, the Trust for Educational Advancement in South Africa, which provided blacks from every part of the Republic with access to quality teaching focused in the areas of mathematics, science and technology. These organizations neither sought publicity nor received much. They somehow never fitted the templates for western media reporting on apartheid. Yet they, unlike visiting Hollywood stars and United Nations resolutions, made a real and measurable difference. Sadly, very little was done to facilitate the teaching of vocational and trade skills, without which an essential black middle class demography could not be created—a mistake which has not yet been corrected twenty-five years after the establishment of South Africa's democracy.

Fortunately, there were also those outside the country who really did invaluable work with focused relevance and positive effect: *Médecins Sans Frontières,* for example, several Roman Catholic teaching orders—the Jesuits and Marist Brothers—and Mormon missionaries who taught artisanal and vocational skills. Most overseas aid and support that mattered was delivered under that radar screen.

It was only in the 1980s that properly researched economic and trade sanctions were applied, at last with strategic focus and specificity. They began to work. The major western nations applied increasingly effective sanctions in the areas of finance and South African agricultural markets, which started to hurt the Nationalists' voter base. Afrikaans farmers were the core of the Nationalist Party, so their most crucial voting block began to feel the pinch. When the apartheid regime was eventually brought to its knees and then to the negotiating table, it was not protest (peaceful or otherwise), not United Nations resolutions, not military force, not insurrection nor terrorism that made the difference: it was the implementation of focused, effective economic sanctions. The Nationalists came to understand they would lose access to capital and oil from the rest of the world. They would lose their pivotal export markets. They understood they were facing imminent national bankruptcy. In the end it was that simple. But the protestocrats around the world couldn't and never did figure that out.

Could I personally have done a better job? Sacrificed more? Should I have been less selfish and less focused on the welfare and comfort of my family? More effective for the betterment of this very strange society? Of course I could have! Could the cost/benefit ratio driving my choices have been more heavily weighted for the greater good and less for my own comfort, progress and ambition? Of course it could! A few years later one young ill-informed American lady indeed accused me of making a career and a good living off the backs of oppressed blacks. While that was clearly untrue, I had suffered no real personal hardship during 17 years in that very strange society.

On the other hand, since I had never set out to be a candidate for canonization, I didn't think that, at the age of forty, I would have been a better or more effective citizen, more socially virtuous, had I chosen America, Australia or Europe as the stage upon which to launch a career in 1958. Would some other continent have provided a better stage upon which to learn my role as an apprentice manager, as a steward of investors' funds? Or as a contributing citizen in the greater community around me? Given the colossal, positive force of South African industry and commerce in creating human progress, I am not persuaded I could have spent those years better elsewhere. Life is a continuum, an ever-changing flow of social norms, events and circumstances, and it is always easy to judge past actions and decisions when you are assisted by years of distance, changed social and political norms, 20/20 hindsight and wider experience. These questions were revisited many times over the following decades, sometimes posed by myself, sometimes by others. My considered conclusion, however, has never materially changed. Neither conscience nor remorse has tortured me.

Departure from the country in January 1977, more than a dozen years before Mandela's release, was guided and prompted by key factors. There was no sign of significant change in the country's socio-political direction, nor any indication that the Nationalists were facing any real obstacle or insuperable threat to their rule. Their dogma, policy and ability to follow through had not yet been effectively challenged by military intervention, violent or peaceful opposition or protest. It seemed likely that the ANC would be contained for years ahead, that the Nats would proceed further down the path of apartheid's unacceptable, hypocritical and untenable "separate but equal" ideology. Leaving the country was an entirely personal decision taken with my perceptive and intelligent seventh generation South African wife, Judy. Neither her views, nor those of her family, on the country's policies differed one jot from mine. This was reflected in her mother's membership in Black Sash and her own work with African Self Help in Soweto. Beyond Alex Page's betrayal, the underlying reasons were almost all generated directly or indirectly by the country's extraordinary politics. Given my publicly expressed views on issues so sensitive to Nationalist policy, I would probably still have a residual fiduciary challenge as head of another public company, if I took another such leadership position in the country. South Africa's long-term prospects as a place to have children grow up were irrefutably questionable, to say the least. Adding some urgency to our growing need for change was the duplicity, lack of leadership and the corporate politics at the top of the Metal Box group in the UK. After a parent company board meeting at which my case had obviously been discussed, just before I resigned, I had received a personal, handwritten letter from Philip Walker, the English outside director, in which he actually advised me to resign.

"Get the hell out of here and find something better to do, with better people who better fit your style."

Having just turned forty, I felt that it was halftime. I wanted to regroup and score a little higher in a rewarding second half. The long love affair with the United States of America drove my aspirations and efforts strongly westward. I may, to a degree, have had stars in my eyes, but there was no *Brolly Brigade* to contend with in the States!

Photo Gallery

John W. Baxter, Chairman & Managing Director (CEO) of Metal Box
South Africa Limited from 1947 to 1970, who took the company public
on the Johannesburg Stock Exchange.

Metal Box South Africa's plastics division start-up in 1960 was housed
in rented premises just south of downtown Johannesburg, on Eloff
Street Extension.

Soweto, the largest of Johannesburg's black townships, housing the vast
majority of the city's labor force

'Partnership the only solution'

SOUTH AFRICA'S only solution lay in finding a mutually acceptable formula for economic partnership, Chief Lucas Mangope, Chief Minister of Bophuthatswana, told about 150 people at the Carlton Hotel yesterday.

CHIEF LUCAS MANGOPE, Chief Minister of Bophuthatswana, answers questions from the audience of 150 Black and White businessmen, industrialists and Government officials who attended a luncheon at the Carlton Hotel yesterday. On the left is Mr C F Heilmann, managing director of Metal Box Company. Right is Mr C B Pearce, vice president of the Johannesburg Chamber of Commerce and a member of "Operational Progress," which organised the luncheon.

The National Management & Development Foundation of South Africa in 1971 convened a multi-racial conference of business and government leaders to address labor and economic development issues. (Rand Daily Mail).

Subsistence *mealie* (maize) farming in the "homelands" of the Transvaal highveld region.

A Swazi labor *induna* (leader) in Ngonini Estate's citrus groves of United Plantations South Africa.

Arthur Goldreich, *Chief Interior Architect of the giant OK Bazaars* retail group—when not playing his leadership role as leader Communist Party's sub-Saharan military wing. Seen here under arrest in Marshall Square police headquarters, Johannesburg 1963.

Lillieasleaf Farm, where Nelson Mandela was in hiding, sheltered
by Arthur Goldreich, a year before Mandela's arrest. Goldreich
and Harald Wolpe were themselves arrested here later.

Flemming Heilmann, newly appointed Managing Director and Chief Executive of Metal Box South Africa Ltd.

The Metal Box stand at the annual Rand Easter Show, South Africa's premier industrial convention. Left to right: Bobbie Locke (four-time British Open golf champion) with his wife, Mary; Sam Cohen (Chairman of the giant OK Bazaars retail empire); and Ed Loughlin (Sales Director of Metal Box South Africa).

Flemming Heilmann presenting one of many long-term service awards to an employee at the company's Cape Town factory.

This image, when first used for the front cover of Metal Box South Africa's 1972 annual report, was intended to reflect management's focus on employee communications. It caused a stir.

Alex Page, Chairman and CEO of the parent Metal Box Company in London, visited a South African plant with Flemming Heilmann in 1973.

A tool room superintendent teaches young apprentices to operate a high-precision metal lathe at the company's Machinery Building Division in Cape Town (note the ethnic composition of the class).

Metal Box South Africa's flagship plant at Vanderbijlpark (minutes away from the site of 1961 Sharpeville massacre).

Plant employees said farewell to Flemming Heilmann at the end of 1976 after a long-term service award ceremony.

B. Nigel Gilson succeeded Flemming
Heilmann in South Africa, rising to
top management of the parent
company in the UK in the 1980s
(photo' from the 1990s).

Dennis Allport as Managing Director
and CEO of the parent Metal Box
Company in the UK in the 1990s.

Sir Alex Page, Chairman of Metal Box Company, being honored at the Savoy Hotel in London upon his retirement.

Warren J. Hayford in the early 1970s, before being appointed President of Continental Can Company, Continental Group's dominant packaging business.

S. Bruce Smart succeeded Robert S. Hatfield as Chairman of
Continental Group in 1982.

Ex-President Gerald Ford is greeted by Bob Hatfield at a Continental Group management conference in Palm Beach.

Bob Hatfield toured Metal Box South Africa's facilities with Flemming Heilmann in 1975.

Attending a 1980 Continental Group conference in Bermuda—left to
right: Donald J. Donahue (Vice-Chairman & CFO); Gerrit van Driel
(Chairman of Thomassen & Drijver and his own Royal Wessanen
group); and Flemming Heilmann.

Donald J. Bainton as President of Continental Can Company introduces
Judy and Flemming Heilmann to Ex-President Gerald Ford at a
management conference in 1981.

Flemming Heilmann, while President of Continental Group of Europe in 1980, introduces Don Bainton to the management of Schmalbach Lubeka Werke at their Braunschweig headquarters.

Gerald W. Schwartz, founder and Chairman of Onex Capital, Toronto,
at the closing of their deal to acquire American Can Canada Inc.

At the Toronto Stock Exchange listing of Onex Packaging Inc. in 1986, left to right: Chairman Gerry Schwartz, President Flemming Heilmann, Vice President & CFO d'Arcy Bird and Vice President of Onex Capital Tony Melman.

John T. Stirrup, President & COO of Brockway Standard at Flemming Heilmann's 80th birthday party in Connecticut, 2016.

Jack Stirrup and Flemming Heilmann cruising in Sydney Harbor while attending a 1993 packaging technology conference in Australia.

Youth exchange participants from Jacob Riis Neighborhood Settlement in Queens, New York, visiting the social reformer's place of birth in Ribe, Denmark, with Executive Director William T. Newlin (3rd from left) in 2006.

Bill Newlin retired as Executive Director of Jacob Riis Neighborhood Settlement in 2013 after more than two decades of dedicated leadership, spearheading a ten-fold growth in the scale and reach of the social services agency.

Chapter V

Brave New World

*"Do not let spacious plans for a new world divert your energies
from saving what good is left of the old."*
Winston S. Churchill

THE ENDURING LOVE affair with the United States of America had
been rekindled during that 1960 business trip to learn about the plastic
packaging business. My warm feelings for America, already in my schoolboy
and undergraduate days, could be attributed to the pivotal role of the US
military when they finally joined the Allies, then the American financing of
Europe's escape from famine and its recovery after World War II—the oft
forgotten Lend Lease Program and Marshall Plan. That perception was
underpinned by the family's wartime experiences in South East Asia and
Australia. The impact of the Truman Doctrine was to be felt everywhere.
MacArthur, Truman and Eisenhower were familiar components of boyhood
learning and student discourse. Already in 1947, glossy magazine
advertisements for Buicks, Desotos, Packards, Kaisers and Studebakers
adorned my dormitory walls at school in Denmark. The spontaneous
heroism of General Clay's rebuttal of Soviet intimidation in the Berlin Airlift
had been stunning. American innovation, technology and scientific advances
affecting everyday life on the planet boggled the mind. US Olympic legends
from Jesse Owens and Harrison Dillard to Bob Mathias were athletic gods.

Corporate icons as disparate as Boeing, Kellogg, Ford, Kodak, Wrigley's, Colgate, Esso and IBM along with countless others had, for decades, been part of daily life. The *Saturday Evening Post*, *Time* and *Life Magazine*. Paul Robeson, Marion Anderson. Martin Luther King. Doris Day, Ava Gardner, Esther Williams, John Wayne, Spencer Tracy, Gregory Peck and James Stewart. The Ink Spots, Bing Crosby, Bob Hope, Dean Martin, Frank Sinatra, Jimmy Durante, Satchmo, Fats Waller, Duke Ellington and Jimmy Dorsey all left their indelible imprint. Irving Berlin, Rodgers & Hammerstein, Gershwin, Bernstein and Copeland. John Steinbeck, Ernest Hemingway, Norman Mailer, Georgia O'Keeffe and Norman Rockwell. Blue jeans, hamburgers and popcorn. Americans, American music, American clothing, American enterprise and innovation, values and candor were all in the eye of life's whirlpool. Especially when seen from South Africa in the 1960s and 70s, America was also making real progress in its legislation in support of civil rights and to curb persistent racialism.

Adolescence and undergraduate years had provided a distant view and spawned my admiration of America's post World War II Golden Age. Despite the Keynesian pessimism of Nobel Laureates Paul Samuelson and Gunnar Myrdal, who predicted that the imperative of debt reduction would lead to unemployment, social unrest and economic collapse, the United States entered a quarter century of boom and prosperity. A conservative Congress had taken over to liberate the economy from excessive central control and the unfettered misuse of Washington's money-printing presses. Price controls were lifted, taxes lowered, investment encouraged and full employment achieved. Government expenditure outside the infrastructure was cut, national debt was pared dramatically, personal consumption and gross private investment rose sharply to support the growth cycle, which endured through the 60s. America's economy and that of many other nations were propelled past recovery into prosperity as automation and productivity raced ahead. Economic activity was boosted by Eisenhower's progressive Interstate Highway system. Chemical fertilizers, innovative combine harvesters, new high-yield crops and ground breaking raw materials such as plastics were commercialized.

Nor had the lessons of failed socialism in so many corners of the globe, including two countries in which I had grown up, gone unnoticed. America's enterprising and venturesome optimism, offensively brash as it sometimes could be, were so much more appealing than Europe's collective claims of entitlement, self-pity and whining. Americans exhibited a refreshing focus on opportunity, rather than the European whining fixation on entitlement that spawned dependence on others (tax payers), discouraging individual responsibility.

America, in matters pertaining to racism, segregation and reinforcing democracy was moving forward, step by step, at 180 degrees to what we had experienced in South Africa. The reforms and multiple desegregation triumphs of the Civil Rights Movement, continuing legislation, Congressional action and disparate social programs didn't get the job done, but directionally the civic approach and social order of America was ad-dressing and making progress in reversing the inequities and injustices of generations past.

Yet, it was that 1960 jolt of excitement over my first exposure to pulsating New York in the steamy heat of July, which triggered a nascent dream of living and working in the United States one day—not yet a specific objective but, as negative developments in South Africa accelerated, it was an increasingly alluring option. Joining Continental Can was an almost natural evolution—a geographic, dimensional and cultural progression within a familiar industry. Several American friendships and my brother John with family in Connecticut since 1968 were hardly a deterrence.

Quite ironically, this was President Carter's America that we had chosen to make our new home. He was into his single term in the White House after narrowly beating a hapless Gerald Ford in the general election and no less than thirteen rival Democratic contenders in 1976 primaries. It was not exactly a thriving America, nor a particularly happy one at the time. It was a confused America struggling with global stagflation and its own Byzantine foreign policy initiatives. The USA was desperately pursuing multiple and muddled "strategies" in a Middle Eastern labyrinth of power politics set in parochial Levantine and Arab intrigue. It was a scenario in part generated by Washington's erratic support of the Afghan *mujahedin* fighting the Soviets, with the brutal Saddam Hussein and faltering Peacock Shah of Iran thrown into the mix—all at various points in time—while also ceding control of the Panama Canal. Waffling through ineffectual SALT II talks with the Soviets. "Normalizing" relations with the People's Republic of China, while snubbing the touchy Taipei government. Carter's international strategic guru while all this was going on, was the equally muddled Dr. Zbigniew Brzezinski, National Security Advisor to one of the country's most ineffectual presidents ever. As a newcomer, ill-informed on US politics, I paid scant attention to the Middle East or the loquacious Ziggie's diplo-babble.

It was all a bit of a mess!

Elsewhere in America, 1977 was marked by events, which an immigrant could only take as a clear reminder that he or she was embracing an exceptional country. Apple Computer and Oracle Corporation were incorporated; the death penalty was reintroduced with Gary Gilmore's execution by firing squad in Utah; Gerald Ford had pardoned Tokyo Rose just before Carter was sworn in as 39th president; the ground breaking TV series *Roots* commenced on ABC; twelve Hanafi Muslims took three buildings in DC, killing three and taking 130 hostages for three days; *Star Wars* was released; 200,000 marchers in San Francisco protested Anita Bryant's anti-gay rantings; Elvis Presley and Led Zeppelin performed their last concerts; New York's 25-hour blackout provided opportunity for wide spread looting and the conception of the innumerable babies born nine months later; serial killer Son of Sam—or David Berkowitz—was at last captured in the Bronx; Ted Turner's *Courageous* won the America's Cup and *Voyager I* was launched; L'il Abner ended his 43-year cartoon series and the expensively elegant supersonic *Concorde*'s transatlantic service was in-augurated, setting up a contest with the workmanlike Boeing 747 Jumbo's low cost airfares. On the socio-political front, the Community Reinvestment Act was passed to put an end to the discriminatory practice of red lining, and Harvey Milk was elected as San Francisco's first openly gay City Supervisor. Secretary of State Cyrus Vance resigned in disagreement with the President even before the failure of Carter's doomed hostage-rescue attempt in Teheran.

However, current affairs did not draw enough of my attention to cause me great concern.

My laser-like focus was locked on building a new career and restoring my domestic finances while the growing family was getting settled. My new surroundings made it abundantly clear that, having been a relatively big fish in a tiny South African pond, I was now but a minnow in the gigantic American ocean.

In 1977, Continental Can Company was a five-billion dollar blue-chip company, originally built on the manufacture of metal consumer goods packaging. It had diversified very logically within the packaging industry, moving into other materials such as plastics and paper, but never glass. By this time, Continental was further diversifying by acquisition of businesses way beyond its historical base and competencies, industries as disparate as gas pipelines and title insurance. At the company's helm, Bob Hatfield was a major part of the company's strong reputation for competence, dependability and integrity. He was perhaps not the planet's most innovative or sophisticated strategist, nor was he a balance sheet gymnast or adventuresome deal maker; but he was a leader of people and an indefatigable competitor, a both-feet-on-the-ground realist and a sound businessman. Despite his commanding stature, his style was low key, occasionally diffident, always warm and open. His unswerving integrity made him an engaging and effective CEO.

"You can take Bob's word to the bank on any commitment he ever makes," said Citicorp chairman Walter Wriston. "Every self-respecting bank should have at least one or two

Bob Hatfields on its board—I sure know we need him on ours. He is so good here on our Citi board, we don't need more than one Hatfield."

Wriston, who with Felix Rohatyn of Lazard, had helped resolve New York City's almost catastrophic financial crisis (caused by years of profligate deficit spending), was not alone in his assessment of Bob. Hatfield at various times served on the boards of Eastman Kodak, Johnson & Johnson, General Motors, Marsh McLennan, Koppers Industries, Nabisco Brands and the New York Stock Exchange. He was an influential member of the Business Round Table and a trustee of Cornell University where, after retirement, he also did a pro bono stint as CEO of Cornell's hospital cum medical school in New York City. Bob loomed large in corporate America and was a respected leader beyond his own company. If Tiny Rowland was the unacceptable face of capitalism, Bob
Hatfield was a paragon of the system.

Within the company, Bob was universally respected and trusted. His integrity allowed him to be extremely direct in otherwise sensitive situations. People inevitably knew where they stood, and if not, could very soon learn the answer to that question. On one such occasion, Bob's personal appointment of a new Vice President of Government Relations caused another ambitious VP of Public Relations and Advertising to have his nose put out of joint. Don Earnshaw made the mistake of attempting to discredit the new rival in the eyes of the CEO. He engineered a 7:30 AM encounter with Hatfield at the coffee machine on the executive floor of headquarters at 333 Third Avenue, and engaged Bob in a conversation. The exchange migrated into the CEO's office, where the portly Don Earnshaw was encouraged to lower himself into an armchair. He proceeded obliquely to imply that the new VP, Tommy Thompson, had flaws in his qualifications and could not serve Continental's cause optimally in Washington, where controversial consumer packaging legislation was being contemplated. Bob's eyebrows jumped skyward as he looked up at Earnshaw from behind his desk.

> "Well, that's an interesting point of view. In fact, the returnable packaging legislation is so critical to the business, that I need to make sure I thoroughly understand the issues and the relevance of what you're saying, Don. We should talk about it—I mean go through the whole thing. Tommy is due to come chat with me right now, at eight o'clock. Please just carry on, and we can get him in to join us, so that we can all share views."

Earnshaw instantly suffered a quasi-convulsion, struggling for air and coping with palpitations. He then managed to stammer that he did not think such a conversation would be productive, or words to that effect. There was but a moment's pause before Hatfield slowly drew himself up from his chair to his full six foot, three inches, leaned across his large mahogany desk, both hands planted on its top and straining his neck as he locked eyes with Earnshaw, who was by now also standing.

> "In that case, Don, get out of my goddamn office, will you!" Bob said very slowly and very deliberately. And then, after a pause, "Right this moment, Don!"

That was consistent with Bob's style and values. To Earnshaw's credit, he related this episode to me himself a year or so later, when we overlapped in Brussels at Continental's European headquarters.

Continental Can Company, Inc., which would soon change its listed name to Continental Group, Inc. (to reflect its diversifications), was in transition mode. The dominant can-making component retained the name Continental Can Company. For half a century the company had been the leader in its domestic market, content to limit its international presence to a network of technical licensees in the major markets of the world, generally writing lucrative technology and service agreements, backed by small minority stock holdings, with the leading national player in each country. Trailing in second place at home and abroad was American Can Company, and then others like Crown Cork & Seal, National Can and Ball Corporation.

Several game-changing forces came into play in the late 1970s as tensions arose between members of what had long been a tight, international Continental Can "family." Along with Metal Box in the UK, there were CCC family members, or licensees, in virtually every West European country. The license agreements were crafted to cover markets within national boundaries, which created a territorial segmentation, or a de facto European market-sharing arrangement. The agreements precluded each licensee from *applying, or selling products utilizing the subject technology outside the licensed territory.* The European Economic Community (EEC) or Common Market was in those years maturing as an entity under an exploding bureaucracy in Brussels. So there were early rumblings from EEC headquarters indicating a determination to dismantle any arrangement that had even a whiff of market-sharing, let alone the stink of a cartel. Corporate lawyers in New York saw cause for concern and a chance to make a fortune in fees. Continental's leadership grew wary of the tightening regulatory situation in Europe. The markets of other licensees in countries such as Japan, Australia, India, Malaysia or New Zealand, were all defined by natural boundaries like sea or impassable mountains, whereas the national markets in Europe were juxta-positioned, with porous borders, many of which were merging into a common market.

The hawks in Continental's top management saw the regulatory threat as an opportunity to terminate the license agreements and abolish the old family club. They considered the old relationships to be self-inflicted barriers to growth. With the exception of Metal Box, many of the licensees were relatively inefficient and complacent, content to work within their own high-margin, largely protected markets. The American hawks relished the prospect of dropping their gloves and engaging in a brawl. They wanted to invest aggressively in territories where Continental's superior technology and scale could be put to work, particularly in the beer and beverage industries. The Metal Box hawks, with far less firing power, weaker management, but more international experience, were also looking for a scrap. The Brits, with some geopolitical justification, regarded the European continent as their natural hunting ground.

"It's OUR back yard, my dear chap!"

"Why don't you just stay on your side of the pond, old boy, in North and Latin America, while we look after our side? That way we can both enjoy our established positions without pissing away profits. The same makes sense for the old Commonwealth territories, where we've been around since Christ was a child—don't you see?"

The European mainland licensees were also content to maintain their cozy relationships with competitors, banks, suppliers and domestic customers. The whole operating environment was changing; the yeast was already at work as the EEC fermented in its pursuit of the economic union, and Brussels spawned dreams of a political European Union. Change lay ahead.

Warren Hayford, as the relatively young President of Continental's dominant metal can business, was in charge of the corporation's largest concentration of assets. He was well placed to lead the charge of CCC's hawks. He was a rising star in the Continental Group firmament. Warren was raised in a strongly Roman Catholic military family, a West Point graduate with an exceptionally sharp intellect. He had an extraordinary talent for numbers and quantitative methodology. He made an impression in any gathering and looked the part of a leader. Well over six-foot, penetrating brown, deep set eyes framed by heavy black-rimmed Rip Kirby glasses, he had sharp, clean cut features. Sartorially, he was as much a prisoner of

Brookes Brothers of the 1960s as any IBM salesman; he wore white button-down shirts, plain ties, dark suits and big, well-polished black brogues. His erect bearing and military heritage shone through an engineered veneer of worldliness and bonhomie. Warren was intense and tirelessly competitive, occasionally prone to take short cuts through best practices, but only when he was confident that he could not be called on them. Meticulous in his due diligence and occasionally ruthless, but a man of his word once a formal deal was struck. He asked incisive questions, the answers to which he listened carefully. He had a keen eye for people of strong intellect, but he was a less effective judge of character. This could lead to some appalling choices of bedfellows. The West Pointer was a top down manager with a keen sense of rank, which he would at times invoke when thwarted. He could be cunning in his use of cleverly selected facts as he pursued his agenda. Warren was not always sensitive to the styles and values of others and could become uncharacteristically insecure in rare situations where he found himself out of his depth. This perhaps explained his strange personal reluctance to court customers face to face—he preferred that others do that.

Religious conviction took him on an annual pilgrimage with his wife to Lourdes. Warren and Mary Lou were counted among the more than 200-million miracle-seeking Catholics, who have flocked there since 1860 to make sure God is on their side, or would help them with some medical or emotional problem.

~~~~

Warren J. Hayford's first charge, upon his 1975 appointment as Executive Vice President of Continental Group and CCC president, was to turn the mighty US can business around from its ailing condition and then grow the business globally. Continental's corporate growth had come largely from the group's other packaging businesses in plastics, paper, or forest products and latterly from acquired diversifications. The very significant turnaround in the US can business had been largely accomplished by 1977, after radically adjusting the capital and human resources employed, reducing working capital and accelerating fixed asset turnover in a saturated market. Short term growth had to come from elsewhere: hence the appetite for expansion of the packaging business abroad. My international background, industry experience and intimate knowledge of Metal Box's dynamics were seen as helpful, but this did not necessarily mean that my views were always instantly appreciated or even understood in Stamford, Connecticut.

The largest CCC licensees in Europe were in the crosshairs of the evolving strategy of the hawks (with which I generally agreed). Schmalbach Lubeca Werke (SLW) in Germany and Thomassen & Drijver-Verblifa (TDV) in the Netherlands dominated their markets with very limited competition. They had both been private, tightly held companies, with Continental holding small minority positions when in the early 70s the American giant acquired 100 percent ownership of them both from the Munte and Drijver families respectively. Between them they added $1.3-billion to Continental's top line. American efforts to take full operating control of these European assets were resisted because the entrenched decision-makers were terrified of change and generally regarded American management style as crass and overly aggressive. By the mid-70s, local management was still directing strategy, day-to-day operations in modus operandi extant. A feeble attempt at European coordination was made by the new owners, who registered an entity called Europemballage in Brussels to "assert control, rationalize and modernize." The CCC strategy team was led by Warren in Connecticut. It was a parochial group when it came to understanding, let alone coping with, dynamics of the European corporate and labor laws of the mid-70s. National cultures and social issues of the day were way beyond their ken. Anything that existed or took place east of the New England coastline was indeed very foreign and confusing to them—inexplicable to a can-maker from Milwaukee, Wisconsin.

Hayford's new CCC headquarters, carefully removed from the corporate HQ on Third Avenue in Manhattan, were located in Rowayton, Connecticut, in an old mansion, which was formerly the home of the wealthy

Farrell shipping dynasty. A large residential stone edifice perched atop a wooded bluff overlooking Long Island Sound, it initially housed a staff of no more than thirty people. Warren, whose personal office quite appropriately had been General Douglas MacArthur's after President Truman fired him, when he was Chairman of Remington Rand. Hayford relished the military connotations of his new command post. This was where I reported for my first day at work in America. Forty years later The Smithy, our treasured little retirement home, happened to be in the same village, near the mouth of Five Mile River on Long Island Sound, just 600 yards from the Farrell mansion, now part of an elegant office park housing a hedge fund.

The initial job in Rowayton carried the title Vice President, Commercial—and was ill defined. It was a staff role as advisor to Warren, particularly on international, marketing and development issues. My years of dealing with the multinational consumer goods companies were useful. CCC's domestic turnaround led by an able if authoritarian manufacturing executive, Don Bainton, had resulted in a tight, secretive management group in Chicago, which was quite evidently skeptical of my alien presence at Warren's side. Bainton's turn-around of the US can business was pivotal to the Continental Group's overall performance, widely lauded and applauded, of course, for the numbers. So Don was quick to feel his oats and reset his already aggressive ambitions. He carefully controlled my contact with any part of the domestic organization: I had little new to offer Chicago's comprehensive but parochial focus on the USA, except relationships giving access to leaders of some major multinational customers. My direct contact with Bainton was at arms-length, awkward but polite because he did not know how to read my relationship with his superiors at the top of the totem pole. Little did he know that I really didn't either.

In 1977 the Europemballage concept and its Dutch leader with support staff in Brussels was abolished. Warren replaced it with a small office and an American President, Don Earnshaw, of a newly registered entity named Continental Group of Europe. It was to be a beachhead from which CCC would control the large German and Dutch subsidiaries after subjugating local management. The objective was to improve flagging performance of the complacent SLW business and to modernize and protect the sustainability of the more profitable TDV. The Dutch company was exposed to self-created vulnerability—very high costs sheltered by the absence of competition and exorbitant pricing. The managers of both businesses were intimidated by muscular labor unions, as was typical throughout most of Europe in that socialistic era, when organized labor bullied the national social democratic governments. TDV was vulnerable to a pincer movement of unsustainable cost of wages and benefits (on which the unions insisted) along with an obese corporate structure and lack of growth on the one side and very high prices on the other. Both companies were facing the inevitability of cross-border competition as the Common Market took shape. They could not see how reality could be so cruel.

The flow of paper from Warren's office to mine instantly became a torrent. Reports on evaluations of African and Asian markets and national economies; copies of the German and Dutch companies' board minutes; memos on talks with Metal Box, or the Australian and Japanese licensees regarding termination of the technology transfer agreements; analyses of metal vs. plastic container costs; focus group reports on the respective merits of steel and aluminum beverage cans; environmental legislation involving litter, energy consumption, returnable containers and recycling; and the corporation's questions on the political and economic outlook for dozens of countries including, of course, those of the British Commonwealth—sovereign risks. My workaday challenge was light years removed from a South African CEO's responsibilities to two divergent groups of shareholders, 5,500 employees and disparate stakeholders.

The Metal Box-Continental conflict quickly came to a head, which in turn led to what proved to be a terminal summit meeting in Brussels at the venerable Hotel Amigo, just off Grand Place. This was Continental's final bout against the heaviest puncher in the global licensee family. This relationship had evolved over forty years from a warm friendship between its founding giants, Sir Robert Barlow in London and Carle Conway in New

York. The Barlow-Conway alliance had led to the preeminence of the
Continental licensees in virtually every market of the global packaging
industry. Now Alex Page and Bob Hatfield led the respective teams, each
pressured by his own hawk-in-chief, Dennis Allport and Warren Hayford
respectively. The priority topic was, of course, territory, with the Brits basing
their claims on "established positions" and what they regarded as "fairness
based on historical understandings." The American strategy was to hone in
on the exact definitions of "licensed technology" in "licensed territory"
written into the legal agreements, which were now expiring with the passage
of time—all in the context of the evolving EEC and the European and US
antitrust laws. The weakness of the Brits' reasoning made it a lop-sided
debate. The Amigo meeting marked the final chapter of Continental Can's
comfortable family history shared with licensees stretching from Tokyo and
Melbourne to Helsinki, from Johannesburg and Delhi to Stockholm. A
courteous if cool divorce process was negotiated, leading to a corporate
decree nisi document a few months later. The terms were based on the solid
legal position of the Americans, which was invulnerable, and decisive:

> "I am truly sorry, my friend, but that's the way it has to be.
> The setting has changed and continues to do so at an
> accelerating pace," said Bob to Alex. "What's yours by law is
> yours, of course, and what's mine by the same yardstick is
> mine."

The Brits had been outmaneuvered by strategic use of relevant jurispru-
dence. Metal Box, true to my own experience with these Brits, had not done
their homework very thoroughly, whereas the Americans had, in full
measure.

Personally, I played my own role, way off-stage, as a guide and
interpreter of Metal Box's approach to the negotiations and their territorial
aspirations. As State Farm's advertisement of today, forty years later, might
say:

I knew a thing or two, because I'd seen a thing or two!

At the summit conference cocktail hour, brushes with my erstwhile senior colleagues from across the Channel were diplomatic and polite, but generally less than convivial. A couple of stunted exchanges with Alex were particularly awkward, in part perhaps because he was deep into a protracted affair with my ex-wife Marilyn (of which I was well informed, courtesy of my children and old friends at Metal Box). Dennis Allport never uttered a word in my direction, beyond a perfunctory initial greeting. He was relishing his recently elevated role in the MB hierarchy, Managing Director, which could be either CEO or COO in the UK context, but Alex was very obviously still at the helm. Allport was by now the clearly anointed crown prince.

However, Hotel Amigo's house Sancerre was crisp, nicely astringent and eagerly gulped by the Brits while the Americans carefully nursed their scotches and martinis. From one of the junior staffers on the Metal Box team I received some interesting commentary. His babbling river of small talk meandered through the delights of the Loire's lowland variety of Sauvignon Blancs into typical Metal Box hallway gossip.

> "Alex is an interesting chap, isn't he? I'm sure you've heard about the Chairman's history of trysts and girlfriends. After all, he does drag them around, quite unashamed—ha ha, why the hell not? To all his official and public functions! Well, the latest buzz is that Mr. Page is running a pretty hot and heavy relationship with a bird called Marilyn Harter, at one time married to one of your senior Continental chaps, who once worked for MB in South Africa. Forgot his name for the moment, but he apparently picked a fight with Page over Reading's meddling in Jo'burg's business, so he left the top spot in Metal Box South Africa and fucked off in a huff— only to join you people at CCC. I'm sure you know him. I

bet he's doing all right over there now, given your US salaries and bonuses. It's a pity this kind of cross-pollination has now got to end, don't you think, old boy? Damned shame, I'd say! It's been a lot of fun over the years, and I wouldn't mind a job in Yankee land myself."

I didn't let on. The poor, ill-informed Englishman would have writhed out of his skin, had he realized to whom he was telling his story. Interestingly, the "cross-pollination" didn't stop as several Metal Boxers were to join Continental over the years ahead as the British company lost its head of steam and Allport (succeeding Page) inexplicably rolled over, allowing Metal Box to get swallowed by the much smaller French company, Carnaud et Forges de Basse Indre, which in turn was gobbled up by Crown Cork & Seal, the emerging force in the global industry. Crown Cork with its relatively humble beginnings, stuck to its last and well-defined objectives, focused on the financial and market realities, eventually becoming dominant.

Hayford quickly put me to work carrying his strategy and theories across the Atlantic to the European subsidiaries. After about ten months, Warren asked that my darling pregnant Judy and I move with our little boy, Per, to Braunschweig, the seat of SLW's headquarters, to be the number two man for Continental's European operations and expansion throughout Europe. From there, I was to lead the implementation of CCC's management reform, rationalization plans and new business development. I would be reporting to a charming, urbane but ineffectual President of Continental Group of Europe in Brussels, none other than ex-VP of corporate Public Relations and old time CCC super salesman, Don Earnshaw. Warren's idea bordered on lunacy.

"You've got a good German surname, Flemming, and a bit of the language. You and Judy will blend in just beautifully in Braunschweig. They'll almost think you are one of them, Herr Heilmann!" said Warren, not sensing how horrified I was. "And the Munte family will give you all their support via their family and friends from over here in the States, where he's now based at corporate headquarters. You'll be spending most of your time with the two national company heads and won't need the Brussels-based staff people on a day-to-day basis. You'll be perfectly placed to light a fire under Dieter Madaus (the recently appointed successor to Munte) and his Germans, or get him out of there. And I'll make sure Don Earnshaw doesn't get in your way." Warren drew breath, clenched his lips and proceeded "We need to build some momentum for change, Flemming, and I believe SLW is the better place to start. They are a bit less stubborn than the Dutch."

The Munte family, succeeding the original Schmalbachs via a marriage, had virtually owned the business before selling to Continental, who promptly removed CEO Hans Herbert Munte, now an affable multimillionaire. He was given a big-title-no-job position in New York. Continental simply wanted him out of the way. Stupidly, Hans Herbert had been allowed to select his own successor as head of SLW before he left Braunschweig. Dieter Madaus soon proved to be a disaster.

The new American owners had no perception of the mutual animosity and distrust between the Germans and the Dutch. Nobody stateside understood that World War II was not yet over for these two companies, that the prior owners had been at loggerheads and that their respective trade unions loathed each other for basic tribal reasons and fear of cross-border competition. The managements and unions resisted any change that could threaten their cozy nests and protective practices. Separately, they were all hell bent on preserving the status quo.

Hayford had developed a theory that I could help the essential melding of the European operations from Braunschweig if I were given sufficient authority. The idea was naïve, ill-informed and without merit. Besides,

Braunschweig was an isolated medieval town near the border of what was then East Germany, with no airport nearer than the provincial city of Hannover. Getting to anywhere from Braunschweig had to involve exorbitant air charter expenses or time wasted, puddle jumping on tiny regional carriers. Moreover, the Dutch saw Braunschweig as a threat to their own isolationist fiefdom based in the little provincial town of Deventer. Anything emanating from Germany was bad news for the Dutch and for TDV. Cautiously and very quietly, I engaged Hayford and persuaded him that the plan was a bad idea, that it would not work and there had to be a better way to skin this cat.

Within a few weeks the next idea was presented: I would be promoted to Executive Vice-President of Continental Group Europe (now referred to as CGE) based in the neutral Brussels office to await Don Earnshaw's repatriation after two or three months, and then I would become President and head of all Europe.

"I see no need to rush Don out of there," said Warren. "You can get on with the rationalization and fixing operations as Don prepares for his return home. He'll just continue to do his glad-handing, which he does so well. From Brussels you can reach TDV's headquarters in Deventer in less than three hours by car, and you have my full authority to use charters to fly to and from Braunschweig, or anywhere else you need to go in Europe. The CGE office already has the financial staffing and controls you need, so what we are lacking there is your understanding of things European and operational moxie on the ground." Warren did his lip clench and exhaled. "Despite your tender age, Flemming, you are far more experienced than Dieter Madaus or Rudy Miolet in Holland. It's one heck of an opportunity for you, my friend, to take this bull by the horns. You have got to stop their stonewalling. We've let these people block every needed change for far too long. You and Judy should plan on being there for three to five years—find a nice house in Brussels, and bring the family home for your vacations over here. By 1982 or '83, you can also get two or three new beverage-can plants established for us in the UK, France, Spain or perhaps Italy," Warren's machine-gun directions sputtered on and on.

"I also want you to draw on your Danish and British networks to break SLW and TDV out of their molds, and engage across borders. Work with potential customers the Dutch and Germans have never talked to—people like Carlsberg, Pripps, Guinness, Schweppes, Whitbread and Scottish & Newcastle. We'll back you up from here in the soda business through our friends at Coke and Pepsi, to support startups outside Holland and Germany. It's one great opportunity, Mr. Heilmann, and you have all it takes!"

Hayford's rapid fire articulation was backed by all sorts of relevant numbers and was driven by an avalanche of ambitious ideas to support his well-reasoned strategy. The quantitative goals were rarely to be faulted and his sense of urgency was an effective motivator, even when he was too impatient. If only he had been more sensitive to cultural differences and had embraced just a touch of humility, Warren could have been an exceptional captain of industry on a global scale.

This time I had little difficulty in buying into Warren's plans, despite my realizing it meant putting Judy and the family through the hoops once more—yet another testing move across the ocean.

The new challenge Warren presented entailed a significant promotion, and this time also made strategic sense. In the context of career building, it was a very exciting opportunity. For the family—now four of us with our youngest Niels born in Connecticut —it was another emotional upheaval, coming so soon after deliberately immigrating from South Africa and assimilating into a new life in a new country. Another set of personal challenges was now facing all four of us. For about three years, home was Avenue Bellevue in Waterloo, at the edge of the gorgeous Foret de Soigne, south of Brussels, on the border of Rhode-Saint-Genese. Our white-painted brick house, with a steep wood-shingle roof, bottle green shutters and doors, surrounded by ancient sycamores and oaks, almost had the feel of a grand New England colonial. Avenue Bellevue itself was an enchanting cobbled street under a canopy of giant linden trees, closed off at one end, so access was confined to its residents. Large villas with mature gardens hinted at the solid affluence of the Belgian neighbors. Brussels' Zaventem international airport was a mere twenty-five minutes away by a highway. Virtually any city in Europe could be reached in an hour or two, and getting to the office required but a fifteen minute commute along the Chaussee de Waterloo. Central Brussels, anchored by its fabulous seventeenth century Grand Place and spectacular culinary offerings, was twenty minutes away via the Chaussee and elegantly residential Avenue Louise. A couple of miles to the south in Waterloo village was the historic battlefield upon which the Duke of Wellington's Allied Coalition, with a little help from Prussia's General Gebhard Blücher, put an end to Napoleon's reign as self-appointed Emperor. These historic surroundings offered no warning that I had my own war to face on the battlefields of Braunschweig and Deventer.

Continental's combined businesses in Europe were lagging in terms of competitive returns to shareholders, given Continental's large investments in the two subsidiaries. The specific management challenges to be addressed in Germany, Holland and in the rest of Europe differed substantially. SLW and TDV each called for reform in quite different business environments and disparate socio-political constraints. In the rest of Europe, growth via startups or acquisitions called for yet another approach.

SLW generated sales of about $850,000,000 and TDV about $500,000,000, but the income performance of the two presented divergent issues. The Germans were parochial, complacent, stodgy and seriously underperforming as measured by return on assets. The Dutch were arrogantly smug, seriously overinvested in fixed and human assets, paying unsustainably high wage rates and granting rich benefits—yet quite profitable thanks to very high prices facilitated by the absence of competition. SLW and TDV had to be integrated into a more cohesive and productive asset base to compete in a free, increasingly open European market. Straightforward stuff by the American business school textbook, but the Americans were new to the challenge of breaking encrusted mindsets, social norms and traditions. They were puzzled, blankly unfamiliar with the relationships between European governments and trade unions, and ignorant of the attendant entitlement-based labor agreements of the Continent. In Chicago and New York, they would have simply closed and rationalized plants, paid termination settlements and sent in the bulldozers. After all, Don Bainton had just fixed CCC's stagnant US Can business exactly that way.

~~~~

West Germany in the 1970s was still struggling under the influence of the heavy-handed socialism of the SPD party. Chancellor Willy Brandt and his government had spent one in every three available (often borrowed) Deutsche Marks on creating cradle-to-grave social welfare: ever-expanding entitlements and ever-shrinking workweeks. It was the era of universal unemployment compensation set at 68 percent of most recent wages and overtime paid, standard six-week annual vacations plus virtually unlimited sick leave, maximum 38-hour workweeks, penal termination costs and full retirement benefits available at middle age. All of this had crippled or obliterated German companies and destroyed Germany's overall competitiveness. In 1976, Willy Brandt was quite appropriately elected head of *Socialist International*. His successor, the more pragmatic Chancellor Helmut Schmidt—famous for his *Ostpolitik* and thawing relations with the Soviets—was less extreme, a little further to the right of Marx and Engel, but still a Keynesian on steroids. As a result, the West German economy and fiscal situation were in near mortal shape, threatening to rival its communist eastern neighbor's performance at a time when Angela Merkel was still a physics student at the University of Leipzig in the People's Republic.

Breaking the remnants of this mold of constraint on SLW's business in the 1970s involved taking on the government-backed unions to alleviate constrictive employment legislation and prohibitive labor costs, all while living with *Mitbestimmung* or co-determination (i.e. labor's voting representation on management and supervisory boards). It did not make it any easier that the huge industrial complex surrounding Volkswagen's HQ and auto unions were in nearby Wolfsburg, only thirty miles from Braunschweig; nor did the steel industry unions of SLW's crucial suppliers. Both were hotbeds of socialist excess, the aspirations of which were effectively communicated to SLW's unions by osmosis.

Mitbestimmung's earliest manifestations arose in the coal and steel industries of the Ruhr region just after World War II. It quickly spread to the auto industry. By 1976, it was established in various iterations throughout German industry, depending on the size of a business and numbers employed. Versions of *Mitbestimmung* had to be implemented in all companies with over 500 employees. The smaller of these companies usually operated under a one-tier management structure, a management board or *Vorstand* representing private owners, who had to appoint an *arbeitsdirektor* or labor-elected representative to that board. Larger companies operating on a two-tier system had the same obligation to appoint an *arbeitsdirektor* to the *Vorstand*, but also had to appoint one or more labor-elected board members to their supervisory board or *Aufsichtsrat*, which represented shareholders. This legislation coupled with an obsessive post war rush to entitlement and guilt-driven political correctness made for daunting obstacles to economic performance and cross-border competitiveness—let alone the creation of financial surplus to fund those entitlements. It was probably never more difficult than in the late 1970s.

Things eventually changed markedly for the better in Germany when reform of labor markets took hold, but that was well after my term in Europe. This eventually allowed a united Germany to become the powerhouse that it is today, the cornerstone and savior of the European Union. Germans had learned a lesson that Mediterranean deficit-financed welfare states refused to learn. The German economy, her relatively strong balance sheet, pragmatic fiscal discipline and leadership of the European Union are quite remarkable, especially after funding the crippling cost of reunification after the Berlin Wall fell. Germany's progression from the Social Democratic Party's vision under its post war leader Kurt Schumacher, to the economic bastion led by Angela Merkel, provides the world with a compelling template, which is sadly so broadly ignored.

Meanwhile, back in 1978, the challenge at SLW was first and foremost to install professional management at the top, and then educate the second and third tier of competent operating managers, who simply lacked understanding of the financial realities. The CEO, Dieter Madaus, was a diminutive, dapper, doe-eyed dreamer. An esoteric, sun-tanned socialite from Hamburg's world of media, advertising and PR. He was married to Gisela, an attractive statuesque Teutonic blonde, in her own right an accomplished social climber of Hamburg's Wedel community on the banks of the Elbe. Dieter had not a clue about industrial management in his gentle persona. Hans Herbert Munte had picked his own successor for "his urbane style and impressive West German network." Poor man was tragically out of his depth, so now poor Dieter had to go. His departure was in due course accomplished, but only after an excruciating review process involving both the *Vorstand* and *Aufsichtsrat*, where there was instant unanimity over his termination, but passionate debate over his termination conditions: the *arbeitsdirektor* pleaded for conditions giving Madaus a lifetime of carefree comfort and indolence. Several bankers on the board, along with the American owner (represented by me), insisted on generously compliant but less utopian retirement conditions. Dieter and his princess lived happily ever after on the affluent banks of the Elbe in Wedel.

The *Aufsichtsrat* conducted its meetings in German (the labor representatives spoke nary a word of English), always in Braunschweig, chaired by a distinguished, immaculately attired little banker from Frankfurt, a silver-maned Herr Doktor Wilhelm Vallentin. The meetings were bureaucratic affairs of process by the book, conducted with painstaking courtesy by the Doktor. Most board members simply concurred lamely and bowed to the process. Only with the help of one or two English-speaking directors could I introduce discussion of operating performance. Any proposal to improve human or capital productivity would instantly jolt somnolent directors into alert participation, because employee entitlements were, of course, to be safeguarded. It was never quite clear to me whether Continental's views and demands were fully and accurately translated for those who spoke no English.

My limited German allowed me to understand much of the social chitchat between the competing bankers on the SLW board, usually over lunch or coffee. My American toes curled in my shoes as I heard them exchange privileged information and swap notes, describing their particular banks' deals and trades. They did so in ways that would have led to incarceration or huge fines under US antitrust laws. With abandon, directors would also discuss confidential product development or pricing practices of competing companies on whose boards they served. The concept of *conflict of interest* appeared alien to the Germans. For example, two of the directors also sat on boards of important SLW customers, and one member sat on the board of its main steel supplier. The contrast between their sanctimonious attention to employee rights and the blatant disregard for fair and responsible practice in conducting business was bizarre. This sort of corporate misconduct could only generate empathy for the EEC's sharpening attention to antitrust issues on the Continent. The UK and the Nordic countries, which by contrast conducted business with respect for best practice and the law, were clear exceptions. German practice, on the other hand, presented an unacceptable face of the capitalist system—misuse and abuse.

Appointing a new CEO was a long and tortuous process in the course of which I personally made serious mistakes of judgment and process—inexcusable despite the unprofessional modus operandi of a greedy Swiss headhunter in Lausanne, who was in too much of a hurry to collect his fee. I had mistakenly given insufficient thought to internal candidates when the executive recruiter introduced a handsome, blond Aryan Adonis in his late forties, who had the usual doctorate and a string of impressively senior appointments in German industry on his CV. Board members had also offered candidates drawn from their circle of cronies. After several long interviews in Brussels, I wanted the handsome Herr Doktor Kurt Metzger looked over by my seniors stateside.

At that very time, 40 top executives of the Continental Group, along with wives, were assembling for a three-day conference in Bermuda, so I had Doktor Metzger fly in to be interviewed by the top brass. Bob Hatfield, Vice Chair & CFO Don Donahue and SLW's chairman Dr. Vallentin took their turns with Metzger after he was blessed by Warren Hayford. All reported positively and gave the thumbs-up. Back in Brussels after the Bermuda meetings I made Metzger the offer, first by telephone call to his car somewhere on the autobahn and then in writing. To my astonishment, the phone conversation was strangely stilted and the German sounded anxious and somewhat hesitant, but I readily accepted that he should have a day or two to consider. From that moment on, I never heard from him again. He vanished. The Lausanne recruiter insisted that he was equally in the dark, claiming he had failed to run him down. However, he was quick to send a hefty bill for fees and expenses incurred in the aborted search. I rejected his invoice by return mail, writing NO WAY in capitals diagonally across it, and never heard another word.

Bewildering rumors of Metzger floated around German industrial circles and Europe's headhunter community for months, snippets of which suggested he had a racy lifestyle. Eventually, he was reported to have landed a short-lived leadership position in a large but failing engineering company and was then rumored to be under treatment for some form of addiction. In

1981, his obituary appeared in the German press. Doktor Kurt Metzger's life had ended in a harbor view suite in Hong Kong's Mandarin Hotel, throat slashed by a man associated with a young Chinese lady he had befriended. The delay in succession to SLW's leadership was damaging. The young German CFO of Continental Group Europe in the Brussels office was eventually promoted to take over. Doktor Helmut Albrecht, smooth, cultured and partly educated in the States, was totally up to speed on SLW's financial affairs.

By this time I had concluded that Germany's *Herr Doktor* population was absolutely the world's largest, not just in per capita terms—*doktor*s were everywhere, doctors of every subject imaginable, from industrial engineering, labor relations through religious philosophy to leadership psychology. There was a time in America when we said, "If you want to get ahead, get a hat," but in Germany it evidently required a doctorate, rather than a hat. Two-a-penny degrees and title inflation in the business world?

SLW's expensive symbols of owners' hubris from the Schmalbach and Munte days were steadily chipped away. Burdensome overheads were chopped, a couple of plants closed, excessive staff was retired and valuable talent redeployed. It was a very deliberate process, but it was implemented without the conspiratorial obstruction encountered in the Netherlands when addressing TDV's rationalization.

Erik Kanovsky, SLW's burly Bavarian manufacturing chief, smart and courageous, had been introduced to American management practices at business school in the USA. He set about the consolidation of bloated production facilities and technical centers with the energy of a young bull. A fat and happy sales organization had its surplus weight trimmed and rich entertainment perks cut to size. The company became very competitive by German standards of that time; turnover of the company's trimmed asset base accelerated dramatically. The blue-eyed, blond Bavarian sported an American crew cut and spoke articulate English with the thickest of accents. He was tenacious and quite cunning as he navigated crosscurrents of union politics, labor legislation and *Mitbestimmung*. The company's performance improved strongly, boosting CCC's aggregate European contribution in support of improving corporate results reported on the New York Stock Exchange. Employees started to enjoy their own accomplishments as Albrecht and Kanovsky built an effective team. The Germans were embracing American performance criteria and started having fun at work.

Thomassen & Drijver and the Dutch were a very different story.

The Dutch are stubborn but pragmatic people. Stubborn to a fault, but pragmatic enough to change course at the last moment if and when real disaster threatens. This was reflected again and again in the tortuous story of CCC's efforts to wrestle operating control of TDV from a capable but misguided management team under the rebellious and supercilious Rudy Mioulet. As head of the sales organization Rudy had prevailed in a power struggle to succeed the previous CEO, Ido Stuit, who had planned to anoint his protégé, head of manufacturing operations, Ben van Asselt. The bitterness of their rivalry was never far below the surface.

A couple of years earlier, in 1976, the previous Europemballage structure in Brussels along with its Dutch President, Ben te Haar, had been removed. Don Earnshaw from New York was installed as President of the new entity named Continental Group Europe. This had triggered alarm and a closing of the ranks in Deventer as the Dutch alertly realized the American owners were moving in on TDV's autonomy. They took full advantage of Earnshaw's lack of action in Brussels, so nothing changed much.

Don mainly used his title as President of CGE to promote PR issues and goodwill objectives. He was a tubby teddy bear, articulate and urbane. Don had persuasive charm, but was distinctly confrontation and conflict averse. A hint of a smile—never a smirk—always lingered on his lips as he engaged in chummy chats with anybody about anything. His approach to pursuing Continental's objectives in Europe was diplomacy: win friends, spread the gospel and thus gradually sell the mission of the American owner—drip by drip. He was the Neville Chamberlain of CCC's situation in Europe. His management reports to home base would always claim "directional progress," with a plea for time to produce tangible results.

Earnshaw's tool box was that of a PR executive and previously a senior salesman, who sold cans to the top brass of breweries and soft drink companies across the United States. He was a deft, high-end *schmoozer*. Don's *tour de force* was accomplished in St Louis, when he beat rival American Can Company to a major contract after stalking and then befriending August Busch III of Anheuser Busch. He caught August on the sidewalk outside the mid-western city's #1 businessmen's restaurant—an upmarket steakhouse. Earnshaw, while having a quick solo lunch at the bar, had spotted the brewery magnate sharing a major repast with somebody at the *Busch Table* in a quiet corner. He knew August would leave the restaurant at some point in time, so he settled his check and set up camp on the sidewalk right outside and waited. Sure enough, about an hour later the young Busch emerged in an evidently benign mood, so Don made his move, fell in step with the beer baron, engaging him in conversation, and *schmoozed* his way into a relationship. This new relationship was eventually consummated with the award of an invaluable Anheuser-Busch beer can supply contract. It was the biggest order a salesman could land in all of the USA. Donald V. Earnshaw's career took off.

However, Don could also be lazy, sloppy and undisciplined. Continental's internal auditors were regularly after him to file documented expense claims. His record-keeping technique was based on multiple shoe boxes kept on the floor of his bedroom, into which he tossed receipts recovered from pockets when his suits were sent to the cleaners.

By the time my succession was announced, his two years in Brussels had generated some goodwill for Continental with independent directors at boardroom level and major customers loved him. Yet he had caused nothing to change in SLW, and he let the Dutch feel their oats and gird for battle.

Rudy Mioulet was an intelligent, headstrong and narcissistic autocrat. In many ways very un-Dutch, quite elegant in demeanor. He was sartorially meticulous, invariably dressed exactly to code for every occasion, never a hair out of place. Very dark brown eyes, a high brow and thin-lipped mouth characterized a clean cut, sallow face. Under Mioulet's relatively new leadership, TDV's performance had temporarily strengthened after a slump under his predecessor, a folksy factory-oriented Hollander named Ido Stuit, who lived close by in retirement and stayed connected through his retained seat on the Supervisory Board. The profitable streak was partly achieved by the sale of a very old, unprofitable but valuable factory building and its associated chunk of real estate in Ruys-Haarlem. The transaction generated a hefty cash surplus and some reduction in fixed and variable costs from abolished workplaces. Stuit's favored Ben van Asselt had a tight group of followers, especially among plant managers, who were wedded to a highly participative management style encouraged by Holland's codetermination practices. Ben and his friends were uncomfortable with Mioulet's authoritarian practices.

Before Continental's takeover deal was closed, the Dutch had squirreled away the cash proceeds from the sale of Ruys-Haarlem, a substantial Dfl. Sixty-million cash chest, in *financiele reserves*—reserves banked separately. The Dutch insiders, acting in isolation, solemnly vowed to keep this money as a Dutch nest egg for strictly domestic purposes, meaning any kind of rainy day in their own judgement, a downturn in performance or other in-house priorities. The new 100% owner had paid full price in acquiring all the assets of TDV, including its cash reserves, of course, and had the final say as to how their *finansiele reserves* should be put to work. However, the Dutch did not recognize that. Deventer's best business practices did not always stretch to the rights of shareholders beyond their national boundaries. Neither the board nor management were particularly sensitive to the interests of US shareholders, nor their view of an acceptable return on funds employed in Holland. As long as the business generated cash flow to cover TDV's perceived requirements, Mioulet deemed performance to be satisfactory. The cash in the *financiele reserves* was considered sacrosanct, invested "very conservatively" outside the business, ready for any Dutch day of need. This specific issue later became a pivotal leverage point in a complex and dirty deal attempted by Mioulet in direct, secret negotiation with the insecure and sometimes devious Bruce Smart, who succeeded Bob Hatfield as Chairman and CEO of Continental Group.

Mioulet was absolutely livid when I cut his capital spending authority to comply with the rules for the rest of CCC worldwide. In his mind, American corporate governance had clipped his wings, limiting his personal authority to expenditures of DFL (Dutch Florin) 100,000 or less. His limit, blessed by TDV's board (which included Earnshaw) and indeed by Brussels until that point in time, had been DFL 30-million. His ego simply couldn't bear it, causing him to rant and rave in public and private. Servan-Schreiber's best seller, *Le Defi Américain (The American Challenge),* became his bible, a favorite source of quotations to support his anti-American vitriol. He bought dozens of copies, which he distributed to anyone who might share his anti-American position. The renowned author's aspiration was to create a European alliance or coalition to stem and reverse the rushing tide of American economic power and competitive superiority. *Le Defi* fit right into Rudy's playbook.

Weeks before anyone else knew of Earnshaw's imminent departure and the impending change of leadership in Brussels, Don convened a European management conference at the famous Turnberry golf links venue on Scotland's southwest coast. Sixty senior managers converged from Germany, the Netherlands, Brussels and the States to attend what would be the last meeting at which Earnshaw presided and addressed the Europeans. I was invited as a "Rowayton observer." CCC's objectives for the subsidiaries were broadly presented by Earnshaw and his Brussels office staff, while Mioulet and Madaus and their managers presented a review of current operations in their respective realms. The meeting was also intended to promote mutual understanding and provide a social interface between the two European groups and between the Americans and the operating managers. Mioulet, in his wrap-up presentation for the Dutch, put a big stick in that wheel by seizing the podium to unload his rancor on a perfectly captive audience.

With a spotlight precisely trained on him in a darkened room, Rudy at his elegant, narcissistic best—poker faced and articulate –launched into a sarcastic and vitriolic attack on American corporate takeovers and management practices. He characterized CCC's management disciplines as bureaucratic limitations on TDV's leadership talent and flexibility. His message was accompanied by random slides showing manipulated macroeconomic metrics and national productivity figures interspersed with custom-drawn cartoons. He mocked management in Brussels and at the CCC headquarters in Connecticut, referring to Continental's acquisition and takeover of the European subsidiaries as being

> "like elephants mating—a clumsy process which takes place at high altitude, makes a lot of noise and takes forever to produce results."

The accompanying slide was a cartoon drawing of two big, trumpeting elephants copulating in front of the Washington DC Capitol building.

While a few of the Germans and many of his own managers applauded enthusiastically, many executives were stunned, particularly Ben van Asselt and his operations managers. They anxiously warned Rudy that his performance would have negative consequences for their company and possibly for himself; but he cared not a jot, strutting around the Turnberry hotel like an aroused peacock in all its colorful glory. Earnshaw merely smiled wistfully. His diplomacy had not worked very well, certainly not with Rudy.

> "Boys will be boys," Don lamented over a nightcap late that night, "but Rudy took this one a little too far. That man is trouble. Although he has some local backing, you should know that the unions and plant management are, at times, united in their distaste for Rudi's style. His haughty manor doesn't sit well with the workforce or many of the staff, particularly the van Asselt group. The Dutch board isn't unaware of what's going on, but Mioulet needs to be corralled and brought to heel—and you are the one who's

going to have to do it. You have some fun and games ahead of you, Flemming," he chuckled, "ha, ha, ha! Rather you than me, I say! Cheers, my young Viking chief and good luck to you!"

Don was delighted to be leaving the scene, but his insight and analysis was right on the mark. At that stage, I was no more than an observer. I had no role at the conference, so I watched the Dutch CEO's performance from the gallery of the auditorium with some trepidation. Mioulet's presentation had certainly thrown down the gauntlet in a very public manner, and as far as I was concerned, it had blown his cover. His performance had gained me a little time to prepare strategy. It allowed me a jump start on getting a good understanding of the Netherlands' corporate governance practices, their employment legislation and de facto rulebook. It was heavily influenced by the Dutch version of co-determination involving the *ondernemingsraad*—or works council, strongly influenced by the unions—and other forms of labor representation in management. A supervisory board—*Raad van Commissarissen*—on which non-executive and a couple of management members were seated, was at the top of the governance pyramid, overseeing the executive management team known as the *directie*.

Don and his wife departed Brussels for Connecticut and I took over the driver's seat and his title.

In Brussels and stateside, Continental anticipated a future in which EEC legislation would open markets to stimulate pan-European trade, with stricter antitrust rules and significantly increased mobility of capital and labor. I was personally in favor of the EEC concept and open markets, but I was also aware of the short-term challenges they presented the two subsidiaries. I demanded that, in addition to traditional operating budgets, management of the subsidiaries develop control budgets, which assumed revenues reduced by competition across borders, lower prices and consequent erosion of the fat margins to which they had become accustomed, particularly in Deventer. Preemptive action plans to lower fixed and variable costs were called for. Mioulet did not like that, so he responded with a perfunctory planning document defining only an arbitrary maximum six percent reduction in the workforce, irrespective of "the too-pessimistic American assumptions." The gauntlet had indeed been thrown down at Turnberry. I quickly established direct and personal communications with the non-executive members of the Dutch board, finding them generally sensitive to the growing risks facing TDV and concerns over Mioulet's behavior and style. They sensed that Mioulet would have to be reined in, conform to CCC policies or be nudged out. So Rudy's maneuver was to backfire on him. He not only took on Brussels, but also his own *Raad van Commissarissen* (Board of Directors).

While all this was developing, Warren's career plans and assumptions had suddenly been dealt a staggering blow. Group Executive Vice Presidents Warren and Bruce Smart had long been rival candidates for the corporate top spot, generally considered way ahead of anyone else in the company. Succession from within had been the expressed preference of the Group's board. Bob Hatfield had two years to go before stepping down as CEO at age 65 according to the rule he had himself introduced. Via synchronized press releases and telex messages throughout the organization he announced Bruce Smart's promotion to President and COO of the Continental Group, thus revealing his choice for succession. The die was cast.

Before the news reached Brussels, Hayford called me. Uncharacteristically, without prologue or greeting, he announced he was leaving Continental immediately to become President and COO of International Harvester under the chairmanship of the renowned Archie McArdle. So, he said, I would immediately have a new boss. (He must have somehow been warned ahead of time that he had missed out at Continental, and then launched an urgent job search.) This came to me completely out of left field, as Bob had, in private conversations over the years, referred to Warren as an amazing leader and a great strategist and intellect—stopping just short of signaling that Hayford was to be his successor. That had been my impression since Bob and I had first discussed my possibly joining

Continental from South Africa. I was flabbergasted and perturbed, despite my occasional questioning of Warren's views and judgement. Random encounters with Bruce Smart had left me less than impressed.

"Good grief, Warren, what the hell are you telling me? Is this some kind of a game you are playing with me?" I blurted out. "You were here in Brussels just last week, talking about our Dutch strategy, plans for the UK, challenging Rasselstein's stranglehold on SLW's steel supply—You can't be serious. You just have to be kidding!"

"No sir! He's not," Bruce Smart interjected out of the blue, his voice coming across the wire from a speakerphone in Hayford's McArthur-style office. He was obviously monitoring and participating in the communications. "This is for real. Warren's already in the process of packing up. You will be reporting to Don Bainton, who will be taking over the can company immediately, and he, in turn, will be reporting directly to me at headquarters. He's also in the process of packing up and moving—to Connecticut from Chicago, that is. Don will be taking over the whole can business, USA and all of international. But there will be no change at all in your responsibilities. Your job hasn't changed one bit, Flemming. Your marching orders remain precisely as they have been—you have a lot on your plate, and we are relying on you to follow through after a good start. Just get it all done there in Europe. Zero change! Just keep going. And I'm sure Don will be very supportive." Bruce paused for a moment, "In fact, he may also have to take a lesson or two from you when it comes to the European scene and the weird way of doing things over there."

Warren had a long-established pattern of holding monthly meetings with his direct reports, known as his *Kitchen Cabinet*, assembling in Connecticut to report on operating results, but above all to receive explicit direction. These meetings would often start late in the day and continue over dinner into the late evening. I flew out of Brussels the very day of that telephone call to attend the last of Hayford's Kitchen Cabinet meetings. He was already driving around Fairfield County in an International Harvester *Scout*—not a tractor, but a jeep-like vehicle, made by his new company. Quite a statement! Warren was never slow to make his point, sometimes right in your face.

Donald J. Bainton was an extraordinarily focused, super ambitious, egotistic and obnoxious man. He was nobody's fool, however, constantly drawing on native thespian talent and a deep baritone voice to command attention. He clearly believed *that all the world's a stage*, and that he was principal amongst its players. His rich voice, which rivaled that of Dave Ross on CBS News 880, somehow belied his overshot toothy mouth, almost chinless jaw and jowly throat. He walked with a swagger, head held high as he looked down his nose, ever ready to be greeted, if not saluted. He wanted all the world to know that he went to Columbia University and that he was a member of the Knights of Columbus. He was obsessed with rank. Beneath all this bravado, I suspected a deeply insecure man.

Bruce Smart couldn't have been more wrong about there being no change in my job. Bainton had little sense of market and ambient business climate, and absolutely no clue when it came to international operations, let alone European etiquette, sociopolitical climate or labor legislation. For the time being, he left me to my own devices, concentrating on maximizing his personal PR around his new global role. Bainton's priorities were reflected in his addiction to the first person singular.

Pretty soon he was determined to spend time in the UK whenever he could possibly justify it. Earnshaw had overseen, with scant respect for cost, the laying of foundations for a British startup company with extravagant offices on Hyde Park Corner and a company apartment in a posh Belgravia enclave. Bainton relished that setting. He was obsessed with all things British and the lifestyle of upper crust London. On frequent visits to London he would stay at the Connaught or the Ritz, buying his way to contrived business encounters to meet titled gentry, prominent politicians, diplomats and luminaries of business and finance. None of them, however, were relevant to CCC's objectives in the UK. On one occasion, he assembled a motley bunch of toffs, including a retired Tory minister, a Roman Catholic Cardinal and an ex-president of Henley's much vaunted Leander Club for a dinner in a cavernous parquet-floored private room at the Ritz. It had a cathedral ceiling, red velvet curtains hanging from eighteen-foot window frames. To fill the yawning emptiness of the room, there were only sixteen chairs around a heavy oaken ball-and-claw dining table at one end. The guests, most of them harboring lifestyle aspirations well beyond their budgets, leaped at the chance of a free meal at the Ritz with good wine, rare vintage port and cigars. Judy and I were only invited in order that I might coach Don in matters of English manners and custom. As I briefed him, the questions tumbled out of him in a verbal avalanche.

"You're a Cambridge grad, aren't you, so you can point me in the right direction, right? Make sure I don't drop the ball in any way?"

"Do you think the dress code should be tuxedo?"

I told him it should be defined as Black Tie.

"They sometimes wear what they call morning coat in the evening, don't they?"

I told him that was not so, unless you were a butler or an undertaker.

"Flemming, how do I go about proposing a *Royal Toast?*

When should I do it? At dinner, right? At the end or at the beginning?
Do I have to stand up when I do it, and should I hold up my glass?"

"And what exactly—and I mean EXACTLY—do I say?"
"And tell me, if a guy is knighted, like Sir Humphrey Winterbotham, do I call him Sir all the time, or just now and then? Do I say Sir Winterbotham, Sir Humphrey, or just Sir?"

"Is Henley the same thing as The Boat Race?"

"When is it that I should say *'Gentlemen, you may smoke'*?"

"And what's this I have heard about the ladies leaving the table when port is served? Do I have to do something to indicate that we're done, I mean ready for port, or at the end of the evening?"

"Flemming, I want you to sit somewhere pretty close by at dinner."

"Judy can act as a kind of first lady. She knows the ropes too, doesn't she? She knows these things from life in South Africa, doesn't she, because of the British Commonwealth? She'll manage the other end of the table and the ladies. Isn't that the way to do it?"

The dinner was particularly enjoyed by the more impoverished of the titled aristocrats, who reveled in the culinary experience, quaffed the wines and chatted animatedly among themselves. The value of the evening to Continental Can was zilch.

On another occasion Bainton, who was himself a decent tennis player, arranged an afternoon party on the outside courts at Wimbledon, co-hosted by the hired-for-a-day Honorary (meaning retired) President of the Wimbledon Lawn Tennis & Croquet Club. The distinguished but impecunious old Brit was of course thrilled to receive such a useful non-declared contribution to his retirement income, along with the cucumber sandwiches, non-vintage champagne and the obligatory strawberries and cream—all on his old stomping grounds, where he no longer had an expense account nor a role to play. There were no customers or suppliers present, nor bankers nor business associates—just influential people, according to Bainton, so that

> "The Continental Can name gets exposure and we become better known in London's business community."

In his new and much enlarged role, Don Bainton became increasingly authoritarian as he surrounded himself with yes-men from his old domestic management team in Chicago. He fawned over people with talent or experience he needed to paper over the cracks in his own knowledge and *savoir faire*. He didn't like Hayford's penchant for conference calls, so he replaced them with a frantic schedule of meetings in the new Stamford offices, including a gathering of direct reports every other Friday. He insisted I report on Europe at these meetings, in person. In other words, Bainton doubled the frequency of my trans-Atlantic trips. This was his way to micromanage, increase personal control and to boost his fragile confidence. My travel schedule was plainly unsustainable. Time in Braunschweig, Deventer and in London, along with development trips to Madrid and Milan already presented an overload of travel, which included calling on potential customers in Copenhagen, Munich and Vienna. The turnaround visit to Stamford every two weeks meant leaving Brussels midday on Thursday to attend Bainton's meeting on Friday morning before flying back to Brussels later in the day. Half of Thursday and all of Friday were taken out of the working week. Half of Saturday would be spent recovering, asleep and out of the family's reach. Management priorities, health and family life were going to hell.

So a compromise was made: by leaving Waterloo at five-thirty AM on Friday morning by chauffeured car, I could catch the nine AM *Concorde* from Charles de Gaulle and be in Stamford for a ten AM meeting lasting into the afternoon, which ruled out the Concorde back to Paris, so I had to take SABENA's overnight 747 subsonic. Half of every second Thursday was thus saved. It was absolute corporate lunacy.

~~~~

The Netherlands of the 1970s was governed by a centrist coalition led by Prime Minister Dries van Agt of the Christian Democratic Appeal (historically a Roman Catholic party, which made van Agt a good guy in Bainton's judgement). However, many of his party's anti-business, but pro-labor employment laws and constraints still set the tone in Dutch industry and corporate governance. Collective bargaining with overt government backing of labor's demands were part of the industrial environment. Rudy Mioulet's authoritarian, hard line style meant that he did not have universal support from his subordinates. Ben van Asselt's production team overtly criticized the CEO's dictatorial and egocentric style. Several letters were addressed to the *Raad van Commissarissen*—the supervisory board—by middle management groups seeking leadership change. Slowly, the supervisory board members came round to my way of thinking, recognizing the legal and economic realities. Our non-executive chairman, Gerrit van Driel, was CEO of nationally known Royal Wessanen, a giant food company. He was the first to get it. He had turned around his own flagging company by breaking the mold of traditional Dutch management in his own shop.

Things came to a head between Mioulet and me. As he sensed that he was cornered, at some point he went around Brussels and Bainton's Stamford office in an attempt to make a personal deal directly with Continental's relatively new Chairman and CEO, Bruce Smart. Somehow, with Don Bainton eventually implicated on the fringes, Mioulet was offered a very well paid, but ill-defined, staff job at corporate headquarters, or in Bainton's office in Connecticut. But, having seen what happened to Hans Herbert Munte of SLW when he was ousted for a cushy but impotent role stateside, Rudy declined. Mioulet was nobody's puppet, or dummy for that matter. So, with the TDV supervisory board members signing off in support, Mioulet was sent on his way in February 1980.

It was much later that I learned of Mioulet's last ditch attempt to make a secret deal with Bruce Smart. The deal would have called for Rudy's immediate release of the DFL 60-million *"financiele reserves"* still held in a Dutch reserve account plus his commitment to full co-operation with CCC and Brussels going forward, all in return for his restored authority to approve capital expenditures up to DFL 30,000,000. The deal was reported to have fallen through because Smart would not agree to put it in writing. Rudy had rightly insisted it should be documented. Nearly forty years later, I have yet to hear of an attempt by a public company CEO to do a dirtier, more lily-livered intra-corporation political deal.

[The sources of these historical details are not limited to personal recollection or private records. Many of the details were gleaned from a book written in Dutch by retired TDV personnel manager, Carel J.H.Wevers, published in 1992 and titled **TERUGblikken.**

The title itself is a Dutch play on words, as "terug" means back or backward and "blikken" means either glances or tin cans! It emerged long after I had been nudged out of Continental. I had no way of knowing about Bruce Smart's or Bainton's duplicity at the time. Had I known earlier, it could have saved me and many other stakeholders a lot of grief in the early 1980's.]

As with the SLW situation, the replacement of Mioulet became a messy process, as both Bainton and Smart blinked and then bungled their roles in authorizing his departure at the very end of my tenure in the Brussels job. The internal politics and machinations of the Dutch also caused missteps. Communications and relationships between the TDV's supervisory board, the pivotal works council, the unions and general management were allowed to become so complex that clarity and action to orchestrate the succession were sabotaged. Eventually a *troika* led by the subsidiary's CFO Rob van der Koppel as *directeur-president*, a senior technical staffer named Gert Brillman and Ben van Asselt took over while a permanent solution was worked out. Reformed management practices and American-led professionalism slowly took hold. By 1980, CCC's European results and performance were more than competitive by any standards, and tensions eased with Mioulet and his Machiavellian scheming gone. He soon got another job as head of a relatively small Dutch food business.

~~~~

Usually without the family, I traveled through most of Western Europe in the course of nearly three-years, but spent no time at all in the Eastern Bloc. Business travels meant rushed exposures but lasting impressions of many cities. Travel within Germany was often by chauffeur-driven car, at nerve-chilling autobahn speeds, but these trips happily exposed a country far more scenic and splendid than its reputation suggests. There is so much to this striking country beyond the tourist destinations of Berlin, the Rhine, Mosel, Munich, Bavaria and the Black Forest. Visits to SLW's plants spanned the country from Karlsruhe and Stuttgart to Bremen and Lubeck. Central Germany's magnificent forested hills and arable dales offered gorgeous contrasts to the northern flatlands of Luneburger Heide and the Hanseatic League towns like gothic Lubeck on the Baltic coast. Munich and Bavaria reflected the softer people and language of the south against the backdrop of the magnificent foothills and dazzling snow-capped peaks of the Alps themselves.

Short but fabulous vacations took the family to the enchanting Mosel and Rhine valleys flanked by their spectacularly steep vineyards. Corsica, flooded in Mediterranean sunlight, was an indelible indulgence in silver beaches, peacock blue sea, scary mountain drives on single track roads through craggy gorges to isolated waterfalls and pools for skinny-dipping.

One-day kayak adventures down the River Meuse. A week in a borrowed villa, perched high above the Cote d'Azur between Cannes and the perfume town of Grasse, where the air itself was scented. Grandstand views of topless girls' volleyball on St. Tropez' beaches—which had our teenage offspring riveted. Sunset family dinners in fishing village bistros of Normandy. A weekend in Reims at the pinnacle of gourmand heights, staying at the very source of Pommery Champagne, exploring the vast storage caves of chalk hills under the immaculate, hallowed vineyards of the Champagne region.

Over a five-day Easter weekend in 1979, at the invitation of Alexis Lichine (acclaimed oenophile, cognoscenti and champion of Bordeaux), Judy and I were the only guests at his onetime Benedictine priory, *Chateau Prieure-Lichine* of the Margaux appellation. In those more private days, the chateau was not open to visitors seven days a week as it is now. The weather was grey and the breeze off the Gironde brisk but dry, so the whole of Bordeaux could be explored, starting with the nearby Lascombes property (of which Alexis had been the owner from 1951–1971 to the immense benefit of its wines), then Kirwan, d'Issan, Palmer, Brane-Cantenac and Chateau Margaux itself; a widening circle day by day took us to the icons of Haut Medoc and Graves, and finally St-Emilion and wonderful Fronsac properties on the right bank. This exploration was all by car and on foot, peering through the protective boundaries of the venerable estates. Back at the *Prieure*, we were pampered by Alexis' folksy housekeeper cum chef, who served bordelaise delights from her cuisine's repertoire of finest country fare, right at the kitchen table, accompanied by the house wine—the less heralded vintages! Yet we never had a bottle that wasn't perfect for the occasion.

Early on Easter Saturday morning, out of the blue, Alexis himself appeared at the kitchen door, directly from the airport in Paris. In New York he had suddenly decided to spend part of Easter at the *Prieure* before meetings in Bordeaux the following week. It was a priceless bonus added to our extraordinary adventure, as Alexis enthusiastically took hours over each of the next two days to show and teach us about his own and the surrounding properties, including Chateau Margaux, where his friend André

Mentzelopoulos was owner and wine maker par excellence. His 1979 vintage was later characterized as "exceptional" by the very top tasters, including Alexis.

Alexis, great maestro of Bordeaux, knew everybody from elite proprietors to local hands in the vineyards. He could explain the soil characteristics of any patch of terroir, the ever-changing mix of clay, sand, gravel and loam, along with every vineyard's elevation, exposure to the elements and natural drainage. With his warm, winning charm and wicked sense of humor he delivered two days of education, entertainment and captivating yarns from his illustrious career.

> "Alexis, would it at some point be possible for me to buy some of this year's Prieure-Lichine *en primeur* to send home to the States?" I asked gingerly at the end of our last delicious dinner in the kitchen, topped by one of Lichine's prized vintages.

> "But of course, dear friends!" he said with bubbly enthusiasm. "Given the early spring, I have high hopes for 1979, but obviously nobody can be sure for some months yet. We'll know more about the vintage by the summer. Summer itself is reasonably predictable, but so much depends on rain, temperature and the amount of sunshine at the right time in September and early October. But we are talking of 1979, no? How much do you want, Flemming?"

> "Oh, I was thinking of a case, as a very special memento of our marvelous adventure here. I would have it properly stored and would keep it for special occasions over the coming years, always to rekindle wonderful memories of the *Prieure*."

"Did you say ONE case? No, no, I must have misheard you, I'm sorry!" Alexis responded, eyebrows incredulously arched and his voice raised a touch. "What did you say? You can't buy less than the ten-case minimum here from the *Prieure*. At a later date you could probably buy a single case *en primeur* from Zachys in Scarsdale, or any old merchant in Connecticut, for that matter. But you don't just want one case. That would mean paying a much higher case price."

"Okay, of course I'll take ten cases, Alexis," I hastened to say, blushing and feeling like a blundering peasant. "We'll drink to you and our lovely memories of the Medoc through all of the coming decade."

From Brussels, the family routinely took fun-filled day trips to exquisite towns of the Middle Ages like Bruges and Ghent, or Zeebrugge on the chilly windswept beaches of the North Sea coastline. Canal-based Bruges was spell-binding. Founded in the eleventh century as a trading post, it was one of several European cities dubbed "Venice of the North," and though it never had Venetian scale or grandeur, it is intimately enchanting. By the twelfth century it was a bustling port, serving a developing textile industry with its merchants, master spinners and weavers. Ships trading in the Hanseatic League called in from the Baltic Sea or the northern rivers and canals. Later the town was home to the acclaimed Flemish School of painters, and it was here that William Caxton had the very first book printed in English. The canals are still bustling with busy barges. Ghent was another gem, built in the Middle Ages at the confluence of the Scheldt and Lys rivers, its medieval architecture dominated by Gravensteen Castle, built in the 1100s by Count Phillipe of Alfonse in the style of the Crusaders' fortresses seen on youthful ventures to the east.

From Brussels, at the very heart of Western Europe, there was unmatched access to myriad centers of culture, history, sunny vacations and hedonistic fun. Exciting weekends in Paris, Amsterdam or London. The Belgian capital was at the core of evolving dreams and fantasies of a united Europe. It was a veritable petri dish for breeding untenable political and social structures and huge EU bureaucracies employing armies of central planners and spawning academic dreamers plunging into economic and monetary theory. Its geography also made Brussels a preferred location for multinational corporate offices, while dozens of international schools became populated by tens of thousands of ex-patriots from around the world. The city was a curious concentration of cosmopolitan stodginess; it just never had the heartbeat, sparkle, humor or excitement of other multicultural capitals such as Paris or London, let alone the pulsating hustle of a city like New York. Yet, its culinary offerings were unequaled by any other metropolis. The strangely drab Belgians somehow managed to quash the potential of Brussels as a mecca of culture, fine architecture, fascinating history, epicurean cuisine and gourmand wines.

The Belgian capital gave birth to separate elite societies, deeply divided between pragmatic and effective financiers, bankers, industrialists and professionals on the one hand, and rhapsodic dreamers, socio-political collectivists and bureaucratic functionaries on the other hand—the latter group in hot pursuit of a romantic but unrealistic dream called the European Union. Some even talked of a United States of Europe. What started as the EEC, a pragmatic and valuable customs union, was to be transformed into a questionable political, fiscal and monetary union of wildly different countries. Billions were being invested in the quest for a grand union, devoid of a common fiscal structure or discipline, with no common language or unifying culture, language or religion, and no common currency at that stage. The population of EEC bureaucrats multiplied year by year like mice in a church belfry. By the millennium, that population had reached 33,000 in Brussels alone, never mind the thousands employed in Strasbourg and by dozens of agencies in other European cities, Washington DC and at the United Nations HQ in New York. The launch of the single Euro currency was still over a decade into the future, yet the Euro skeptics were already making themselves felt in several sovereign legislatures. Delors and other leading Euro-proponents had not yet acquired their fame and high profiles. The billions being spent were, of course, all contributed by taxpayers across the member countries. This spending spree never decelerated. By the second decade of the new millennium, the Euro skeptics of the UK (which never joined the Euro Zone) were screaming blue murder over Britain's annual contribution for its EU membership, ever thankful that they were not party to the common currency debacle. The later Brexit shock was partly prompted by British dismay and scorn for the centralist overreach and wasteful spending. Yet the dream lives on: In the post-millennium teens, the European Parliament in Strasbourg consumes an estimated annual expenditure of $250-million for transport alone, so that over 750 members (MEPs) can use the Strasbourg edifice three days a month. All the legislative work, aside from the political posturing, is done in Brussels. Not even the prodigality of today's Washington can match the EU's performance on a proportionate basis.

Countless international businessmen and their families were efficiently located in Brussels for reasons of logistics and easy access to the continent's many markets. This utility of location made it efficient for multinational companies to manage global regions from this city, whether it is Europe, per se, or the Middle East and Africa. This highly diverse community was a welcome source of conviviality and fun, divested of the wan smugness and pretensions of the city's *apparatchick* population. Its social life was spiced with the traditions and customs of an eclectic and itinerant population, which turned over and churned like a whitewater river. The city's restaurants tempted with the best cuisine on the continent, supported by the world's best and amply stocked wine cellars—even outdoing Paris. If only the aboriginal Belgians were themselves a little more loveable! Walloons and Flemish alike seemed very parochial, like Pieter Breughel's bucolic characters, and rather dull unless temporarily inflamed by internecine quarrels.

Belgium's national government wallowed in the wasteful bureaucracy of obsessive bilingualism, territorialism, tribal jealousy and religious exclusion, which was enervating even for the temporary expatriate. It was all so inefficient. For example, it took a week or longer to get an exit permit when leaving the country for good, contingent upon your obtaining a receipt for your returned *poubelle* (assigned municipal garbage can) printed in the designated language—French or Flemish depending on where you lived. Curiously, nobody cared whether your taxes had been paid before you took off.

The most testing moments of daily life in Brussels were endured in the inescapable confinement of the city's undersized, fully-loaded elevators at peak commuting hours: the whiffy odor of the unwashed, wearing their ring-around-the-collar shirts, exhaling traces of last night's garlic intake—all of which got trapped in the elevator's stagnant air. It was a public health risk, which would never be tolerated in countries like Denmark or the USA. This daily test of human tolerance was only matched by a single childhood experience, making the trek across the city of Madras (now Chenai) in an overloaded bus packed with Tamil stevedores at the end of a long stint in the docks under tropical sun.

~~~~

CCC's efforts to establish a beverage can project in Spain were stalled in 1979. A deal involving a small Spanish can-making company with secured sales to Coca Cola and a local brewery just would not gel, so meetings were arranged with private equity investors in Madrid. Continental's team was in the hands of a fabulously flamboyant Spaniard named Ignacio Gomez-Acebo, commonly known as Paddy among Anglophones. He was six-foot-four and the sometime Chairman of Chrysler Motor's Spanish subsidiary. He was also Chairman of the European Advisory Board of the New York Stock Exchange, wired into Spanish political circles and power brokers. The gregarious Paddy had an umbilical cord into Bank Santander. So, within hours of our first encounter, he had arranged introductions to several new leads. Elaborate al fresco lunches at three in the afternoon, dinners at eleven o'clock PM, followed by night clubs or *juergas* jumping with Flamenco singers and dancers on tabletops, all to staccato Andalusian rhythms of castanets, guitars and *palmas*—into the wee hours of the morning. Santander Bank ferried us around Madrid in shiny black Bentleys or Daimlers escorted by Paddy on his Ducati 1200cc Multistrada wearing goggles and a streaming red silk scarf. He would always take off just ahead of us, to ensure that we were welcomed at the doorstep by his next "good friend and long-time associate." After three exhausting days and nights, the return to home and kids in Brussels was a blessed respite. Promising connections had been made in the mercurial manner of Spanish banking. My departure from Brussels meant that it would fall to somebody else to convert those leads into opportunities for CCC investment.

Towards the end of 1980, a call from Bainton informed me of a change in structure in the Continental Group, which placed all of its many packaging businesses (except those based in forest products) under a President of Continental Packaging Company, which was to be Mr. Donald J. Bainton. As Bruce Smart's candidate, he had just been elected to the group board. His extended empire was to span not just the metal can businesses to be led by a colleague named Dick Hoffmann, but also the non-metal packaging and auto component businesses to be managed under an entity known as Continental Diversified Industries. I was to head up this latter unit and had been elected an executive vice president of the corporation. The family was to head home to Connecticut right after the year-end holidays.

A round of farewell visits to Braunschweig, Deventer and Windsor— now home to an appropriately downsized and modest office for CCC's British venture—was no cause for strong emotions either way. It had been a challenging three years in Europe, fraught with tensions and some hard feelings here and there, but generally very rewarding as I had made a few good friends. Back home, at corporate headquarters my tenure as head of

European operations was generously acknowledged by the usually xenophobic Bruce Smart.

The new appointment to head up the diversified packaging business
based in Connecticut was all-absorbing, demanding strategic initiatives and
action as diverse as the name of the business unit suggested. It was focused
on domestic US markets, except for Continental's Canadian interests—
including a full range of packaging products and a sizable auto parts business.
Family life was to benefit enormously from the less frantic travel schedule
and a beautiful Greenwich home. There was little change in terms of
business scale or the top line, but the challenge was quite complex in that it
spanned six distinctly different consumer packaging businesses and some
industrial components. In the words of Glyn Jones's entry level textbook,
Essentials of Economics, it was all about the creation of incremental wealth via
the production of goods and services attained by the employment of four
factors of production: land, labor, capital and organization. This job had
enormous appeal because of its multifaceted challenges, and it was a perfect
fit with lessons learned and experienced in South Africa and Europe, and
because performance was so clearly measurable. It was a dream job for as
long as it lasted.

Chapter VI

Sinking American Roots

"Immigration is not just compatible with but a necessary component of economic growth."
- Rupert Murdoch

REPATRIATION FROM BRUSSELS afforded the first chance to settle down for the long haul in our adopted American environment, to live American lives as an American family, armed with green cards and feeling very welcome as the community once again opened its arms to us. We lived in Greenwich, which was still a warm, family-friendly commuter town in those days. As soon as we had possessed our green cards long enough to qualify, the family applied for citizenship, not only based on a strong distaste for taxation without representation, but because we wanted to be real American citizens in our new homeland. Business travel was predominantly in-and-out visits to plants, offices and customers in urban centers all over the USA, often allowing a same-day return to home base, thanks to productive use of corporate air transport. Business travel provided tantalizing glimpses of America's extraordinary diversity and beauty, which kindled a yearning to explore the continent and drink in its human diversity, its stunning natural treasures of mountain and plain, desert and pasture, shoreline and river, forest and prairie. The ambition to make such a long, slow exploration was only to be satisfied twenty years later, starting the week after 9/11 in 2001.

There were also regular trips to the Canadian cities and many smaller towns within the narrow 4,000-mile strip running across the continent north of the 49th parallel, the 100-mile-wide belt where most Canadians live. To some extent, Canada beckoned in the way the fifty American states did, but the attitudes of locals from time to time got in the way. Canadians somehow seemed to have difficulty with their national identity, either because of their colonial roots, or the Queen's silhouette on their postage stamps. It could also have been because of bilingual issues, or because provincial ambitions and territorial envy got in the way. Free-flow of trade and commerce between Canada's own ten provinces was absurdly impeded by petty protectionism and fatuous language laws, which forced the use of French in irrelevant places like Anglophone Alberta, nearly 2,000 miles from the border of French-speaking Quebec. Ottawa has, for generations, been slow or reluctant to commit to national positions on global issues of import. The brilliant Canadian actor, Michael J. Fox, once captured this famously for millions on TV: Asked by the host to define the Canadian equivalent of the American adage *"As American as Apple Pie,"* Fox thought for just a moment before answering with a mischievous smile on his lips.

> "We Canadians are not that assertive," he pointed out, "and we never like to offend anybody, eh? We are such sensitive and caring people and wedded to individual rights. You see, some Canadians may not really like apples, and it is their inviolable right to dislike apples and, by logical extension, to dislike apple pie. So we have to be careful! And it would, of course, also have to be a bilingual adage or maybe two adages, equally acceptable to all Canadians—maybe even ten adages, one for each province. They don't talk much about Canada over there in Quebec, but I believe we might get away with an English language equivalent to your American apple pie slogan … We could try *"As Canadian as possible under the circumstances!"*

At a social gathering during a trip to Toronto, my British accent had, quite understandably, led one poor man to assume that I was an Englishman, so he asked where I lived in the UK.

> "No actually, I'm a Danish-American," I explained. "I am on a business trip from the States. I live and work in Connecticut, pretty close to New York—I'm just visiting your lovely city for twenty-four hours. America is my home now."

The Ontarian's eyebrows were drawn to a heavy frown over troubled eyes. He leaned forward and put his hand gently on my shoulder as he sought to comfort me.

> "You poor bastard!" he whispered. "But I suppose someone has to live there, eh!"

Little did I know that three years later the family would move to Toronto for an extended sojourn in a very different role.

The retirement of Robert S. Hatfield as Chairman and Chief Executive had rippled through the whole Continental organization, triggering S. Bruce Smart's pre-announced succession. A game changing event. Bob handed over the baton at the end of a huge conference of top and middle management held at the Rye Town Hilton in the woods of Westchester County when the leaves were turning and the fall colors were at their most brilliant. In his somewhat self-effacing style, he made a moving speech expressing his gratitude to the people with whom he had worked for four decades. Bob was retiring at 65 according to the rules he had written, which also allowed him two more years as a non-executive member of the board. Nearly two hundred men gave Bob a standing ovation as he made his exit, pausing at the bottom of the podium steps, right hand held high in salute before walking slowly through the length of the cavernous room, shaking hands as he went, a bit like a popular US president leaving the chamber after a state of the union address. That was about all the fanfare and ceremony he allowed himself. I could not stem the tears. Bob had played a pivotal role in my life.

The new leadership inherited a six-billion dollar company in respectable shape, much admired as a sound blue chip industrial enterprise enjoying a strong cash flow from its base business, but it was not exactly the most exciting stock on Wall Street. The packaging industry was perceived as one which offered limited growth, while facing some crucial technological and strategic choices to be made, which clearly required decisive leadership and some intestinal fortitude. Recent acquisitions outside Continental's historical business base presented new and unfamiliar issues, and the stock market failed to get excited about the diversification. It was a stimulating opportunity for a new and creative leader, including the enlistment of support and loyalty from seasoned business leaders at the head of acquired businesses, such as Virginia Life, and a title insurance company, and an oil and gas pipeline company called Florida Gas. These men became friends within the corporate family.

The head of Florida Gas was an obviously brilliant, youngish mover and shaker named Ken Lay. He was a fiercely independent and outspoken leader of his business, who happily called a spade a fucking shovel in any company. He was always a great colleague and fun to be with. Because of his competence as a manager of a business so alien to Continental's base, and because of his grasp of infinite detail, he could get away with murder under Bruce Smart—and did!

Years later, of course, he became infamous as the Enron crash and scandal broke. His insistent claims that he knew nothing of the criminal behavior of the corporate executives under him never persuaded me. Ken was a total control freak with incredible retention and command of detail at Florida Gas. They would not have been perishable talents at his attained age when Enron happened.

I sensed at the time that Chairman Smart had some testing times exerting his leadership of these new, strong managers now under Continental Group's tent.

Bruce, the MIT graduate was indelibly Yankee, six-foot-three, with wide-set eyes, a pugilist's nose, jutting chin anchoring a square-jawed physiognomy below a heavy head of silver hair combed to the side from a ruler-straight parting. He walked with a distinctive bounce to his stride, almost rising on his toes with every step. In public he habitually wore a hint of a smile, irrespective of the occasion, perhaps to suggest he was totally unflappable and master of every situation. Hollywood's top casting agencies could not have found a physically more perfect Captain America of the corporate world. The first months of the S. Bruce Smart era were quiet in terms of executive action—no change of direction or style was immediately evident. Some observers saw this as appropriate deliberation before coming to grips with the accelerating rate of change in the company's business environment.

Continental Diversified Packaging did well, and its performance was competitive with, or better than, other major components of the corporation in terms of return on capital employed, so I was happily left to my own devices, with limited oversight and direction. Several of the businesses were expanding fast—which was welcomed in board meetings, where directors were pushing very hard for growth to boost the stock price. Although I was never a director, I reported on performance of Diversified Packaging to the board at monthly meetings. This fostered some lasting relationships, including a friendship with Frank Rhodes, President of Cornell University. The connection to Cornell was, in time, to become important in a very different context.

The board had some interesting members. Colby Chandler of Eastman Kodak, who took charge of his company in its Halcyon days, the pre-digital era, when it had 90 percent of America's film market. Jack Parker, Vice Chairman of GE, who slept through board reports that he found less than fascinating. The most impressive director was Pete Peterson, who started his career in advertising before becoming a co-founder of Blackstone. He was an MIT dropout from Chicago who later went back to take his studies more seriously, graduated and took an MBA at The University of Chicago Booth School of Business. In the boardroom and elsewhere, he clearly loved his own voice, often pontificating; but it was always worth heeding his words. This champion of national fiscal responsibility served the country well in sundry roles under Republican and Democratic administrations from the early 1970s into the new millennium. He was, for example Nixon's Secretary of Commerce, later castigating his own party as he watched the GOP succumb to crippling deficit spending.

> "I remain a Republican," said Pete, "but the Republicans have become a much more faith-based party, not troubling with evidence."

Peterson was in due course invited by Bill Clinton to serve on his Commission on Entitlement and Tax Reform. The Blackstone Group grew to be an invaluable contributor and stabilizing factor in America's industrial and financial sectors. The firm originally focused on the business of advising challenged companies but, as originally planned by Peterson and his co-founder Schwartzman, moved deliberately into private equity and eventually into broad financial asset management. Blackstone was a paragon of that time and remains so, despite media bias and the Obama administration's name calling—labeling it and other companies like Bain & Co., the Carlisle Group and KKR as *vile vulture capitalists*.

My work on the job was regularly interrupted. Don Bainton constantly involved me in meetings to explore projects that would cause directors to give him attention in the boardroom. This was part of his expressly declared strategy to become Chairman and CEO of the corporation. He obsessively embarked on all sorts of ideas from new products to organizational restructuring, all of them attention seeking. His behavior became progressively devious and narcissistic. Some initiatives costing millions of unauthorized dollars were funded by padding legitimate capital expenditure applications that were approved at board level. At other times he would devise changes in management structure exclusively to improve the position of his henchmen and stooges, or to pull the rug from under the feet of able managers he saw as potential threats. One such target in Don's sights was Dick Hoffmann, his immediate subordinate at the head of CCC, the metal can business. He thought Hoffmann had the evident support of Bruce Smart, which Bainton found unwelcome.

He also persisted in his bizarre quest for exposure in British society under the guise of acquiring influential friends for Continental in London. The disgraced Lord Jellicoe, leader of the House of Lords before admitting to casual relations with call girls from *Mayfair Escorts*, was a dinner guest on at least one occasion—perhaps a situation not fully comprehended by his host. Less irresponsible, but still over the top, were endless meetings with, and reckless entertainment of, John Sculley, President of Pepsi-Cola at the time. Bainton wanted to garner support for the development of an aluminum bottle, at vast cost—a new package for carbonated soft drinks. It was an absurd idea in the context of early 1980s technology and costs, but Don saw it as a path to world fame and a boost to his career. Thirty years later, a similar concept was brought to market, but limited to a tiny market segment, super-premium beer packaging.

In the fall of 1982, Bainton called me at the office late on a Thursday evening to say he wanted me to join him for a seven o'clock breakfast the next morning at the Showboat Inn in Greenwich, where we both lived. Seated at a quiet corner table after putting in a wholesome order, Bainton cleared his throat and dialed in his best baritone broadcasting voice, which he did whenever he needed to make an impression. He had thespian talent.

"I need your help, and you need to help yourself in the process," he said. "Flemming, you know that I will, in due course, be Chairman and Chief Executive of the Continental Group. That's a given! It's a question of when, not if, and you'll do extremely well out of that." For effect he paused to wipe his mouth carefully with his napkin. "And please look ahead. Recognize that you are young enough to go on to succeed ME one day. I will want to move on after a while, to other corporate boards and maybe a senior government job after my stint at the head of Continental. So now listen carefully, my friend." He bared his teeth in a frigid smile over his receding chin. "Because Smart and some of his chums on the board have this strange preoccupation with Dick Hoffmann, I need to make sure he is neutralized and out of the way. I need a new organizational structure for Continental Packaging, which must make you my clear deputy, with a really strong staff, so we can keep corporate at bay, keep them guessing. Bruce and some of those guys have orgasms whenever Hoffmann appears before the board—I'm sure you have already observed that, Flemming—you've seen it for yourself. I bet he blabs to Bruce behind our backs. Well, the reorganization will give you a nice promotion and then isolate that son of a bitch. But to accomplish that, I really must have your help in designing the structure and picking the right people for the key slots. You're in good standing with the directors after the job you did in Europe, and your results in Diversified are just fine, so I want you to help me with the plan and then support me in leaning on Smart to buy in. I can then present a done deal to my board colleagues. None of those buffoons heading up our new businesses in insurance and goddamned pipelines have the clout or history that I have, so the next corporate CEO simply has to come out of packaging. By the way, I can tell you that Bruce has been talking confidentially about moving Hoffmann to a corporate strategy job on the executive floor—just down the hall from Smart. That bothers me." Another pause for drama. "I want you to think about this over the weekend, Flemming, so we will meet here again on Monday morning, same time and same place, to seal the deal, then talk through the details of how we move this thing along." Bainton stopped for air. "Got it? Have I made myself clear? And all this is, of course, completely off the record. There'll be no way anybody outside the board could ever know about your involvement in the plan."

Bainton continued his soliloquy over the next half hour. His machinations were beyond the Machiavellian, almost psychotic. All the while, he was chomping on a full English breakfast with a calorie count breaking the 2,000 mark. Fried eggs, sausage, bacon, tomato—and biscuits to add an American touch of the South.

I sat there, speechless, and watched Bainton give his mouth a final wipe, flash his weak-chinned grin, rise from his chair and pat me on the shoulder as he made for the exit.

"See you Monday, Flemming!" he said as he headed out. "Use the weekend to think clearly about this thing! Have a good one!"

Getting to the office late, completely and utterly distracted, I had a useless day. I could barely make sense when communicating with colleagues, bungling conversations with outside associates. At home that evening after the kids were in bed, Judy and I had an interminable discussion, exploring the very limited options in responding to Bainton. It made for a short night's sleep. The immediately obvious and firm conclusion was that I had to cut off the Bainton conversation, making it crystal-clear that I would have nothing to do with this poisonous plot, then or ever in the future.

I called Bainton next morning before he could leave home for golf.

"Well, hi there, Flemming, isn't this a gorgeous day?" boomed the baritone. "Glad you caught me, as I'm on my way out the door. You have good news for me!"

"I know it's Saturday morning and that you would be on your way early to the course," I said, "but I had call you right away to avoid any waste of your time—I mean regarding your proposal over breakfast yesterday. Don, there will be no need for you to take time out for breakfast together on Monday. I simply cannot consider being part of the project you described to me, nor can I put my name to the objectives as you explained them. Dick Hoffmann is not my closest buddy, but he *IS* a colleague, and I haven't any reason to distrust him, nor to believe he does not trust me. The kind of move you have in mind just doesn't fit my playbook—and I don't care how private, off-the-record or confidential you claim it to be. I can't have any part in it, now or going forward."

There was a long, deep silence at the other end. So I continued.

"I can be more explicit at some point, if you like, but I just could not wait through the weekend to let you know where I stand. You have to know right now, unequivocally, that I can have no part in your project."

This time there was an even longer pause before Don responded in a calm and matter-of-fact mode.

"Well, my good friend, we'll have breakfast exactly as planned. You obviously need to understand and appreciate what I'm asking of you and what I'm offering you. Think this thing through, man! You have to look further than your own fucking nose, and you must give yourself more time, and reconsider the implications of what you have just said." Then he quickly said, "Gotta run, Flemming! See you seven o'clock Monday! At the Showboat, right? Bye now!"

Bainton hung up.

Monday's breakfast was an extraordinary ordeal. Fortunately, the dining room was practically empty, but the experience was as disconcerting as any I ever had in a personal relationship. It required every bit of self-control I could muster. I knew how much was at stake. After I repeated my position exactly as conveyed to him over the phone, Bainton literally pleaded that I listen carefully and avoid committing what he described as "a suicidal mistake." He was by then less composed, dark eyes fixed on mine, shaking his head and ponderous jowls, teeth bared again in that frozen grin.

> "Why do you have to fall on your fucking sword?" he admonished me as his voice rose. "Please, Flemming, listen to me—please! You're too old to be a boy scout. Don't be so goddamned naïve. You've enjoyed one hell of a rapid rise through the ranks since joining the company. You simply cannot squander the unique opportunity I'm presenting to you. Others would give their right arm for it."

> "Don, you also have to listen to me," I countered, struggling to keep calm. "I am simply not going to weigh in for this kind of fight. I am, not in any way, going to be part of any move or scheme that clearly contrives to undercut a colleague of mine, whether he's a kindred spirit or not. I simply will not do it! I regard the plan you have outlined as completely out of bounds, according to my own rule book. Just count me out. I have been given a job to do at

Diversified Packaging and I just want to get on with it, working within my own bailiwick. I expect to be judged by my results and I expect my future to reflect whatever performance I am able to deliver. I am very happy to play by those rules, but there's no way that I'm signing up for this scheme of yours."

I sensed that Don perhaps understood that he could face some seriously negative exposure if I were to choose an overtly confrontational course of action. This time, Bainton did not take long to finish his coffee and toast. No full English breakfast this time. He again folded his napkin deliberately, rose from his seat and stood behind his chair, both hands grasping its back like a preacher in his pulpit:

"Flemming, I'm afraid you'll regret this 'til your dying day. Didn't I tell you that I shall be running this company before long, and you could be there drinking sherry by the fireside with me, sharing the rewards of our work together? You really are being a silly little boy scout! You have some time to come to your senses and call me. I'm your boss, you know. But it's your call to make. Bye for now!"

Stunned, I sat in my chair for several minutes and then took a long scenic drive to the office. Don did not raise the subject of our two meetings over the coming weeks, and for some time I had no calls from him. Although he rarely addressed me or asked questions, our public interface at scheduled meetings remained apparently unaltered, as if the exchange had never taken place.

One day, a month or so later, Bruce Smart left a message for me at the office while I was away on a short trip to Europe, visiting operations in Belgium and Germany. He wanted to chat with me, it said, and I was asked to call upon my return. I did so from JFK, where I had checked for messages before going directly to Stamford. No cell phones in those days. Bruce said he would come to my office, rather than have me go over to HQ, and that my secretary should let his office know when I got there.

Bruce was coming down from on high, as if he wanted it to be a covert visit. That told me something unusual was up. He duly arrived in my office half an hour after I checked in. Walking straight through the wide-open door, he did not wait for my secretary to show him in, but quietly and deliberately closed the door. Smart bid me good afternoon, asking how my trip had been, before he lowered his big frame into one of the comfortable armchairs by my coffee table.

> "Diversified Packaging is doing pretty darn well, Flemming, and that has not escaped the Board's attention. I want you to know that. The pipeline and insurance businesses are doing fine, too. All good!" the chairman said, rambling on with no perceptible direction or purpose. "So, speaking of diversification, and given the board's pressure on us to create growth, I want to accelerate the company's investments in the many opportunities out there, outside the world of packaging. Tell me your thoughts on that, coach!" the chairman suggested.

Bruce, for some reason called me "coach" in private, which was a habit originated in Europe when I spent a week showing him around the operations.

> "Well, you can hardly look to me for ideas on financial services, the energy game or any of the other industries you have talked about, but if its growth we are after, we have lots of growing we could do within our own base industry. That's how I see it. I know there are many attractive growth opportunities in packaging all around the world, by organic

expansion and by acquisition. There's low hanging fruit in all sorts of places, all in the industry where we are clearly global leaders, already nicely deployed for expansion. Our learning curve, whether in start-ups or acquisitions in new territories, would be very manageable were we to move further afield. That's where I would like to see us go, and I'm sure it would serve our stockholders well," I ventured. "We're in great shape to grow in Asia and we could be doing much more in South America. We could even take a crack at Southern Africa, where I know Metal Box and Crown Cork have some vulnerabilities …and I'm only half-joking, Bruce!"

I had for a long-time observed Bruce's parochial and xenophobic fear of international exposure, and recalled his neurotic fear that the Soviets would invade West Germany, causing us to lose Schmalbach. One of his early actions after taking over as Chairman was to hire an Indian PhD. in international relations, a Dr Bhalla, to evaluate "Continental's exposure to sovereign risk" in each of our operations located in a non-US territory. On one occasion he and his minions attempted to withdraw from a planned beverage can startup business in South Korea, which in fact went on to become one of the most profitable units in the corporation for decades.

"Come on, Flemming, that story doesn't get me or Continental Group on the cover of Business Week!" chuckled Smart, pretending HE was joking. "Geographic diversification is not newsworthy enough, it's not sexy enough. I need to make a less predictable move, something a bit more dramatic, and I have to goose the stock price." He then changed the subject abruptly as he settled back in the chair, trying to look relaxed. "Tell me, how are you getting on with Mr. Bainton, your ambitious boss?"

We had now come to the point, I concluded, the real object of the exercise. Bainton was his real reason for the unprecedented visit to my office. For so many months I had been troubled by my peripheral involvement in some of Don's escapades at home and abroad. Perhaps Smart had perceived that. So I decided to let rip.

> "I am not sure I welcome your question at this particular juncture, Bruce, and I'm damn sure you'll not welcome my answer, not one bit. But you asked, so I am going to tell it to you straight. I am not happy! I'll give you the facts and leave you in no doubt as to what I think. I'll let the chips fall as they may," I said with my heart now pounding and my temples throbbing. "You asked the tough question, so here goes—what I tell you about Don Bainton's style, his maneuvers and motivations, as I see them, will shock you— even if I only tell you half the story. And this has, in fact, been going on for a couple of years, since he arrived here from Chicago to take over from Warren. As you have come to see me here, away from your own office, I'm pretty sure you have heard something from somewhere else and don't like what you've heard. So don't just shoot this particular messenger, Bruce! I'll be pretty brutal because it's also pretty ugly."

I went on to recount much of what I had experienced of Bainton in Europe and after my return to Stamford. I told the new chairman quite bluntly what I felt about the man's conduct in Europe, and in his leadership of the packaging business. I told him of Bainton's bizarre social aspirations and spending habits abroad, especially in England. I pointed to padded capital expenditure applications used to create cash to fund unauthorized product development adventures. I even told him of Don's obsession with elaborate executive bathrooms installed adjacent to every office he ever occupied over time. However, I did not tell Smart about Don's attempt to lure me into his restructuring scheme designed to promote himself and derail Hoffmann—that was probably my very first mistake, and I still don't know why I made it.

It was a near-soliloquy, as Bruce just sat there, at moments involuntarily wide-eyed and physically squirming in the armchair. When I came to a halt, Bruce exhaled deeply, but seemed quickly to pull himself together, dragging himself up to his full height and then silently shook my hand. He said nothing, but looked me in the eye, apparently attempting to show that he was in absolute control of the situation, knowing exactly what to do.

> "Thank you, Flemming, you've obviously had a lot on your mind. I appreciate that, but don't do anything rash now! Don't worry! I will deal with this. Be assured I will deal with this," he repeated. "Don't you speak to a soul about this thing, not a soul! Just leave it with me. I'll sort it out. And you'll be hearing from me, of course."

Smart normally had that spring to his step, but now he was on his heels as he shuffled out of my office, closing the door very gingerly behind him as if to avoid being seen or heard. However, after no more than a minute or so, the door was slowly pushed ajar and then half-opened again as Bruce peered in and then poked his head past the doorframe:

> "Flemming, where does all this leave you in terms of working for your present boss, reporting to Bainton? Where are you on that one?"

> "Obviously I can't work for Bainton in the long run. That must be so obvious. You just told me not to do anything rash. You said you would get back to me. So I'll be a good soldier and will await your thoughts. I'm a big boy, Bruce, and I do understand that discretion is called for. Meanwhile,

I'll do my job as best I can. I guess the next move is yours since you told me I should leave it with you, sir."

Smart just nodded.

"Yes, just leave it to me!"

The expressionless chairman pulled his head back as he eased the door closed once more and disappeared.

Weeks went by and business was its unusual self as I continued to work at arm's length with Bainton. Smart's behavior could easily have suggested he had forgotten all about our extraordinary exchange, appearing to be his normal self at our regular meetings. That was, however, most unlikely, given the facts—if I spilled the beans or the story somehow leaked, all hell could break loose. I waited patiently, but could not help speculating as to what the resolution would be. Something had to give.

Finally, Bruce broke the silence. At the very end of 1982, Smart offered me a new job.

I was to move to headquarters as EVP and Chief Administrative Officer of the corporation to take charge of all staff functions except finance, strategic planning and legal. That meant managing corporate officers in charge of human resources and employee benefits, government relations, external affairs including investor relations, communications, advertising and PR. One had to wonder who Smart might have consulted. As a relatively new arrival in the USA, equipped with a limey accent, seventeen years of experience on the southern tip of Africa and carrying a Danish passport, I was to oversee Continental's lobbying efforts in Washington and manage the corporation's image to an American audience, while navigating US labor laws and fighting Chicago-based unions faced with plant closures! All this against the background of my entire career focused on operations management, marketing and technological issues. I vainly thought the title was somehow impressive and alluring, and that new challenges in unfamiliar areas would be stimulating. The job would get me out from under Bainton, I reasoned, and I could not see him lasting long in Continental anyhow, so there was potential for a natural transition back to line management ahead of me.

I was a sucker and fell for it—a very stupid and monumental mistake!

My acceptance of Bruce Smart's offer was the most idiotic business decision of my whole career. It was naïve and spineless. Knowing that Smart was Bainton's champion in proposing him for the board of directors, the transparency of Bruce Smart's cowardice should have been obvious. He feared questions from the directors, and he was right to do so. I could have blown his cover and caused pandemonium. I had a good track record before joining Continental, then with the CCC European assignment and now in the States with Diversified Industries. I had all the leverage, yet put none of it to work for me. Had I wished to exploit the situation for financial gain, I could even have taken Smart and the company to the cleaners by resigning quietly in return for a life-changing golden handshake. However, allowing the title and the phony job description to hoodwink me, I was as cowardly as Smart himself in making the asinine decision to accept.

This was not wasted on Don Bainton, whose derisive smirk told the whole story. Dick Hoffmann was also given a sideways promotion from CCC to Chief Strategic Officer for Continental Group. His gutless vanity matched my own.

I proceeded to do a poor job at corporate headquarters. This could be partly attributed to my lacking relevant experience and knowledge, and partly to Smart's lack of support. He really wanted to shoot the messenger—his inability to forgive me for taking a position over Bainton prompted him to isolate me gradually in the organization, going around me to pursue issues directly with my subordinates. Bainton put up every barrier he could possibly erect in the way of my work to get things done across the face of the company: He was the line manager in charge of 60 percent of the territory in which corporate staff functions had to work. It was agonizing, frustrating, and it took me too long to realize I was on a hiding to nothing, meaning I was in a serious, no-win situation. My mistake was soon compounded when events finally caught up with Bainton. A rising star in the packaging business, Greg Horrigan, with several of his colleagues, blew the whistle on Bainton, much more publicly than I had. This time Smart could not sidestep the issue, and Bainton was terminated, thrilled with his very generous and comfortable golden handshake. With Don gone, I thought, the road would again open up to top line management positions. This, however, was not to be. This was another major mistake on my part.

Smart's stated position was that he could not let any whistleblower benefit from getting his or her boss into trouble. The Chief Financial Officer, Phil Silver, who had risen from the acquired gas pipeline business was given Bainton's packaging job, putting an end to my own aspirations in that direction. Just after becoming an American citizen along with the rest of the family in October 1983, my constructive termination at Continental was evidently under way; but Smart lacked the guts to address the situation he had himself created. He would not confront me face-to-face. He used his colleagues and henchmen, including Vice Chairman Don Donahue, to deliver warm and friendly advice on how to cut a deal, and make an exit, which I eventually did, but with much less leverage than I would have had earlier. Smart tried to get cheap with me, but collapsed like a house of cards when I warned him quite directly that anything short of fair treatment would do the company and his reputation no good at all. On the other hand, I demanded nothing beyond decent termination practice by the corporate standards of the day. I formally resigned.

For the last time, I enjoyed the gorgeous top floor view from my office all the way across Stamford's opulent Harbor Plaza Marina right below me, and Long Island Sound beyond, as I packed up my desk on February 24, 1984. No generous golden handshake; but I did insist on a measure of security for a year or two and a pension annuity well in excess of the formula governed by years of service. I demanded to be considered vested at the ten-year level, despite having barely served eight. I had been invited to join Continental in 1977, sharing the mutual expectation of a lifelong association. Smart, always anxious, made a final, fatuous attempt to improve the cosmetics of the situation by setting up a formal farewell luncheon at the nearby Stamford Yacht Club, ironically assembling the Group's top management at the home of the acclaimed and very popular Annual America-Denmark Friendship Race.

I passed on the opportunity.

Chapter VII

Wheelers, Dealers and Cheaters

"You don't go wheeling and dealing for money. You do it for fun. Money's just a way to keep score."
Henry Tyroon, Texan tycoon character in MGM movie "The Wheeler Dealers."

FROM A SMALL rented office on Arch Street in hometown Greenwich, I started casting around for a new job. While my research quickly led to some minor non-executive directorships and consulting projects, several seemingly attractive leadership jobs eluded me. Advanced conversations in London with Babcock International, chaired by Margaret Thatcher's chum Lord King, Baron of Warnaby, came to an abrupt end when the Brits finally addressed the issue of my CEO's remuneration. John King was also chairman of British Air, credited with the airline's impressive turnaround and rescue from the brink of collapse. He is still known for his "dirty tricks" used to combat growing competition from upstart Richard Branson's Virgin Air, who countered with libel suits that were eventually settled out of court by British Air paying Branson and his airline a total of three-point-six million pounds Sterling—a telling sum of money in the mid-80s. King conducted some of our interviews in the presence of all his assembled directors, or solo over gourmand lunches at Browns, complete with vintage port to round off the repast. Lord King comported himself as he thought a baron should, but I wouldn't really have cared if he were the King of Siam.

Another near miss was a small company named Raybestos, which produced automotive brakes and clutches for cars and industrial equipment—all involving asbestos materials. A career there would have plunged me into years of vicious litigation over workers' injuries from exposure to this dangerous material. Looking outside the established corporate arena came naturally, especially as leveraged buy-outs (LBOs), mergers, restructuring deals and turn-around projects proliferated in the mid-80s. European companies seeking landfall in the USA were also of interest. Even the Pitcairn family, who controlled the renowned PPG paint company, was looking for a CEO with industrial experience to lead the family's holding company, which oversaw their eclectic investments, but they rightly found me short of corporate finance skills. I was in touch with a lot of investment banks. There was not yet reason to worry about mortgage payments, Greenwich living expenses or the education for the three kids, who were far from done with schools and university—but I certainly endured some waking hours, thinking about unwelcome *what if's*.

About two months after departing the somewhat complacent Continental Group, the company was shaken to its very core when Sir James Goldsmith, the controversial Anglo-French financier, often characterized as a corporate raider, fired a salvo smack across Bruce Smart's bow. Goldsmith was a major figure in the UK, and indeed on the European continent, before his major American initiatives made him famous here. Mightily successful all his life as an active and very shrewd private equity investor and deal maker, the smartly tailored financier also enjoyed a colorful romantic life. Goldsmith and Smart were from different planets. Sir James administered the shock personally by 'phoning from out of the blue to lob in a dollar-defined bid to acquire the whole of Continental—lock, stock and barrel.'

Continental Group, almost four years into Bruce Smart's term as Chairman and CEO, had become a somewhat complex company to understand, so its stock underperformed commensurately. Part of Smart's problem was that he and his board never explained their diversification strategy to the market—assuming for a moment they ever had one—nor did they market its strengths, such as the can company's industrial preeminence, its dependably strong cash flow and relative immunity to business cycles. Continental's diversifications outside the packaging industry never moved the needle on the stock price, as the market failed to see synergies between packaging and insurance businesses, or gas pipe lines. The core packaging business was very slow to grow, so the price of the group's shares sagged sadly to book value or below. Goldsmith, as he had done so often, spotted greater value in the sum of its many components than reflected in the group's share price.

Apparently, panic and pandemonium erupted as Bruce Smart's xenophobic heart swooned. The situation could not have been more alien to him or his minions. What worse situation could befall the preppy, parochial Yankee than a brash European Jew with an upper crust English accent humiliating him? And then having his company chopped up and sold off in chunks? The chairman wrung his hands as the board was called in for multiple emergency sessions convening, as usual, in the GM building opposite the Plaza in Manhattan. Bankers were engaged, legal advisors appointed and the offer was pompously rejected. In the nervous aftermath of shock, Vice-Chairman Don Donahue was dispatched on corporate flights across the USA to seek a white knight to save Continental and Bruce Smart from the "marauding, wheeling and dealing Anglo-French Jew."

The news reached me via early morning business news on TV, and a day or two later, one of Smart's loyal henchmen, Jess Belser, called to extend a lunch invitation. He had been a ranking colleague with whom I had rubbed shoulders at executive meetings, but I had never been close to the man on a personal basis and was astonished to get the call. Jess was Jewish, but did not like to be categorized as such. He liked to hob nob with the New England huntin', shootin' and fishin' types and wore tweed suits on weekends. Bob Hatfield had at one time unsuccessfully proposed him as a member of Greenwich Country Club and had admirably resigned his own membership when Jess was blackballed. It took decades for that club to shake its covertly anti-Semitic ways. Smart, in fact, had just recently deposed

Jess from his job running Continental's important forest products businesses, to take a staff role as the chairman's adviser on strategic and organizational issues—a situation which was, in some ways, similar to my own demise. I was dying with curiosity to know what Jess's motivation was.

> "What a pleasant surprise, Jess! How are you? I guess it has been a great spring for you and the sheep up at your place in Vermont. It must be lambing time," I speculated. "This is very kind of you, Jess, but what prompts the invitation at this particular juncture, with all that's going on at Continental?"

> "Nothing in particular, pal. Just wondering how you were faring, so I thought I'd give you a call to see if you were free to meet for a bite. No agenda, though, just to shoot the breeze! You did leave Harbor Plaza without giving us much of a chance to wish you well, so I was just keen to know how things were going."

The ruse was obvious, but its underlying purpose was still a mystery to me. A *puzzlement*, as the King of Siam would have described the unexpected conversation.

Smart's chronic Yankee xenophobia was consistent and had many symptoms. He never liked the idea of investing abroad. He would shrink from overseas investment proposals, calling for endless sovereign risk analyses. He literally winced at the pale blue socks and beige summer suit worn by an English manager, Pat Barrett, in charge of the UK operations. Smart's idea of proper business attire was a dark box-like Brooks Brothers suit with that bizarre buttonhole half way up the lapel, a white button-down shirt, plain navy blue or Ivy League tie, and black wingtips. He and his henchmen conspired to mock those of us who dared to wear colored or striped shirts and tailored suits, perhaps with double-vented jackets. Foulard patterned ties were taboo. Non-American accents caused him discomfort.

So, Smart's funk in reaction to Goldsmith's attack was totally predictable, as was the resulting scramble for a red blooded, American savior in the form of a white knight.

Over lunch at The Red Lantern in Greenwich, the initial conversation with Belser covered the wind and the weather, the stock market and then the Vermont farm. After nearly an hour he took the cover off the inane rationale for his surprising, improbable lunch invitation.

"What do you think about this whole Goldsmith affair, Flemming? Isn't it appalling that our system allows a disreputable financial cowboy like him to cause this much disruption, without having to account for what he is doing? And he's doing it all with zero at stake? He may get away with it in Europe, but it's nothing short of nefarious, and it shouldn't be tolerated in our American system. You know, he's one of these guys who uses the acquisition target's assets as collateral to finance his own purchase, goddammit! Can you believe it?" complained Belser, shaking his heavy head of thick graying hair—his lack of financial understanding made me look as if I were an old hand in corporate finance. "They call these schemes leveraged buyouts, or somethin' like that—its crazy! By the way, how well do you know him? Didn't you run into him in Europe, in Brussels, or was it in your Metal Box days?"

"Good grief, Jess, what the hell are you thinking? Do you really believe I know Goldsmith? Of course I have read and heard a ton about Sir Jimmy, his many fantastic deals and his enterprising love life; but I've never set eyes on the bloody man himself. The billionaire financier is way out of my league—and yours, Jess, and poor old Bruce's. I have to tell you, he knows what he's doing, and I believe he'll be doing a lot more here in the States." I paused for a moment. "Oh Jess, I really do wish I did, in fact, know him!"

I wanted to make the most of having the upper hand for once and so continued.

"He has saved a lot of failing businesses and made brilliant successes out of some mediocre ones. He has often replaced stagnation with profitable growth and has either saved or generated hundreds of thousands of jobs—scoring time after time, far outweighing his rare failures. He's always ahead of the game. Heavens above, Jess, you were in charge of Continental's one-and-a-half million acres of timberland, so with your knowledge of the forest industry you should know that! Goldsmith's far and away the largest owner of US forest lands, and that's because he spotted our idiotic treatment of amortized American forest property values on corporate balance sheets. He does great things by acquiring mismanaged or undervalued assets, or just unleashing the intrinsic value of underutilized assets. Jimmy Goldsmith may be a bit of a buccaneer, but he's also a big-time philanthropist and a really colorful character! He has a lot more moxie and brains than anyone Continental has confronted before this."

Disconcerted, Belser's jaw dropped and his face went blank. I relished his discomfort as I plunged in.

"You know, he runs two families. One with his wife and one with his mistress, and everybody involved is extremely well looked after and both ladies claim to be very happy! You know, Jess, two summers ago he had his wife plus kids on vacation on the island of Sardinia, while his girlfriend and second family were on holiday two or three miles away, just across the sound, on Corsica—or was it the other way 'round? I simply don't recall. Anyhow, Judy and I were there on Corsica with our own family at the time, and the local gossip was that Jimmy G., as they called him, would have lunch and afternoon tea with the one family, then take off in his high-powered speedboat for dinner and the evening with t' other. How's that for good asset utilization, Jess?"

I paused to let Jess catch his breath.

"He is also hugely generous, doing great stuff for the underprivileged in the UK, France and around the world, all very efficiently, demanding great discipline—famously cost effective, he is. He didn't get knighted for nothing! Jess, you might get on very well with him were he to become your boss. You might have more in common with Goldsmith than you think—I've read that he does like shooting quail."

Belser was not amused by the last remark, but quickly recovered decorum and proceeded to unload the whole story. The financier's blunt call had apparently paralyzed Smart. Coming across the wire from nowhere, Goldsmith's rapid fire, carefree style and upper-crust English accent spooked the hell out of him. According to Jess, who by now had his tongue loosened by several glasses of nice Burgundy, Bruce was rendered paranoid. As Smart had tried to retrace events leading up to the attack, he somehow got the idea that a "disgruntled Flemming Heilmann, with his own English accent and Savile Row tastes," could have approached Sir James to plant the buyout idea, offering him the benefit of inside knowledge accumulated over eight years at Continental. Smart had apparently noted aloud that I was under no contractual constraints, no non-compete conditions, as I left Continental to seek a future elsewhere.

"You know, Flemming, it's really not absurd to think you
had a relationship with this Brit. You do come across as a bit
of a limey—*birds of a feather* and all that! Ha, ha, ha!" joked
Belser awkwardly. "After all, you are looking for something
new to do, and most of your friends at Continental know you
are no great fan of S. Bruce Smart, Jr. You've got a pretty
damned good résumé and track record with lots of
background in the UK. Why wouldn't you give it a shot if
you knew the guy? It's not that crazy of a thought, is it?"
"You flatter me, Jess! Thank you!"

Belser was looking rather sheepish by the time we had enjoyed coffee,
and he limped home, presumably to report on his mission's outcome. The
chairman had sent Jess to test his dark conjecture, which, in retrospect, I
found neither out of character nor offensive to me. In fact, it made me regret
not having had the gumption to think of contacting Goldsmith myself. He
was known to be a most approachable fellow; I could have been very useful
to him in a due diligence process, and perhaps beyond—why not?. The
episode strengthened my developing interest in the private equity business
and the leveraged buyout methods that were being so widely used in the
1980s. As Jess left The Red Lantern, he made his exit from my life.

In May 1984, the Wall Street Journal reported that Continental's great
rival, American Can Company, rushing to raise cash to fund its own
fashionable diversifications by acquisition, was attempting to sell its
Canadian can business. The closing of an LBO deal with Sam Belzberg's
First City Financial of Vancouver had fallen through. This grabbed my
attention because all of Continental's Canadian business, including the can
business, had been part of my portfolio as head of Diversified Industries. I
knew the Canadian business environment and its stakeholders across all ten
provinces. A call to Bill Woodside, Chairman of American Can in
Greenwich, drew an encouraging response. Apparently, Belzberg had
attempted to move the goalposts just before the final whistle, thus delaying

the scheduled closing. This, of course, caused much ire at American Can and precipitated their walkout. In answer to my question, Woodside said he would listen to any credible group interested in acquiring his subsidiary, but also claimed that he was preparing for discussions with other interested parties. However, he would be pleased to discuss a deal with a credible group.

> "If your group were industrialists, especially with experience in packaging, we would be happy to talk, but you better get on your bicycle," he said. "The vultures are already circling, young man!"

This call jump-started a feverish week spent writing a crude business plan for American Can Canada, Inc.—known as ACCI—as best I could from recollections of the Canadian industry and dozens of conversations with Canadian contacts, erstwhile customers, suppliers and even union leaders. ACCI was a business with fifteen plants across Canada, sales of about C$480-million, a bunch of blue-chip customers and a much-neglected asset base. Plant maintenance and investment in new technology had been given short shrift as a part of American Can's strategy of siphoning off cash to finance diversified acquisitions—in this case financial services, gramophone records and other areas totally alien to the core business. The Canadian company was operating at about breakeven, with a heavy fixed cost structure and a tired management, discouraged by the lack of capital to maintain their assets, keep up with changing technology, let alone grow the business. The company and its employees were on a slow, sad march to nowhere. A twelve-page document was put together, reflecting my capacity to address operating issues, but also my lack of expertise as a balance sheet gymnast—I had little idea of how to go about financing the notion of a leveraged buy-out. I proceeded to pound the sidewalks of Manhattan, calling on people like Forstman Little, KKR, Shroder, Warburg Pincus, Morgan Stanley and Lazard. I tried Pete Peterson, using our passing acquaintance at

Continental, but was turned away. He quickly but courteously made it clear he had bigger fish to fry. With metaphorical and physical pats on the back, all the bankers thanked me politely and encouraged me to move right along.

Except for Lazard.

I had met Dave Dillard socially a few times in Greenwich, and he was a general partner at Lazard, New York. He had worked with Continental's leadership from time to time. When he checked out my CV and heard about my exit, he volunteered that Smart and his leadership talent had never impressed him, so had not been surprised at Jimmy Goldsmith's shot at the group. Dave quickly grasped the notion that, given appropriate management and capital capacity, there was value to be built in ACCI and opportunity for a profitable turnaround, even a potential for growth. A creative breakfast discussion at Lazard's Rockefeller Center office was set up. As the resulting conversation concluded, and I moved to catch Metro North back to Greenwich, he promised to show the document to Felix Rohatyn, Lazard's renowned New York chairman.

Back in Greenwich just over an hour later, as I checked in to collect messages at the front desk of the little office on Arch Street, an urgent note to call Dave was waiting for me.

> "Thanks for the chat this morning, Dave. I've this moment got in to find your message that you wanted me to call—so what's up?"

> "Get right back on the train, Flemming! I unexpectedly got a chance to show Felix your paper right away, and after a quick read says he likes it." Dave continued after drawing on his cigarette (Dave would often pause when expressing ideas as they came to his very sharp mind). "As it happens, we have Gerry Schwartz of Onex Capital in Toronto coming in to see Felix early this afternoon, and he wants you to be here for a possible conversation with Gerry. Your ACCI idea

could be just the kind of project Onex is looking for right now. Schwartz is relatively new to the LBO game and wants to do something industrial, which he's never done before, something bigger than he's done before. And Felix likes the look of your resume, pal. If you get a train right away, you can be here in time to have a chat with me to prepare for a possible conversation with both Felix and Gerry. And they could get a chance to talk a bit about ACCI and also size you up. There's just a chance this could turn out to be good for us all. You better scramble!"

I was ushered into a small but elegant conference room next to Rohatyn's office the moment I arrived, a little out of breath from a brisk walk from Grand Central's uptown 47th Street exit. I was glad to have a moment alone to gird my loins. Before many minutes had gone by, Dave Dillard arrived to coach me on responding to the strategic questions he expected the two financiers to ask. He said he would try to handle the acquisition financing issues. Half an hour later Felix Rohatyn and Gerry Schwartz walked in for the chat, which turned out to be a lengthy discussion. Each of them was armed with a copy of my simplistic document. Rohatyn was all business, courteously deferential to Schwartz. Gerry greeted me with a winning smile. All three of them were acquainted with Sam Belzberg, and Felix knew Bill Woodside, so they all knew about the aborted deal. ACCI's potential, as described in my paper, seemed real to them. Gerry appeared keen to look at a first industrial LBO with some scale to it. Onex Capital was Canada's fledgling equivalent of KKR, with Schwartz its founder and a rising star in Toronto's financial and political communities, eager to show his paces. It was decided that Gerry, as a first step, would contact Bill Woodside, referring to my earlier conversation with him, and take it from there. Gerry invited me to come see him the next week in Toronto, irrespective of the outcome with Woodside.

"If this thing moves forward, I would like to chat with you about playing a role as our industrial consultant on this deal and leading the due diligence on operations and assets. And if it doesn't go anywhere, you could possibly help us with other industrial opportunities as our Onex man in New York. Would you be open to that?" he asked. "Onex' experience has been mostly limited to service businesses—media and advertising—no manufacturing stuff or consumer goods to speak of yet."

Gerald W. Schwartz was an engaging man with a quick sense of humor and ready smile. It was not surprising that Woodside and Gerry hit it off. Gerry had a winning charm and an eye for the unconventional. He quickly picked up on Bill Woodside's artsy long hair and laid-back style. American Can was apparently talking to several other Canadian investors, including a mini-conglomerate rooted in brick production and construction. The Onex group was, perhaps, especially welcome at American Can's office complex in sylvan Greenwich for Gerry's relationship with Lazard and Rohatyn himself. The fact that American Can was aware of my career in packaging did not do any harm either. Exploration and initial sparring quickly moved into negotiating mode. Due diligence soon proceeded at a pace. Negotiations to secure mezzanine and other financing were dramatically lubricated by the fact that Lazard offered to take a 15 percent equity stake in Newco in lieu of its normal fees, if the acquisition were made. That was a tremendous feather in Gerry's cap and a compliment to the business plan's logic and specific goals. The deal closed in early November 1984, just six months after my initial conversation with Dave Dillard, but only after hectic work on financing and a feverish due diligence exercise that took me from coast to coast across Canada. I enjoyed the process and my role in fleshing out the business plan to be implemented under a new and different management philosophy, deriving particular pride from my success in persuading Gerry to invite about twenty senior managers of the company to invest in Newco alongside the principals,

The Unacceptable Face

on identical terms. About fifteen of these key people invested at modest but varying levels, some with funds generated from second mortgages on their homes. It proved to be a winning formula. A very effective motivator.

Half way through this process I told Gerry that I would like to invest in Newco, albeit modestly, given my limited resources. This conversation happened while he and I were in the back of a car being driven to the airport in Richmond, VA, where we had been to see the head of Reynolds Metals, a major supplier of aluminum. His reaction took me by surprise as he turned to me, slapped me on the shoulder with one hand and grabbed my right hand and shook it demonstrably.

> "That's just fabulous, Flemming, that's the best news we've had since embarking on this deal. Just the best. The banks will love it."

While all this was happening, Continental Group was acquired by Kiewit Brothers of Omaha, Nebraska, in the biggest acquisition by a private US company on record at the time. Kiewit was a huge privately-owned civil engineering and construction enterprise sitting on mountains of cash. Their press releases told the world that they were seeking to invest in manufacturing and natural resources. While that was probably true, they had also understood that Continental's assets were seriously underperforming in terms of total return to its stockholders. Don Donahue was credited with finding the white knight to protect Continental from the evil marauder, Goldsmith. David Murdoch, the powerful Los Angeles financier and developer joined forces with Kiewit, taking a 20 percent position in the buyout, only to sell out again just over a year later. He did not want any part in Continental's continuing can business while the individual business units were sold off as going concerns. In fact, the men from Omaha did very well in the can business over the next ten years, as growth in its markets resumed. Kiewit's acquisition was heralded by Bruce Smart in his own press releases and letters to employees as a triumph *"because the Kiewit people are our kind of people.*" But a few months later, his pronouncements to the press changed markedly. In answer to a reporter's question about the affinity he felt for Kiewit, he said of their leaders, David H. Murdock and Walter Scott Jr.:

> "[They] all come from business cultures completely different than ours. None of them worked for large, publicly owned companies. They're much more entrepreneurial, much more numbers-orientated and deal orientated and less process and building orientated."

Bruce was fending off reported views that he was himself driven by process and organization, rather than strategy and growth in changing markets. Smart believed that organizational structure should provide the answer to changing circumstances. He went on to plead that there was nothing he could have done to prevent or preempt the takeover once Sir James had taken that first shot across his bow. (Greenwich Time 11/7/84)

So Smart was soon shown the door, along with much of CGI's top echelon as Kiewit's designated Don Sturm embarked upon a ten-year dismantling of Continental Group, but steadfastly optimizing performance in ongoing operations as he went. Kiewit, having paid Continental's shareholders an attractive premium, sold off the pieces, while deftly supervising the management of the enduring operations exactly as Jimmy Goldsmith, the alien "asset stripper" or "vulture capitalist" would have done. Kiewit's cumulative reward was colossal as they lowered costs, earned good profits from continuing operations and then took gains from the disposal of each business in turn. Rumor had it that they netted ten-billion pre-tax dollars over the decade it took, including the income from operations over the years. In 1985 dollar values this was big stuff. Their last asset sale was hardly material, but it was fascinating for some veterans of Continental: None other than Don Bainton paid an inflated price for the rights to the *Continental Can Company* name. He also overpaid for the company's boardroom table, a polished mahogany relic that allowed him to complete his fantasy. Donald J. Bainton had bought his way to his desired title as Chairman and Chief Executive of Continental Can Company, a name he bestowed on his two-bit assemblage of packaging-related businesses.

As Kiewit sold divisions and segments of the packaging business, the most entrepreneurial of Continental's competent managers acquired a few of them and developed some of them brilliantly. Phil Silver and Greg Horrigan built a significant packaging empire over time, which was taken public on NASDAQ as a corporation named Silgan. (We were to cross paths again at a later date.) Many middle managers ended up with Crown Cork & Seal, which gradually became the leading global packaging company. Crown picked up pieces from several major players in the packaging field as they aborted or sold off, in country after country—some of them not having the appetite for heavy investment in technological change.

Ironically and despite his xenophobic handicap, Smart talked his way into a short stint as Assistant Secretary of Commerce for International Trade (one of multiple assistant secretaries ranked below Under Secretary of Commerce) in Reagan's administration before a precipitous and unexplained resignation (rumor had it that he was passed over for promotion), which led him to a new career in horse breeding in the equestrian farmland of Virginia. Bruce's 2019 obituary in the Wall Street Journal noted that he had been "felled" by a corporate take-over.

Bainton actually had some measure of success with his small collection of boutique packaging related businesses under a NYSE listing he wrestled from his brother's aerial surveying company. Somewhere along the way he settled a nasty insider trading case with the government.

~~~~

For less than a year, I served as Onex's oversight consultant on the board of the acquired American Can Canada company in Toronto, spending a couple of days a week in the Toronto offices or visiting plants and customers across the country. When the incumbent President and CEO of ACCI, a Brit named Barry Pocock was caught misusing company resources to address his struggling finances on a little farm he owned north of the city, I was assigned to terminate his position and send him on his way. I took his place as President and CEO under Gerry Schwartz's non-executive chairmanship, so the family and I moved to Toronto in the summer of 1985. With limited assets to my name, I had invested modestly in the acquisition, but then more than doubled that stake by buying the stock owned by Pocock (taking a mortgage on our new home in Toronto). Lazard Freres and American Can in Greenwich, each with their 15 percent equity stake, were represented on the board by Dave Dillard and Bill Woodside respectively, with the balance of the board drawn from Canadian financial services companies and sundry friends of Schwartz. Early progress was rapid and the company was renamed Onex Packaging before being taken public on the Toronto Stock Exchange in late 1986 via an Initial Public Offering underwritten by Dominion Securities.

From a family viewpoint, the timing of the move to Canada was miserable, since it was right after three of us had become naturalized American citizens; Niels had been born in Connecticut. Leaving the country to which we had just sworn allegiance was upsetting and especially confusing to the two boys. However, the five years in Toronto proved to be a rewarding experience. Living in the greenest part of Etobicoke hard by St. George's Golf Club, with good public schooling and excellent public transport, offered the preteen boys a happy and healthy life in a real world, far from coddled Greenwich's privileges and pretensions. They moved around the safe, clean metropolis with an independent ease almost unknown back home in urban USA. Toronto's cosmopolitan and eclectic cultures and community rewarded the family at every level, from youth hockey, access to sailing on Lake Ontario, an outstanding symphony orchestra, the famed Group of Seven Canadian painters, international gourmet cuisine and Rocky Mountain vacations.

Canada was in transition. A newly elected Prime Minister, Brian Mulroney, had taken over after the truncated tenure of John Turner. The mercurial Pierre Trudeau's second term had ended earlier in 1984, marking the curtain-fall on a Liberal-dominated era. Deserting his early socialist roots, Trudeau had, in the mid-60s, joined the Liberal Party, which he was soon to control from his Quebec stronghold, and he became Prime Minister in 1968. Trudeau claimed he believed in national unity and the merits of keeping the British Dominion of Canada intact as one country. He is credited with defeat of the separatist Quebecois. In international affairs he was a consistent proponent of NATO, but strangely unpredictable on other issues. For example, he claimed a solid friendship with Fidel Castro, declaring his admiration of the Cuban leader's vision and many of his controversial positions. Trudeau also established a formal relationship with China's leadership well before Nixon did the same for the USA. At home, however, he was finally held accountable for mismanaging the economy, excessive deficit spending and over-reaching for central federal powers and control of the western provinces and Canada's energy resources. As with other national leaders over time, Trudeau's charisma and the support of enthralled media had propelled him to international icon status, which proved vulnerable.

Brian Mulroney, on the other hand, had a good measure of success in leading the Progressive Conservative Party's fiscal and monetary reforms, putting Canada back on her economic feet while promoting successful free trade agreements with the United States and others. The Mulroney government was helped along the way by burgeoning exploration and development of oil, gas and mineral resources, particularly in the western provinces. The economy's turnaround was reflected in the value of the Canadian dollar during our four-year sojourn. Too often Canada's weird territorialism, however, got in the way of the country's enormous potential, and it interfered directly with the effective use of capital in both public and private sectors. Inter-provincial jealousies were embodied in provincial and federal legislation, which created totally artificial barriers to logical development, growth and the economies of scale on a national basis. There were even tariffs in the way of normal inter-provincial trade and commerce, which robbed the economy of the benefits of national scale—territorialism broke up the Canadian market into sub-competitive provincial markets.

Quebec's provincial economy was heavily endowed with, and dependent on, low cost hydro-electric power for domestic consumption and export to the USA. Consequently, the power-intensive aluminum industry was a major driver of Quebec's finances and policies, with huge investments made by Alcoa, Pechiney, Alcan and other aluminum producers and processors. The province wrote protectionist laws to shelter its key industries. For example, all beer and soft drink cans made or used in Quebec had to be made of aluminum rather than steel, the competitive option. This prohibited cost savings from scale and meant duplication of technological and equipment costs because in neighboring Ontario the exact opposite provincial intervention prevailed: To appease the steel workers' union and prop up the province's jobs and capital invested in the giant coal powered steel mills in Hamilton, all beverage cans had to be made of steel. Beer brewed in one province was not to be quaffed in another without a severe cross-border tariff applied. The result was that the national beer brands like Molson, Labatt and Carling were brewed on a sub-optimal scale in multiple small breweries located in each province, using packaging materials dictated by local union politics rather than logic and economics.

It got worse.

In the late 1980s, the town fathers of a bucolic Quebecois village a few miles in from the Ontario border decided that its sidewalks on Main Street were in shameful disrepair and needed replacement. Budget was allocated for smart new concrete replacement walkways, which were to be celebrated with a village street party. However, at the town budget meeting days before the party, a nitpicking Quebecois separatist discovered that the cement used in the concrete was imported from Ontario. The immediate calamity prompted an allocation of fresh new dollars, demolition of the offending new sidewalks, so rebuilt, identical walkways could use concrete mixed with Quebecois cement from a compliant plant in distant Montreal.

Canada is probably rivaled only by Belgium in the realm of fatuous territorial, religious and language bigotry, or perhaps South Africa in the 1970s, where you could add race and tribal considerations to the monstrous mix.

Both latent and overt anti-Americanism were occasional features of life, which some Canadians attribute to unwarranted feelings of inferiority. Our English and South African accents regularly tempted locals to assume it safe to spill venom and vitriol on their southern neighbors. And yet Canadian popular culture was firmly built on the north-south axes across the 49th parallel. The population of British Columbia related much more closely to the coastal Pacific states of the USA than to Canada as a country; the same applied to the Atlantic Provinces and the states of Maine, New Hampshire, Vermont and New York. Ontarians looked across The Freedom Bridge to Buffalo, NY, for their value-shopping and vacations. All this resulted in an uneasy Canadian search for national identity. Subliminal expression of distaste or fear of things American had unfortunate effects on the 27-million population of this decent, fair-minded, friendly and caring nation.

Family vacations were mostly spent south of the 49th, where we quite deliberately bought a vacation home in the Adirondack wilderness, on tranquil Blue Mountain Lake, which could be relatively easily reached from Toronto. The lakeside camp was surrounded by *Forever Wild* forest preserved under the auspices of the Adirondack Park Agency of New York and a conservation trust established by the Hochschild family of American Metals Climax or Amax fame. Harold Hochschild was a co-author of the legislation that underpinned the APA and the management of America's largest state park covering six million acres of forest lands, rivers and lakes. Pristine Blue Mountain Lake, with its many islands, is sparsely populated to this very day because so much of its shoreline is preserved, as are thousands of surrounding acres of state forest. The major objective of the purchase was to ensure that the family nurtured its roots in our newly adopted home country. It seemed crucial to remind the young boys regularly of their newly won US citizenship. Over the following decades the gorgeous property, christened *Calumet*, became a treasured all-season vacation refuge and reunion point for the extended family.

Blue Mountain itself, which reaches almost 4,000 feet, provides the gorgeous backdrop to any view looking north or east across the lake and islands dotted around it. Views to the south and west deliver the same islands and exquisite sunsets behind the smaller peak of Castle Rock and surrounding sylvan hills. The entire environment is an ever wild mix of coniferous and deciduous forest, which in the fall bursts into a kaleidoscopic explosion of flaming red, orange and golden hues, unmatched in the world.

~~~~

Slight of stature, Gerry's boyish Levantine features, big brown eyes and black curly hair made him look young for his age. He was quite brilliant, quietly spoken, charming and quick to flash an infectious smile. He dressed simply but was always meticulously elegant, presenting an understated self-confidence, behind which lurked an ego anxious for exposure and recognition. Gerry's sharp intellect was particularly evident in plotting deal strategy, conducting any negotiation and closing the deal. He and his wife Heather Reisman were active Liberals and prominent fundraisers for the Party while also giving generously (often Onex money) to fashionable charities and many Jewish causes. They worked hard to build their profile among the movers and shakers of Canada and loved rubbing shoulders with Toronto's not-so-old money couples. Over time, they acquired homes in Palm Beach, Malibu and Nantucket while holding endless soirees at home in their elegant Rosedale mansion—a niche just north of downtown Toronto where there was also plenty of real-old-money residing in gracious, but less ritzy, digs. The hot spots of Europe were not left out, Cap d'Antibes was a favorite. Gerald W. Schwartz was an easy guy to like in the early phases of the crucial relationship between the controlling shareholder of the company and its executive management, yet working with him became increasingly difficult for me personally as differences arose and tensions grew.

The determined young Schwartz, with roots in an unremarkable Jewish immigrant family in Winnipeg, grew up wanting to make it big. At one stage he had a summer job with the infamous Bernie Cornfeld's Investors Overseas Services, which collapsed in 1973. He soon worked his way to a top law degree from the local university and went on to Harvard's B-School. Diving into finance, he cut his teeth alongside Messrs. Kohlberg, Kravis and Roberts, in private equity at Bear Stearns in New York as LBO deals became ever more popular. After spending some time learning the LBO trade's intricacies, Gerry returned home to Winnipeg to join another entrepreneur, Izzy Asper, to form a private equity group known as CanWest Capital. From Saskatchewan, they made some less than earth-shattering acquisitions in media, advertising and retail before quarreling and a very public fallout. This was when Schwartz moved his shop to Toronto in the early 1980s, retaining control of a small, unsuccessful fertilizer company, Na-Churs Plant Food, and the Canadian small-town retailer McLeod Stedman as part of his settlement with Izzy. Neither of these two relatively small positions survived very long, but that did not stop Schwartz, who committed two million of his own dollars and a $50-million loan to launch Onex Capital, which over time became one of Canada's largest and most successful financial and industrial empires. He became one of the country's wealthiest men, described by Maclean's Magazine in 1999 as having "a strong sense of public service—real, not fake."

Onex Capital monitored the management of their first industrial baby closely through the financial reports. The objective was, of course, to build value by turning breakeven performance into profitability, restoring the asset base for future development and growth. The industrial realities of time lag incurred in generating acceptable returns on new and incremental capital investment were new to the controlling shareholder and his team. The importance of technology, engineering and maintenance were new to them. Onex Capital held control via a hefty block of multiple-vote shares, so the chairman could freely select his board and did so to meet his different needs. Representation of the lead investors' circle of associates and chums led to obvious appointments. Less obvious were the choices intended to lend gravitas and profile to this, his first public company—his biggest project yet, by far. He loved having Bill Woodside's name there: an American captain of industry, sometime economist and Chairman of New York's Whitney Museum of Modern Art. Jacques Drouin, the head of the prominent Laurentian Group in Quebec. A high-quality appointment, Gail Bennet, was added from her perch as a senior executive and director of Manufacturers Life Insurance. David Dillard's name added the panache of Lazard Freres. However, Gerry's henchmen and pals could not be left out. John Elder of Fraser & Beatty, Onex Corp.'s tamed external counsel was more active behind the scenes than he was as a director; Tony Melman, the extremely bright, adroit and innovative Vice President of Onex Capital was Gerry's useful lapdog. By far the most colorful director was Gerry Pencer, a blatantly suspect wheeler-dealer with an uncommonly checkered career. He was yet to reach his pinnacle of infamy when he joined the ACCI board. The result was an extraordinary amalgam of contrasting business experience, principles, standards and philosophies. The governance and oversight emanating from the boardroom over the years were to become inconsistent, not always reconcilable with best practices in a public company.

In rapid succession, Onex Capital proceeded to acquire AMR's (American Airlines') in-flight catering business, Sky Chefs, a courier company named Purolator, and Beatrice Foods Canada. Onex Capital made healthy rates of return before going public itself in an oversubscribed IPO. Gerald W. Schwartz was on his way, big time.

Schwartz in the early days was particularly anxious to be popular with the management of acquired companies. He saw to it that annual bonus awards generously reflected progress and good results, and he enjoyed marking success with personal gifts and elaborate events. In early 1986, Heather and Gerry gave an elegant dinner party at home in Rosedale for the top ten or so members of ACCI's management, with spouses included. A gold women's Rolex Oyster was placed on the napkin at each spouse's table setting to convey Gerry's personal message of *"Thanks to a true ACCI partner"* engraved on the back—a reference to the fact that every manager at the dinner was invested at some level in the company. However, the Rolex on Heather's napkin at the end of the table was a little different—it was a little bit bigger and had a ring of eight sizable diamonds sparkling on the rim around its elegant face. The Bay Street jeweler's bill for the ten plain watches plus the one diamond-enhanced time piece arrived at ACCI the following week.

The invoice from the caterer arrived, too. Our CFO, D'Arcy Bird, a diminutive Catholic copperhead with Celtic freckles, stormed into my office, puce in the face and about to choke. The aggregate cost of the thank you dinner, now charged back to those being thanked, was unreservedly outrageous. Once the two of us had calmed down, we eventually rejected various forms of protest. We decided we would let the matter be, pay the bills and tell nobody on our management team. It was a personal copout on my part, the shame of which has lingered on, but we were not yet a public company. Gerry had the freedom and voting power to do almost whatever he liked.

The business made rapid progress for a couple of years, both before and immediately after it was taken public on the Toronto Exchange later in 1986 and renamed Onex Packaging. Cutting excessive costs, improving working capital management and manufacturing productivity had been priorities from day one and had yielded good results very quickly. However, the technology and machinery employed in the burgeoning beverage can business were outdated and ill-maintained under the previous ownership, so it needed upgrading if the company were to survive and grow. As I personally had led the pre-acquisition evaluation of operations and physical plant, I could only blame myself for some underestimation of required capital spending. I should have put a more conservative value to it, even allowing for American Can's skillful window-dressing. American Can's two representatives on the board had some awkward moments, but for me it was a *mea maxima culpa* situation! The consequence was a heavier burden of capital expenditure than foreseen and incremental implementation costs.

This depressed the company's performance, leading to a very unsettling short-term operating loss, which precipitated a drop in the company's stock. Along with production equipment, many engineering and management skills had to be upgraded. Schwartz, Melman, Pencer and some of the other financial engineers on the board almost lost their nerve. Only Dillard, Woodside and his sidekick, John Polk from American Can, grasped that it would take time and a dip in profitability before the 100-million dollar Canadian capital spending program could yield a decent return. That's what it took to fix the company's manufacturing base and position it for longer term growth and development. Woodside and Polk had, of course, presided over the milking of cash from their Canadian business and the deliberate neglect of maintenance and technology upgrade. They were uncomfortably circumspect in their commentary, but there were no surprises for them! At no stage did they hint that they would seek to do anything but stick with their 15 percent stake in the company

Schwartz and Tony Melman, became extremely nervous and jumpy. They simply could not fathom the industrial dynamics and implications of upgrading technology, a neglected manufacturing base and plant management while continuing to satisfy the needs of customers, all world-class consumer goods companies in a highly competitive environment. As the problem was reflected in a sliding share price, they panicked and even persuaded the board to approve a 20 percent dividend increase in the face of depressed profits *in order to show confidence to public shareholders,* according to the board minutes written by John Elder, the tamed Onex lawyer. Gail Bennett from Manufacturer's Life was the only director to vote with me in opposition to the bogus dividend boost. My opposing vote sat very badly with Gerry, and the incident marked the beginning of escalating tensions, which would only tighten between management (particularly me) and the Onex Capital downtown office at Commerce Court West.

The existing beverage can equipment and technology, inherited from American Can Company, was derived from a continuing technology agreement and license from Daiwa Can Company of Japan. Management's corrective actions were not made easier by Japan being thousands of miles away and Daiwa's limited ability to communicate in English. Nor did it help that American Can sidestepped their contractual obligations to keep supporting the technology they sold to us. Onex Packaging was now out on a bit of a technological limb and had to scramble.

I was personally able to strike up a warm and productive relationship with Daiwa Can's authoritarian founder, chairman and controlling shareholder, Yamaguchisan. Trips to Tokyo led to amended technical agreements and an assistance protocol based on teams of Japanese technicians being assigned to our Canadian beverage can plants at our cost, but with Daiwa's license fees and royalties payable on a scale strictly based on production performance metrics. No quantified progress, no payments to Daiwa! In negotiating the terms, Daiwa's reputation in North America was a wonderful leverage factor. The possibility of Daiwa and Yamaguchisan *losing face* was introduced with good effect. Selective investments in equipment upgrades were to be paid for only upon achieving guaranteed performance.

The visits to Tokyo prompted memories of trips to Japan from Johannesburg with Ed Loughlin in the early 1970s. Little had changed in terms of Japanese business practice, although the players were quite different. Back in the 70s, the mission had been to secure steel supplies during a world shortage, and our dealings were with the huge trading houses representing Nippon Steel, Kawasaki and others—all enormous, highly structured organizations in which decision making was ponderous, sometimes excruciatingly slow. Privately owned Daiwa Can, on the other hand, despite its impressive dimensions and scope, was almost a one-man show, where Yamaguchi called all the shots, and implementation was instant, with draconian discipline. You still had to be on your toes to cut a square deal, but Japanese courtesy and hospitality remained constant, and this time they also stuck to their word from the get-go. Yamaguchi had built an impressive industrial empire thwarting bias and discrimination arising from his Korean immigrant background and in the face of strong competition from the even larger Toyo Seikan Company, which was pre-eminent in the Japanese market. In xenophobic, homogeneous Japan, a huge population of Korean immigrants confronted institutionalized prejudice against them. Yamaguchi was no exception. In contrast, Toyo Seikan's chairman, Yoshiro Takasaki from an old Japanese family, was an entrenched establishment insider with great political clout and connections. His daughter, Tatsuko, had married Prime Minister Miki's son, the urbane and charming American-educated Hiro Miki, who was in due course to succeed to the Toyo Seikan throne.

Daiwa had scores of factories, development laboratories and machinery-building plants throughout the country. Japanese consumer goods packaging was innovative and sophisticated, bringing new convenience and promotional features to the marketing of everything from carbonated beverages to canned coffee, from toothpaste to tuna fish, and from hair spray to marine paints. Every visit to this fascinating country was a welcome education. It was also a culinary adventure. Yamaguchi personally arranged exotic dinners in elegant, traditional settings attended by late twentieth century Geisha-type hostesses who looked after every need—almost—thus reminiscent of Tokyo trips from Johannesburg in the 70s. No detail was overlooked. An ample stock of canned Sapporo, Asahi and Kirin ("musta sahpport orrr our custoomah," our host explained) and 18-year-old Suntory or Nikka whisky. Ancient tradition requiring you to dine at a low table, seated cross-legged on the floor, was no longer *de rigueur*: the regular western table with its normal length legs was planted in a deep rectangular well, where western diners, sitting at floor level on cushions, could plant their feet and be spared the gymnastics of old.

"Mistah Whoolemming Heirrmann, pleess enchoy!" Yamaguchisan would plead as we took our places, "I lecommend you test evellissing we plesent for you—all dish *ichiban*, I plomiss. Theess fish velly goot for sushi and sashimi. Cow meat velly goot for your sukiyaki. Whisky better zan Canada Lye whisky! Ha-ha-ha! Suntory my favoolet whisky. Suntory goot custoomah, you know, also put Pepsi in Daiwa cans. Soon make beer too, I think. All beer custoomah here. Daiwa make cans for all kind-off *Nippon* beer."

Yamaguchi was referring to the fact that the giant distiller Suntory was in the process of negotiating exclusive rights to bottle or can Pepsi Cola's range of products in Japan, and had its eye on one of the leading domestic breweries, too.

The patriarch of Daiwa took a deep personal interest in Onex Packaging's problems, particularly where they might reflect on his company's technology or, worse still, its machinery and equipment. It was a matter of great pride that American Can Company and its Canadian subsidiary had taken licenses on Daiwa's technology and machinery. (Arch rival Toyo Seikan, despite its own technological strength, had been licensees of Continental Can.) Yamaguchi's personal oversight had a direct effect on the pace of progress in Canada. On December 13th, 1987, I was in his vast teak-paneled office, almost due to return to Toronto with the details of the new technology transfer agreement in place. All his meetings, including gatherings of his Board of Directors were held in this large room, which was dominated by an enormous old teak table, unusually elevated high above the floor on sturdy hand-carved legs grounded in clawed lions' feet. Twenty-four people could be seated around the table in richly upholstered chairs. The old scion, ensconced behind his regular desk by the window, was checking some minutia of the agreement when suddenly the room started to sway and everything in it was unexpectedly shaking. An immense bronze chandelier swung back and forth like a great pendulum. The traffic noise in the street below was hushed. The lights flickered as emergency generators kicked in to maintain the power supply. A mild earthquake at 6.3 on the Richter scale was occurring. And it continued to rumble causing tremors and shaking for minutes at a time in waves.

Yamaguchi raised his hand to reassure me, smiled knowingly and calmly indicated we had better take some precautions, which I assumed would involve moving to some secure space elsewhere in the building. But no! The old man simply said that it would be safer to be under the big old teak table than at his desk by the window. He ushered me politely to a crouch under the massive table top and told me to sit on the floor at one end, while he took his position at the other. Here we spent an hour or so wrapping up our discussion as a tea tray for each of us was placed elegantly on the floor, our heads bowed to avoid the table top above us. The earth's bowels seemed to settle just as midday arrived at the conclusion to our discussion. My host knew I was booked to fly home late that evening.

> "Whoolemmingsan!" my host said, "Tokyo now big mess! Evellissing velly soon stop. My chauffah take you to airloport now in my car. You wait for plane in airloport, before evellising stop there too and you miss airloplane for Tolonto. You see, erssqueke will make evellising stop. I will lite detail letter finishing goot talk and velly goot agleement for make good can in Canada. Now you must go, pliss my fliend."

So, after picking up my bag at the hotel, the long trip to Narita in Yamaguchi's huge black 1980 Chrysler Imperial was an exhibition in pragmatic Japanese public discipline. Police and other first responders appeared in hordes from nowhere to guide and control traffic disrupted by fallen telephone poles and displaced power lines. Here and there, walls had toppled into the streets and sidewalks. Drivers waited their turn to move forward and around obstacles in the road, abstaining from normal honking or other displays of impatience. Bricks, tiles, mortar or plaster spilled onto roadways; but the rubble was immediately cleared by laborers in orange vests and numbered helmets. They were assisted by citizens, who simply volunteered spontaneously and went to work as directed by officials.

The approaches to Narita's international terminal were heavily guarded at check points as cars and passengers were hustled on their way, allowed only to stop briefly to disgorge travelers and luggage. So insistent was the police hustling that in the rush, I forgot my beautiful old Dunhill pipe in the ashtray of Yamaguchi's Chrysler. At that very moment twenty years of addiction to tobacco was terminated. In the back of the car I had inhaled my very last drag of Mac Baren Scottish Blend. The immediate and most acute withdrawal symptoms were survived on a 15-hour JAL flight to Toronto, during which no smoking was permitted in any event. I was helped en route by a copious flow of scotch and wine administered by a delightfully flirtatious hostess. Two young sons and Judy saw to it that deprivation was extended into strict and lasting abstinence—from tobacco, that is.

Recapitalizing and modernizing the company's beverage can production was expensive and took time. Simultaneous restructuring of the overall manufacturing organization continued, so profits remained depressed into the second half of 1988. The gratifying early returns on the LBO could not be sustained while this was going on. The impatience, sometimes desperation, of Schwartz and Melman was never fully reflected in the boardroom discussions, thanks in part to the maturity of industrial veterans like Woodside, Polk and the experienced Dillard. Outside the board Gerry started demanding detailed reports on productivity, headcount numbers, quality control data and many of the other performance measurements, on which we had always relied as everyday management tools. However, in the hands of the financiers—industrial neophytes—it only prompted myriad questions, which gobbled management's time. Tensions tightened, especially in direct communications between me and Melman, who became Gerry's messenger.

Boardroom practices were not entirely conventional. Gerry Pencer, for example, was blatantly abusing his access to confidential, insider information. By 1988, he was CEO and the controlling shareholder of a beverage canning and bottling business named Cotts, (one of our customers) in obvious conflict with his directorship in Onex Packaging—and Onex

Capital). When pricing and contractual matters pertaining to Pepsi, our biggest customer, were discussed, Pencer would take details of the pricing and volumes, only to rush out during the meeting to transmit the information to his own small company, where his buyer would use the information against us in our can supply dealings with Cotts. Schwartz's feelings for me were not helped by my personal boardroom challenges on a number of issues, including an up-front $350,000 "investment" in a corporate box in the new Sky Dome stadium under construction in Toronto, with an annual $35,000 fee commitment to follow. Neither did he like my questioning of his direct orders to the manager of our Baie d'Urfe plant in Quebec to register a phantom job for his daughter's fiancé from Eastern Europe in order to lubricate his landed immigrant application. I also opposed a $600,000 reserve requested by Gerry for a second corporate name change—an attempt to distance Onex Capital's name from our current problems. The second name change actually never happened, but my vocal objections lingered long in Schwartz's mind.

> "Don't be such a precious little prick," Gerry warned. "It's not a perfect world, and we don't all have to be saints, Flemming. I happen to control this company!"

On another occasion, I was called to his office and reprimanded for something critical I had said about Gerry's spending of shareholders' funds, inappropriately within earshot of his chauffeur. For once, I had a measure of sympathy with his point, but kept that to myself.

> "Gerry, I didn't say anything I wouldn't say to you directly— and I have regularly expressed myself much more critically to your face. You know I don't pull my punches on that sort of issue!"

"Just don't let me ever again hear that sort of shit from you indirectly, from a third party," said Gerry angrily as he swiveled away from me on his desk chair, signaling my dismissal.

Gerry Pencer at age 42, going on 70, was bad news. His appearance did little to alleviate the repulsive aura about him. He was a fat, swarthy little man with an expansive shiny pate and a full, unkempt black beard, as if to compensate. His beady black eyes peered through dark oversized rims of pseudo-cerebral horn-rimmed spectacles; his tight shiny suits were far too small, middle button permanently straining at limit over his ample belly. According to a 1973-1976 Quebec Commission of Enquiry into Organized Crime, cited by Toronto's Financial Post, he was *kind of a lynch pin among Montreal criminals. He acted as the money mover for the mob,"* the Commission said, *"hiding the proceeds of crime and putting them in legitimate businesses.*

~~~~

A history of Pencer's career in the *Financial Post*, September 1988, said his early career in bubble gum vending machines and low-end Montreal restaurants had him associating with another money-mover for organized crime back in the early 1970s. The man in question, William Obront, was serving a 30-year sentence in the USA for trafficking in narcotics at the time of the article. In 1978, Pencer settled a one-million dollar civil fraud suit with Calgary meat packer Burns Foods for $600,000—no pittance in those days. He later got involved in car dealerships, real estate development in different parts of Canada and then a brokerage known as Walwyn Inc., a base from which he proceeded to build a financial services conglomerate. By 1988, Pencer was chairman and CEO of high profile Financial Trustco, financed with two-billion dollars Canadian of investors' and depositors' money, which was then suddenly *thrust into outside hands* for a relatively low selling price. The *Financial Post* went on to comment that:

The suddenness of the corporate manoeuvre reaffirmed to many in the trust industry the tenuous position of the financial services holding company and its 45 percent controlling shareholder Pencer," [who] has long occasioned a sense of skepticism in some circles of the financial community].

Sandy Fife of *The Financial Times of Canada* expressed his views like this on September 12th:

Why Gerald Pencer cut his flagship adrift

Financial Trustco faced a potential run on deposits in the wake of allegations against its founder.

Financial Trust's affairs have been under close scrutiny by Ontario trust regulators and federal deposit- insurance officials. A source close to Financial Trustco says that under Pencer the trust company was improperly involved in non-arms-length transactions."

Fife went on to say that *"a newspaper story alleging past Pencer dealings with the Montreal underworld was about to be published. The story would surely have led to a run on Financial Trust by depositors. And its other high profile business—investment dealer Walwyn Inc.—is also likely to be sold. A Financial Trustco insider says regulators found 'a lot' of self-dealing on the trust's books, in violation of the spirit of the law."*

~~~~

By innuendo, the media fueled speculation as to the true value of Financial Trustco at the very time it was being sold. Its recent losses might just have been worse than its financial reports claimed. The value of Pencer's crumbling empire was propped up by its holding in Onex Capital's subsidiary, Sky Chefs. Pencer remained on Onex Capital's executive committee and board of directors and, to my chagrin, the board of Onex Packaging. This became the subject of escalating chatter among senior Canadian business leaders. Pencer's hasty retreat caused him to reconnect with his family's beverage canning and bottling business, Cott Corp., and somehow took it over in short order. He stayed at the helm of Cott for some years, taking it through another roller coaster of startling growth, precipitous losses, a public offering and, along the way, some "aggressive accounting" (as described by Forbes magazine in a snip headed "From sizzle to fizzle")— and eventually, Cott's demise.

Pencer died prematurely of a brain tumor in the early 90s. Memories of his early history had faded, and the family received a measure of public acceptance, even admiration, for significant philanthropy heavily orientated towards research into ailments of the brain. Yet for many, Gerald Pencer remained an unpleasant, if not universally unacceptable, face of capitalism.

The two Gerries went back a long way. Cash flows thicker than water! That was presumably the basis for Schwartz's extraordinary loyalty to Pencer, which surprised many people on Bay Street. In late 1989, the magazine *Canadian Business* quoted Schwartz's views on loyalty in the context of press reports about his friend's (Pencer's) reputation for self-dealing and aggressive accounting:

> *I don't think it's appropriate of me to abandon Gerry Pencer when he's having troubles. He was a good shareholder and he's a good friend. One thing I've learned in politics is that loyalty is a starting point. If you don't have loyalty, which is a two-way street, you don't have anything.*

In 1987, the Schwartz-Melman panic escalated seriously. Provided with copies of all our internal management reports and metrics beyond their comprehension, Melman buzzed around like a fly trapped in a bottle, seeking one-on-one "consultations" with staff, and even ex-managers fired for incompetence or neglect. One of these disgruntled ex-managers, from whom Melman was covertly seeking "background information," eventually got hold of a shareholder register, which he later used to communicate directly with stockholders. He was protesting his termination and accused Onex of mismanaging shareholder funds at both holding company and operating company levels.

Gerry ordered that outside consultants be secretly hired behind my back. Management only became aware of them as these well rewarded parasites from New York had to be briefed, learning first about the industry and then the business, through endless, time-gobbling Q & A sessions. The distraction was enormous. The management team had been greatly strengthened, particularly in the manufacturing operations now headed by a smooth-talking but hard-nosed Dutchman, Andries Mellema. He was a bright and well-educated opportunist who brought excellent communications and modern disciplines to plant management and the factory floor. Mellema had developed a template of turnaround actions he had applied to the restructuring and streamlining of manufacturing operations elsewhere. He was the man for the moment. D'Arcy Bird, who was little more than an experienced cost accountant, serving as CFO, was now underpinned by a very bright young treasurer, Ray Seabrook, recruited from Coopers & Lybrand, quarterbacked the corporate finance function and improved the focus of prioritized operating reports. Much later, he went on to become treasurer and then global COO of America's Ball Corporation.

Two consultants, both McKinsey dropouts, who called themselves *Management Practice LLC,* were hired by Commerce Court and then fired after eight weeks at significant cost to our shareholders. After a very disruptive month of teaching them our business, it took two weeks for them to produce a seven-page paper written in consulto-babble, entitled "Findings." All it did for us was to illuminate their total ineptitude.

Communications with Schwartz almost ground to a halt as Melman's information requirements inundated our Rexdale offices. Gerry Schwartz did, however, make odd visits to Rexdale at lunchtime to check out how we spent our lunch breaks.

Late in 1987 Frank Connor, unemployed ex-president and COO of American Can in Connecticut, was brought in by Gerry to "advise" me and then report to Commerce Court on management actions. He had become redundant as Gerry Tsai took over American Can from Bill Woodside, renamed it Primerica and converted it into a company focused primarily on the embryonic on-line retail businesses and financial services. Almost certainly Bill had something to do with Frank's recruitment—after all, they had been joined at the hip at American Can and were both now looking for a job, something at rarified altitude in any industry that would hire them. For his pains, Connor immediately received the first installment of a healthy retainer plus 200,000 share options, which rewarded him undeservedly within a year for reasons totally unconnected with his "advice." Management's methodical, carefully executed plans from 1987 kicked in quite dramatically early in 1988, delivering nicely increased profits and renewed growth, sending the depressed share price soaring.

By this time, Schwartz was quite besotted with Bill Woodside, the long-haired, hippy-tinged economist, and had given him the chairmanship of Onex's Sky Chefs company. This did not sit well with Sky Chefs' CEO, who shared his frustration with me, but what could he do? It was a private company.

Primerica's packaging business was sold to relatively new players in the LBO game, Nelson Peltz and Peter May of Triangle Industries, (later named Trian of activist fame). They had just bought control of National Can, ranked among the top five of America's consumer packaging companies. These two nimble private equity investors had come out of nowhere during the junk-bond-driven LBO boom of the 1980s. They had worked with the notorious Michael Milken of Drexel Burnham along the way. Sitting now at the pinnacle of the packaging industry, atop the merged American National Can Company, they took over Woodside's and Polk's seats on the Onex Packaging board, having inherited American Can's 15 percent equity stake in the company. The change had little impact on the business. As soon as it was announced, I had rushed all the way to Beverly Hills to meet Peltz and

May for an urgent breakfast meeting, as I wanted to give my own account of Onex Packaging's condition and progress; I also had concerns that American Can's already weakened technical support, to which we were entitled, would be further weakened or even cut off by the new owners. On the flight back from LAX to Toronto I bumped into Gerry and Heather returning, well-tanned, from a Pacific beach vacation. Gerry wanted to know what the hell I was "doing in California while the company was collapsing?" He winced as I told him.

At his first board meeting, Nelson Peltz from behind his aviator-shaped spectacles flashed a big horsey smile as he proclaimed Triangle's new-found, undying commitment to the consumer goods packaging industry and our prosperous future together.

> "We're industry people at heart, you should all know, we
> don't invest just to flip companies. We invest for the long
> haul, to improve and build our companies."

Peltz was ever anxious to counter media depictions, their accusations of opportunism and short-term orientation among "LBO artists." He was prone to describing himself, his partner Peter May, and Triangle or Trian as serious industrial investors. Not everyone could swallow that message. Connie Bruck, in her riveting commentary on this LBO and junk bond era, "The Predators' Ball," cites one of her advisors for the book:

> *Nelson Peltz is floating Nelson Peltz the industrialist—In your book,*
> *you call him 'Nelson the industrialist' and it makes us all vomit.*

The advisor had said Peltz was a sham, self-proclaimed industrialist, and her description of Peltz and May as industrialists simply made him and his colleagues scoff at her. Bruck also wrote that Felix Rohatyn decried the creation of such highly leveraged empires as being achieved "with mirrors."

In the fall of 1987, when it was already clear to management that the turnaround was taking hold and financial performance was about to surge, Schwartz and Melman did not believe us. They were still in panic mode and failed to comprehend the emerging evidence. In late summer, I had personally made a declared insider purchase of a block of Onex Packaging stock on the Toronto Exchange, making a meaningful investment given my personal net worth, at a price of about four or five dollars, just above the share's lowest ebb. The financial press noted it, but Commerce Court had no comment.

In January of 1988, my old colleagues at Continental Can, Phil Silver and Greg Horrigan, who were successfully building their Silgan packaging enterprise via piece-by-piece acquisitions and Greg's very competent management of operations, quietly approached Gerry Schwartz to make a bid for Onex Packaging. They had been introduced by an extraordinarily well-informed packaging industry analyst, Art Stupay, of Bear Stearns. Not surprisingly, Gerry was quite keen to talk, but immediately swore them to secrecy with regard to communicating their interest to me. As related by Phil years later, several positive conversations took place, so he and Greg had felt very confident that they were about to make a deal. However, in mid-February, Gerry suddenly decided to bring me into a pivotal meeting with them. Gerry described it as a "fish-or-cut-bait" session at Onex Capital's offices. With no apology and without giving me much of a briefing, Gerry said he wanted to hear my view on whatever they might offer and their rationale behind it. So, feeling some strong emotions, with juices flowing, I arrived in Gerry's office at the appointed time.

As they arrived, Phil and Greg were quite evidently surprised to see me included, but we immediately exchanged the warmest of greetings as old friends. I had always felt a particular kinship with Greg back in Continental Can days. My old colleagues presented an impudent lowball proposition involving some cash, preferred convertible paper and a mix of debt anchored to a current share price of five dollars, for immediate control plus future options to take Onex right out. Phil was the financial talent and Greg the operating professional; and both were very good at what they did. As old hands in the industry, they had obviously understood the nature and depth of our manufacturing restructuring and the technology conversions undertaken; but they had no way of knowing how firmly the turnaround had taken hold. Without comment or warning signal of any sort, Gerry turned to me the moment Phil concluded his pitch and asked me what we should do.

"Well, what do you think, Flemming? Should we be taking this thing any further with your old pals? Do we really have something to talk about here, or should we just pass?"

I was stunned by Gerry's sudden appetite for my opinion after so many months of overt skepticism and vocal criticism. But there was, of course, absolutely no doubt in my mind. Not for a moment.

"Good grief, Gerry! Much as I love and admire my old friends, I can't believe what I'm hearing—they simply cannot be serious! This proposal is a lowball joke, if not a bloody insult!" I said as I turned to the visitors. "And Phil, you of course, know it! I can't believe what you guys are saying. Seriously, you wouldn't really expect me to buy into this, would you? You both know what it takes to go through a major solder to welding conversion and a capital-intensive upgrade into two-piece can technology. Greg, you were right in the middle of Continental's struggles in the USA under Don Bainton just a few years ago. I'm sure Silgan is tackling exactly the same sort of situation in some of your newly acquired properties, which have been similarly starved of capital and milked for cash. You have lived through the burden of heavy capital expenditures and their associated short-term losses. We've been at it for almost two years now, so we're at last on the brink of reaping some real reward for our dollars and efforts. Back to decent returns, good growth and a sharp hike in our stock price. But maybe Gerry and Tony haven't conveyed any of that to you."

It was never clear what Gerry was expecting of me, but he very deftly picked up the conversation before I could get another word in edgeways. Oozing charm, as Gerry certainly could, he reminded the Silgan boys that they had been invited to Toronto to put forward their "best effort and last offer," a final show of good faith. He said he indeed had confidence in an imminent share-price recovery and in the future health of Onex Packaging (words I had not heard from him or Melman for a long, long time). Gerry swiftly announced his conclusion that this discussion would not go anywhere useful, so it was time to say thank you and call it a day.

Twenty years later, when Judy and I had a glass of wine with Phil, Greg and their brides back home in Connecticut, I saluted their stellar achievements with Silgan, and we reminisced over bygone days in the can and plastic container businesses. Apparently, Phil had forever been puzzled by Schwartz's abrupt change of demeanor and his termination of their talks with Onex.

"What on earth happened, Flemming, at that last meeting in Toronto? Greg and I flew in quite positive we had a deal with Gerry in the palms of our hands. We really thought it was in the bag, and you personally had welcomed the chance to cash out. Rumor had it that you were having problems with Schwartz and Melman. But when you joined the party and said what you said, Gerry all of a sudden went stone cold and sent us packing."

"I never got to know all the details, guys," I countered. "But I don't think Gerry or Tony ever grasped the industrial dynamics of the cap-ex program we undertook and its short term operating implications. I knew nothing of your earlier talks with Onex—I think you guys were aware of that. I guess I could have saved everybody a lot of time, had I been given the chance to say what I finally did in your presence. We were Gerry's very first foray into manufacturing, and both he and Melman got spooked by the capex and the time lag in getting a return. I'm sure he didn't have real faith in me—until the numbers started to come through so strongly. Nothing new to you guys, of course. In his time of near panic, I'm sure he welcomed the chance to talk to you about an exit. When we met, it was the first I heard about your cheeky lowball offer to steal the business from right under my nose, so you can't blame me for being a little unhappy. You'll recall I was pretty frank." Greg and Phil chuckled quite openly. "Another factor may have been that I had personally made a declared insider purchase of our stock a month or two earlier—Gerry must have noticed that, since it was in the papers. Who knows? Sorry, guys! You didn't get away with that one, but I'm sure you don't hold that against me today!"

"It takes a thief to catch a thief," Gregg laughed. "And you were, of course, right. A shame, though, because we could all have ended up on the same team!"

"But you were right, of course," interjected Phil. "You had made your declared stock purchase at well below our five-dollar mark, and you were taken out at nearly triple that when Onex and Ball took you private!"

We all laughed. In retrospect I could be tempted to speculate over the possibilities, had I become a part of Silgan at the time, as it has continued to flourish and grow. Greg and Phil were good men and extremely competent. They are excellent examples of how much good can be done with high-leverage acquisitions, given managers of integrity, who know what they are doing.

My CEO's eight-page report to the board on first quarter 1988 performance described the latest progress and results reflecting early signs of a solid turnaround; a competitive net earnings forecast was defined for the full year. In conclusion, the report stated that

> " … after 15 months of corrective actions taken by management under uncommonly difficult conditions, we are now starting to earn returns on our aggressive capital spending programs, albeit a little late."

In July the Globe & Mail's Kimberly Noble reported that

> "OPI [stock symbol for Onex Packaging Inc] is delivering profit increases that astonish investment analysts and exceeded even its own (announced) expectations. While first half sales grew a respectable 6% to $216-million, productivity improvements and ruthless cost-cutting finally paid off in profit of $10.1-million, 120% higher than prior year. Profit for the three months ended June 30th took an even more dramatic upturn to almost $7-million—more than triple what was reported in the year earlier period.

> Onex Packaging President Flemming Heilmann said the company is "finally beginning to reap the benefits of our capital improvement program, albeit it a little late.

> Analysts said this illustrates that the dramatic improvement was internal, not in the market place, where the packaging

industry is enjoying a comfortable but not spectacular summer—the season when most beer and soft drinks are consumed, when most crops are harvested and preserved, and the one that annually makes or breaks a can maker's fortune."

On October 18th, the *Globe & Mail*, in its business section's *Briefly* column (covering major company reports) headlined OPI's performance with one word: "Booming." It reported nine months earnings up 94 percent before an extraordinary gain from the sale of the plastics division to American National Can. Sales for the period were reported up by more than three percent at $344.5-million, headed for a projected $460-million for the full year.

Before and while all this was going on, the industry's jungle drums were beating out the news of OPI's imminent recovery across North America, and smoke signals reached Ball Corporation of Muncie, Indiana, or at least their top packaging executives based in Westminster, Colorado. They wanted to acquire this potential Canadian extension to Ball's growing international packaging business. By September, Ball's corporate leaders were in negotiations with Onex Capital while our own top people showed their highly professional packaging team around OPI's plants and assisted with their due diligence. A partnership with Ball and Onex would take OPI private again, delisting the stock from the Toronto exchange. Ball's CEO, Dick Ringoen, was a gregarious and affable engineer in charge of a whole team of mechanical engineers who ran their businesses with characteristic discipline. They were no-frills industrial managers, who constantly referred to their company's commitment to the long term and to integrity in all their doings. They worked hard as a tight-knit group, but they were also quick to put their feet up with Ringoen at the end of the day to review their findings over a healthy shot of bourbon—or two. For some time, I was included in these sessions with their top packaging executive Delmont Davis and their intended successor to my job, Bill Lincoln, another serious engineer. The idea of my joining Ball to help steer their ambitious international expansion from Westminster was floated, leading to my making briefing and information trips to Colorado and their corporate HQ in Muncie, Indiana.

The negotiations moved forward without major hitches, but I grew nervous about a concurrent avalanche of negative headline publicity on Pencer. I feared his historical closeness to Schwartz and his role on Onex Capital's board and executive committee could spook Ball, given the extensive media comments on his murky history and their current questioning of his Trustco and Walwyn situations. Gerry Pencer was not exactly their kind of guy, so I feared negotiations with Ball could be jeopardized. Despite OPI's well publicized turnaround, tensions between me, Schwartz and Melman were still as tight as a drum when I called Gerry (apparently with Tony on the speakerphone), and told him I felt that Pencer should be isolated from discussions with the Ball group. Particularly worrying was a planned weekend at the Boulders Resort in Arizona, where directors and top management of both companies, with spouses, were to assemble for mutual briefing sessions. The idea was to encourage *bonhomie* and pave the way to an early closing. Right or wrong, my position triggered an immediate outburst from Gerry Schwartz. He decided to ban Judy and me from the Boulders meeting and had Melman write me a letter, which was hand-delivered before the end of the day.

Dear Flemming,

This is a short note to confirm our conversation this morning.

Given the concerns that you have raised and the circumstances pertaining to the pending Ball/Onex transaction, on balance I consider that it would not be appropriate for you to attend the Conference at The Boulders.

Yours sincerely,

Tony

ARM:mpb

cc: Mr. Gerald W. Schwartz

Predictably, my isolation from the negotiations and details of the transaction became absolute, and the earlier indications that Ball had an interest in my joining them in the States died on the vine. Schwartz had probably poisoned that well. I prepared a draft press release from OPI announcing that after fully supporting the Ball transaction and the transition to Ball Corp.'s management, I would upon closing be selling my stock into the deal and would then be headed home to the USA with my family. Coincidently, a couple of weeks earlier, I had received a call from Warren Hayford in Chicago asking if I would help him with a due diligence exercise on a potential packaging business acquisition he was considering.

Right before the Ball deal was to close formally, a junior lawyer, whom I knew quite well from Fraser & Beatty, paid a surprise evening visit to our home. Charles Baker, having knocked on the front door, looked sheepish as he stood on the doorstep holding a large buff-colored envelope. It contained a brief but all-encompassing release document, the acknowledgment of which was sought via my signature. I glanced through it in a matter of 90 seconds. The release would have me forfeit and forego any and every right, claim or complaint I might ever have against Gerald W. Schwartz, any of his companies or associates past, present or future, forever and ever. Poor Charles, a decent and impeccably mannered Canadian alumnus of Cambridge University, was left on the doorstep in chilly autumnal dark while I quickly skipped inside to make a photocopy of the document before handing it back to him—unsigned, of course.

> "For heaven's sake, Charles, you know me better than that! You know I wouldn't sign that thing in a month of Sundays. You and I didn't need Tort lectures in the Old Schools (13th century home of the law school at Cambridge University) to fathom what's going on here. It's quite obvious why they want a release, isn't it? I suppose they're scared I might turn nasty once this deal is done and everybody has been paid

out—or maybe Gerry still fears that I am too much of a 'boy scout' or 'pious prick' for his own safety? Oh dear, oh dear, oh me!" I paused for effect. "Now that I've made that clear, would you like to come in for a drink, Charles? You look frozen."

The invitation was sheepishly declined.

"You know, Charles, this makes me think I should get my own lawyer to make sure I don't get screwed as we proceed to close out this thing. It's getting potentially messy. Meanwhile, you know what you can tell Schwartz and John Elder to do with their shitty little release paper. Yes, Charles, right up!" Another pause. "But I'm sorry you had to go through this embarrassment. No hard feelings between us two! You, of course, know the details and background to all this, and I know that you personally had no option but to do as you're told. Just tell'em I said, 'nice try, but not tonight, Josephine'!"

I patted Baker on the back as he turned and went on his way, bidding me good night, large buff-colored envelope again in hand.

Charles actually did very well as a result of the Ball Corp deal, as he was soon stateside, hired by the Ball people and eventually became their general counsel and corporate secretary. When I asked him many years later to fill in some gaps in my understanding of the details behind this episode, he declined.

"Well, Flemming, I'm a lawyer, and you should know that lawyers tend to suffer an occupational amnesia problem. I'm afraid I can't discuss any details of that whole Fraser & Beatty relationship with Onex and what transpired with Ball. I also had some difficult personal issues with my firm at the time. Even though it's ancient history now, I can't go there!"

The shareholders' meeting authorizing the Ball/Onex transaction was completed without major hiccups, despite multiple stockholders' complaints that the $11.50 price was not high enough. The disgruntled ex-manager who had obtained the shareholder register stood up to comment sarcastically on "Gerald W. Schwartz's reputation for making gold out of everything he touches," before he proceeded to say that Onex Capital had turned "this gem of a company into a lump of coal." He caused nary a ripple, except for a some giggles among a few shareholders in the crowd. Otherwise, it was a carefully scripted process during which the outgoing President and CEO of Onex Packaging was in fact scripted right out of the proceedings. I did vote by hand to endorse the deal as CEO. A small posse of reporters, who had gathered around me after the proceedings to ask of my personal plans, caused some anxious glances in my direction from Tony Melman. In fact, the media simply quoted me and confirmed my press release.

> *Heilmann says he plans to return home to Connecticut with his family after his four-year stint at the helm of OPI in Toronto. He may or may not give his attention to the packaging industry, which he considers 'a happy hunting ground for an industrial guy like me.'*

~~~~

The family set about preparing for the move home, but not without misgivings. The Canadian adventure had been a good one, for the boys in particular, and many wonderful Canadians had become equally wonderful friends, young and old. Toronto had offered extraordinary opportunities, which were happily enjoyed. Inevitably, the young boys' ice hockey had become a cornerstone of family life, a new tradition, which was transported home to Connecticut and led to constant travel to all corners of New England and well beyond.

Canada's natural beauty is vast, often dramatic, varied and stunning, yet not quite as diverse as that of the USA, constrained as it is by the climate of far northern latitudes and more limited exposure to solar light and dry heat. Yet, scenic Canada gives extraordinary moments of enchantment and breath-catching excitement. Living in Toronto gave easy access to the crowded but still lovely wooded Muskoka Lakes, to which thousands upon thousands of Torontonians flock every summer Friday, starting at noon, for their prerequisite weekends at "the cottage." Treasured summer days of boating, water sports and tending meticulously to window boxes on their lakefront boathouses, one cottage-dweller outdoing the next in competitive lakeshore horticulture. Canadians—if you put ice hockey aside—are not born to be the most competitive of nations; but on the ice rink and when it comes to boathouse window boxes, look out!

Also within reasonable reach of Toronto are spectacular destinations like Lake Huron's Georgian Bay or the Algonquin Park. No coffee table photo book will ever quite capture their ever-changing ruggedness, colors, light and scenic dimensions as do the magical work of Canada's *Group of Seven* painters. The original members were born between the late 1870s and 1890s, and the Group's most important work, in styles somewhat reminiscent of the Post Impressionists, was done over a period of fifteen years starting in 1920. Had Cezanne or van Gogh been Canucks, they might well have been members. Ironically, the greatest single influence on the *Group of Seven* was Tom Thompson, who died before the group was officially formed or named—drowning mysteriously in Canoe Lake in his beloved Algonquin region. Lawren Harris, one of the Seven, wrote that Thompson was "a part of the movement before we put a label on it." The Rockies and western regions are not represented in the group's work; but their collective genius encapsulates the astounding nature of Ontario and the eastern provinces. The shoreline of Lake Huron's Georgian Bay, where huge gnarled white pines lean eastward yielding to the prevailing wind, exposed roots clinging to rugged granite outcrops. Gorgeous forested wilderness of the Algonquin, where autumnal colors are luminous. Wild Atlantic landscapes of the Maritime Provinces. Fertile farmlands separating pristine villages of southern Quebec's Eastern Townships.

Trips to the glorious Canadian Rockies included the 1988 Calgary Winter Olympics, where Italy's Alberto Tomba, *La Bomba,* famously captured gold in both the slalom and giant slalom, along with the hearts of infatuated women across Canada and around the globe. They included Katerina Witt, the sexy, statuesque East German figure skater whom he courted in macho style in front of a million camera flashes. A summer exploration of these magical Rockies took the family from Calgary through the Banff wonderland, glacial ice fields, the Kamloops flatland and finally down to Vancouver. A highlight was Lake Louise, set like a smooth Cambridge blue gem beneath a rocky alpine backdrop, glowing turquoise as sunlight caught the glacial *rock flour* particles suspended in its deep, dead-calm waters. When the sun shone, Vancouver showed off its treasured vistas, which might compete with those of Cape Town, Hong Kong or Rio, with its captivating maritime mountain views of the city across the twinkling waters of Burrard Inlet, off the Strait of Georgia. Bright, glimmering days were sunlit rewards for enduring the region's prevalent blanket of misty moisture and persistent precipitation.

More than three thousand miles to the east, across the prairies, boundless wheat lands and forested lake-land wilderness of central Canada, the weathered maritime Atlantic Provinces, also etched fond memories. The stormy Atlantic coastline's brave little villages were home to one of the world's toughest fishing communities, forever battling the mighty ocean's pounding elements. On calm sunny days in summer, stretches of Newfoundland's shoreline seemed akin to the northern reaches of Sweden's rocky Baltic coast. The topography and charmingly variegated vistas of the Eastern Townships south of the St. Lawrence Seaway also projected a Nordic ambiance.

Canada's cities are at least as diverse as those of the United States. No urban contrast is starker than that of Montreal's mellow tradition, French folk lore and architecture on one hand, and landlocked Calgary's strutting oil-town architecture and western stampede culture on the other. Reflecting the north-south cultural axes across the 49th parallel, however, Vancouver and Seattle are partnered; Calgary with Denver; Toronto with Chicago; and the isolated villages of Nova Scotia with those of northern Maine. Only Montreal and Quebec City are uniquely differentiated in this respect— francophone gems unto themselves on that imposing St. Lawrence Seaway, the very lifeblood of so much of mid-America, Ontario and Canada's breadbasket provinces. Regrettably, we never experienced the tundra of the Northwestern Territories or the lonely wilderness of the Yukon. The unfathomable vastness and scenic dimensions of Canada are staggering.

~~~~

Before the ink had dried on the Onex/Ball deal, I found myself diving into a due diligence exercise to evaluate the present state and the development potential of Brockway Standard Inc. It was a subsidiary of Owens-Illinois, the world's top glass container company newly acquired by the private equity firm KKR. The LBO kings were hell bent on debt reduction via disposal of what were deemed to be non-strategic assets. Brockway Standard, which produced metal and plastic packaging, fell outside the core glass business and was for sale as a non-strategic corner of the business. A small group of industrial operators, led by Warren Hayford and another ex-Continental executive, Marvin Pomerantz, was being assembled to consider a leveraged acquisition of Brockway. Pomerantz and Hayford had been partners in building their own little empire in the corrugated board business, Gaylord Containers, incurring a ton of debt. Hayford had called me in Toronto to ask about my future plans, and said he was wondering whether I might be interested in looking at Brockway Standard, evaluating its potential. It was an intriguing invitation.

Newly taken private again, the Ball/Onex venture went well at the outset, but after a year or so, some real tension arose between the partners as the North American Free Trade Agreement, *NAFTA*, kicked in, and the removal of some trade barriers opened segments of the Canadian market to competition from south of the border. Prices came under pressure, market share was challenged by imports, and as stellar results started to slip, squabbles arose between the engineers running the business for the long term and the impatient balance sheet gymnasts seeking instant gratification. Onex again became frustrated in the absence of the high returns and equity growth expected from highly leveraged investments. The quarrel evolved into a showdown and a reportedly vitriolic divorce. Ball finally bought Schwartz out of a manufactured bankruptcy. Onex, however, had long since recouped their original investment, and then some. Schwartz had done well.

The 1984 LBO had literally rescued a business and did a lot of good for a lot of people, all sorts of stakeholders ranging from employees to customers, suppliers and local communities across Canada through more than a decade. A moribund company was extricated from terminal neglect as the previous owners siphoned off cash. It was turned around, albeit more painfully than planned, and new products and new jobs were brought to the Canadian marketplace. Despite early layoffs and two plant closings to ensure a competitive, viable cost base, hundreds of jobs were saved and many more new jobs created on an incremental basis. Any suggestion that Gerry Schwartz was a "vulture capitalist" or "asset stripper," in the lingo of the media and omniscient politicians, was inaccurate and grossly unfair. Many such politically motivated allegations at the time, north and south of the 49th parallel, were just that. In real life, of course, you can't expect to win 'em all; but this leveraged buy-out of ACCI in 1984, and most others undertaken by Onex Capital, had positive impacts on their related industries, consumers and stakeholders including the people employed.

Chapter VIII

Shipwreck Refloated

"You may not control all the events that happen to you,
but you can decide not to be reduced by them,"
-Maya Angelou

DECEMBER 1989 BROUGHT a fond farewell to Canada, the family's return home to life in America and fresh opportunity. It was the end of a turbulent decade in industry and finance characterized by fast-paced and sometimes outrageous deals and mergers, racy leveraged buyouts, abuse of shareholders' funds, corporate fraud, insider trading and gross over-reach in the junk bond business. Michael Milken embarked on his country club incarceration. Other headline-grabbing movers and shakers ranged from those convicted of fraud and insider trading, to self-enriching corporate larceny and executives living obscenely hedonistic lives off shareholders' funds. This was a decade of systematic and unacceptable abuse of capitalism, and once again there were too many of the individual abusers and perpetrators who got away with that.

On the other side of the equation there were hundreds, if not thousands of entrepreneurial investors, saviors and fixers of mismanaged companies and corporate giants on the brink of collapse, which averted catastrophe for hundreds of thousands of good employees and other stakeholders. The much-maligned leveraged buyout methodology for financing business acquisitions was often the salvation of otherwise moribund businesses. By the end of the decade the LBO technique had become a widely used tool of private equity in America and Europe. Some of these transactions, of course, did fail, usually because they were over-leveraged and vulnerable to cashflow crises, but they were certainly in the minority except in the eyes of anti-business reporters and politicians. Thousands of successful acquisitions and turnarounds received no attention from the media. Unwarranted misrepresentation and vilification of the high leverage financing technique escalated steadily and persistently, but only reached their peak much later, well after the Lehman crash. Barak Obama's 2012 re-election campaign against GOP candidate Mitt Romney labeled the latter a "vulture capitalist" par excellence, "asset stripper" and "Wall Street Fat Cat" who exploited the less privileged. Romney was but a greedy member of the "one per centers." Ironically, Obama's starting Treasury Secretary, Tim Geithner, ever at the President's side, was soon to leave public office to join Warburg Pincus's private equity operation described by Bloomberg News as a "deft practitioner in LBO acquisitions."

The turn of the decade saw tumultuous developments around the globe. It was the time of Czechoslovakia's Velvet Revolution; the Soviets made their exit from Afghanistan; the brutality of Tiananmen Square shocked the world; Blacks rioted in apartheid's South African townships causing 2,500 to die; Lech Walesa's Solidarity movement blossomed in the Lenin Shipyard of Gdansk; the Berlin Wall was torn down; the US Galileo spacecraft was launched; the Supreme Court ruled that the First Amendment of the Constitution protected the people's right to burn the national flag; the Exxon Valdez spilled 11,000,000 gallons of crude oil into Alaskan waters; Leona Helmsley was put in the slammer for her extensive tax fraud; Nintendo released Game Boy; Ayatollah Khomeini ordered his *fatwa* on Salman Rushdie for publishing *The Satanic Verses*; and the world saw the first episode of The Simpsons on TV.

The 1980s had seen entrepreneurial start-ups blossom and new enterprises grow to national and international dimensions, such as

Bloomberg, Microsoft, Starbucks, Apple and Cypress Semiconductor. American business leaders gave invaluable service to the nation in government roles, while some broke every existing boundary of global philanthropy for the benefit of countless millions of starving, sick and underprivileged people around the world—the dimensions of their joint philanthropy exceeded the GDP of whole nations. It was a fantastic decade of turmoil and innovation, of both negative and positive extremes.

If the business world had a 1980s Rogues Gallery as well as a Hall of Fame, there would have been plenty of candidates for them both to choose from. Some of the big names generated debate as to which of these two characterizations they should be assigned. Common decency and good judgement, titillated by constant media coverage, quite understandably placed people like Ivan Boesky, Michael Milken, Leona Helmsley, Ross Johnson, Victor Posner, Martin Siegel, Charles Keating and countless others amongst the rogues. Many, but not enough, of them ended as convicted felons. Some managed to abuse the system criminally and cheat investors without incarceration, legal penalty, shareholder redress or other serious consequences. All of the rogues cheated on the capitalist system. All of them broke the trust upon which any civilized society, sustainable civic order and organizational entity has to be built, the trust that is the *sine qua non* of every sustainable system of governance or civic order. It was not the democratic free market capitalist system that wrought havoc; it was those who broke trust and abused it at the expense of their fellow citizens.

Candidates for the 1980s business Hall of Fame would include people like Pete Peterson, Warren Buffett, Bill Gates, Lou Gerstner, Ted Forstmann, Michael Bloomberg and perhaps people such as John Mackey of Whole Foods, T. J. Rodgers of Cypress Semiconductor and Starbucks' Howard Schultz, either for what they fixed or what they started in the course of the decade. Bill Gates for his global positive impact in so many directions and lesser known James E. Burke would surely qualify for his record as corporate leader, reasserting and living up to the famous *Johnson & Johnson Credo* of integrity and good business conduct—not least for his decisive, transparent handling of the Tylenol crisis in 1982 (involving deaths from cyanide contamination of McNeil Laboratories' over-the-counter painkillers). Over time, they and their vast cohort have collectively done more good for humankind by generating sustainable economic enterprise and growth than any governmental stimulus program, federal policy or legislation ever devised. Their economic and philanthropic promotion of social progress at home and abroad was and still is massive, strategically focused and effective, making the efforts of many European countries, the UN and most NGOs look paltry and wasteful. However, these leaders and visionaries received much less ink than the cheaters and thieves because the media and their ill-informed audience prefer to focus on the sensational, the violent, the sexy and the repellent, rather than the events and forces for good.

~~~~

Before the family left Toronto, Warren Hayford invited me to meet him in Dallas along with Jack Stirrup, a highly intelligent, degreed ceramic engineer who had been a senior manufacturing and procurement executive with Owens-Illinois, or O-I. The meeting was called in order to plan a tour of Brockway Standard's plants and offices and to discuss the potential for individual participation if there was a sensible LBO project in sight.

Warren had been in discussion with Jack for some time before he knew I was leaving Canada. Much later it became apparent to me that Warren had indicated to Jack that if there were to be an acquisition and he elected to invest, he would be president of the new company. Jack could hardly be faulted then for assuming that this meant he would run the business.

At the Dallas meeting Warren evidently startled Jack by offering me the opportunity to invest and become Chairman and CEO, with Stirrup reporting to me as President in the role of COO. Jack, the ultimate gentleman, did no more than swallow hard and recover his composure. It was the first of a thousand instances of Warren's insensitive and often imperious way of doing things. Jack and I quickly grew to appreciate and trust each and, over time, learned that Warren could play word games when explaining away earlier pronouncements and contradictions. When cornered, he was a master at redefining the meaning of words he had previously uttered. Hayford's duplicity would mar what could and should have been an unusually harmonious partnership in Brockway Standard's ownership and management. The four principals were all industrialists, builders and more patient and conservative investors than the balance sheet gymnasts and asset flippers of the private equity world. Jack Stirrup was a major force in developing the successful business that Brockway became. He sported a neat Clark Gable mustache, stood about six-foot-three, played to a single-digit golf handicap and brought a keen intellect and pragmatism to operations management. Strong personal values and high standards completed Jack's personification of what is best in American industrial leadership. The two of us enjoyed an unreserved trust in each other, which underpinned an excellent partnership and a lasting friendship.

We took a tour of Brockway's nine plants spread across the Deep South, from Dallas to Homerville in Georgia's Okefenokee Blackwater Swamp, and one in Chicago. There were sales offices and customers to be checked out across the country while lawyers of Kirkland & Ellis and financial advisors at Bankers Trust put together the structure of the transaction. Due diligence was conducted by three of the four principals. Marvin Pomerantz was too busy running his own empire, which included the corrugated carton company Gaylord Container, of which Warren was a subordinate but active director, partner and had the title of COO.

Like American Can's business in Canada, Brockway had been neglected and starved of both capital and senior management attention, partly because it operated in low-growth, unsexy segments of the packaging industry and partly because it was not about glass—and only glass had the attention of O-I's top brass. Due diligence revealed dilapidated, underperforming plants, ill-maintained equipment, poor working capital management and some demotivated managers fast asleep at the switch. There were warehouses full of obsolete inventory buried in dust, but still valued at cost on the balance sheet.

We were looking at a shipwreck.

On the other hand, there were also some specialized products serving niche markets and a sound base of still loyal customers, some of them household names, who made no secret of welcoming the prospect of ownership change.

The acquisition was concluded smoothly with Bankers Trust playing a leading role for the controlling shareholders Pomerantz and Hayford, who took exactly equal 35 percent stakes, with Stirrup and Heilmann each holding about 15 percent of Newco, the latter as CEO and Jack as COO. The company was eventually listed as BWAY Corporation when it was taken public. Immediately after closing, I had little trouble persuading Hayford and Pomerantz to invite members of middle management to invest alongside us (repeating our Onex Packaging approach), which caused a negligible measure of dilution of the principals' position, but fired up the enthusiasm of people who would help us implement our strategic plan through effective day-to-day action at mid-management level. It was a wonderful motivator.

Management was refocused and with customers sensing positive change, Brockway Standard was in business with a new sense of urgency. Jack mainly addressed the manufacturing operations, the supply chain and inventory control, while my focus was on customers, working capital tied up in debtors accounts, communications, access to technology sources and motivation of management when not working with Warren on strategy and business development. The authoritarian in Hayford ensured clarity of purpose, to say the least, and that was positive; but his constant attempts at micromanagement, his obsession with experimental technologies and his habit of placing unqualified family members and chums in the business would, at times, jeopardize progress. In pursuing financial performance, Warren set clear and intelligent priorities, which were generally helpful to management. Jack and I had to ensure that our operational priorities were not derailed by his theoretical obsessions—sometimes garnered from articles in management magazines. Unlike his Continental Group situation back in the 70s, Warren was no longer constrained by corporate decorum, chains of command or competition for favor with the Board of Directors. Between them, Chairman Pomerantz and President Hayford also owned the Board of Gaylord Container, which was larger than Brockway and Warren's prime focus—for the time being.

The extraordinarily intelligent Warren J. Hayford never learned to curb his ambition and certain personal characteristics after losing out on the top job at Continental. When he left Connecticut in 1979, he immediately took on the job of President and COO of International Harvester, or IH, under its imperious chairman Archie McArdle. The company was in the process of recovering from a recent slump, thanks to the newly appointed McArdle's deep, far reaching cost reductions, but was soon in turmoil again with marketing problems at home and abroad. The UAW (United Autoworkers Union) had engaged in a vicious war with IH because the company demanded that employee benefits and compensation to be trimmed. The union went on strike for six months, which crippled cash flow and drained working capital. The assertive Hayford was almost immediately at loggerheads with his authoritarian boss, and neither of them lasted too long as International Harvester faltered. While at IH, he had brought in his old pal, Marvin Pomerantz from his Continental days, as an Executive Vice President and strategic consultant. By the end of 1982, all three of them were gone. Warren left with a lustrous golden handshake, the terms of which he had negotiated upon entry.

Pretty soon Hayford was back in his determined pursuit of a CEO role in a major, high profile American corporation. The O'Neil family, which controlled General Tire, had decided they should put a non-family member at the helm of their Akron based empire, so they chose Hayford to be their President and COO. This time, however, his appointment contract clearly required that he be made Chairman and CEO within two years. His first challenge was to restructure the highly diversified group, which involved the establishment of Gencorp as a holding company for its disparate business units—from automobile and tractor tires to film studios and broadcasting. History soon repeated itself with the outbreak of squabbles between the controlling shareholders and their Chairman and CEO-elect. Rumors had it that Warren was having "chemistry problems" with the O'Neil family. In 1983, within twenty-four hours of a scheduled Genco press release announcing a restructuring, Warren resigned. This time, the impressive dimensions of his termination were defined by his employment contract from the get-go.

Having become a veritable champion of lucrative corporate exits, Warren could now pursue his ambitions armed with an empowering personal capital base sans concern over continuing income stream. Warren J. Hayford was ready for further action in the leveraged investment environment of the day. Yet again, he partnered with Marvin Pomerantz, who had made a fortune, originally earned from the sale of his family's Des Moines paper bag and sack business to Continental in 1971. Pomerantz had stayed with Continental for five years after his sale to them and had befriended Hayford at that time. Together they had embarked on building Gaylord Container Corporation, a liner board and corrugated carton business in the "brown paper" industry sector. They did this by doing a series of rapid-fire acquisitions—a practice known as a "roll-up."

The softly spoken Pomerantz was an appealing caricature of a merchant hustler from Des Moines, Iowa. He was barely five-foot-four-inches, quite spherical, florid and usually perspiring, irrespective of ambient temperature. He had a shiny pate, an aquiline nose separating his poppy eyes, ever gregarious, courteous and ready with a warm smile for everybody he engaged. The buttons of his gray pinstriped jacket were constantly strained to the limit as they served protocol's purpose. His nickname at Brockway was immediately Mr. Michelin. Behind this cartoon figure hid a shrewd, sometimes aggressive investor, who was not afraid to engage intelligent risk. Marvin was top dog at Gaylord with a controlling interest and the chairmanship; Warren was President. Initially, they expanded rapidly in a burgeoning market and invested very aggressively in upgrading technology and environmental improvements in acquired mills. In the late 1980s, before these investments had a chance to yield a return, they suddenly found themselves in an industry-specific cyclical downturn, so typical of the whole paper industry (in contrast to less cyclical consumer packaging with its predicable cash flow). The corrugated board industry was plagued with over-capacity, high costs and terrible prices for their products. Some years after their Brockway acquisition, by the late 90s, Gaylord was actually bankrupt and only emerged from a dramatic restructuring to be acquired by Temple-Inland in 2001.

Marvin was a people-oriented operator. He understood Warren as few others did. For Marvin, the Brockway project afforded an opportunity to not only make a promising investment, but also to give Warren a chance to have his own baby to manage, nurture and grow. Brockway could be the vehicle for Warren to score, make waves, satisfy his ego and burnish his image. That was the background for the very personal deal Hayford and Pomerantz made between them without informing their new junior partners, Heilmann and Stirrup, who were eventually short changed. It also became clear at a later date that Marvin valued the opportunity to get Warren out of the way at Gaylord Container, where he was causing problems in relationships between the board and key senior managers.

The structural and financial strategies Warren defined for Brockway were intelligent and sound, and they succeeded because management had the people skills he lacked to implement and execute. It was an effective combination when he did not intervene directly in the day-to-day business. A dozen or so middle managers had invested alongside the principals, so there was little difficulty in defining shared objectives. The acquisition was highly leveraged, but the sources and level of risk had been minutely assessed. We had identified plenty of opportunities for debt reduction and to build equity, especially in managing working capital. It was very early on that I regretted not having made a bigger personal bet than I had. The first phase was all about adjusting physical, financial and human assets to fit the scale of the redefined business base for longer term growth. A couple of plants were closed and product segments selectively sold off as the workforce was reduced commensurately and working capital was quite dramatically reduced. Turnover of the trimmed asset base was accelerated via productivity improvements and sales growth. As a matter of management style, financial results were widely shared with middle management.

Brockway Standard was off to the races.

Motivated employees could hardly wait to see the operating accounts because they knew that improved performance would lead to improved wages, and some of them watched their own equity values leap as operating earnings strengthened and acquisition debt was reduced.

The Deep South was home to most of the original nine plants acquired. The Birmingham factory could not be saved because of its obsolete equipment, low-margin product line and a labor force rendered uncompetitive because of wage and benefit hikes conceded by a complacent corporate management at OI headquarters in Toledo, OH. They had simply rolled over and agreed to the United Steel Workers' demands for crippling wages and benefits. The USW actually dominated Birmingham's steel-based industries, so when we attempted to negotiate adjustments, trimming total labor costs to make the plant viable, the workers would not give an inch to the new owner. All but one of Brockway's other plants were non-union; they all became competitive and thus enjoyed healthy growth as part of the company in the years ahead.

As the steel industry hit hard times, Birmingham's industrial base eroded. US Steel's huge plant and other companies had become sadly uncompetitive, largely because of their labor costs. The population shrank dramatically year after year until the city's transformation was launched, at the very end of the century, by attracting financial, banking, and other service industries.

The Homerville plant was a different story. Deep in southern Georgia's swampland, not far from the Suwannee River, it was surrounded by endless thousands of acres of Loblolly and Southern White Pine plantation. In 1990, the town's population of 2,800 had a median income per household of

$17,500 a year. Brockway's role in this struggling rural economy provided about 500 jobs; the average annual income earned per employee was $30,000, which in turn generated an annual total of $15-million dollars in before-tax wages flowing into the town's economy and tax base. The plant housed some complex machinery and a specifically skilled workforce producing a wide range of packaging products, some of which were quite unique. Apart from industry staples like paint and coffee cans, battery cases or cans for WD-40, this remote Homerville plant produced a series of highly specialized ammunition boxes for US defense establishments and exported to other NATO countries like Germany, France and the UK. These heavy steel containers had to withstand drop tests, fully loaded, from 25 feet and then remain 100 percent water-tight when completely submerged—a business school example of "high-value-added, differentiated product." At the other extreme were the plant's commodity products made on old, neglected equipment, which provided the new ownership with attractive opportunities to improve engineering and maintenance practices, upgrade productivity, raise quality and expand sales. The Homerville business was to thrive and grow again. The new owners not only kept the town alive, it generated income growth and a higher standard of living in the Okefenokee Swamp. Brockway drained that swamp pretty well—more effectively than politicians claiming to be draining another swamp far, far north of the Okefenokee. This leveraged buyout was not the product of vulture capitalists in the perception of this once moribund community.

Homerville was a somnolent, deeply southern town. Time and social evolution do their work slowly here. The drab grayness of sleepy live oaks bedecked with Spanish moss somehow matched the community's sluggish acceptance of change. Ill-maintained homes and rusty car wrecks in junky backyards told of despondent sloth. Employment outside Brockway's plant and its directly dependent commerce was difficult to find in sub-par public education and healthcare. The town's deeply segregated demographics were reflected in the plant's employees. Almost exactly half were African American, a few American Indians and Latinos and the rest were White. In its culture, verbal expression and attitudes, the Caucasian segment of Homerville was reminiscent of apartheid's Boer population of rural South Africa or the "poor Whites" of the country's railroad system—in fact, disturbingly similar. But in the USA, the country's legislation and attitudes were steadily moving in the opposite direction, albeit too slowly. In the Brockway plant, however, the diverse workforce worked harmoniously, yes even cheerfully, in well trained production teams based on specific skills required, blind to ethnicity—some production line supervisors were black. Whether such convivial relations ever reached into their personal lives in neighborhoods around town was a different question. Homerville was not a progressive stronghold. All of society and local culture was built around deep-fried everything, barbecues, pulled pork, peanuts, bourbon and Miller Lite. One female supervisor from the plant grew subtropical fruit and even some grapes in her yard at home, inside a huge barbed wire cage. She explained that this structure was to

"keep them naaaitives out and stop'em thieeevin'!"

Yet, in the midst of this occasionally bilious setting, the Brockway plant was a catalyst for change and personal improvement, as its jobs were prized and offered opportunity. The plant was a ladder for upward mobility. The training provided by the business created opportunities for not only jobs, but also education, training along with enhanced living standards—for those who sought them, which was not everybody. It was disconcerting to see that some groups with low self-esteem, who had the most to gain, seemed to be the least motivated or interested in making use of the opportunities offered them. This reality was equally troubling in other locations, where Brockway plants were located in poor urban neighborhoods.

Another force, away from the Brockway plant, that glued the community together in rare unity of purpose and good fellowship was high school football. The game was the cornerstone of the region's social life and leisure priorities. Nearby Valdosta High, hard by the Florida border, had won more statewide high school championships than any other school in all of Georgia. The alumni, town hall, local businesses, players and players' parents from all walks of life, saw to it that the school's football department lacked absolutely nothing, was well financed to provide any and all desired equipment, uniforms, merchandise and transportation, not to mention coaching—all in support of revered Valdosta football teams year after year. The Valdosta football community was colorblind, more black than white, with no detectable prejudice, discrimination of any sort, while socializing as supporters of the team at games and social events or not. It was one united community 24/7.

The new Brockway Standard played a similar restorative role in even tinier Picayune, Mississippi, near New Orleans, thirty miles east of the Lake Pontchartrain causeway and bridge. Like Homerville, it was in a vast, flat and swampy softwood plantation area, where people's lives rarely broke the bounds and constraints of poverty. Outside the plantations, pulp mills and lumberyards, jobs were few and far between. The plant presented welcome opportunity and a path to progress for those who sought them. Again, the population's appetite for work or self-improvement was not overwhelming—undoubtedly a symptom of very poor education or total lack of it. Only about 250 jobs were offered by the plant, but they represented solid employment, good benefits and upward mobility. The plant provided training beyond the strictly vocational, such as reading, writing and basic math skills for jobs in dispatch, production control, and new quality measurement or inventory control jobs introduced by the new Brockway. For the more ambitious who grasped at opportunity, it was an attractive and socially beneficial alternative to the pulp mills, plantations, and the cotton picking or crop sharing of yore. Yet, too many showed stubborn disinterest, no eagerness to improve their lot in life, which tended to be funded by low wages for unskilled labor and food stamps. In seeking reasons for the social stagnation of these rural southern communities, one had to conclude that the most obvious cause was the lack of adequate public education and civic leadership.

The factory produced a variety of round tinplate cans for consumer products, but especially Folgers Coffee cans—by the tens of millions—for Procter & Gamble's giant coffee roasting facility in New Orleans, where most of their imported raw coffee was landed from Latin America.

Picayune was a tiny, poor village bereft of charm and romance, but next to its solitary gas station, right on the rail track, it did have a spectacular diner, "Abner's Place," in the traditional southern style. Locals and visitors from as far away as New Orleans would indulge in the very best of hedonistic southern fare—from morn 'til dark of night. Deep fried catfish or chicken, always striking that perfect combination of savory tender-moist with crunchy, crusty delight; pulled pork with mustard sauce or tomato-based sweet sauce and hushpuppies; deep-pit barbecued beef dishes derived from Cajun or Creole cuisine. Collard greens. Breakfast of imperative grits along with fried eggs, sausage and thickly-sliced bacon; corn bread or corn pones and biscuits. The Picayune diner's fare was the Sunbelt's ultimate challenge to Pfizer's famed Lipitor anti-cholesterol medicine.

Despite nearby New Orleans' respected colleges, its wealthy residential corner, its captivating Vieux Carre, and despite its African American and Creole cultures and cuisine, fabulous jazz and carousing 24/7 high-jinks, the city was for me an uncomfortable stopover on quarterly business trips. I chose to bypass the city tracts frequented by tourists. Massive civic corruption indulged or encouraged by a succession of mayors, chronic destitution, despair, moldy disrepair, and overt substance abuse along with its attendant crime, hovered at every turn if one took a step or two outside the privileged areas. It was worse than I had experienced in other troubled American cities. A welcome alternative to smart hotels in the French Quarter or downtown was a spartan but clean motel in Slidell on the eastern shore of Lake Pontchartrain, off Interstate 10. No contrived merrymaking, no glass bead necklaces or tourist traps here; unpretentious but quite comfortable, offering a pleasant terrace with a gorgeous view of the setting sun over the expansive lake. Creating a more equitable New Orleans was not my mission.

In larger urban areas like Chicago and Atlanta the revitalizing effect of Brockway's revival was far less obvious, affecting relatively small communities or neighborhoods. There is no doubt, however, that struggling plants in Dallas and Memphis would have died, along with the whole business, had they not been acquired as a turnaround investment opportunity. With new and focused owners, the otherwise moribund Brockway Standard was energetically nurtured back to health and then, through agile marketing and careful investment, to a healthy growth pattern. Steady organic growth was bolstered by selective, digestible acquisitions in niche markets across the country as the original acquisition debt was paid down. Constant rationalization of resources and investment in equipment upgrades rendered the company competitive. The business almost doubled its size by the time it was taken public after about five years. Net increase in jobs did not quite match the company's pace of growth in sales and earnings, but several hundreds of incremental jobs were created and thousands of workplaces saved (i.e., jobs that would have otherwise disappeared—lost to business closure).

One of Brockway's smaller but most entrepreneurial customers had built his business from scratch, starting with a schoolboy savings account. He could have been the subject of a good movie or novel. His story was that of the aspiring American; he believed his opportunities were boundless, provided he was alert to them and embraced them. Jerry Whitlock was born into poverty and raised by his single mom in Ft. Gibson, Oklahoma, near Muskogee, 50 miles east of Tulsa. He left school at sixteen to become a fireman because he reckoned the hose company's hours, although unpredictable, would afford him a lot of time to do other things on his ambitious agenda. By working hard and saving, Jerry, in his late teens, was a budding entrepreneur and small-scale real estate developer. His savings account at Ft. Gibson's local bank allowed him to borrow enough to buy an empty lot located centrally on the main drag. With single-story buildings on either side, Jerry built a double-storied one with his own hands, to house a retail site at street level and an apartment or office above. With the rental income banked, sustained frugality and energy, Jerry was able to finance a few more purchases and rebuilding projects to become the mover and shaker of Ft. Gibson. Meanwhile he had also worked hard at his favorite sports, cruising on Harley Davidsons, riding bareback bulls, and horses for competitive tie-down roping of steers from the saddle. Before he turned twenty, he had biked through more than forty-five states and had become a serial "All Round Rodeo Champion of Oklahoma State."

In nearby Muskogee, one of the giant paper companies suffering a down-cycle had decided to close their underutilized tissue conversion plant, so Jerry jumped in to buy it. The plant had produced a complex, multi-specification range of tissue products such as toilet paper, cosmetic tissues, all sorts of napkins and paper towels for many different customers. Before confirming his bid for the plant, Jerry rode his Harley over to Walmart's headquarters in Bentonville, Arkansas, a mere 100 miles away. There he talked his way into a huge multiyear contract to supply cheap toilet paper in bulk—just one single product, with one low-end specification and no variations at all, which meant that production costs could be cut to the bone. He would have no machine downtime for changeovers to different specifications, and his production capacity would be loaded at over 95 percent. He had calculated his breakeven point at 58 percent capacity usage. Jerry had aced the perfect deal with Walmart and did not have to give thought or attention to other customers or products. Before that contract terminated, Jerry could leverage his balance sheet to start up a contract beverage canning and bottling business, Whitlock Packaging Company. It became a prime supplier to blue chip customers like Pepsi, General Foods and Proctor & Gamble, bottling or canning only non-carbonated drinks from pure fruit juices to artificially colored belly-wash. At the end of his contact with Walmart, he sold off his inventory and paper processing machinery, so he could use the fully amortized building as a warehouse and distribution center for the new drinks business.

Jerry's education had been basic, at best, but he had other personal assets. He was intelligent, tall, with handsomely clean-cut features, a thick dark thatch and an athletic physique. He was all about having fun. His gregarious personality was matched by his open smile and the friendly mischief ever lurking in his Celtic blue eyes. He wore white shirts with bootlace ties or medallion pendants, nicely tailored cowboy jackets and tightly tapered black trousers on his long legs. Jerry's physical presence and native intelligence was only surpassed by his tireless can-do attitude and determination. He lived life to the full. Overcoming his limited Ft. Gibson education, he would suck in knowledge from any source and learn quickly from experience, from studying the media and listening intensely to anyone he perceived to be smart, knowledgeable or successful. Jerry would flirt with any and every attractive woman who crossed his path, with astonishing success. He could draw them as a magnet draws iron shavings off a toolroom floor. Having married and divorced at a very young age, he trawled any and every gathering for pretty women, enjoying endless hot affairs with an eclectic range, from local bimbos to mezzo-sopranos of touring opera companies, from starry TV anchors to brainy Rand Corporation analysts. Taking some time off from his energetic commitment to his businesses, Jerry rode one of his many Harleys on a solo trip through Iran and Turkey across the Caucasus range and into Soviet Asia, before turning north to traverse the Urals and finally reach Moscow. On another vacation, he rode through the length of Vietnam into Cambodia and Laos, seeking and finding hospitality in rural villages. Jerry Whitlock was a renaissance cowboy, agile entrepreneur and his talent for snaring beautiful women outshone even his mastery of bucking bulls and his ability to bring steers to ground. Unfortunately, over the years he developed some less healthy habits, ingesting all manner of stimulants and downers to excess. Just in time, he installed a capable successor and withdrew from operating management of his business; but he continues to contribute to the welfare of many communities across the country by employing many hundreds of people, paying his taxes and giving charitably. Jerry still underpins the finances of Ft. Gibson Hose Company and all manner of social services within fifty miles, especially those serving truly needy native American communities.

With Brockway headquartered a long way from home in Atlanta, I was left with spare evenings on my own, so I got involved in the local Danish community. This caused me to show up on the radar screen of the Danish Olympic Committee, which in 1993 was preparing for the '96 Games in Atlanta. They were looking for a US representative to protect and promote their interests as the host city planned and made decisions affecting the Danish team's conditions and circumstances for participation. At a later date, after I parted company with Brockway, this volunteer work introduced me to some of the darker aspects of the Olympic movement's practices and abuses. Very few non-profits are completely immune to organizational politics and self-serving agendas, but Atlanta's ACOG (Atlanta's Committee for the Olympic Games) was unprecedented in my experience of volunteer organizations. It was headed by a hustling, jumped up real estate developer, Billy Payne, who had also led the city's successful bid for the Games back in 1990. He consigned the Danish team's leadership and administrative group to windowless offices two stories below ground level in a downtown high-rise building. There was poor ventilation and no wireless communications capability, so the US representative for the Danes was sent in to fight the Danish cause. I went directly to Payne's office and told his secretary what was on my mind. Sitting in a waiting room outside his office when she announced me, I overheard him declare that Denmark was a "two-bit country" without athletic or political clout. He felt that he had to see me, but was quite sure that, whatever I was seeking, it would be no problem to "avoid changing any of our well laid plans and send the guy packing." It was clear that forceful persuasion was called for, so I walked straight through his office door.

"Mr. Payne, I heard every word you just said while I was out there." His rimless glasses almost fell off his face as his jaw dropped. "Depending on what you do for me now, every media representative in Atlanta, including your own CNN friends, and every paper up and down the East Coast, is going to get chapter and verse of this little episode, complete with quotes. ACOG's treatment of my TWO-BIT country's modest request will hit the wires nationally and certainly back in Denmark."

ACOG's CEO, William Payne, restored the Olympic spirit of fairness in a nanosecond. The Danish Olympic Committee was allocated commodious, sunlit space, high up on the 15th floor of the same building, with flawless communication facilities and an attractive view of Atlanta's green park areas. The Danish Olympians, drawn from a tiny population half the size of Georgia's, won eight medals at the Games, four of them gold. Denmark punched way above her weight in 1996.

Atlanta's Olympics were marred, through no fault of Billy Payne or ACOG, by the infamous "Olympic Bomber" incident in downtown Centennial Olympic Park, which was to serve as the town hall square of the Games. As crowds were assembling for a concert, official security guard Richard Jewell discovered a remote-controlled bomb placed outside a busy bar and immediately alerted the appropriate authorities so that people could be warned and the bomb neutralized or disarmed. However, the bomb exploded before the whole crowd could be dispersed, killing one man and injuring 111 others. Based on a flimsy lead and wild assumptions, the media enjoyed a feeding frenzy over the incident, as is their wont. They virtually accused Richard Jewell of being the perpetrator of the explosion, harassing him and his family at home and wherever they went for weeks. The authorities, however, were responsibly deliberate and measured in their response, so a few months later a terrorist, Eric Robert Rudolph, was arrested and found guilty of the murder. As an activist, he had been seeking to have the Games disrupted for the anti-abortion cause. Meanwhile, Jewell's life, and that of his family, had been destroyed, and yet the media simply went on their merry way unscathed. In fact, the TV network only benefited from a freakish peak in viewership and, of course, nice ratings.

Billy Payne's Olympics were seen by the IOC as "over-commer-cialized," but they were financially sound, and his new concept of corporate sponsorship of the Olympics became a template for future organizers. Thanks to excellent management, in 1984, Peter Ueberroth was the first Olympic organizer to finance the games almost entirely from private funds. His Los Angeles games were widely applauded as the most successful ever held. He finished with a $250-million surplus—a substantial sum in those days—which was donated to public youth and athletic programs across the USA. Compared with Ueberroth, Billy Payne got a B+. Ten years later his peers among the good old boys of Georgia, selected Payne to be Chairman of Augusta National, where in 2012 Condoleezza Rice and Georgia financier Darla More were the first women to be invited, not only to watch the Masters from the club house, but to become actual members.

Warren Hayford's very effective role in all facets of corporate finance and strategic acquisitions was unquestionable. His effect on management's motivation and focus was less positive. Warren had a bullying element to his style because he was really a thinly disguised drill sergeant, albeit a very intelligent one. I spent far too much time acting as a buffer between him and senior managers and restraining his nepotistic instincts, which inevitably caused consternation among senior staff in the company, especially when family members performed sub-optimally. His obsession with selected, unproven technical developments would absorb management time and cost a fortune as they failed to produce results or were aborted. Brockway was a small, relatively low-tech company generally producing commodity products for customers who sought quality, reliability and service rather than cutting edge innovations. If those customers needed expensive research or ground-breaking inventions, they would go to the big boys of the industry, like Ball or Crown Cork & Seal. The imperious Hayford did not want to trust the standard operating reports, so he would demand new information and even placed moles in the accounting function to obtain it. He even parachuted his seriously underqualified son, David, in as CFO; but that was after I had retired.

The business grew, organically and by acquisition, to a point where an exit strategy could be contemplated. A key element was the private deal struck between Hayford and Pomerantz, allowing Hayford to keep his stock in Gaylord but forego his management role, while Pomerantz would stay out of Brockway's affairs, giving Warren free rein, and would sell his Brockway shares on the same terms as all other shareholders. Since the acquisition of Brockway, Marvin had served as a healthy constraint on Hayford and had, from time to time, indeed reined him in. But Warren now took the bit between his teeth. Meanwhile, Jack Stirrup and I still did not know about the deal that had been struck between our two controlling shareholders, or that Warren had acquired de facto control and was flying solo.

While this little Brockway saga was evolving, George H. W. Bush at his inauguration—perhaps thinking of Harold Macmillan's famous *"Winds of Change"* speech—spoke of a "new breeze blowing" through the world and "the totalitarian era passing." Tectonic geopolitical shifts initiated by Reagan actually came to fruition under Bush 41: The Berlin Wall crumbled under communism's failure, and the forces for freedom and individual responsibility, choice and open markets surged. The Soviet Union collapsed. Tyranny was a thing of the past, George H.W. Bush told us, now that we were moving into a better and truly democratic world. He made the shallow claim that the bullies of the world had been dealt with. In the real world, the West Germans immediately addressed the gigantic task of reunifying their nation and rehabilitating a devastated socialist East Germany. It was the turning point of West Germany's withdrawal from the very brink of economic disaster wrought by excessive social welfare expenditures and suicidal employment policies. Unified Germany, slowly but steadfastly, applied fiscal discipline and reforms across the social spectrum to permit the financing of the reunification and consolidation, the cost of which was crushing. The Germans, step by step, embarked upon the task of building their twenty-first century powerhouse, the savior of the European Union and, later, the Euro zone. The other former Soviet countries followed suit with the Poles and the Czechs leading the way. Soviet totalitarian rule beyond its Russian borders was terminated—to that extent, George H. W. Bush was right.

At Brockway Standard authoritarianism, alas, was not a thing of the past. It was alive and well.

Given Marvin's capitulation, the bully in Warren had been let loose, with all the power and control of voting rights in a private company. Whenever Warren was busy with acquisition projects, which he led very effectively, operating management could freely go about the business of improving the company's performance, reducing debt to normal gearing levels, growing the customer base and thus generating organic growth and healthy returns. Equity was rapidly building in the business, the book value of its stock rising commensurately. But on the other hand, whenever he was not engaged in an acquisition, Warren would fill his days in pursuit of his pet theories, seeking covert conversations with middle managers, some of whom were understandably scared to challenge him. Relevance was not always apparent. He would cause distractions, confusion and crossed wires, especially for Jack, the CFO Harry Payton and myself. As CEO, it fell upon me to shield operating management from the chairman's obsessions and interventions, as best I could.

At the end of a board meeting, over dinner at *Antoine's* in New Orleans' French Quarter, Warren abruptly launched into an obviously prepared monologue calling for a re-leveraging of the company. Acquisition debt had been effectively paid down, thanks to the disciplined efforts of management. All the directors including Marvin, the hired lawyer from Kirkland & Ellis and a couple of key managers provided a politely captive audience. Warren's thesis *du jour* was that operating performance is inevitably sharpened when managers have a heavy burden of debt hanging over them.

"We must talk to Bankers Trust," proclaimed Warren over dessert in good West Point form. "The balance sheet is in great shape to take on a bunch of new debt, which will give us ammunition for acquisitions and, more importantly, reimpose the pressure on operations to perform and keep management focused. I also want access to more cash." Warren exhaled. "But I know that the immediate benefit will come from you guys and the plants working with a sharpened sense of urgency. That will be the real payback!"

Utter silence fell upon the table. Even people at neighboring tables turned our way with enquiring expressions on their faces to see what had happened.

"What the hell are you saying, Warren? You really can't be serious," I spluttered in disbelief. "This team of ours has done one hell of a job paying down acquisition debt at a clip, with tough and disciplined management of costs, controlling inventory, creditors and payables. They've really goosed productivity, grown the top line and wrung margin improvements out of competitive prices—delivering great cash flow, a cleaned-up balance sheet—and now you want to take on unnecessary new debt in order to create a SHARPENED SENSE OF URGENCY? Good grief, Warren! That's just insulting and very unfair! I don't buy it!" I needed to snatch a breath or two before continuing. "When we have identified the next acquisition target and determined its scale, we can talk to any bank of your choosing about new financing. With our track record since 1990, the banks are falling all over Brockway Standard today, and our friends at Bankers Trust know that. There's tons of low hanging credit on offer out there to be plucked at will, whenever we might need it. Tell me what I have missed here? Please explain to me! I can see from Jack's face and Harry's that I'm not alone."

The rush of blood to my cheeks made me sweat, my chest was heaving and my hands trembling. Warren compressed his lips, as was his habit, exhaling again through flared nostrils like an excited stallion. Around the table spoons had dropped into bowls of ice cream and hot chocolate sauce, some of them falling onto the table, causing a few brown splotches on the pristine linen. For some time, not a word was said as the diners audibly gulped at wine or water. Jack and Brockway's very bright operations analyst, Rita Ferrazzano, looked aghast. Pomerantz said not a word, as he stared at the menu, contemplating augmentation of his ice cream desert with some additional Gallic delicacy. After a long silence, Warren again filled the airwaves. He dropped the debt issue, but delivered a cascade of pontification on an array of pet issues. Marvin the Michelin Man facilitated an end to the uncomfortable proceedings by simply rising to his full five foot four inches, leaving the table with a smile.

"That's all for now folks, thanks and good night!"

Next morning in the hotel lobby Warren greeted me, evident sarcasm lacing his icy white smile.

> "Well, Flemming, did you have a good rest? You certainly got a load off your chest at dinner with the guys last night. I would say that was quite an unburdening, quite a clear statement of yours. I am pleased to know of your thoughts, but I'd normally expect you to talk to me privately rather than publicly debate an issue like that. You somehow found last night's dinner to be a better forum."

> "You do have a point there," I confessed, "and that's exactly what I would normally do, and you know that, given our association since 1977. But, Warren, it was you, who chose the occasion to proclaim, out of the blue, your total reversal

on managing leverage in front of that particular group, including Rita and the local plant manager. That was YOUR choice of forum. You had plenty of opportunity all day yesterday, or in the board meeting, for example, to talk about refinancing, or to Jack and me with Marvin in the car on the way to or from Picayune. Warren, what's good for the goose is also good for the fucking gander!'"

For once there was no immediate comment from Warren, as we each went on our way with a perfunctory goodbye. No visible gauntlet was yet thrown, but a duel was certainly in the making. And Warren was better armed.

Of the several acquisitions made, Armstrong Can based in Chicago was the biggest, with multiple plants in the Midwest and California. It allowed an expanded Brockway to go national, which bolstered our position with countrywide customers. Jack Stirrup was masterful in rationalizing and integrating the acquired facilities; he was also deft at making the best of enlarged scale in managing our procurement and supply lines. The company grew, enlarging its established customer base with household names like General Foods, Clorox, Sherwin Williams, Behr Paints and Benjamin Moore. The value of the enterprise was escalating and preparatory steps were taken with potential underwriters for an IPO.

Hayford and I clashed more often, more directly and with growing intensity. In seeking some sort of solution, I asked Pomerantz for a private conversation. I thought he could help me explore some options for resolving the increasingly tense situation. I had no idea yet that he had abdicated his voting rights in the deal to get his old pal Warren out of his own Gaylord business. I had no way of knowing that the benefit of his normal businesslike approach and pragmatism in addressing Brockway's issues had been bargained away. In Marvin's 45th floor apartment in downtown Chicago, with a generous 18-year-old scotch in hand, I watched a brilliant sunset over distant O'Hare to the west, as jets sliced through the orange sky on their glide path to touchdown. When he sank heavily into his favorite armchair, similarly armed with his favorite tipple, I laid out my concerns to the kindly Michelin Man.

Marvin seemed sympathetic and nodded as I spoke, without letting on that he and his own Gaylord managers had gone through painfully similar problems with Warren. Angry conflicts had nearly cost them their able Irish CFO, who had been about to resign in the face of distractions caused by Hayford's frenetic interventions. Marvin's response was to express his opinion that Brockway Standard's limited dimensions cramped the very different styles of Hayford and me. He felt that it had worked for four years because Warren (while still active in Gaylord) had confined his role to Brockway's boardroom issues and acquisitions while Jack and I ran the business. Marvin went on to further comment:

> "Warren says that he is having difficulties communicating with you on key issues. This, he says, is getting in the way. He says it is causing misunderstandings between you, which could easily be avoided if you communicated properly and cooperated. He says he doesn't have the same problem with Jack Stirrup or the others." Marvin sipped at his drink. "Brockway is probably not big enough for the two of you. You're both pretty strong characters, and neither of you pull your punches. It's unfortunate for you that he outvotes you by so much."

There could be no misunderstanding Marvin's message. He knew I talked back at Warren and that his old partner had the upper hand with twice my number of votes plus Marvin's tacit but pledged backing.

> "You said he has problems with my communications?" I asked, and without waiting for an answer I continued "Marvin, you know that's total bullshit! I have communicated in four

different languages with people all over the world for fifty years. I've had problems and disagreements in the course of a career in umpteen different countries and cultures without the slightest problem in communicating—very easily and clearly! That has never been a challenge for me. I've never been anything less than an eager listener. Difficulties in communicating? That's wildly absurd. You know very well that Warren's own hearing is highly selective! The problem is that I am telling it like it is, speaking for all of Brockway's top management, when I object to some of his machinations, especially when he causes confusion or promotes the needs and wants of his personal and family aspirations. I am the insulation protecting management from Warren's dictates, and I dare say I am also taking positions in the best interest of shareholders other than Chairman Hayford."

This time Marvin took a deep draw on his scotch, looking out at the fading sunset before he turned to me with a manufactured smile.

"I hear you, Flemming. But I'm not sure I know how we deal with this thing. I'll do what I can, but you must recognize that a long and valued relationship, and some commitments made to my friend, do constrain me somewhat. They limit the options open to me. You and he are both strong characters and the problem, as I've already said, is that Brockway may not be a big enough space to accommodate both of you. From experience, I am pretty sure that given Warren's makeup, some sort of a division-of-labor deal between you two at the top would not work. He doesn't respect boundaries."

Another pull at the scotch as he again paused to revisit the sunset, while I waited for Marvin to finish his line of thought. But he didn't.

"Now, my friend, don't go and do anything rash," he advised. "Promise me to give it some time. A whole new situation will surely arise before too long if you all keep performing as you are. All sorts of options will open when we go public, sell or engineer some sort of exit within a year or so. Please, Flemming, may we just leave it at that for the moment?"

"Okay, Marvin, but I am only willing to soldier on if you can assure me you will personally stay invested for the duration, as a director and alongside Warren as controlling shareholders. You made that commitment going in, when Jack and I invested and made our own commitment to managing the business. I know Jack and the other top guys also feel this way. Apart from me, you are seen to be the only constraint on Hayford. As you now point out, you and Hayford have more votes than Jack and I have! That's very clear, but I've got to preserve and protect my stake and my exit, just as you do, Marvin. Like it or not, there's a responsibility to all shareholders, including smaller holders in management. If you were to sell and then take off before we are all free to do so, it would be a most unfortunate change of course, even a breach of faith. I would need to exercise my rights to do the same, quite publicly and on exactly the same terms as yours. Whether it's an IPO or a sale. Isn't that the deal?"

"Yes, pardner!" he looked me in the eye and nodded, with just a suggestion of discomfort in his uncertain smile. "You got it!"

Now I knew that Marvin Pomerantz had copped out.

He was protecting his much bigger Gaylord investment while preserving his rewarding Brockway stake, under the new and different deal he had quietly struck with Warren.

The business continued to make good progress, and before the year was out Bear Sterns had been chosen by Warren to underwrite and advise Brockway in preparing for an IPO. Warren's day-to-day activity in the company's management accelerated as he tried to tighten his control. By devious means, he sought access to detailed plant level cost accounting information behind Jack's and the CFO's back. He placed a very obvious mole as a "financial management consultant," Perry Schwartz, ex-CFO of Heekin Can Company. Hayford announced that he was to advise on how to "modernize and strengthen financial controls and management practices." Perry was to report to CFO Harry Payton on paper, but he spoke a lot more to Warren over the phone than he ever talked to poor Harry in the next-door office. Warren started having private meetings with middle managers and even with Jack, who Warren probably found more pliable than me.

He summoned me to a series of *tête-à-tête* sessions at his Hobe Sound vacation home, in hotel suites, at Greenwich Country Club and airport conference rooms. He would issue his customary marching orders and then, prompted by notes, pick on "negative developments," or challenges faced in the business, within and outside of my control. By innuendo, he started to question my performance as CEO. He expressed displeasure over my resistance to some of his dictates.

"I want to make it clear, Flemming, that although you and I may not always agree on what's right or wrong for Brockway, shareholder votes are what count," said Warren at the

Helmsley Palace in New York. "The fact remains that I am
the guy who is BUYING in this situation, and you are the
one who is SELLING—I want to be very clear. You are the
guy who needs to please! That's just the way it is. So, I want
you to think hard about that. By the way, I understand you've
had conversations with Marvin on the side, but you should
know that it won't get you anywhere."

I could not have had it explained more clearly.

Meanwhile he continued very ably and professionally to quarterback
several acquisitions, which certainly complemented our organic growth. The
company forged ahead for a successful public offering; but before that came
to fruition, things came to a head between Hayford and me.

Hayford called me to another one-on-one meeting, this time in leafy
Winnetka, north of Chicago, where he lived in his commodious primary
residence, cheek by jowl with Midwestern captains of industry, prominent
lawyers, leaders of finance and commerce. He had set up a nearby mini-
headquarters for Brockway's holding company, BS Holdings Inc., which
served as his command post. The space was modest, just two offices and a
decent meeting room, staffed only by the 20-something Susan Hayford. She
was one of Warren's seven children, three of them or more, enjoyed
sheltered employment or consulting roles at Brockway over the years.

A big black shiny limo was at O'Hare to pick me up, and the reception
prepared for me in Winnetka oozed warmth and camaraderie. Soft spoken
pleasantries were conscientiously observed, coffee was served by Susan.
Compliments on management's performance and the progress of Brockway
Standard "here on the home straight and over the years" were expressed in
grateful terms. For a while all was sweetness and light. Quite suddenly,
however, Warren was on a script. I was to understand that it had become
clear to the "controlling shareholders," whom he also characterized as "the
owners," that I was apparently unwilling to "toe the line." I was seen as
unwilling to "accept the realities." It was clear to the "owners" that

Heilmann, as chief executive of the company, was not willing to "respond appropriately to majority shareholder direction." I could almost hear the voice of Bill Kirsch, the enlisted Kirkland & Ellis lawyer on our board.

> "Since your little chat with Marvin, he and I, as the owners, have revisited the question of how we play our respective roles. You and I have also talked about this more than enough, Flemming, and it has to be resolved. Marvin says Brockway Standard is too small to accommodate both of us." Warren paused, compressing his lips again to punctuate the point, and then exhaled through the flared nostrils. "Now, we have two ways of doing this thing. It can be very friendly and easily concluded in a really harmonious way to our mutual benefit and comfort, or it could become hostile and unnecessarily unpleasant—and the latter would probably also cost you some—rather than yield a very nice recognition of your role in building Brockway's success." Another slight pause for the compressing of lips before Warren reengaged me through his heavy horn-rimmed glasses. "So I'm asking you to resign, on your own terms, and provided the terms are reasonable, you can write your own ticket! Whatever you think is reasonable for the owners to consider. You'll obviously do as well as anybody, scoring very nicely alongside us in the IPO, as you certainly deserve."

Warren switched freely from the first person singular to a royal "We." He did not acknowledge that all my rights as a shareholder were *ab initio* protected anyway, under contract alongside all the original investors.

> "Should you, for any reason, want to sell your stock, I have to tell you that we cannot make exceptions here, as neither Brockway nor Bear Sterns would allow the current CEO to

sell and then head for the hills just as we go about pricing the
IPO. But of course, Flemming, you wouldn't want to sell at
book value before the IPO and miss out on our expected
premium, would you?"

He paused, and I wondered why he thought I could be stupid enough
to consider selling.

"Now take your time, my friend, use the conference room
next door, and the phone if you need it. Write your own
ticket, and let's talk about your ideas whenever you're ready.
Susan can get you anything else you need."

If there were options that made sense, I could not see any at that point.
I had no appetite at all for a fight that could end up destroying value. I had
successfully invested money, effort and five years in Brockway Standard, and
at this point in life I did not have significant concerns over the cosmetics of
the situation. I did not quite write my own ticket; but the ticket we agreed
upon was very reasonable and quite fair, given the realities I had to face.

Thus went the dissolution of yet another confrontational, yet ultimately
productive, relationship. Neither this nor any of the previous clashes with
Alex Page, Don Bainton, Bruce Smart or Gerry Schwartz had been totally
unavoidable. So I could ask myself whether these confrontations should
indeed have been averted—they could have been averted.

Many admirable and responsible men would have compromised,
choosing to embrace a more pliant stance. After all, in an imperfect world,
one can choose a route of compromise to avoid confrontation and conflict,
or to get things done and make progress without causing a fight. So why had
I not done so previously? Why not now? I could have drawn in my horns,
raised the white flag, conformed to Hayford's needs until the time was ripe—
quietly sitting it out until the imminent IPO was behind us, and then either
walk away or pick a very public fight, possibly armed with significantly

greater leverage. But I chose not to, out of self-respect and perhaps a bit of a stubborn streak in me. I thought that giving way to Warren would have been a copout. But who knows? Life is a constant flow of changing circumstances that offer an infinite choice of actions; yet choices have to be made. Second guessing past decisions is a mug's game, and history suggests that the particular options I chose along the way have been generally beneficial. They have not hurt me in the longer term, or the people dear to me.

You can't win 'em all!

Chapter IX

Disengagement is Never an Option

"To retire is to die"
-Pablo Casals

AS I DEPARTED Brockway and the IPO was successfully completed, I was busy as the American Representative of the Danish Olympic Committee in preparation for their stellar participation in the 1996 Olympic Games. There were also directorships and consulting work for various packaging businesses. Jerry Whitlock's contract packaging company, a cellophane producer called Flexel, and another packaging business called Wheaton Inc. were all fascinating situations involving every manner of business, social, family and ethical conundrums. A directorship in Porter Chadburn PLC, a public company in London, offered a welcome return to the British business arena and that city's singular appeal, which I had missed since the Metal Box days ended.

Wheaton Inc., a billion-dollar, 100 percent family-owned company was by far the most challenging boardroom scene. I had been recruited to the board, along with the CFO of a New Jersey pharmaceutical startup, by a head hunter engaged by an insurgent group of Wheaton family shareholders, who used their collective voting power to force the appointment of two outside, non-family directors for the first time in the company's history. The century-old business manufactured sophisticated glass and plastics vials, tubes and bottles, along with laboratory vessels and equipment. Until the 1980s, it had been very successful, profitable and highly regarded. Technological innovation was the genesis and driver of the business. The founder and his early successors had invented groundbreaking techniques for converting glass and plastic. In the early 90s two unfortunate characters, Messrs George Straubmuller and John Vegte, took control as Chairman and CEO respectively, both of them married to Wheaton heiresses who owned large blocks of shares. A combination of arrogant complacence, incompetence, nepotism and gross misuse of shareholders' (other family members') funds had plunged the company into a downward spiral of operating losses, excessive debt and unsustainable interest costs.

Healthy family-owned enterprises are a vital feature of America's free market capitalism underpinning the economy. Hundreds of thousands of small businesses and scores of our largest private companies employ endless millions and consistently contribute economic growth to fund the nation and its social services. They are just as important as public companies in generating enduring progress for the USA. Rarely does their relative freedom from regulation and scrutiny prompt private companies to behave unethically; but the leadership of Wheaton was certainly an ugly exception. Operating management was consistently distracted by family infighting, shareholder lawsuits, bankers and lenders pressing for redress, broken loan covenants and frequent IRS audits. Shareholders filed complaints over the personal junkets and free spending of Vegte and Straubmuller. These two executives even bungled the board-approved exit strategy (sale of the business). As the ship was sinking, they were simply too busy seeking personal gain at the expense other shareholders. As two outside directors, our responsibility was to protect the rights and asset values of all shareholders. Vegte's irregularities as a brazen *bon viveur* included trysts and racy vacations in Paris with a female associate employed by Wheaton's French subsidiary; Straubmuller's predilections were in the world of motor yachts and fancy ocean front real estate. The boardroom cross fire, as bankers and family members fought to protect their turf, was an ugly illustration of the unacceptable face of capitalism at work. Fortunately, the assets of the company, diminished and devalued as they were, ended up in more competent hands. The employees and other stakeholders were in a better place when the company was eventually sold and merged with better-managed entities. The sale generated some relief for some family shareholders, but many had already been forced to adjust lifestyles, trim expenditures and lower their sights in preparing for retirement. It is safe to say, however, that their fate would have been worse, had it not been for the constraints imposed on the two rogue executives by a board strengthened by outside directors. That was certainly the message that my independent colleague and I got as we bid the victimized family members farewell.

A more widely discussed and better-known private enterprise was that of Koch Industries and its affiliates led by two of four Koch brothers. It was the second largest private company in the United States and quite profitable. The Koch's and their company were and still are vilified by left-leaning media and politicians because they are active and outspoken libertarians on a very large scale. They are commonly labeled Republican extremists. In fact, they have massively financed PACs and campaigns promoting libertarian views, sometimes seriously at odds with the Republican Party line. The Koch's are, for example, pro same-sex marriage (one of the four brothers is gay) and have argued for progressive tax increases in combination with public spending cuts to get closer to a sustainable fiscal policy and a balanced budget. Not surprisingly Paul Krugman describes them as "evil doers," while Harry Reid from his Senate pulpit said they are "un-American" and have "no conscience." The biscuit probably goes to David Axelrod who categorized them as the political equivalent of "contract killers." Surprisingly, Daniel Schulman of leftist Mother Jones magazine was more balanced and much closer to the truth in writing about the extended Koch family. During Obama's reign the left were audibly rattled, not so much by the wealth of the Koch's, as by their ideas. Suddenly forgotten were the left wing's own equivalents, such as the secretive George Soros who was convicted by France's and Europe's highest courts for insider trading. Or Rob McKay of

Taco Bell fame, or Peter Lewis of Progressive Insurance, who match the libertarians in political use of money. However, they are no match for the Koch brothers' munificence in support of education, science, culture and art—and their massive financial support of dozens of institutions from MIT to Lincoln Center.

Private companies, large and small, are irreplaceable contributors to the welfare of our democracy.

~~~~

My personal business commitments were winding down, so more time was soon given to volunteer work, including a directorship on the board of a social service agency in the inner city of New York. The Jacob A. Riis Neighborhood Settlement House was to become a major preoccupation and a treasured lifetime experience of learning and discovery. It is located in the heart of Queensbridge Houses, America's largest public housing project in Long Island City, stretching north along the Queens side of the East River from the 59th Street Bridge (later named for Ed Koch).

In the mid-90s, the Danish Consul General in New York, Hans Grunnet, called one day to suggest that I check out the agency named for the famous Danish-born photojournalist and social reformer. Hans wanted an evaluation of its work and to see if he or I could be of help in some relevant way if the work of the agency lived up to its reputation and that of the Danish reformer. Riis Settlement's executive director, Bill Newlin, was an engaging personality, a singular leader and the driving force behind an exceptional organization. The agency's effective programs in support of the needy in western Queens were carefully targeted and always relevant to the true needs of its local citizens. It differed from the run-of-the-mill New York charitable organizations serving the poor because it was always focused on offering opportunity for self-improvement, rather than unconditional handouts, grants or subsidies. Its work was particularly effective because it was, and still is today, guided by the prioritized needs of its participants' pursuit of social and financial self-sufficiency.

The agency was founded in Manhattan's Lower East Side district in 1890s when the settlement house movement was imported from its English roots in London's East End. The adopted concept offered programs that would give poor people access to education, vocational training and trade skills, healthy and hygienic living habits, and the skills or knowledge necessary to become contributing citizens. The settlement house was located in an area adjacent to the infamous tenement house district near today's Chinatown and The Bowery, where Riis did his photo-journalistic work exposing the sordid living conditions and abusive exploitation of immigrants, who were streaming into New York. It was during those years that Jacob Riis drew the attention of Teddy Roosevelt, then Police commissioner for Manhattan, to the wretched situation in the tenement houses. The two men became lifelong friends, with Riis acting as Roosevelt's advisor on all his social reform initiatives. Roosevelt became known as America's "reform president."

After World War II, as returning GIs sought housing and jobs, the US government built the Queensbridge Houses to provide for their immediate needs; but within a few years as the war veterans reintegrated into American society and moved on, the housing project became home to tens of thousands of African Americans migrating from the southern states—many of them seeking to escape from the Jim Crow South and its persistent racism. By 1990, when Bill Newlin took over as executive director of the Jacob A. Riis Neighborhood Settlement, the population of Queensbridge was about 95 percent black, with a few Latino and a sprinkling of Asian immigrants, but hardly any Caucasians.

Bill Newlin's ancestors had moved north from the Sunbelt states to Harlem. His mother later moved to the Lower East side, where he himself became a product of the settlement house movement. Bill's early days as a participant at Henry Street Settlement set him on course to educate himself, eventually earning a master's degree in social science at Hunter College and embarking on a career in the City's education system. He then moved to New York's Equal Employment Opportunity Commission, where he worked for some years before taking on the leadership of the Jacob Riis Settlement in 1990. In the Queensbridge Houses, he was faced with a failing agency under threat of closure at the hands of the City because its prior leadership and board had allowed it to become a hub for drug dealers and pimps, rather than pursuing its intended mission. This was in the pre-Giuliani years of Mayors Koch and Dinkins, when New York City teetered on the brink of urban calamity, fiscal implosion, crime, gang warfare and filth in the streets. Bill's arrival was not welcomed by those who lived off the criminal activities surrounding Riis Settlement House. On several occasions he would find the tires of his parked car slashed, or its windows shattered. It was only as he personally connected with the mothers of the surrounding 15,000 population—of which single parent families were heavily predominant—that he could start turning the tide against violence, drug dealing and other crime in the housing project. The single moms soon saw that Riis Settlement, managed properly, could provide their children a path to progress and escape from the misery of poverty. This was the realization that persuaded the local residents, especially the single moms, to join forces with Bill and Riis Settlement to turn the community around. At the time of his assuming leadership in 1990, the agency's annual operating budget was $150,000, funded almost entirely by the public sector.

By 1996, when the Danish Consul General encouraged me to visit Bill Newlin, his budget had doubled to $300,000 and was still largely funded by public dollars from the federal government, the State of New York and the City. His early progress in turning the agency around had encouraged city authorities to increase support gradually as the number of programs and participants swelled. New York was beginning to reap the benefits of Rudi Giuliani's sometimes ruthless cleanup, and Queensbridge Houses responded with the enthusiastic encouragement of local citizens. Relative order, hygiene and safety returned to the streets; piled up garbage and filth on sidewalks was dealt with. Community street life tentatively emerged from the shadows of the project's six-story brown-brick apartment houses. Although no Republican voter was to be found within miles, residents of the Queensbridge Houses shouted the praises of Mayor Giuliani, who was freely credited with the turnaround of the Western Queens neighborhood. (One has to wish that his focus in later years had not run off the tracks). Riis Settlement was by then offering access to after-school academic assistance along with youth programs addressing substance abuse, health and hygiene, safe sex, vocational training, summer employment and, for the few, counseling on college education. Modest programs providing social interaction and some health services for isolated seniors in the neighborhood had started. The agency's reputation and support had also benefited from generosity of Danes and Danish Americans in the city, and the sincere interest shown in the Settlement's work by its new Patron, Her Royal Highness Princess Benedikte, sister of the Queen of Denmark.

By 2012, Riis Settlement's annual operating budget had grown to $3.3 million, of which 30 percent was now funded by private sector philanthropy. The agency's mission and programs to this day reflect Jacob Riis's personal philosophy and reformist ideas: He loathed self-pity and was critical of unconditional grants and handouts, which he saw as a root cause of persistent complacency and dependence on the generosity and efforts of others. His approach was to work for equality of access to the requisite knowledge and skills needed to become a contributing citizen. He toiled for the eradication of exploitation of the underprivileged by landlords of tenement houses occupied by endless thousands of immigrants in the nineteenth and early twentieth centuries. He wrote extensively, in journals, newspapers and revealing books, such as his acclaimed exposé "How the Other Half Lives."

At that point, in 2012, Riis Settlement was offering its programs on five different "campuses," of which two were sites in the housing projects of Queensbridge and Ravenswood and three more in western Queens public schools after hours. One third of the budget was now allocated to programs for immigrants arriving mainly from Latin America, but also growing numbers from sub-Saharan Africa, Asia and Eastern Europe. By this time immigrants accounted for 30 percent of the Western Queens population. English language, American citizenship, the legal system, financial literacy, job search and immigrants' rights were all components of these programs. The latter involved some practice of the *don't ask, don't tell* approach while dozens were guided through the legal naturalization process to productive citizenship. In the year 2013, no less than 40 immigrants were successfully naturalized. In all Riis Settlement programs, at every level, participants had to make demonstrable effort and show commitment in order to continue participating. No free rides were allowed. It was made quite clear that your shot at social progress and a better life came with assumption of responsibility for yourself as an individual and, indeed, for those around you.

Bill's presence anywhere, at any time, commanded attention. Tall and handsome, sharply turned out for any given occasion, with neatly trimmed salt-and-pepper hair and periodically sporting a closely trimmed beard, he exuded a personal charm, warmth, and humor, usually accompanied by a generous smile. With a self-effacing style that belied a steely determination, he would set realistic priorities and then focus his effort and finite resources on those foremost issues, attempting only what was possible. Always pragmatic, ever persuasive and sensitive to the personal needs and feelings of people around him, Bill had great human judgement and attracted the best of staff for each level of his talented organization. New sources of funding opened and grew as it was evident that the agency's resources were frugally managed and always laser-focused on the real needs of the evolving demographics of the community. This was guided by insightful representatives of the local community elected to the board (in my own experience as chair, I received invaluable, insightful guidance from them— sometimes privately outside board meetings). A constant emphasis was on academic education. Average high school graduation rates in the Queensbridge and Ravenswood projects and surrounding areas were an abysmal 48 percent, whereas Riis Settlement participants on average graduated at an 88 percent rate. Programs were promptly abolished if they became under-subscribed or obsolete. New programs were added with the guidance of participants, local board representatives and local residents in focus groups. Working with Bill was a tonic. We both saw how much we had to learn from each other, so a deep friendship developed, which for me became a treasured relationship. The friendship thrived well beyond our respective retirements from day-to-day involvement in the Jacob Riis organization. I stepped down as chair in 2012, and Bill as Executive Director a year or two later.

Work in the non-profit sector illuminated the unmatched generosity and philanthropy of productive Americans. Somehow the traditional American commitment to take individual responsibility translates into stunning generosity and concern for our society, not just among the affluent and reviled one-percenters, but throughout the productive population. Middle class giving by Americans who earn as little as $35- $50,000 far exceeds the per capita rate of any comparable society in the world, including those in relatively wealthy western European countries. Moreover, the US private sector's contribution to serving the needy (via registered charities) is a lot more efficient and cost-effective than most government departments and services at federal, state or local levels. The public sector's performance in the area of social services is poorly measured or evaluated, and too many programs tend to be wasteful if not corrupt.

In Connecticut, as just one example, a 2013 Hartford city project was intended to promote new commerce in support of revival in its downtown area. One grant made by the city was to sponsor a modest retail site for a startup letterpress print business and retail outlet. Three enterprising young women worked with diligence and energy, investing scarce working capital to build inventory to stock their shop, create marketing materials and a PR program as they prepared to open with a modest event involving the closing of their street on the date the city had promised availability of the space. However, it took so long for the city bureaucracy to figure out their own muddled paperwork, that the young entrepreneurs' startup business could not open for weeks after the agreed time and thus suffered commensurate losses—with wasted expenditures and premature commitment of scarce resources. Bureaucracy handicapped the enterprise before it could get out of the starting blocks. Only private support and generosity saved the business from being stillborn.

In New York City, Jacob Riis Settlement, in the aftermath of the 2008 financial crisis, was asked to accept help in the form of a federal government "stimulus package" worth some $75,000. The stated objective was to create two incremental full-time jobs and extend the agency's programs, which Bill Newlin gladly accepted. The next day, a delivery van arrived with a dozen boxes of official questionnaires and report-documents, which had to be completed by a tight deadline date. They represented weeks of work for the two temporary people who had to be hired for that short-term purpose only. The net result was no stimulus to the ongoing work or growth of the Riis Settlement, but it created short term make-work for two people who did nothing for economic growth. In the end, and in real terms, the stimulus package cost Riis Settlement more money than was granted, for no net gain at all. The two involved temporary employees were back in the job market when all the forms were completed—way past the deadline and to no avail. When a second round of "stimulus" was offered, it was firmly declined despite political threats from public administrators charged with implementing the policy.

By contrast, private sector non-profit organizations have difficulty raising funds if they cannot demonstrate compliance with strict standards of cost control and performance. For example, the Better Business Bureau will recognize only agencies that comply with best practices. With their official recognition, however, fund raising capacity can be materially enhanced.

A few years into the new millennium, the global Giving Pledge project, initiated by Bill and Melinda Gates, and then supported by Warren Buffet, had quickly enlisted 115 billionaires, mostly but not all American, to give or pledge at least half their fortune to charitable organizations and causes. By 2013, that added up to half of one trillion US dollars and counting. That was roughly equal to Belgium's gross domestic product. Those who pledge tend to set high standards for the productive use of their funds. They tend to be very focused on *ad hoc* funds, cost efficiently applied to their chosen causes, in a manner that public funds are rarely managed. The Giving Pledge project continues to grow internationally, as Europe's participation lags and Asia remains largely untapped—but America's productive billionaires keep joining at a clip. The Bill and Melinda Gates Foundation, in 2012 alone, made multiple contributions like those of $1.5 billion to GAVI for vaccination programs around the world and $1.5 billion to the United Negro College Fund for scholarships. Left wing bigotry was quick to attribute this philanthropy to the "guilt of the wealthy over increasing inequality of income."

The surge in inequality of income (which is of course a very grave and threatening issue) was in fact exacerbated by artificially low interest rates engineered by the federal government in a succession of *quantitative easing* programs, which failed to create jobs as intended. The manipulated near-zero interest rates favored investors and Wall Street, but were of no use whatsoever to those who had nothing to invest. The poor and the middle class didn't own stocks and were still looking for jobs after a succession of government stimulus packages. Stakeholders in the equity and other asset markets were given one super ride as the Fed fixed the price of risk near zero and drove stock prices to record levels while middle class wage earners and the poor stood still, at best. Nevertheless, inequality was put back at the top of Obama's second term agenda with QE II, QE III (three "Quantitative Easing" programs) and the Fed holding interest rates at near zero. Vilification of Wall Street, vulture capitalists, the one-percenters and other "beneficiaries of income inequality" were hallmarks of the 2012 re-election campaign.

My industrial career and two turnaround projects were rounded off by some rewarding years working with non-profit initiatives. Many lessons were learned, all sorts of misconceptions exposed, lots of conventional wisdom debunked, and mindsets adjusted by realities encountered. A host of enduring and treasured relationships were spawned. Cornerstone values evolved, with change and adjustment prompted by the realities experienced along the way.

Chapter X

Quod Erat Demonstrandum?

"Travel is fatal to prejudice, bigotry and narrow-mindedness, and many people need it sorely on these accounts. Broad, wholesome, charitable views of men and things cannot be acquired by vegetating in one little corner of the earth."
-Mark Twain

WHAT WAS REALLY learned in the course of this odyssey of over three quarters of a century? What did these adventures demonstrate— experiences of a Malayan childhood in complacent, colonial comfort in the midst of benign Islamic culture and astonishing diversity; the geopolitical and personal convulsions of World War II; education in socialist post-war Scandinavia and tradition-bound England; making a living under South Africa's apartheid; North American business pursuits in a free market capitalist environment—all the way to retirement in cosseted, coddled Fairfield County in fiscally imperiled Connecticut?

Between the bookends are varying degrees of exposure to Japanese, German and South African iterations of totalitarianism or fascism; Scandinavia's post war crescendo of socialism; Britain's and Germany's socio-economic disasters wrought by socialist nationalization, deficit spending, unfunded benefits and trade union tyranny; primeval African stagnation and deprivation; and then, finally, America's democratic free market capitalism now being eroded after driving progress for three hundred years at home and around the world. What beliefs, priorities and values were spawned and fostered by experience and careful observation on four continents over more than three quarters of a century? And, yes, what *hobby horses* were developed? Merriam-Webster defines a hobby horse as *"a topic to which one constantly reverts,"* which might suggest I have fallen prey to a surplus of them, not uncommonly among older people, methinks! However, I would not be the first to suffer that fate. In his "Contemplations Moral and Devine," written in 1676, English jurist and writer Sir Matthew Hale said:

> *Almost every person hath some hobby horse or other wherein he prides himself.*

Four of them have caused me the most questioning and deliberation:

- EDUCATION–paramount prerequisite for effective and durable democracy
- WASTE–horrifying practices, particularly of developed countries;
- RELIGION–its positive effects and its overbearing misuse and abuse;
- DEMOCRATIC CAPITALISM–its essential role in human progress and its vulnerabilities.

One never knows it all—indeed one never knows anywhere near enough! It is extremely rare that a person knows enough to justify being as assertive as most of us are in everyday life. Omniscience is a claim far too commonly made, especially in our youth. Fortunately, age and experience tend to blunt this absurd misconception (which is inevitably coupled with a sense of infallibility), but it is only through collisions with reality and bumping into the unfamiliar that the necessary corrections are made. Even in maturity, those of us who have never been immersed in unfamiliar cultures, never been driven out of house and home, nor experienced war or enemy occupation, can easily fall prey to preconception and parochial group-think. Without personal immersion in truly disparate and sometimes alien cultures, people (understandably) can find it almost impossible to accept that different times and different cultures have quite different norms.

Even without education in philosophy or scholarly analysis, valid lessons can be learned—by osmosis and honest observation. So, late in life it would surely be a dreadful mistake not to revisit and learn from object lessons that life has presented. In fact, it would be a dreadful waste if indeed they are worth sharing.

So much has been said and written about education by scholars and experts, that I shall only use a couple of quotations to supplement some simple thoughts on education, a subject that has for so long been a hobby horse.

Nearly all of the world's gravest problems could be more easily addressed, if not solved, if the average voter were adequately educated. The vulnerabilities of democracy proliferate in direct proportion to voters' ignorance; totalitarianism and populism thrive in direct proportion to the population's ignorance.

FDR said that

> "democracy cannot succeed unless those who express their choice are prepared to choose wisely. The real safeguard of democracy is education."

And John Dewey said that

> "the quality of mental process, not the production of correct answers, is the measure of educative growth."

Churchill reminded us that

> "the best argument against democracy is a five-minute conversation with the average voter."

By education, I do not mean to confine the process of learning to academics. Preparing youth for the realities of life also has to address social and civic skills, vocational and trade skills, responsibility for self and community, self-discipline and control. Today's American politicians, for example, fixate on "college education for every kid." It's an absurd notion, if they would only stop to think. Ten years after the great recession started in 2008, hundreds of thousands of jobs remained unfilled for lack of semi-skilled or trade-skilled labor. Bigotry and racism are spawned by ignorance, and both were unwelcome features of that same period. Without adequate education self-esteem is usually prohibited. Disease is perpetuated if not caused by lack of knowledge. And yet education, in its broader sense, is with stubborn persistence neglected by those who set the local, national and international agenda—all politicians talk about public education in unctuous tones; yet no top politician, let alone a political party, has presented serious, comprehensive proposals to remedy the American disaster. Sadly, too many parents also neglect their responsibility for guiding their children and preparing them for an appropriate education. There are too many deadbeat dads and too many struggling single moms. We cannot blame it all on politicians.

In countries where education and training are best addressed, a more holistic and realistic approach is applied to preparing children and youth for citizenship and a life of productive and rewarding work. Trade or vocational teaching and training are recognized to be as important as academics, and while private schooling is certainly not discouraged, access to, and the quality of, public education is engaged as a national priority, and is most commonly nationally funded—from professional care in creches to research centers at and beyond Ph. D. level. Corporations and other private sector entities play a major role in financing and establishing apprenticeship systems to answer the needs of industry, commerce and the public sector. The education and training of teachers is tailored to focus on appropriate, relevant types and levels of sophistication. By lamentable contrast, the failing American concept of funding public schools with property taxes (i.e. by postal zip code or district) can but guarantee continuing disparity and a downward spiral of poor quality and lack of access in the local systems "serving" lower income groups in the poorer districts of America. Meanwhile, wealthy districts, with their higher property values yielding commensurate taxes, get the good schools for which they pay. And America does not have anything like the national or regional apprenticeship systems that work so well elsewhere, especially in northern Europe. Many US states and municipalities make superficial attempts at establishing technical or trade schools, but most of them lack rigor, are relatively superficial and are demonstrably failing to meet the country's needs.

In Africa, the British colonial educational system was government funded and was far better than those in other colonial territories. In Botswana, for example, Seretse Khama, took over and built upon the British system when they left, and this is reflected in their relatively strong democracy, healthy economy, lack of corruption and relatively high standard of living. A sad comparison is provided by neighboring Zimbabwe, where the school system was even stronger, but every remnant and legacy of colonial administration was to be trashed, burned or stolen—leaving millions illiterate, uninformed, starving and destitute.

Public education obviously cannot fulfill its proper and essential role with insufficient funding, but it surely takes more than money. The national attitude to and perception of teachers' crucial role, value and status in society has to encourage quality and performance in the profession. Here again, the United States fails, particularly in poorer districts. If funding is inadequate, so too is teacher training, along with disciplined insistence on performance and results—prerequisites to the status and respect good teachers deserve. Many teachers' unions don't get that.

Waste tragically pervades almost everything mankind does. Unthinking and sometimes deliberate waste of time and human life, waste of both finite and renewable resources: food, money, energy, knowledge and time, including waste of opportunity—too many fail to realize that opportunity is very often a perishable commodity; left unused, opportunity fades or disappears. All waste depletes man's finite resources and reduces the potential for progress and well being. And yet waste is very rarely a subject that draws sufficient attention, let alone corrective action. Is that because curing waste requires such radical change in behavior? Reversal of bad habits, which could cause loss of creature comforts, is rarely popular. Elimination of waste may call for reduction of the self-indulgence endemic in life across the planet, but particularly in America and the West generally. Most forms of waste are right out there for everybody to observe, but they continue to be ignored. We look the other way. An exhaustive litany of wasteful behavior is neither possible nor helpful, but ghastly waste of criminal dimensions is ingrained in everyday behavior.

Food waste tops the list, be it discarded leftovers destined for the trashcan from billions of excessive servings in our homes, restaurants, fast food outlets—or even the poorest of households. Wasting food is tragically pervasive. Unthinking mothers heaping ridiculous piles of food onto the plates of children, way beyond their capacity to ingest, only to toss 60 percent of it in the garbage when the innocent child is stuffed to the brim less than half way through. Teenagers and adults, particularly in America, persistently help themselves to portions that never get consumed and end up at the same destination. Many restaurants don't give their diners any choice in the matter, delivering grossly overloaded plates to the table. Ubiquitous, irresponsible, self-centered and revolting waste.

According to the World Resources Institute the USA wastes twice as much food as Europeans and nearly three times as much as the people of Southeast Asia, measured in terms of calories of food produced per capita. Developed countries worldwide account for 60 percent of all food wastage, while the balance of 40 percent occurs in under- or less- developed areas that are much more heavily populated. Americans are exceptionally generous to the seagulls and other scavengers living off our dumped waste.

Wasted opportunity to address starvation is another unjustifiable reality. Unscientific prejudice and dogma get seriously in the way of solving major food shortages. Hysteria over genetically modified (GM) foods is spread by ignorant consumers, misinformed media and omniscient environmentalists. These groups broadly claim genetically modified crops are health risks, despite the grounds for such claims being scientifically discredited and debunked. The anti-GM activists love to attack companies like Monsanto in the plant science industry, so they use cherry-picked studies and flawed science to promote their cause. One such study was published by the respected journal *Food and Chemical Toxicology*, which claimed mortality and tumors in rats feeding on genetically modified corn, based on work of scientists at the University of Caen. Several other studies found no evidence at all to support this particular journal's position, but it was nevertheless promoted by the activists to the extent that Russia suspended imports of the crop and Kenya banned all GM foods. The French Prime Minister pressed for a ban of GM corn across Europe. The EU countries generally drank the Kool-Aid, lifting their glasses in toasts to Prince Charles, who had the identical thirst. Meanwhile, science continued to discredit *Food and Chemical Toxicology*'s claims, which were then unreservedly retracted by the publication. There is now no serious evidence that responsibly modified crops pose a realistic threat to human health. (The Economist, December 2013) Since the early dawn of history, misuse of scientific method has led to harmful results from time to time; but had such misuse—intentional or accidental—been allowed to stand in the way of scientific advance for the benefit of mankind, we would be in a sorry place today. Don't blame the system or the technology, folks! Expose and punish those who misuse them. The arrogant prejudgment and often dishonest representations of extremists persist, however. In 2013, extreme environmentalists vandalized a crop of Golden Rice—a GM strain of rice—grown for research purposes in the Philippines. The experimental grain, which carries beta-carotene, has the potential for solving vitamin A deficiencies, which cause premature death and blindness in hundreds of thousands of people around the world.

In his 2018 book, "Seeds of Science," British environmentalist Mark Lynes calls for responsible use of GM foods to improve the plight of man, citing dozens of peer approved studies. He totally reversed his youthful opposition to GM practices: "Science won the debate," he explains today.

By 2050, Earth will be home to between nine and ten billion people. This means we have to find a way to double the production of food on the finite arable acreage of this planet without using any more water and with fewer chemicals. GM seeds or foods are not a panacea, and they cannot alone address the challenge of feeding the world's growing population in decades and centuries to come, but they can help, for example, in managing our forecasted climate change. As Kate Balchelder of the Wall Street Journal points out, citing the Service for the Acquisition of Agro-Biotech Applications:

> *"Thanks to fewer sprays and less tillage, GM crops in 2012 reduced carbon emissions by 26.7 billion kilograms—the equivalent of taking 11.8 million cars off the road for a year."*

Over 90 percent of all the acres now planted with corn and soybeans are GM crops. The greater part of these crops are typically fed to livestock and used as ingredients in other foods that represent 80 percent of the products on American grocery shelves. Biotech-derived products consumed by the American public are the most strictly tested and regulated of all our foods. By law, Monsanto's GM products made with a new seed have to pass muster with the Department of Agriculture and are voluntarily checked by the FDA (Food & Drug Administration). Moreover, if a GM product involves insecticides or pesticides, the EPA (Environmental Protection Agency) also has to pass on them. Meanwhile, crops that are traditionally bred, undergo zero testing. So the extremists placate their fads by forming groups like *Occupy Monsanto* and label the company *Monsatan* and its products *Frankenfood.* Fortunately, the GM faddists are perfectly free to choose; they can buy their certified organic foods at the premium, which privileged and wasteful Americans can afford. If the actual effects of climate change were to validate the predictions of creditworthy scientists, our essential crops will also have to be much more resistant to droughts and floods than they are now. We have come a long way since Malthus and his dire predictions (of starvation caused by overpopulation) made nearly 200 years ago; but this time it is an even bigger challenge. Remarkably, with little or no scientific base, the GM faddists argue that the answer is organic farming. But since when has organic farming delivered a productivity increase? The opposite is closer to the truth.

Who is kidding whom? And for how long can it go on?

What is there not to like in organically produced products? But if agricultural yields had stayed at the prevailing 1960 levels before the Green revolution, the world's food production would today be catastrophically inadequate, even if every acre of the earth's workable soil had been put under cultivation; even if the Russian and Canadian tundra were transformed into bountiful prairies of corn or wheat fields; even if the whole Amazon basin were one big soya bean field instead of rain forest. GM crops have been made disease resistant, pest resistant, less dependent on chemicals and better able to withstand the climate extremes attributed to global warming. Future genetic research could lead to much more lifesaving improvement in agricultural productivity. Like the vitamin A benefit in the Filipino rice case, new GM cereals could soon fix their own nitrogen.

The Economist had it right when it pointed out that

> *Vandalising GM field trials is a bit like the campaign of some religious leaders to prevent smallpox inoculations: it causes misery, even death, in the name of obscurantism and unscientific belief.*

Those vain dogma-driven ideologues in the Philippines (an association of NGOs and "biodiversity" fanatics called *MASIPAG*) who trashed the GM rice trials, were financed by none other than the Swedish government. Fortunately, the US government does not pay a lot of attention to this GM ideology with which Europe seems so obsessed. Yet stubborn vilification of GM food by the mainstream American media and *Occupy* groups persists, but fortunately with a few exceptions, such as the *Wall Street Journal* editorial quoted below, and the scientific analysis of The Economist.

The *Wall Street Journal* chose to differ with the faddists. (WSJ Kate Bachelder, 8/23–24/2014) The editorial in question pointed out that if you were to Google-search "Monsanto employees," your computer's search engine would bring up "Monsanto evil" before you could finish typing in the request.

Energy waste is everywhere to behold in limitless iterations such as waste from gas-guzzling mega-sedans and SUVs used only to carry a driver and perhaps one passenger to permanently overcooled or overheated office buildings; waste from billions of lights left on in high-rise buildings 24/7 in Los Angeles during media-hyped threats of statewide blackouts. Waste owing to untapped natural oil and gas resources withheld as a result of science-deprived, hip-shooting opposition, or waste of opportunity to tap endless sources of economic solar energy in sun-drenched regions. Illogical squandering of fuel as Air Force One is used to fly to political fundraisers less than 250 miles from the White House. Energy wasted because wind turbine projects are obstructed or banned by the efforts of *NIMBY* (Not In My Backyard) populations that do not like turbines featuring in their landscapes, or by relatively minute loss of bird life inanely attributed to wind turbines. And so it goes on with complete disregard for cost/benefit consideration.

Monumental waste of money is infinite and pervasive, especially when people are spending other people's money. Bureaucracies of governments and collective international organizations, almost without exception, lead the world on the evil highway of monetary waste and unforgivable prodigality. Private sector corporate funds "invested" in monumental overhead costs and the hubris of corporate leaders, their elaborate headquarters and their boondoggles are favorite mechanisms for wasting other people's money. Corporate executive narcissism drives inexcusable misuse of funds on a gigantic scale. Hollywood and the corporate world continue, unchallenged, to squander funds and resources on an appalling scale, wasting money on totally unproductive narcissism.

This is a very dark side of free market capitalism, which feeds live ammunition to the chattering machine guns of the system's opponents. These opponents then blame the system rather than its abusers, whom they forgive with startling alacrity. Think of what happened to General Electric as a result of Jeff Immelt's antics and predilections of a decade and a half.

Meanwhile, the empirical damage wrought by ALL corporate waste in totality is a mere pinprick compared with the numbers chalked up in avoidable waste by governments, national and international collectives in the name of social services, and in pursuit of political optics.

The United Nations organization is history's largest, most deliberately organized and legitimized generator of waste. Seen through the lens of any reasonable and honest cost/benefit analysis, the United Nations organization is but futility funded by the foolish, for the benefit of the feckless. Its staggering prodigality has been obvious from the organization's very start, when it replaced the League of Nations. It is to America's deep discredit that this vast organ of ineptitude has not only survived since 1946, but has grown and flourished unfairly on the backs of US taxpayers. The USA, as one of 193 member nations, disproportionately funds at least 22 percent of the regular UN budget and over 27 percent of its peacekeeping activities. America's return on this absurd investment might be better justified if the UN were not so consistently ineffective in pursuing its chartered purposes of *keeping the peace,* and *securing human rights* and *promoting democracies.* American funds should, of course, play their rightful role in financing UN initiatives that spawn demonstrable progress in the human condition, but the chronic failure to accomplish that meaningful progress is hidden behind the UN's opacity. The United Nations administration is completely immune to accountability while its charter guarantees *sovereign immunity* of the body (or any employee) from prosecution and punishment for wrong doing. So Americans continue to bankroll the iconic body's waste on an astronomic scale.

My personal observations of UN antics started in the 1960s as my business travel regularly included destinations popular with rookie African diplomats, such as London, Frankfurt and Paris, as they extended their regular trips to the UN's New York headquarters. The normally hushed elegance of lobbies in the Dorchester, Frankfurterhof or Bristol hotels would be shattered by inebriated posses of apparatchiks competing for attention as they quaffed their Tanqueray Number Ten, Reinhold Haart Riesling or Louis Roederer champagne. No attempts to move beyond their hotel were made without shiny black Bentley or Mercedes limousines to help colorfully attired couples on their way. These were merely peripheral symptoms of UN extravagance, far from its temple of prodigality on Manhattan's East Side.

Unchallenged expansion of the UN's administration and reach has run riot under nine or more Secretaries General, drawn from academia, diplomacy or government bureaucracies, where basic principles of effective management and administration are neither known nor sought. These leaders have repeatedly been found ineffectual or even publicly disgraced.

Think of Kurt Waldheim, disgraced Nazi. Think of Boutros Boutros-Ghali, presiding over the UN as he and the whole organization sat on their hands through the protracted genocide that killed over 800,000 people in Rwanda around 2009. Think of Ban Ki-Moon, nick-named "Slippery Eel" by his peer bureaucrats in the South Korean administration, whose "oversight" of the Darfur genocide costing 200,000 lives, and counting. His UN actions to "protect and stabilize" disaster-stricken Haiti led to blue-helmeted Peace Keepers reintroducing cholera, after the country had been free of that scourge for many decades, causing an epidemic that killed 8,000 and sickened 600,000 suffering Haitians. (According to NPR bulletins and Yale University reports). UN immunity has allowed Ban Ki-Moon to deny responsibility and reject Haitian claims for compensation. The world has fawned over the articulate, impeccably tailored Kofi Anan who arrived in the hallowed chambers on the Upper East Side promising to be the champion of "organization and management repair." His regime oversaw the UN implication in the infamous "oil for food" scandal, and his "repairs" to management led to an enquiry into UN practices headed by former Fed Chair Paul Volcker, who quite specifically decried the organization's unchanged management structure and the sterile impotence of the Security Council at the body's very core.

Examples of monstrous waste in the UN are boundless, but enough said!

Happily, the world does derive some real value from UN activity outside the central UN umbrella organization itself. Without being able to make specific cost/benefit judgements, it appears clear that the world is relatively well served by some of the individual agencies under the auspices of the UN, such as UNICEF (United Nations International Children's Emergency Fund), FAO (Food & Agriculture Organization) and WFP (World Food Program), which facilitate supply and access to food (FAO actually strives to reduce the staggering $750-billion of annual food waste occurring in the world today). There's also UNAIDS, which addresses HIV/AIDS issues and does essential statistical research. However, most of these agencies are funded outside the core budget of the United Nations organization per se and cannot, therefore, be considered reflective of the mother body's value. It is almost impossible to make a judgment on each element, but some excellent management and productivity characterizes some of them. For example, a full 90.4 percent of UNICEF's total revenue goes directly to children's programs, only 6.7 percent to fundraising and a frugal 2.9 percent to administrative and management costs. The last percentage matches or betters the performance of some effective private sector philanthropies.

The cost of the UN peace-keeping charade, however, is a staggering demonstration of waste. Estimates of the total cost vary widely in a range from $7.5-billion to $12-billion depending on who is counting and according to which contributions are defined as "outside UN financial management." Too much of the accounting is fudged. Meanwhile, estimates of total US contributions to the whole of the UN, as published by responsible newspapers and journals, seem to exceed $7-billion. The UN's own numbers indicate that the USA contributes 28.4 percent of all revenue reported by the UN for peacekeeping, 10.8 percent from Japan, 7.2 percent from France, 7.1 percent from Germany, with the UK chipping in 6.8 percent. Apparently, Russia and other countries are less avid supporters. Perhaps they are more seriously concerned with value for their money? Meanwhile they get the benefit of effortless access to the podium in the global forum that is the UN's General Assembly, its infinite councils, commissions and committees—and endless media coverage. It is difficult to blame them!

Who knows what all this is worth? Even the most conservative numbers of genocide victims in the Sub-Saharan areas are utterly outrageous: As already noted, in Rwanda Burundi 800,000 to 1,000,000; Darfur 100,000 to 250,000, Liberia 200,000, just to mention a couple of the tragedies occurring under UN peace keeping or observation. Who can guess what value the UN might eventually bring to the Syrian conflict, where the death toll raced past 100,000 in its first two years.

The value of maintaining the United Nations organization has to be seen and gauged in the context of its two controlling power groups: its cornerstone Security Council and its Human Rights Council (which succeeded the original Council on Human Rights from 1946). The former serves as little more than a well-publicized theater in which national views and positions get a global hearing. It is systemically rendered impotent by its composition, with totalitarian Russia and China as two of the five permanent members with veto rights over any resolution they don't like. A single veto by a permanent member leaves the other four dead in the water, alongside the fifteen rotating council members. Russia's or China's authoritarian rulers can and do, single-handedly, scuttle the consensus of the rest of the world.

Given its stated mission, the Human Rights Council's composition is often quite fantastic. Regularly, council members are drawn from countries like Pakistan, Zimbabwe, Congo, Syria, Egypt, Uganda and—believe it or not—Rwanda (classes of 1995 and 2013), hardly champions for human rights. The UN persistently puts the inmates in position to rule the prison.

~~~~

As the winds of change were steadily gaining strength in sub-Saharan Africa, I spent seventeen years in the Republic of South Africa under evolving apartheid and traveled widely through neighboring countries. I lived and worked in an environment where no thinking person could but have deep concerns over the African continent's often primeval condition and the plight of its many different peoples.

East Africa was the crucible from which Homo Erectus and then Homo Sapiens evolved. Over time, groups migrated from Kenya's Rift Valley, moving mostly to the north and eastward, and then in every direction across the globe. The migrant groups became increasingly sophisticated in controlling their destiny; but those who stayed behind did not fare as well. Most of the continent south of the great Sahara Desert remained relatively stagnant in economic, cultural and civic terms over the millennia, while Indo-European, Mesopotamian, Levantine, Asian, and Central American civilizations evolved and blossomed. The cultures and civic progress of Mediterranean North Africa eclipsed their southern counterparts through the ages, driven by Hamitic, Judaic and Semitic cultures and their Muslim and Hebraic scholarship and learning. By contrast, when Europeans first settled the southern sub-continent of Africa many thousands of years later, native Africans were yet to develop written language or script, and had not yet adopted the use of the wheel. There was no literature, so history and culture and tradition were passed down orally, often through vocal music. In attempting to explain the different rates of progression, anthropologists and other social scientists have flirted with theories suggesting that the planet's different ethnic strains or groupings evolved from different species of hominid. That speculation was finally debunked, however, by serial discoveries of extraordinarily well-preserved skulls, reportedly from about two million years ago in Georgia, not far from the Black Sea, linking us all to the same species, a common human ancestry. Sub-Saharan Africans, if you go back those millions of years, were derived from the very same species as Mongolians or eastern Asians, Indo-Europeans, Polynesians, Incas and Mayas, etc. The migrants who took the initiative to leave Africa's crucible of mankind as hunters and gatherers did a lot better, even in inhospitable climates and barren environments. After more recent periods of colonization by Europeans some benefits of education, infrastructure, economic development and civic systems have accelerated the progression of living standards, civic order and governance—in some countries, in varying degrees. And these advances have benefited the native populations despite their brutal exploitation and suppression by the colonists in the 19th and 20th centuries. Sadly, many of the newly independent African "democracies" (as their totalitarian regimes still characterize themselves) have failed or are in tragic, self-inflicted decline. Sub-Saharan Africa is still in more urgent need of support and help than any other region on the planet—and it has to be prioritized support, applied with discipline and integrity to be effective.

How to define, prioritize, fund and deliver that support and help ensure enduring, sustainable progress?

The destitution and suffering of the sub-continent endures, for lack of a disciplined approach and prioritized focus of those people and organizations that want to help. The West's attempts at establishing or promoting post-colonial, independent democracies have generally failed because of tribalism, pervasive corruption and cronyism, which in turn have exacerbated inequality of income, inequality of access to education and training. So these countries desperately need and deserve help—but how?

Interfering with self-determination or the government of sovereign states (in Africa or elsewhere) is unavoidably problematic, irrespective of how badly they are failing. The preeminent reason for repeated failures in country after country, is the scattered, wildly random and uncoordinated nature of the aid being given. That does not mean, of course, that they should not be assisted or supported generously; but it requires realism, strategic planning and coordination so that effective action can be taken on a prioritized basis.

So, why couldn't an international organization or group of truly qualified people focus on just the three most transforming issues on a strictly prioritized basis and develop a coordinated strategy of applying finite resources to attain realistic and carefully targeted results? (That's what the UN was meant to do, but has not yet done, since its inception) Having observed socio-economic calamities and the plight of the destitute over decades, my instinct is that the three most transforming imperatives are:

EDUCATION
CLEAN WATER and
HEALTH CARE

Africa's ubiquitous cancer of corruption and cronyism (tribal and/or political)—the biggest obstacle in the way of social progress—is best addressed by making public education and vocational training the #1 priority—just as it should be in every country.

Sub-Saharan Africa is home to between12 and 14 percent of the world's population. About 48 percent or 40 to 45 million Sub-Saharan children do not go to school at all, and about 66 percent of those children are girls, most of whom are married off before they are 14 and are very soon expected to be having children and running households struggling to put food on the table. Lack of even the most basic education tragically hinders social and civic progress across the entire region in question.

Primary education is and always has been civilization's single most effective mechanism for breaking the worldwide poverty cycle. Nowhere is that more true than in Africa. Those who receive even the most basic education in the bare essentials generally see to it that their own children will get, at the very least, an equal measure of education. The benefits of effective education are cumulative, long-term, self-sustaining—more so than most other social benefits the world can bestow.

Clean water is also a key to the remediation of the Sub-Saharan human condition. It's one of my *hobby horses* because, world- wide, about 750-million people do not have access to clean water and 320-million of them are in this region. Millions upon millions of school days in the region are lost to water-related sickness, while one in five deaths under the age of five is caused by diseases like dysentery, typhoid, hepatitis A, cholera and diarrhea—all spread by dirty water. Lack of clean water creates sanitation and hygiene crises, and half of the region's primary schools do not have access to water-based sanitation. In Sub-Saharan Africa, 40-billion hours per annum are devoted to collecting (hopefully clean) water from distant wells, streams and other bodies of water—that is the equivalent of France's annual total labor supply. (Statistics from The Water Project, Concord NH and World Health Organization)

An effective pan-African strategy for the provision of access to clean water should be a top priority, but that is understood and heeded by very few. Brilliant exceptions are The Water Project and the Bill & Melinda Gates Foundation. The problem is entirely solvable over the medium term if global attention and resources were prioritized and applied in a coordinated way. It would cure many African ills and alleviate myriad medical, social, economic and even political problems.

My third *hobby horse* is the importance of access to adequate health care. It is difficult to overstate. The tragic loss of life from water-borne diseases is multiplied by so many others like malaria, Ebola, HIV/AIDS, yellow fever and tuberculosis, with thousands of avoidable deaths owing to lack of access to adequate and timely healthcare. Again, progress toward disease containment and sustainable access to basic care are attainable, if only the world's resources and capacity were pooled in pursuit of prioritized and focused action. But that is far from today's random chaos, fraud, corruption, waste and duplication in the international efforts to provide aid for healthcare in Africa. Until that changes, the developed world (sometimes called the first world!) remains an accomplice to despicable neglect of Sub-Saharan Africa's people in the twenty-first century.

Uncoordinated, disorganized attempts to effect positive change are initiated by the UN, by individual nations and by literally thousands of

NGOs. Too few of these programs are effective. Waste, corruption, fraud, politics and vanity get in the way. In April 2017, there were countless thousands of independent and self-governing NGOs actually registered in South Africa and its neighboring countries. One example would be *IMK* (International Knowledge Management), which helps other NGOs decide where they should direct their resources and efforts. Another would be *Genderlinks*, which promotes gender equality in rural and urban areas of South Africa, where most often the top priority at any given hour is feeding the baby, putting food on the table for the family or getting medical attention for somebody dying of malnutrition, malaria, cholera or TB. Imagine if the resources, objectives and efforts of these countless organizations were coordinated and their missions prioritized for results in the short, medium and long terms. Just imagine the potential for economies of scale, the reduction in duplication of effort and expenditure, and the acceleration of progress for millions of deprived people.

This certainly does not mean that intelligently targeted, well managed NGOs cannot make invaluable contributions. There always will be cracks in any system of governance, where effective NGOs can make a positive difference. There is already a system in place to register NGOs. It follows that there has to be a way to identify and evaluate them for their effectiveness and their relevance to the priority needs. This would, however, require cooperation, transparency of funding (sources), expenditures and the results achieved, as judged by donors and by intended beneficiaries.

The work of the Bill & Melinda Gates Foundation installing sanitary pipelines and building water treatment plants along the banks of the Zambezi and the River Niger is absolutely invaluable, effective and highly relevant. The Gates Foundation is also laser-focused on treatment and prevention of malaria through disciplined, targeted and result-derived management action—as malaria is an even more devastating killer than HIV/AIDS. Meanwhile, the UN and USAID pour endless millions of dollars of anti-Malaria medicines into Sub-Saharan Africa only to have 30 percent consistently stolen and sold in the thriving black markets, because the whole exercise lacks management, discipline and accountability.

Teaching the Ndebeles, Tswanas, Ibos, Swahilis, Hausas and Biafrans to read, write and count, along with trade skills, is an obvious priority with predictable results. On the other hand, promoting Matabele "women's rights to equal pay" among chronically unemployed mothers, who are struggling every hour of the day to feed their infants in Bulawayo's townships, is neither effective nor relevant on a priority basis. What comes first? How can equal pay be relevant until there is a job in place, for which compensation is paid? It's that simplistic. Persuading Mafuta Dhlamini in Kwazulu to choose Jesus ahead of her local witch doctor's *tokulosh* may allow missionaries to feel good but it will not necessarily improve the plight of Zulus living in desperate poverty. The media and their celebrities, however, don't get this—it's far more sexy to broadcast images of Hollywood stars or hirsute American college kids talking to sweet little township girls dressed in rags, or hedge fund managers funding "cross cultural sensitivity courses" for Hutus and Tutsis between serial episodes of genocidal massacre. (Matt Damon may be an exception to the Hollywood model, given his low key but informed concentration on the clean water priority).

The world's media could play a pivotal role in achieving social and civic progress, but they rarely do—certainly not when it comes to Africa. Instead, the media are accomplices in failure, giving limelight and encouragement to colossal wastes of time, human effort, money and other finite resources. Most of our modern media don't get this. Journalism as defined by Merriam-Webster is:

> *writing characterized by a direct presentation of facts or description of events without an attempt at interpretation.*

Thus defined, journalism was, for centuries, a crucial instrument of continuing education and cultural development; but today's journalism by this definition is on the critically endangered species list.

As seniority encourages one to develop hobby horses, it fortunately also prompts reviews and testing of popular tenets and social catechisms, and the revisiting of conventional wisdom and preconceptions. Thus, the role of different religions in public life observed while living on three continents caused me concerns. Accumulated knowledge of its misuse over the millennia prompted serious questioning. Whenever Christian values and norms are at the foundation of enduring democratic governance and civic order, and when those principles and precepts are the bedrock underlying a humane code of conduct, religion has served man well. If religion serves as the glue that helps preserve a nation's democratic structure and sound values, it serves great purpose. Faith has certainly alleviated pain suffered by millions of the needy and the sick, by giving succor, solace and comfort. Christianity has no monopoly in this context—the basic tenets of all major religions have so much in common. On balance, they may have done more good than harm. It's difficult to measure or judge.

However, religion's role in government and public policy today is surely overrated. The promotion or reliance on faith to fill gaps in knowledge and understanding has too often reduced or retarded mankind's capacity to address life's realities. Religions demand leaps of faith as they manufacture answers to man's unresolved issues and unanswerable questions, including those concerning the origin and meaning of life itself. Major religions even predict, define and promise life after death, despite the total absence of evidence to support those pipe dreams. Believers by the billion have made such leaps of faith, following each other like lemmings. Religious faith sometimes merges with superstition to more negative effect than positive. And blind faith certainly facilitates outrageous hijacking of religions, urging whole nations, ethnic groups and members of a given faith to overpower, subjugate and discriminate against others, even precipitate genocide. There is no shortage of history to validate the evil and devastating misuse of religion.

The role of religion in sports, social affairs or politics is overt and obnoxious to thinking citizens.

An early experience as a spectator of American high school football, soon after immigrating, gave warning of things to come. Before a local rivalry was to be settled on the playing field, each team of strapping, clean-cut, hyped-up boys in splendid uniforms, helmets piously held in hand, knelt in a circle to engage in coach-led supplication of the Almighty. Each group prayed for God's intervention to secure defeat of their rivals kneeling in prayer on the same turf twenty feet away. The game resulted in a close victory for one team, the other having been deprived of the Lord's favor on that day—the losers just got screwed by their God on this occasion. The same ludicrous claim on the Almighty's partiality occurs every time a batter points his grateful finger heavenward as he steps onto home plate after a home run: This time God screwed the pious pitcher who crossed himself before throwing that fateful pitch at the bottom of the ninth.

Most presidential election campaigns bow to the electorate's concern for the candidate's religious credentials. Whether it be Bill Clinton, George W. Bush or Barack Obama, the media never fails to present images of them in their nice blue suits, with bible tucked under one arm and their wives clutching the other, as they approach the church door in unctuous Sunday ritual.

Unquestioning faith ensnares almost a billion Roman Catholics on morality issues such as abortion or divorce, while far too many of their clergy embezzle funds or leave children devastated by sexual abuse. Other sectarian Christians invite avoidable disease and even death by prohibiting modern medicines and practices. While the United States Constitution calls for separation of church and state, religious preconceptions and biases are pervasive in America's politics and public life. Islam enshrines the deprivation and mistreatment of women. From time to time, even Buddhism calls for persecution and genocidal murder of adherents of non-Buddhist religions.

Such is the persuasive power of religion. Its role is arguably overrated.

The role of capitalism (in its various iterations) as a system of governance has been a *hobby horse* for most of my life, since my undergraduate years at Cambridge caused me to abandon early egalitarian preconceptions and convictions. The balance of its positive and negative aspects, and its power to promote human progress has occupied me for at least sixty years. This yarn you are now reading will end with some views developed over forty active years in industry on three continents and decades of observing the realities of life in under-served urban communities from Johannesburg's Soweto to Essen's post-war residential rubble, from Bangkok's slums to New York's inner city.

Self-interest, the drive for individual freedom and the quest for individual choice are bestowed on us by nature. They drive evolution and progress—be it intellectual, social, technological or artistic progress. Self-interest, pursued within the boundaries of a socially viable and economically sustainable civic order, preserves and builds upon civilization today. However, when man's self-interest breaks those boundaries, it becomes egocentric and excludes the imperative consideration of fellow citizens; it causes injustice and pain, so the community eventually fails. Versions of democratic free market capitalism, built on man's freedom to pursue his own well-being (happiness), have generally served us well; but they cannot endure when individual citizens fail to take responsibility for themselves and, crucially, share responsibility for the extended community of which they are part.

History has demonstrated through thousands of years that improvement in the human condition is contingent upon the creation of surplus, or incremental wealth, or profit—i.e., a condition in which man generates more resources and assets than he needs for subsistence and survival. Without that generation of surplus, society stagnates and then, as the population grows, it regresses.

Inability to create some degree of surplus constrained early man. He could do no more than forage, harvest or kill whatever it took to survive and procreate. His condition remained near stagnant. Collectivists, communists and socialists don't get that. That's why they disparage "profits" and the enterprises that generate incremental wealth to fund their "rights," their "entitlements" and "social standards" for a growing population- they even despise capitalism and work hard to demolish it, often claiming that the world owes them a living to be financed by other people's money or money printed on the government's printing presses. Those earliest migrants from today's Rift Valley in Kenya somehow, at some point, sought something better and were inspired to cause change for the better in their condition. Their quest triggered their initiative to find a way via East Africa's northern territories to the fertile Nile Valley and Mediterranean shores, into Mesopotamia and then far beyond, wherever the environment, climate and soil allowed their individual effort to surpass survival mode, to pursue improvement in their plight. Self-interest drove them to seek what today we call a better standard of living. The surplus they created allowed them to accelerate the attainment of improvements to life, new comforts, new stability; they could extend their capacity for communication, innovation, self-expression and even artistic creation. Social progress stimulated the establishment of new and different systems of civic order, new ways of thinking (the birth of philosophy?) and, yes, new religions. Meanwhile, they also learned that properly organized collective effort could achieve more than the sum of individual efforts in certain circumstances. The surplus they created permitted time and opportunity to think and to innovate.

The capitalist system's many iterations are neither perfect nor bullet proof, as we have seen so many times, and again in the early 2000s. For example, free market capitalist systems throughout the world were once again dealt a devastating blow by egregious abuse by the government, business in the private sector and criminally irresponsible individuals leading up to the 2008 financial crisis. It was the result of many factors including Wall Street's irresponsible risk-taking, fraudulent persuasion of borrowers and avaricious cheating. Ironically, the very earliest roots of the mortgage-based debacle at the center of the 2008 crash stem from President Clinton's much vaunted *National Home Ownership Policy* with Robert Rubin aiding and abetting in the Treasury. It was intended to facilitate attainment of the American dream of owning your own home. But, instead, it led to countless thousands of Americans owning a home they could not afford. But Clinton was certainly not alone, as George W. Bush and his administration embraced the policy and compounded the felony, with accomplices like Chair of the Federal Reserve of the United States, Alan Greenspan, government agencies such as HUD (Housing and Urban Development), and Government's mortgage financing agencies Fannie Mae and Freddie Mac. Cumulatively and collectively, they engineered artificially low mortgage rates, paper-thin down payments and insanely lax lending standards. Wall Street joined the game, creating securities and "bundled mortgage" derivatives, all of which pumped explosive gas into the ever-expanding housing bubble. Government's interference with market-determined interest rates (amounting to fixing the price of money or debt) and distortion of the housing market worked alongside Wall Street to trigger the bubble's explosion and the financial industry's implosion of 2007—2008.

Four years later unemployment lingered at 7.5 percent or above. The national debt, which George W. Bush had doubled, was then to be tripled by Barack Obama. The economy was barely growing at a paltry rate, way below two percent, so the Federal Reserve imposed near-zero interest rates alongside multiple stimulus packages (quantitative easements or QEs and TARPs—Troubled Assets Relief Programs). They all failed to generate sufficient growth or create the requisite new jobs, which in turn prolonged the recession and led to the slowest recovery yet in the country's economic history. Oceans of cash and capital resources across the USA and around the globe remained idle or underemployed because of uncertainty, excessive regulation and the opacity of the government's policies. Obama's administration, now in its second term, had not worked within an approved budget for four years.

The price of money or debt was subsidized by Bernanke's Fed. Near-zero interest rates goosed equity markets and other asset values to record levels, generating enormous new wealth at the upper end of the social scale. The lower and middle classes, which cannot afford stocks or real estate investments, stagnated or lost ground; the poor and unemployed remained poor because the stimulus wasn't doing anything for them. The very real evils of income inequality were exacerbated. Politicians blamed Wall Street and "the one-percenters" as they plied voters with populist name calling—pointing to "Wall Street pigs," the "vulture capitalists" and the "filthy rich."

An unacceptable face of capitalism? Misuse of the system? Of course it was.

Far from perfect, the capitalist free market system remains quite fallible, quite vulnerable and open to abuse. Corporations are often vilified and blackened as the villains when things go wrong, sometimes deservedly. However, it is surely those responsible, the perpetrators, the people leading, managing and setting corporate policy, who must be held to account. They are the abusers of the trust upon which the whole system is constructed. White collar crime is so common and so devastating that it is truly shocking that society, the legislature, the judiciary and our whole legal system does not commensurately exact retribution. Those who break the law to enrich themselves, cheating innocent individuals and society as a whole, far too often walk away unscathed or much too lightly punished. This is a situation where government does not intrude enough, failing to do its constitutional duty of upholding the law, protecting voters' rights and property. Occasionally someone like Bernie Madoff gets put away for life, but far too often the prison sentence for criminal offenders is lenient, too short, or far too comfortable, i.e. in a country-club-style detention center for white collar criminals. Massive corporate larceny, embezzlement, misuse of shareholder funds, fraud and insider trading crimes are frequently settled by dollar payments out of corporate reserves (sometimes specifically created for the purpose) at the expense of shareholders, while the actual perpetrators go scot-free. Individual managers guilty of obscene negligence or near-criminal irresponsibility, who facilitated crimes, are allowed to head for the hills with "contractual benefits," compensation for past service, or various other forms of golden handshake. This leniency itself just lowers the risk of committing or perpetrating crime. Trust is the essential key to, and foundation for, any civic order that can serve mankind and endure. Without trust, no form of societal organization can survive, so those who breach that trust must truly be made to suffer—personally and painfully.

The Business Hall of Shame leaderboard of the 1980s has to be extended to include more recent abusers of our system in the new millennium, such as SAC and Steve Cohen or MF Global and Jon Corzine—the last mentioned also breaching the trust of New Jersey voters in terms of political, personal and financial morals. Willingness to give wrongdoers a second chance has its merits, but overdone leniency is simple injustice and it damages the viability of our systems and institutions. Another prize example, and candidate for the Hall of Shame, Dennis Kozlowski, CEO of Tyco International, was convicted in 2005 for systematically looting the company. He did so in cahoots with its CFO, Mark Swartz. With great gobs of shareholders' funds, Kozlowski enjoyed a hedonistic lifestyle, bought art treasures, and lived in luxurious penthouses where he entertained racy friends. Included in his improper compensation were lavish parties—one for his second wife, which was a two-million dollar birthday bash, featuring an ice sculpture in the image of Michelangelo's *David* and music performed by Jimmy Buffet. Found guilty on 22 of 23 counts, ranging from grand larceny to securities fraud, he was sentenced to "eight-and-a-third years to twenty-five years." After serving some time in an upstate New York correctional facility, he was allowed to move to a minimum security facility in midtown Manhattan so he could hold down a job! At a 2012 parole hearing, Kozlowski was cited for "theft of over $100-million from Tyco," which was found "incompatible with the welfare of society at large." And after all this, on appeal, he was set for parole in January 2014. (WSJ, 12/4/2013) The judicial system had just lowered the risk of committing outrageous crime against "the welfare of society at large."

But don't blame capitalism, don't decry the whole concept, let alone dismantle it (as so many *protestocrats* want to do). Instead, punish the hell out of people who misuse it, cheat on it and jeopardize the only form of governance and civic order that can fund our social services, fund an imperative social safety net, cultural and technological progress on a sustainable basis. There is nothing mutually exclusive or incompatible between the capitalist system and a progressive taxation protocol to fund access to decent living standards for all but the indolent and irresponsible.

There is much to be learned from the effective and demonstrably sustainable social safety net for the truly needy built into the contemporary Danish model of free market capitalism. Unlike the disastrous post-war 40-year socialist regime, which nearly caused the implosion of its economy, today's Denmark enjoys uncommonly wide sharing of prosperity, while financing comprehensive social services and benefits for all citizens via a realistically sloped progressive tax protocol and consumption taxes. A productive balance is maintained with legislation that encourages domestic and international investment, mobility of labor, innovation, job creation. The nation's economy does better than most of its European peers (a condition beyond the comprehension of omniscient Tracy Regan, of Fox News, who equated Denmark with socialist Venezuela). Denmark is a thriving endorsement of Alan Binder's position that there is no real incompatibility between vibrant capitalism and a strong social safety net for the truly needy. Denmark is also a testament to the soundness of Ray Dalio's 2019 views on maintaining and protecting the democratic characteristics of democratic capitalism. (New York Times and Wall Street Journal, April 2019)

Infidels should quit the dogma, the shrill protestations, the slogans and then visit or revisit Economics 101 (even if they can't pass), or invent a specifically defined system better for us all!

Few would deny that the consequences of gross, avoidable, excessive inequality of income and living conditions are widespread, repugnant and destructive. They must be minimized to the greatest possible extent, to avoid ultimate and inevitable anarchy. However, it is a challenge that is rarely addressed pragmatically, logically or for enduring effect because the selected actions and initiatives of politicians and activists are so often driven by no more than facile rhetoric or populist grandstanding. (Ray Dalio's 2019 publications are great exceptions, but not given due attention by the press or TV channels—and therefore side-stepped by media and politicians). The media predictably chooses to highlight issues for their advertising or ratings value, rather than social import. Legislation trying to impose universal "equality" inevitably fail. Mandating draconian redistribution of resources (which are then misdirected and wasted by ill-informed legislators) or laws favoring one segment of society at the expense of another, continue to miss the point and thus fail to cause positive change.

To cause positive change in our society, informed voters must install lawmakers who ensure ever greater EQUALITY OF ACCESS to opportunity, access to the tools—knowledge and skills—and civic conditions required for fostering good citizenship. That means spawning responsible and contributing citizens via:

- Access to quality education & vocational training, Kindergarten through high school;
- Access to adequate health care;
- Absolutely equal treatment before the law;
- Incentives to encourage responsibility for stable family structure and parental responsibility, paternal as well as maternal; and
- Incentives to embrace individual responsibility (rather than prevalent focus on entitlements and "rights" that create dependence on others)
- Clarification that birth does not entitle a person to a comfortable living.

Partisan protestation and public rage are no substitute for an agenda or an articulated plan. Pragmatic, prioritized policy proposals to attain defined results make an agenda.

Major, seriously organized marches and mass protests of change-making scale have historically drawn sufficient attention and created pressure for needed action, so from time to time, they can contribute to good effect.

On the other hand, knee jerk attention-seeking does not. Think of the myriad causes of ineffectual marches, sit-ins, chanting crowds, and traffic-blocking demonstrations calling for their cause *du jour*—*Occupy Wall Street, Occupy Oakland, Occupy Monsanto*, etc.—endless protests against or for issues on the steps of the Capitol or the Supreme Court, pro-gun antics by leather clad bikers, red-necks' pick-up trucks fitted with black smoke generators, and tattooed white supremacist gangs waving Confederate flags or Swastika flags , etc. ad infinitum. Very rarely do these *protestocrats* cause or even promote real movement, or anything meaningful. More often than not, they simply generate counterproductive animus and fuel for the media to boost TV ratings.

In 1994, reversal of apartheid's abhorrent income inequality was pronounced very clearly as a top priority of Mandela's nascent democracy. *Black Economic Empowerment* (BEE) legislation was the chosen mechanism of the African National Congress (ANC) for reducing inequality of income and living standards. It was universally understood that the development of a massive black middle class was the urgent prerequisite in tackling inequality. However, the BEE measures, as legislated, were nothing but affirmative action programs based on quotas, divested of all recognition that education and broad vocational training were absolutely crucial to qualify millions of blacks for existing job opportunities, and the BEE measures were also divested of any plan or incentive that would encourage investment to create sufficient new jobs to support the fast growing Black population. It merely dictated the placement of thousands of uneducated or under-qualified people in jobs at every level of industry, commerce, finance and government, including boardroom seats, government posts and public councils or commissions. The resulting mismatch on this colossal scale quickly caused a deceleration of economic activity, discouraged foreign and domestic investment and strangled growth of the GDP (Gross Domestic Product). It caused private and publicly owned businesses to under-perform or fail, public institutions to malfunction or crash. It cut capital spending and locked the country into a pattern of soaring unemployment, especially in the black under-30 demographic.

There can be a valid case, a time and place, for pragmatic affirmative action mechanisms to be applied for a specified time period, with a clearly stated purpose, to attain defined results in order to break the unacceptable mold of entrenched, institutionalized discrimination and/or segregation. Affirmative action can kick start imperative change. But when affirmative action initiatives are unconditional, put in place for an indeterminate period without defined objectives, they usually become obstacles in the way of society's sustainable progress. Social progress has to be driven by the whole population's collective pool of talent, competence and industrious effort, sometimes necessitating a deliberate division of labor which addresses the needs of each segment of population. Affirmative action can very easily get in the way of the requisite meritocracy and may even become a seriously counterproductive tool for the corrupt and a prop for the indolent, as it has in Zimbabwe and to an alarming extent in South Africa.

The most frequently debated affirmative action initiatives are those applied by academic institutions. The worst of them are nothing but arbitrary quotas, mostly disconnected from any national demographic distribution. The better ones attempt to promote a diverse student body that approximates or reflects the ethnic demographics of the country, and seek to counterbalance the effects of poverty on academic opportunity and performance. In a 2003 discrimination case, Justice Sandra Day O'Connor and the Supreme Court found in favor of a University of Chicago Law School admissions policy considering race, arguing that the school had a "compelling interest" to achieve racial diversity up to a point (the referenced "point" remains undefined today). Her written opinion suggested that affirmative action policies should be temporary and that colleges should not need race-based admissions policies in 25 years—meaning that society should have eliminated the need by 2028! Neither Justice O'Connor nor the rest of America addressed the underlying issue: access to quality public schooling from kindergarten through high school.

There can be little doubt that affirmative action (with or without quotas) has not worked well in primary, secondary or higher education. Should we not de-emphasize the "minority" notion, and instead, give more weight to assiduousness, persistence and straight grit in qualified applicants, to boost the admission of those, who irrespective of class and race, conquer poverty, survive absentee parenting and overcome poor quality or failing schools? Unfortunately, the term "minority" is used disingenuously to disguise focus on blacks and Latinos, sometimes at the expense of Asian and white college applicants, who have been denied admission despite demonstrably stronger qualifications.

So is it not time to challenge the course of our thinking on affirmative action programs, since they seem to be failing? Have we not got the cart before the horse?

To eradicate disparities, as Ibram X. Kendi wrote in his Afrocentric but scholarly 515-page analysis of American racism, *Stamped from the Beginning*, the solution lies in "stamping out discrimination and in providing resources to close the gaps." He is obviously right, but the gaps to be closed are those that exist and penalize any and all groups, irrespective of race, color or creed. Kendi is sadly short on practicable proposals and suggestions, given his meticulously detailed history, analysis and critical classification of reformers and agents for positive change (black and white) in America's history. However, he is surely right about discrimination and access to empowering resources beyond just money. The latter would be readily fixable if our education system produced better-informed voters, who might elect better representatives to take the cause forward.

In South Africa, there is no doubt that BEE's affirmative action legislation has fallen dramatically short as a means of reducing inequality of income, wealth and living standards. To put this into context, one has to look at the population's ethnic segments. The total population in 2018 was around 57 million, of which over 44 milion were black, 4.7 million *Coloured*, 4.5 million white, and the balance Asian; so over 75% were black. Endless statistics and metrics (both South African and international) point to only marginal improvement from the apartheid era's income inequality between blacks and whites by 2015; that small reduction is derived from a despicable accumulation of quite incredible wealth by an absolutely tiny, elitist group of black politicians and their oligarch friends. However, when the focus is on intra-black inequality, meaning within the black majority population, the numbers show a tragic INCREASE in inequality, by a multiple of three or more, depending on the source and who is counting. This under-reported regression is linked quite directly to the massive accumulation of wealth by the ANC's leaders, insiders and ANC cronies linked to its ruling establishment. BEE has been the prime vehicle for South Africa's ruinous corruption, state capture, collapse of utilities, embezzlement of public funds and disastrous incompetence in leadership roles. As the total population continued to soar, unemployment levels rose to between 25 percent and 35 percent; and it was even higher for Africans under 30. South Africa is but one example of failed affirmative action. The worst example is probably Zimbabwe, next door neighbor to the north. BEE on its own does not prove that all such programs have failed, or will. However, it remains difficult to pinpoint an example of successful affirmative action programs anywhere.

Why can't the American voter learn from history?

Nobody can claim that it isn't tough to be born at the bottom of the socio-economic scale, irrespective of geography. And yet, in a lot of countries, it is a lot tougher than it is in the US, because we have, in the course of 200 years, developed a system of national wealth creation, which allows our safety net, warts and all, to help us progressively ensure that being born and raised in Homerville, GA, Birmingham, AL, the Bronx, South Side LA or downtown Detroit—or, for that matter, anywhere in the rust belt or the *Hill Billy* country of West Virginia—is a lot less hopeless and devoid of opportunity than being born in Kano, in a Caracas favela or in Kolkata's slums. In the USA, well into the new millennium, there is at least a 50:50 chance of moving up a quintile on the social scale in the course of a lifetime. About half of those in the bottom quintile had moved up to a higher income group in the course of the preceding decade or two. Economic growth has caused rising incomes for over 50 percent (US Treasury Department report, November 13, 2007) but this trend was interrupted in the years 2007–2017 by the recession and an historically slow recovery before resuming. That is only possible because we are a society where those who are most productive are motivated to take risk, to invest and produce, so the economy can grow, and employment opportunity can expand to keep pace with population growth. Over the long haul, despite the business cycles, the wealth created in a sound investment environment will do infinitely more to fund social services and finance social progress than legislation can. When economic growth occurs and employment opportunities expand, the unemployed and under-served at the bottom of the scale benefit in socially significant and nationally relevant terms, but unfortunately not always equally for all.

Maximizing equality of opportunity, meaning equality of access to all the tools necessary for self-improvement, is the indisputable priority and exquisite goal on which the world must focus—in every country, at any time, under any viable system of government. Despite its dark history of slavery, persistent discrimination and bigotry, the USA is better placed to make progress than most countries on this planet, thanks to incremental reform and advances over 200 years, and driven by America's fundamental democratic tenets. We could have done a lot better if we had not neglected the education and training of our children and youth, That, of course, would not in itself secure remediation of past injustices (if indeed that were somehow possible in practicable terms), nor does it ensure essential reform for the future; but America is well positioned and equipped in this context. Along with the right educational reforms, we need sound political or civic leadership and assumption of individual responsibility. If this notion is difficult for the parochial American reader to accept, direct exposure to the life of ordinary people in Zimbabwe, Democratic Congo or in the Republic of Chad is recommended; alternatively try the Xin Jiang Province of China, Sudan, Afghanistan, Yemen or Bangladesh.

Perfect equality of opportunity and access cannot be legislated; something closer to it has to be attained, building block by building block, through investment in education in its broadest sense, investment in health via access to clean water, adequate nutrition and medicine, and an infrastructure that serves all. It also takes a market-based system of governance where self-interest and investment in sound economic activity can create the surplus (also called profit) with which to finance social programs essential to the extension of equal opportunity and access.

Nice but failing socialistic theory and unrealistic, egalitarian obsessions have been granted credibility for so long that "they have been ossified into dogma." (Nicholas Wade, New York Times, June 2014) Neither speculation in social science nor populist legislation will deliver universal equality of access, let alone equality of income, capacity or talent.

> *"The way to stop discrimination on the basis of race is to stop discriminating on the basis of race."* (Chief Justice John G. Roberts)

There is absolutely nothing unsustainable about laws forbidding and punishing discrimination in a manner that is a true deterrent; nor is there anything counterproductive about deliberate, realistic progressive taxation protocols that can help fund the essential roles of government and social services. Even if it does not balance the national budget, a steeper curve applied to progressive income taxes would make a lot of political sense. The optics would be good, and would be helpful in unifying a very divided society. This approach would likely help less-informed American voters better understand and buy into the free market capitalist system that sustains them. The sharing of such concepts across the country's political divide, however, is obstructed on both sides by identity politics, populist name calling, inane slogans, unfocused and scatter-shot protests, and the closed minds of people who only read and listen to what they want to see and hear. The trouble is that too often

"Conservatives think liberals are stupid. Liberals think that conservatives are evil." (Charles Krauthammer, 2017)

The two concepts or notions EQUALITY and EQUAL ACCESS, meaning equal treatment, remain confused (if indeed understood) in popular socio-politics around the world. Certainly too many misinformed voters persist in confusing the two concepts, and so perpetuate the problem of placing their faith and aspirations in the wishful, unfounded notion that all men are equal and therefore equally endowed with talent and capacity, rather than focusing on the paramount, imperative quest for equal opportunity, equal treatment under the law and equal access to the tools and attributes that facilitate fulfillment and the pursuit of happiness.

Anybody heard of Darwin?

~~~~

"You can't go back and change the beginning, but you can start where you are and change the ending."
-C. S. Lewis

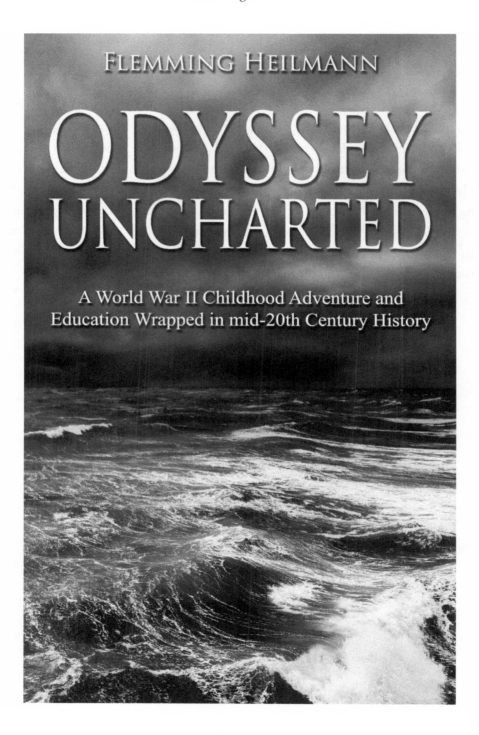

FLEMMING HEILMANN

ODYSSEY UNCHARTED

A World War II Childhood Adventure and
Education Wrapped in mid-20th Century History

Chapter I

Fortress Singapore

" … the worst disaster and largest capitulation in British history."
Winston S. Churchill

A FEARFUL, TEARFUL farewell in a monsoon deluge. My weeping mother, *Mor* (Danish for mom), my big brother John clearly distressed, and I myself at age five quite confused and frightened, all three of us completely saturated on the deck of the evacuation vessel. We were watching the small dark silhouette of *Far* (as Danish kids call their dads) melt into the gray monsoon cascade obscuring the quayside as the ship inched silently sideways from the dock, its lines being cast off, and then slipping out into murky Singapore Harbor like a retreating ghost stealthily disappearing into its own shadowy nowhere.

This is a true and indelible memory among my very earliest childhood recollections.

The very memories are difficult to pinpoint and define, because one never knows which of them might have been instilled by the anecdotes of parents or by images in old photo albums, and which of them are truly pulled from the bottom of the jumbled pile of remembered childhood crises and excitements. In my own case, the nether reaches of that pile are all Malay images: memories drawn from my first five years, spent in Perak on a rubber plantation called Jendarata Estate. It was the headquarters of a Danish-owned enterprise encompassing five plantation properties, literally chopped out of the tropical lowland jungle at the foot of the Malay Peninsula's mountainous spine, which runs from the Thai border to the southern sultanate of Johor just north of Singapore. Here the rubber trees, oil, and coconut palms were planted by the thousands along the northern bank of the slothful Bernam River separating the sultanates of Selangor and Perak as it meanders in slow motion across the steamy flats toward the Straits of Malacca.

I also remember my very best Malay playmate, Fatimah, with crystal clarity. I adored her unreservedly and she remains a vivid picture in my mind seventy-five years later. Immaculate glowing-gold complexion, huge ebony-black eyes in which you could not tell pupil from iris, immense curling lashes, finely chiseled nose and sculpted lips, smiley dimples, and shimmering blue-black hair falling softly in waves to the small of her back. We played together incessantly with her dolls, gorgeously dressed in miniature *sarongs* and silk *baju tutops* of stunning color, just as she would herself be dressed on *Hari Suci*, sacred Muslim days. We played the games of five-year-olds anywhere in the world, communicating freely in the simple Malay of children. It was my preferred language, ahead of the Danish and English spoken by my parents and European adults in the world around me.

Again with unbridled affection, I recall my tight relationship with Fatimah's father, our *syce* or driver, Abdul bin Rahman. Abdul welcomed me into the bosom of Malay Muslim values and traditions. Whenever he wasn't busy driving the big black shiny 1936 Buick for my parents, he would happily sit for hours, relaxed on his haunches, coaching me in Malay mores, Islam's five core principles, its rules, and good Muslim manners, including what foods were off limits and how to eat with only my left hand. Abdul was my gentle Malay mentor, a small, wiry, soft-spoken man with high cheekbones and a broad brow below his carefully combed-back black hair, visible only when he was not wearing his *songkok*. I could never negotiate enough time with Fatimah and Abdul.

From infancy I was assigned to the fussing care of my Chinese *amah*, who preferred to have me play at home inside the bungalow or in the garden, where in *Mor's* sight she could display her hovering attention to my every need, real or concocted, and so justify her employment. Every white child and the children of wealthy Chinese had an *amah*. The majority of them were recent immigrants or expatriates from China's largest province of Guangdong, also known as Canton. Typically they would send most of their earnings home to their families, as their cost of living in Malaya was virtually covered by their employers, who provided lodging, meals, medical attention when needed, and complete sets of new clothing every Chinese New Year (including the mandatory black silky pants and white button-up cotton tunics, which were the trade uniform of *amahs*). They did not have a formal trade union as such, but they organized welfare associations to which they paid a modest subscription and elected leaders by ballot. These groups would rent a whole floor of a local shop house, typically a town house with a retail establishment on the ground floor and residential space above, where they would gather on their days off to gossip and relax, and they would use the space for storage of prized possessions acquired in Malaya and treasured memorabilia, which they had brought with them from China. These women were entrusted with the basic raising and well-being of thousands upon thousands of European and Chinese children, while their mothers enjoyed ample free time for tea parties, social pastimes, card games, and gossip at the club. *Amahs* dramatically lightened moms' burden of mothering throughout colonial Malaya. They could also have considerable influence over a child's early learning processes and values. My own *amah* would often talk of the need to work hard because hard work brought opportunity to make progress and to become wealthy:

> "Amah tell you, Flemmin,' you work hard, it make lucky," she would say, "and lucky make you rich man! When you are big, when you are rich daddy, I come take care your children. Flemmin', I tell you, work hard!"

Another indelible memory is that of "Uncle Gillah" (*gillah* is Malay for crazy) the wild Danish bachelor in charge of one of the plantation divisions, who in his Tiger Moth would buzz our Jendarata bungalow and parachute our birthday and Christmas presents onto the front lawn of the large garden, taking care not to have the precious package land in the crown of the huge Banyan tree at its center. This is a genuine memory, not the product of repeated anecdote.

It is more doubtful that I truly recollect the king cobra, which made itself comfortably at home coiled up in my cot one night at bedtime. That story was told and embellished so often by *Mor* at family gatherings over the next fifty years, I have no way of knowing. However, the story goes on to relate how *Far* shot the cobra and destroyed its nest, which was eventually found between my bedroom's floorboards and the ceiling of the dining room below. In my mind's eye, I still see the thieving monkeys, leaping from branch to branch, swinging tree to tree to strip the back garden of papaya, mangoes, bananas, and crimson rambutans. All sorts including Gibbons, Macaques, and Silver Leafed monkeys. I still hear the staccato chatter and excited screeching of the primates.

I still dream of that quiet, pampered, plantation childhood with ever-hovering *Amah* treating me like a delicate piece of Meissner porcelain—a collage of disconnected scenes from that placid tropical daily routine. The large, rambling bungalow (all white people's houses were "bungalows" in Malaya, as were the homes of rich Chinese *towkays* or merchants, whether the house had one or two stories). It was built to capture every hint of a breeze, with a deep shadowy porch encompassing the whole house on both levels; no glass, but permanent mosquito netting stretched across each window frame downstairs; and upstairs fine cotton netting suspended from the ceiling to the four corner posts of each bed and down to the floor, as there were no windows in the sleeping quarters. The *chichows*, tiny green lizards, clinging to the walls at night. *Far*, feigning conspiracy, whispered as he taught me to cause the little critters to drop their tails in shock reaction to the crack of clapped hands or the stomp of a leather sole on the polished red tile of the floor. *Far* dispelled my initial tears of horror by assuring me that their tails would grow right back, which indeed they did in a couple of days, ready for the next round of my dad's fun and games.

Sauntering strolls around the expansive rectangular *padang*—Malay equivalent of an English village green—in heavy late-afternoon heat, while *Amah* exchanged her stream of gossip in lilting Cantonese with passing women in baggy black cotton pants and white blouses buttoned at the throat. If I stepped off the road, *Amah* would command me to stay out of the *lalang*, the long grassy weeds where a cobra might well be lurking. Scorpions were also a threat if they were disturbed, as they arched their tail segments, venomous stingers primed to strike.

The garden was dominated by a beautiful giant banyan, which has forever been my personal symbol of that Malayan childhood. An ancient, sturdy trunk in the middle of the expansive front lawn supporting a wide parasol crown and drooping limbs from which occasional tentacles reached back down to the ground, striking new roots in the soil. The banyan was home to exotic technicolor birds, green doves or *punai*, and the common yellow-vented bulbul who would signal the arrival of every single sunrise within a minute or two of 6:45, continuing its repetitious call to action for about ten minutes until his daily duty was done. Mynas with yellow face masks, black-and-yellow sunbirds and melodious Oriental magpies, for some reason dubbed *Prosperity Birds* by the Chinese.

An artist's work in Malaya called for a palette loaded with every hue and shade. The country's flora, fauna and human life produced constant explosions of startling color bursting from flowers, fruits, butterflies, birds or snakes of every ilk; more colors radiating from saris, sarongs, and turbans of the Sikhs.

Europeans in crisply starched white shirts and slacks or calf-length skirts grunting and squealing their way through mixed doubles, sweat jumping from their brows and hot pink cheeks. Off court, others would await their turn as they cheered a good shot or confirmed a line call while sipping their iced lemon-barley water. The pale yellow four o'clock sun would cast blue shadows, lengthening quickly as they warned of approaching short-lived dusk. *Chocras*, little Tamil ball boys, scurried around to retrieve errant tennis balls like busy squirrels gathering nuts. They rejoiced in the 10 Malay cents each earned for ninety minutes of busy work.

Children's tea parties were as refined as the delicately sliced cucumber sandwiches prepared for the adults. Heftier jam sandwiches sans crust for the kids. Ice cream, chilled sago with dark rich molasses known as *gullah malacca*, doting mummies with their cups of steaming tea, and of course, hovering *amahs*. European women chatting while knitting white balaclavas and mittens for the heroic Finnish freedom fighters thousands of miles away, skiing around in distant Nordic woods draped in white camouflage of bed sheets, sniping at barbaric Bolsheviks. Colonial ladies of Malaya helped save Finland and the planet from those bloodthirsty Slav invaders from the Russian steppes.

Endless thousands of dark green rubber trees stood smartly at attention in ruler-straight rows like a tropical battalion of guardsmen blocking the advance of the pressing jungle. The white NCO chevron patterns carved into the tree trunks by rubber tappers added to their military bearing. By contrast, the scruffy sprawling oil palms offered shelter and nourishment to evil slithering snakes and plump, scampering rats.

Rubber still dominated the Malay plantation industry in the 1930s, but was already losing ground to oil palms as chemically produced alternatives displaced rubber and latex in making tires, and the demand for vegetable oils for food products, soap, and cosmetics escalated. Coconuts, on the other hand, have never yielded their role in the Malayan plantation industry, nor their picturesque place in the lowland landscape and along fairytale tropical shorelines. Easy access to their husky fruit enhanced many of the dishes offered at *Mor's* curry lunches or *tiffins*, and gave Tamil laborers convenient access to juice for brewing *samsu*, their party libation and source of comfort and mirth.

All of a sudden, the late afternoon's thin sunlight would fade and then surrender to the precipitous descent of a blue-black velvet curtain, as if a chandelier were deliberately darkened on a dimmer-switch, allowing but a few minutes of heat-fevered dusk. High-density darkness, heralded first by a unison burst of cicadas lying in wait for the exact, predetermined moment. Minutes into the darkness a shattering cacophony of wide-awake noises, which would then persist through the dead of night until the horizon allowed dawn's early grey to lift the blue-black velvet curtain again. The impenetrable black of night was pierced only by the dizzy, darting white glow of a million fireflies. Isolated, always breathless, moments of silence and drama would be prompted by the blood-curdling strike of some prowling predator hitting its nocturnal quarry.

Playmates at the Plantation School, where employees' young children of all Malaya's races received a simple but solid start in English, reading, writing, and arithmetic, at first learning by rote and group recital, or by singing monotone chants in unison like little Buddhist monks or oriental Gregorians. That was the modus operandi, and it worked well to prepare them for local schools. Discipline reigned and facilitated a natural appetite for learning

Wherever there were people, blue smoke would suspend a thousand distinct scents, aromas and smells, now perfumed by flowers, now spiced by *kampong* or Malay village cooking, then acrid from the burning of buffalo dung or waste, or just plain old woody from ever glowing communal fires; but the smoke was always turquoise blue. On the hottest airless days bereft of breeze, when not a single palm frond would stir, the stagnant smoke would hang dead-still, a ghostly wisp suspended over flimsy stilted *kampong* huts with woven reed or *attap* roofs. A whole day could pass before the air again stirred enough to nudge the spent smoke away, only to be promptly replaced by gentle billows from the smoldering village embers awakened by the breeze. Dreamy wafts of scent from exotic fruits, whiffs of a hundred different curries cooking, incense drifting from joss sticks in a nearby Buddhist or Hindu temple, smells of fresh buffalo dung, the stink of newly cut durian fruit, sickly-sweet steam clouds from a palm-oil refinery, sour steaming vapor from a latex-curing plant. Interpretive smells of Malaya.

Mor would regularly invite the company's half dozen bachelor planters for Sunday *tiffin,* an elaborate curry lunch, involving servants in crisp white cotton uniforms and silly little white Nehru hats, extending to white gloves and red sashes across their chests for visiting VIPs and special occasions. A couple of pink gins or gin 'n tonics would precede the feast. Blistering *curry-nasi,* the Malay meal of steamed white and yellow rice, and an oft changing variety of curried fish, chicken and beef, sinuous *ikan kring* or dried fish, salty prawns known as *udang,* crispy deep-fried Indian *poppadums* and floppy *chapattis* both of which are Indian varieties of bread, mango chutney and scorching chili or *sambal*—all quenched by cold Tiger Beer. Red spiny rambutan, equally juicy lichee, papaya, mango, and other exotic fruit and dessert of *pisang goring*—fried banana—and ice cream, or perhaps *gullah Malacca* on a kind of ice-cold sago pudding to cool the tongue and palate.

Dipping a pinkie finger in my mother's solitary evening tipple of Harvey's Bristol Cream just before bed time; *Far's* not-so-solitary *stengahs,* meaning half soda water without ice and half Johnny Walker Red. Good old Cantonese *Cookie,* who was in charge of the kitchen and considered himself a chef, made little Chinese and other Asian cocktail snacks called *makan kichil,* literally meaning small food in Malay. *Mor* taught him to prepare the odd Danish dish according to the availability of ingredients. Cookie was competent and reliable, but addicted to a daily visit to his local opium den somewhere in the employee housing complex, where he would go for his "siesta" every day, as soon as lunch had been cleared away.

Apart from Cookie and *Amah,* the domestic staff consisted of Condaya the Telegu houseboy and gardener and a *tukan ayer* or the water bearer, both of whom were Tamils. They all lived in the roomy whitewashed servants' quarters on the far side of a kitchen courtyard at the back of the bungalow.

Hindu funeral processions, escorted by pulsating percussion groups and a couple of wailing Indian *nadaswaram* reed instruments, dozens of white-robed and turbaned pall bearers, women ululating and moaning, mounds of fragrant flower petals inundating the coffin to be interred on a consecrated burial lot at the end of the service road leading into the dark green rubber trees.

Slow moving Malay men in earth colored sarongs and white cotton shirts, occasionally with a ceremonial k*ris*—an ornate dagger—tucked in at the waist in response to a *fatwa*, some wearing the round white skullcap, proud symbol of the revered *Hajj* or a pilgrimage to Mecca. The women wore cheerfully colored and patterned sarongs and *bajus* or blouses, covering their heads only with simple scarves in those earlier colonial days before stricter orthodox Islamic practice took hold.

Pounding thunder, detonating sheets and spears of lightning, gusts of wind propelling cascades of raindrops the size of marbles. Huge post-storm puddles teeming with busy tadpoles; sticky-green frogs with ugly warts on slimy backs, sucking in gulps of steamy air in the post-deluge sunlight. Midday heat so intense the air seemed to vibrate in the shimmering white light, which cooked the earth. Skin itching from the rash of prickly heat, floppy cotton sunhats, clammy sweat-soaked shirts. Bilious attacks with fever and diarrhea, malaria and dysentery. *Mor's* cure-all antidote of castor oil poured into an egg cup of lukewarm, preserved orange juice. Billions of ever-present, ever-whining mosquitoes. Millions of brown and gray moths, hundreds of spectacular multicolored butterflies flaunting their décor and, as darkness fell, the dizzy dance of mesmerizing fireflies. The "Ice House Lorry" from Teluk Anson arriving twice a week, sputtering, creaking and straining under its crushing load of quarter-ton oblong slabs of ice to help preserve household perishables for a day or two, keep the butter solid, and the bottled beer cool. It also supplied the plantation ice house, a less than foolproof repository for local medicine supplies, which had to be protected from the heat.

Torpid *kampongs* along the banks of the opaque café-au-lait Bernam River oozing along its slothful path, giving home to child-snatching crocodiles as it made its lazy way west across Perak's fertile alluvial flatland. The ever-threatening jungle forcing riparian Malay villagers into reluctant action with *parangs* (very sharp wide-bladed knives) and *chunkils*, agricultural hoes, chopping away to beat it back and allowing them breathing room to tend their modest rice paddies, vegetable crops and banana palms. Women cooking rice and fish or chicken over ever-glowing embers between the *attap*-thatched huts perched on stilts. Little rural markets where hustling Chinese shopkeepers or itinerant vendors haggled loudly over the last cent for a pound of rice, bags of *ikan kring* or *udang*, pineapples, passion fruit, durian, a bolt of white cotton, three yards of brilliant silk or a pair of lacquered chopsticks.

Far, whose given names were Poul Bent, was known as PB to those friends and associates who didn't call him Mr. Heilmann or *Tuan,* Malay for Mr. or Sir, figured large in the landscape. In his starched white safari shirt, knee-length shorts, white cotton knee-stockings and polished black shoes, he would march resolutely across the *padang*—the large rectangular expanse of lawn around which houses and other estate buildings were deployed—to his office in the slanting light of morning, just minutes after the hurried sunrise. The administrative offices shared a building with the plantation's clubhouse, where the white *mems* or madams and *tuans* gossiped in woven reed or *ratan* chairs, sipping lemonade and barley water or tea. *Stengahs* and Pimm's or pink gins would take over later when the day's work was done. Ladies playing mah jong or bridge, interrupted regularly for chatter and gossip sessions.

Some of these many memories are derived from family anecdotes and photo albums, but most are vivid recollections drawn from early childhood realities. I certainly have no personal recollection of big brother John crashing into me on his bike as he rounded the bamboo hedge at the end of the bungalow's driveway. The impact sent both *Amah* and me literally hurtling through air to a hard landing a few yards up the road. The estate doctor was called in to confirm that nothing was broken and that *Amah* was not concussed. The story has it that I was left with a debilitating stutter for a month or so.

Then there was the story about me and Roman Catholics. John had, from the age of six, been sent to boarding school at a little Roman Catholic convent in the cooler climate of Cameron Highlands. So, at the age of nearly five I wanted to know what "Catholic" meant. My mother, with her infinite Lutheran tolerance and readiness to embrace all things Christian, defined and explained in diplomatic tones:

> "God can be served in many different ways, Flemming," she told me, "and the Catholics, who are very nice people, do some things differently and have some special rules. Their priests and nuns are not allowed to marry and have families, and they wear unusual clothes. They are allowed to eat meat six days a week, but only fish on Fridays. You know, other people like the Jews and Muslims, don't eat pork at all. Catholics go to confession every week to tell their priest whenever they have been naughty, and they go to something called mass every day to pray in church, where they use special smoke and holy water, and tinkle-bells—all to please God. And they do something called genuflecting and crossing themselves in front of the altar," she explained as she illustrated the maneuvers in a kind of curtsy, while making horizontal and vertical hand movements across her ample bosom, "just like this!"

Her explanation, as the story relates, prompted a prolonged and troubled silence on my part as I left her bedroom to ponder. After some time I returned to give vent to my concern:

> "I don't like that Catholic stuff, *Mor*! Why does John have to go to that kind of strange school? I don't want to go there when I am six. Please, *Mor*, I don't want to be a Catholic, I would rather just be a Dane."

Those early sentiments endured despite the enormous respect I developed over the years for Jesuit education around the world. Jesuit schools have brought enlightenment and progress to so many isolated and needy communities around the world over several centuries.

The undying personal memory of the anxiety experienced as Malaya faced imminent invasion by the Japanese is still crystal clear: leaving my father behind as we were dispatched to an unknown destination in Australia, the departure with *Mor* and brother John from Singapore Harbor on board the evacuation vessel *M/V Boissevain* on a dark drenching monsoon day remains sharply etched in my mind.

~~~~

Life in Malaya, not to mention the daily news, had for months been dominated by stories of Japanese military aggression to the north, the occupation of parts of China, attacks on French Indochina, and menacing threats to Britain's colonial possessions. The Colonial authorities in Malaya never came close to admitting substantive danger. The government resorted to naïve propaganda and bombast, which was supposed to reassure the population that all was well in the eastern reaches of His Majesty's far flung Empire. *Far*, however, did not buy into the British party line, sensing that a Japanese invasion of the Malay Peninsula was in fact a very real and imminent threat. *Mor* had observantly noted an escalation in the number of Japanese people in hotels and restaurants in Ipoh and Kuala Lumpur. There were visiting Japanese businessmen, miners and journalists all over the place. The Colonial regime tried pathetically to calm nerves through 1940 by solemnly repeating that the Empire of the Rising Sun was no match for that of His Imperial Majesty King George VI, and that the Japanese were "safely contained" by the omnipotent Royal Navy deployed to the north and east of Singapore in the China Sea.

"Fortress Singapore is absolutely invulnerable," the news broadcasts assured us.

"The Royal Navy rules the Indian Ocean, the South China Sea and the western Pacific. The Royal Air Force provides cover wherever needed and vigilant reconnaissance from above."

"The RAF's Singapore and Johore bases secure ownership of the air from Bangkok to Batavia. The Army and colonial police forces control every inch of the Malay Peninsula and Borneo, from Kelantan to Sarawak."

"Wild rumors are to be ignored. They are unpatriotic and distracting," directed His Majesty's government via the airwaves from Kuala Lumpur and Singapore.

Behind the broadcaster's voice, the Band of the Coldstream Guards could be heard in the background, playing "Rule Britannia" and "There'll always be an England."

In the planters' community of Perak, PB was never quite accepted by the more blimpish of the Brits and, because of his skepticism, even less so as the war threat escalated. He did, of course, have a funny accent, and Europe was being ravaged by the Germans; so a "kraut" name like Heilmann was hardly an asset, nor was his clearly expressed judgment concerning Malaya's readiness for war. The Brits rarely called him by his "outlandish" Danish name, preferring PB. His forthright attitude and disregard of social rank didn't always fit, and it was known that Denmark's government was not exactly heroic in its stand against Hitler's threats. *Far's* approach to his job was uncommonly energetic and pragmatic. For example, he had long expressed non-conforming views on the planting industry's labor relations and employment conditions. His management style certainly differed from entrenched local practices, and he rarely bought the colonial party line.

> "God knows where he went to school," said Simon Spencer-Worthington in the Teluk Anson club bar. "We have to assume the poor chap went to some village outfit in the boonies of rural Denmark."

> "Strange little country he comes from! Doesn't have the clout of Holland, or even Belgium, does it! Danes know a bit about ships, rearing pigs, and dairy farming, I'm told, but that doesn't do him much good right here in Teluk Anson, eh? We're not exactly deep into the bacon or cheese business here, are we, old boy?"

> "Poor old Hamlet Heilmann! Something's rotten in the state of Denmark all right, and he's certainly got it arse about face here in Malaya. Never had the benefit of our Empire experience and background, of course!"

After Malaysian independence in 1957, Teluk Anson was renamed Teluk Intan, meaning Bay of Diamonds. The old name was in honor of Sir Archibald Edward Harbord Anson, first Lieutenant-Governor of Penang under British rule. After the British hand-over, Anson was no longer an appropriate hero for whom a good Malaysian market town could be named under the Malaysian *bumi putera* (sons of the earth) mantra.

At the Club, over too many pink gins or *stengah*s, the British propaganda was translated into planters' inane bar-room ramblings:

> "Listen old boy, the Japs only have aeroplanes made of varnished *papier mache*," said Godfrey Winterbotham. "Sod it! There's absolutely nothing to fret about! I know the French

are messing up in Europe and Indochina, but we are British, after all. Different kettle of fish, dear chap!"

The reality was that brand new Japanese Zero fighters were to outnumber and outperform the Royal Airforce's obsolescent Brewster Buffaloes, leaving the British ground forces totally defenseless without air cover, as virtually all the RAF's planes were eventually destroyed in their hangars or on the tarmac aprons of their airbases before Singapore fell.

> "The bloody Jap navy is simply no match for *HMS Repulse* or the *Prince of Wales*—and then we have all our other men o' war lying off Singapore. Totally in charge of the South China Sea. They'll have no problem protecting Malaya—and the rest of the world for that matter—from those little yellow slit-eyed buggers. And they can, of course, only get at Malaya from the China Sea via Singapore. No other darn way to take this country on, old boy. Safe as a bloody bank, we are!" declared Humphrey Sandys-Wynch.

> "It's quite impossible for the Nips to get at our backs by air, you know, nor by land! The Siamese jungle to the north does that for us. With the China Sea nicely covered from Hong Kong to Singapore, the Navy's protecting our flanks, my dear chap—we're in excellent hands," said Jock MacTavish, "So, cheers, chaps! Bottoms up!"

In fact, General Tomoyuki Yamashita, the Japanese commanding officer running the war in Southeast Asia, had meticulously planned the surprise landing on the northern Malaya beaches of Kelantan, and every detail was precisely prepared months before, plotted and charted by civilian advance men—the Japanese visitors *Mor* had noticed in hotels and restaurants. The Nippon spy network had in truth done a meticulous job, right under the noses of the colonial government.

> "The Japs just won't know what the hell hit 'em if they try any monkey tricks on Singapore. You just wait and see! They'll scarper at the very first skirmish. Between 'em, the Royal Navy and the RAF will have those little yellow bastards for breakfast. Fuck Tojo, fuck the bloody emperor and fuck his rising sun, too!"

> "Japan's a pretty backward nation, you know. Crude, they are—I'd say bloody medieval. All they know about is Sumo wrestling and making swords, but that's all about fat fellows, samurai and that sort of stuff, not about modern war. And they have strange eating habits, I tell you! That's why they're all midgets and bow-legged. Weak bones! They can't even feed themselves properly. They eat too much rice and uncooked fish. Primitive lot, they are! So, there's naught to worry about, old cock! Keep your pecker up, old boy!"

And so the chatter and braggadocio went on. PB became a less frequent presence at the club, choosing to have his end-of-the-day *stengahs* in more carefully selected company. *Mor* and *Far* spent more time with good friends among the senior people of leading British plantation and trading companies like Harrison Crosfields, Sime Darby and Guthries, as well as some ranking colonial service officers.

The Malayan colonial government was populated by very different categories of civil servant. The top echelon generally consisted of bright people, well educated and urbane, usually with impeccable manners. The British Empire was still enjoying its heyday, and thousands of Britain's *upper crust* who had not chosen careers at home took challenging exams to join the senior ranks of the colonial service in leadership positions, where they often did valuable work on behalf of the Empire and its subjects in many different parts of the world from Hong Kong to Lagos. On the other hand, the lower ranks, including many DO's or district officers were often less educated, leaving them insecure in the colonial environment, where their station in life tended to outstrip whatever perch they might have climbed to back in the UK. These more junior servants of the realm could be overly preoccupied with the pedigree, as they all wanted to claim *upper crust* status or be seen by their peer group to have it. Vocabulary and given accents classified some as *"Non-U,"* suggesting they were not upper crust. Collectively, however, the British Colonial Service, which governed huge territories around the globe, was a far better colonist than its French, German, Belgian, Spanish, Italian or Portuguese counterparts. Its legacy was to leave behind much stronger educational and judicial systems and better infrastructures from which the local population could benefit, if they so chose. The colonial Brits were also solidly loyal to the Crown and extraordinarily incorruptible, unlike their counterparts from the European continent. If only their indigenous successors and rulers in Africa and Asia had emulated them in this respect, billions of people would be a lot better off today.

The irony in 1940 was that the British Colonial Service, while spinning this web of naïve drivel about the strength of the military forces, was at the same time broadcasting offers of free passage to women and children on chartered evacuation vessels from Singapore to safe territory in India, Australia or New Zealand. From their Whitehall home base, the British government was busily contracting with owners of passenger liners and smaller vessels anywhere they could be found, irrespective of flag or registration, as long as they were not of the enemy Axis. The objective was to provide safe evacuation for hundreds of women and thousands of children. Many had boarded these vessels in Shanghai and Hong Kong as the Japanese threatened British strongholds. All of them called on Singapore en route. Dozens of the ships that set course for the UK ended up in Australia, having been forced to turn around and head south again as the North Atlantic had become increasingly perilous. The mighty German Navy, starting in 1940, wrought its U-boat terror on civilian shipping, just as they had in World War I. These evacuation ships generally steamed for Freemantle, Western Australia's largest port serving Perth, or to Darwin. The majority of evacuation vessels from Southeast Asia, however, headed straight for Australia from Fortress Singapore, landing their precious cargo safely in Brisbane, Sidney, or occasionally in Melbourne.

The family had lived in Malaya through the 1930s because *Far* had made his career there with Copenhagen-based United Plantations Limited, a group of five Danish-owned properties, which grew rubber trees, oil and coconut palms, and produced latex, palm oil and coconut products, or copra. The Danish company was founded before World War I as cultivated, commercially grown rubber was being promoted by the British colonial government. Rubber was not native to Malaya, but originated in Brazil's rainforests, where British botanists "stole" 70,000 seeds that were sent to the Kew Botanical Gardens in England. A fraction of them germinated and were forwarded to the colonies in Southeast Asia. Another source of rubber at the time was the French Congo.

The United Plantations properties were located along the banks of the Bernam River, the boundary between the sultanates of Perak and Selangor. Furthest downriver, nearest the Straits of Malacca, was Kuala Bernam (*kuala* meaning river mouth); and way upriver, not far from the foothills of the Cameron Highlands, was Ulu Bernam. The word *ulu* signaled that the place was close to the river's source. At one time they also invested in tea, experimenting with crops on beautiful plantations rolling over the misty hills high in the Cameron Highlands. Jendarata Estate was the biggest property and home to UP's Malayan headquarters, some ten miles from Teluk Anson. Travelling between the estates meant either very long boat rides up and down the wildly meandering Bernam with its oxbow twists and turns, or quick ten to fifteen minute plane rides. Every property had simple grass or dirt airstrips to accommodate small planes like Tiger Moths, piloted by the planters themselves.

~~~~

Poul Bent was the younger of twin boys, by half an hour, born on a mid-size farm in Denmark, in 1901. According to Danish practice and lore of the time, his older brother by thirty minutes inherited the farm. All the family's liquid resources, and multiple loans secured by the farm, had been spent on the training and education of the twins' much older sister. Ellen had, from a very young age, shown extraordinary musical talent, especially for the piano. In fact, she must have been quite an exceptional pianist. She had spent three months as a pupil of the great Arthur Schnabel in Berlin during the summer of 1936, at the peak of his fame as one of the world's very top pianists. Ellen then had a successful debut in 1938 at the renowned Odd Fellow Palace in Copenhagen before contracting an aggressive, racing cancer from which she died within months in her mid-forties. When PB came to the end of his teens as World War I ended, there was no spare cash and no farming career open to him at home, so it was made clear that he was to move right along and make a living elsewhere. Far did just that, with a clear realization that his academic qualifications were meager, and that his narrow reservoir of skills and knowledge lay in agriculture, gleaned through his childhood and teen years working on the farm. According to history as related by the family, he took the train to Copenhagen where he could stay with relatives and launch his job search. He apparently used that era's equivalent of the Copenhagen telephone directory to seek out names of companies and employers with connections to, or actually engaged in agriculture or forestry. One of these companies was United Plantations, or UP, in which he discovered there were some distant cousins involved. This was how PB started his transformation from a modestly educated son of a farmer in rural east Jutland to a career pioneer in groundbreaking agricultural initiatives in distant undeveloped countries. He was selected and employed as a trainee planter (then commonly known as cadets) in Southeast Asia, building on his experience of growing things out of the ground. He was not impeded by the fact that he was a young man of pragmatic intelligence, courage, iron will—and he had little fear of taking considered risk. He did not shrink from the voyage half way around the world and taking a plunge into the unknown. He was going to make the best of the opportunity, sink or swim.

A planter's work in Malaya was no cakewalk. It was an especially tough daily routine for rookie planters and young managers on the smaller estates. The usual elementary conveniences and comforts provided by urban employers were not always there to alleviate the hardships of life at the edge of the tropical jungle. Rising at four-thirty to be ready for muster, the *coolies'* roll call by lamp light at five o'clock. Directing labor to the day's first workplace before the morning mist trapped by the trees could melt away, the dense canopy dripping from over head, the ground dank under foot as snakes slithered out of the way and the mosquitoes attacked. Explaining the foremen's—*mandors'* or *kanganis'*—marching orders. Kickstarting the actual rubber tapping and palm fruit harvesting. Opening the morning shift at the latex-curing and oil-extraction plants. Supervising the recording clerks— *keranis*—in the field. Back to the bungalow for a quick breakfast at nine-thirty. Clear the desk at the office by eleven, check out the latex or palm fruit weigh-ins at the processing plants, plot the acreage yields from the areas being tapped or harvested. Back for lunch at one o'clock. A one-hour *lie off* or siesta. Another round through the fieldwork locations, solving problems on the fly. Back to the office to complete the day's paperwork until darkness fell abruptly two or three minutes either side of six o'clock, depending on the time of year. Only then could the planter say *sudah habis*—all done—and make his way to the bungalow for a cold shower and his first relaxing *stengah* of the evening with his feet up. This pace was maintained five-and-a-half days a week through two o'clock on Saturday afternoons.

Tapping rubber requires more skill than harvesting palm fruit, and some judgment, too. Armed with special grooving tools and knives, the tapper cuts V-shaped channels through tree bark, from which white latex oozes into collection cups suspended at the lowest point of the V. The tapper moves onto the next tree when the latex flow slows to a near stop, signaling exhaustion of that particular tapping. The process leaves repeated tapping grooves which form chevron-type markings like the insignia of a military non-commissioned officer. All this work is performed in Malaya's heavy, incessant humidity and pounding heat. Flaming sun or drenching monsoon torrents. The anopheles mosquito always lurking. Malaria, dysentery and scrub typhus always threatening, especially on the estates where health and hygiene were not given the Danish management's high priority. Apart from the abbreviated weekends, planters' downtime was limited to two free days per month, four days over the Christmas holiday, and four at *Hari Raya*, the big annual Islamic holiday marking the end of Ramadan with feasts of multiple curries and *rendang*, a spicy meat dish. *Hari Raya* is the most important of Malay holidays, when Muslim families gather as Americans do for Thanksgiving, but with a faith-based, benign Islam's emphasis on philanthropy, forgiveness, and good neighborliness.

Far had to learn to speak effective Malay, Tamil, and Hokkien, a Chinese dialect, to qualify for promotion and his free home-leave passage after the initial five-year tour of duty. Failure would mean a one-way ticket home for his own account. He could effectively communicate with UP's employees in all three languages: the Tamil labor force at the less skilled levels and the administrative staff which was multiracial, mainly Chinese and Telegu Indian. The enlightened Danish management style went the extra mile to emphasize respect for all people at all levels, communicating with them in their own language and appreciating cultural mores and sensitivities. It was truly a merit-based management philosophy, which earned UP a reputation as the Malaysian industry's model employer.

UP's success in the plantation business was closely coupled with management's ability to motivate people—that is all sorts of people. This is true of almost any industrial and commercial undertaking, of course, but good communication had special significance when working with such a multi-ethnic, multilingual, multicultural and often uneducated human resource. Hokkien and Cantonese, Tamil, Telegu and Punjabi, and Malay had to be navigated along with Muslim, Hindu, Sikh, Buddhist, Roman Catholic and non-conformist Christian faiths. One had to contend with the influences of class perception and income level among Chinese and Europeans, and divisions by caste structure among the Indians. All these elements guaranteed that few management issues were straight forward and simple.

The enthralling and uncommonly enchanting diversity of Malaya called for uncommon linguistic efforts and skills. On the estates, Hokkien was the commonly used Chinese tongue, reflecting the earlier migrant *coolie* population drawn from China in the first two decades of the 20th century, which then graduated to mercantile and administrative jobs such as clerks on the plantations, at timber companies, and in the trading firms. Hindi, Urdu and Punjabi were also spoken by the ubiquitous Indian tradespeople and money lenders, the turbaned Sikhs.

Native Malays constituted 60 percent of the total population, which meant that the Muslim faith predominated. This was before the start of extremist Islam's steady encroachment into the Malays' moderate, tolerant practice of Mohammedan faith. Many were devout, but very few were extremist. Islam arrived in Malaya with Arab traders in the 13th century and only gradually replaced Buddhism and Hinduism with an unorthodox Muslim faith. Its spread accelerated in the 15th century under the influence of the Sultan of Malacca, reaching up the Malay Peninsula and south into the Indonesian archipelago

United Plantation's cadets, trainees, or "first tour" planters were not allowed to marry on their maiden five-year tour of duty. Young planters lived modestly in bungalows located in the areas or *divisions* in their charge. The local Malay girls were almost universally alluring, often ready for a little infidel romance and the perks which went with it, especially in the most isolated plantation areas. Romance within their own Malay community was hard to come by, because good Muslim practice demanded female abstention until the wedding night, after marrying by arrangement. The taboos and prejudices of white colonial Malaya dictated that Eurasian matrimony would almost inevitably lead to difficult social and workplace complications, so the Danish company preempted the possibility of a cadet planter getting excessively involved with some lovely Malay or Chinese girl and deciding to marry her. The theory was that if it was the right relationship, it would survive the wait for the young man's second tour. Among the Brits it was an environment, where "fraternizing" across the ethnic divides, let alone overt romantic liaison, was verboten, and could be career-ending. Conservative as the colonial rules were, the Danish management's measured tolerance of the cadets' amorous escapades was almost as liberal as the permissive free-love practices in post-war Scandinavia. UP's management had a pragmatic don't ask, don't tell practice, akin to a Danish wink and a nod. Six decades later in Connecticut, reminiscing over a second *stengah*, *Far* would allude to these romantic adventures from his time as a rookie manager on the isolated Sungei Bernam estate, where his bungalow and the employee compound was surrounded by uninterrupted acres of oil and coconut palms. With a conspiratorial hint of a smile at the corners of his mouth and mischief in his eyes he would tell me "between-us-boys" stories.

> "Those were the days—long gone," PB would say almost wistfully, "Those were the good old days, I must say! I'd just love to turn the clock back fifty years—just for a few more of those young and carefree days, or—ha-ha—should I say nights? Too bloody bad they're long gone. But then I'm past it now anyhow, my boy! Much too old for those tricks."

> "Those good old days. What is it they call them, Flemming? Halcyon days?" he asked.

> "*Skaal*, my boy!"

The financial crash of all time and following worldwide slump hit with a vengeance at the end of the 1920s. The Weimar Republic had come crashing down with rampant inflation. Germans were famously lighting cigars with 10,000,000 Deutschmark bills. In 1921, the Reichsmark was valued at 272 to one U.S. dollar, as post-World War I Germany had established its first democratically elected government in the central city of Weimar. Ironically, before Weimar became associated with the disastrous years of the republic to which it gave name, the city was known for centuries as a center of culture, art, and learning associated with names like Goethe, Schiller, or Frantz Liszt. Throughout the country deep depression, unemployment, labor strife, massive public protest, and hyperinflation were hallmarks of the time. The catastrophic inflation was fueled by reckless government spending on "passive worker resistance" and other national and social crises. This was facilitated by simply working the printing presses to create ludicrous, unlimited amounts of new Reichmarks. Soon, one single U.S. dollar bought 4.2-billion Reichsmarks. The utter chaos of Germany eventually led to the installation of Adolf Hitler as Chancellor. As leader of the Nazi party he had been in and out of prison several times in 1933. *Der Fuhrer* was on his triumphal way, but the world around him was stuck in the depths of the Great Depression.

The global depression took its punishing toll on every financial and industrial enterprise, and the commodity markets of the whole world. As palm oil, copra, and rubber prices just imploded, Malaya's plantation industry became a financial quagmire and a management nightmare. The tin mining industry and teak logging fared no better. In 1925, rubber was priced at five shillings a pound; by the end of 1929 it bottomed out at just over a single penny in Sterling currency, a 98 percent plunge. In the phraseology of millennium-age industry and commerce, the downsizing of every company was absolutely devastating. Planters were dismissed and sent home to the UK in droves; that was the fate of almost half the staff on most of British-owned estates. Some properties were simply shuttered; others were amalgamated with neighboring properties to cut costs to the bone as they struggled to survive. Hundreds of thousands in the labor force across the Malay Peninsula were rendered jobless. There were no colonial government bail-outs in the Great Depression of 1929 or during the 1930's. Nobody was too big to fail.

The desperate Danish general manager of the five United Plantations properties was overwhelmed and just could not cope with the pressure. He buckled mentally, panicked, and then sought to end it all. He electrocuted himself in dramatic fashion by walking barefoot into a flooded drainage trench holding live cables in each hand. PB, who had already won early promotion to estate manager of one of the smaller properties at a tender age, succeeded him instantly, appointed by telegram from the chairman of the UP Board in distant Copenhagen. *Far* was thus catapulted into the leadership of a large enterprise in crisis, the *tuan besar*—big Mr.—head man of a substantial business by Malayan or any other standards of the time. PB endured a baptism by fire at the height of the Great Depression, receiving ill-informed and unrealistic directives from a very nervous board of directors, as shareholders panicked in far-removed Copenhagen, where United Plantations Limited was listed on *Borsen*, the Danish stock exchange. As general manager on the spot, his focus had to be on simply keeping the wheels turning, propping up the morale of management and remaining staff, holding the surviving work force together, keeping all variable costs to the absolute minimum. He put a complete stop to all capital expenditure, had to cut corners on maintenance of equipment, and pared all fixed assets. Production had to be reduced to the minimum level dictated by cash flow requirements, leaving oil palm fruit and coconut crops rotting on the ground and rubber trees untapped. It was a unique challenge for a young 30-year-old rookie manager.

Things were no better in Europe. In the USA, Franklin D. Roosevelt was busy spending taxpayers' newly printed money to construct his New Deal which, despite the massive public spending, was to fail him and America until the economy, a full decade later, was eventually dragged out of its rut by the stimulus of World War II.

At Jendarata, *Far* worked 14-hour days, smoking a round tin of fifty English Gold Flake cigarettes each day. The world economy recovered at glacial pace as demand for industrial and agricultural staples was restored by tiny increments in the course of the 1930s. The frantic demands and pressures from the distant UP board of directors and shareholders back in relatively stable Copenhagen were enough to test any veteran manager, let alone a rookie. There was no Roosevelt-type New Deal, no 21st century Stimulus Package, TARP money, QE measures nor other attempts to assist Malaya's economy. Far had a very lonely job, hell-bent on protecting the interests of all stakeholders in a precarious balancing act. His impatient masters were far removed from the rough and tumble of the realities.

Only the jungle was immune to the tyranny of the Great Depression: it never ceased pressing in, attempting to creep in to regain territory lost to the agricultural initiative of the European planter. The jungle's appetite for revenge was irrepressible and simply had to be conquered. Banks, creditors, and suppliers also had to be beaten back. Meanwhile creditors had to be placated as cash flow was managed by delaying payments to the limits of the law while debtors were cudgeled for prompt response to billing. PB weathered the storm by leading from the front, working himself to the bone, commanding the respect of employees at every level and every race on the five estates along the Bernam River. UP finally pulled through and was returned to profitability. By the mid-30s, the price of rubber was slowly recovering from its lowest levels and some of Malaya's rubber plantations, which had been laid dormant, were cautiously brought back into production. Along with United Plantations, the strongest British companies like Harris & Crosfields, Sime Darby, Dunlop Estates and Guthries had survived. Long closed independent small holdings, owned mostly by Chinese, started to come back more slowly.

~~~~

After five years in Malaya, on his first three-month home leave, *Far* reconnected with *Mor* in Jutland and soon asked her to marry him. *Mor* was the younger daughter of a modest soft goods merchant on *Soendergade*, the main street of Horsens, a small market town in eastern Jutland, where they both had gone to school. *Far's* home farm, *Tammestrup*, was just eighteen kilometers north of Horsens on the highway to Aarhus, Denmark's second largest city. They had originally met during a summer when *Mor* was learning housekeeping as a kind of domestic summer intern on the farm, before she started training as a pediatric nurse in Copenhagen. The courtship was a whirlwind of visits to friends and relations before their wedding in the tiny Ousted village church nearby the family farm. It was a 16th century whitewashed stone church, with walls a meter thick, a stubby square tower capped by a modest beaten copper steeple. Three generations of the family were baptized, married, and buried at that same small church. Today it still commands a singularly captivating view from the zenith of Denmark's highlands, across a broad patchwork of cereal, rape, mustard and beat crops, pastures and woodlands undulating down to Horsens Fjord to the south. The typical Danish countryside usually presents enchantingly intimate landscapes and views, but this particular vista has grand dimensions rare in this Lilliput land. Denmark's highest point, all of 178 meters or 550 feet, is but a stone's throw from Ousted church.

Mor's career as a pediatric nurse was promptly dropped, and the newlywed couple embarked for Malaya, where, in 1931, brother John came to this world in a primitive missionary hospital in Batu Gajah (*Batu Gajah* literally means stone of the elephant), a tiny outpost at the edge of the jungle of Cameron Highlands' foothills. *Mor* lost a baby girl a couple of years later, and I arrived in 1936, in the much more comfortable environs of a hospital in Penang. After giving birth to John in a bare-bones missionary hospital, *Mor* had chosen the relatively modern conveniences of a government hospital in the crown colony. I was born with a hair lip, which *Mor's* health care theories immediately attributed to tropical climate, preserved foods and poor vegetables deprived of the vitamins and minerals found in good Danish food—or maybe it was the human waste used by Chinese horticulturalists as fertilizer. *Mor* had these little medical fixations, often embellished by a touch of the hypochondriac's less than scientific speculation. Fortunately, my physical defect did not bring with it the oft-associated cleft palate, so the issue was shelved and later fixed when the family of four enjoyed a 1938 home leave in Denmark. My hair lip was mended in Copenhagen by an extraordinarily skillful plastic surgeon.

As always, the family's home leave in 1938 was spent catching up with relatives, getting acquainted with new arrivals to the clan, and mourning departures. It was the last time I as a two-year-old was to see my four grandparents and my aunt Ellen, the brilliant pianist. After seven years of World War II they were all gone, as was any childhood recollection of them.

Meanwhile, through the 1930s, the complacent western world simply ignored the increasingly ominous rumblings of Hitler and his viciously racist Nazi party, or made excuses to minimize its actions. Left-leaning commentators, many of whom were infatuated with the Bolshevik experiment, labeled any opposition to the coming rape of Europe as warmongering or arrogant imperialism. Others, like FDR and Chamberlain, waffled ad infinitum and looked the other way. At the end of the 30s, Europe, USA and the rest of the world were in deep denial. Only Britain's Secretary of the Admiralty, Winston Churchill, vociferously warned of the catastrophe that lay ahead if the Nazis were not checked. It cost him dearly— his left wing critics and revisionists still paint him as an imperialistic, warmongering blimp of the British aristocracy. Japan's bellicose moves were written off as Tojo's theatrical saber-rattling. Mussolini's fascist bullying and acquisitive African adventures were reported as harmless "Mediterranean posturing." The world's socialists and media, in an unholy alliance with philosophers, suffragettes, preachers and peaceniks, looked away and turned the other cheek. Their response to any serious threat was to advocate centralist socialism at home while encouraging cross-boundary labor alliances and appeasement. The empowered fraternity of labor, they declared, would never allow workers of the world to fight against their brothers in another country when the real enemy was the establishment and the ruling class at home. Doing nothing was so easy. In any event, they claimed, western democracy was under no substantive threat. Millions of tormented Jews lost their homes, their assets and livelihoods to Hitler's monstrous "redistribution," but that was not allowed to be an issue of note.

Europe and America kept right on course, whistling past the graveyard. PB was never in doubt that his duty and job was the stewardship of the properties of UP headquartered on Jendarata Estate; but he grew anxious over what he saw and heard of Europe and was no less concerned over Japan's aggressive moves on China

Early in the fall of 1938, the family returned to Malaya on one of East Asiatic Company's vessels, Denmark's favorite passenger-cargo link to the Far East. A leisurely voyage back to the heat and routine of British colonial surroundings. John was again sent off to his convent up in the cool of Cameron Highlands. I was largely in *Amah's* doting care on Jendarata Estate in the throbbing heat, where I got both dysentery and malaria. This second time round, *Mor* fell into that Malayan routine more readily. Her first arrival years earlier had presented challenges of language, culture and the sometimes pretentious demands of life as a *memsahib*, wife of the boss. She had by now mastered two new languages and learned to handle the pseudo-genteel antics of English colonial women and to speak up for herself. She had, in fact, also learned to enjoy being spoiled by some aspects of a privileged colonial lifestyle.

~~~~

With the escalating aggression of Tojo's Japan to the north, *Far* had decided to take the Brits up on their offer of evacuation passages for women and children. While the government offered free evacuation passages, they did so in hesitant and inconspicuous ways. Singapore's *Straits Times* reported that supreme commander of British forces, General Arthur Percival, had warned that "overt European evacuation programs would have a negative psychological effect on the native Asian population of Malaya," so booking such a passage took proactive perseverance. This was how the families of less farsighted Brits later got trapped by the invasion.

PB booked us on the government-chartered Dutch vessel, *M/V Boissevain*, headed out of Singapore for Sydney under contract to the Brits.

He equipped *Mor* with Thomas Cook travelers checks and an Australian bank account, to provide funds estimated to last up to six months. Everybody, even skeptical *Far*, was persuaded that the Japanese situation in Southeast Asia would be sorted out in a matter of months. This was the expectation despite what was going on in Europe as Mussolini sided with Hitler and every indication was that the Axis could take over that whole continent from Moscow to Madrid. *Far* had only scorn for Neville Chamberlain's wobbly appeasement of Hitler; he scoffed at the Prime Minister's pathetic promise of "peace in our time" upon returning from Munich, waving a piece of paper signed by the *der fuhrer*. He noted how the Vichy French viewed the situation through their own xenophobic lens of elitist complacency. He saw that the Americans were not even vaguely interested in getting involved in what they characterized as a confluence of European issues that did not concern America, even with Japanese aggression in China and the western Pacific region. *Far* wanted us out of Malaya, and yet did not foresee that there were five years of brutal World War II ahead.

He took a lot of flack from peer group planters at the Teluk Anson Club, almost all of whom were contented Brits under the spell of the government's propaganda and spin. Ironically, some of these colonial blimps—hard drinking, bloviating planters, accountants, and lower rank colonial service functionaries—were the first to take off when the situation later threatened them directly. They and their booze-induced bravado would vanish like the morning mist. Meanwhile, *Far* was quite determined to get his family out of harm's way while he would stay on to do his job. He was possessed by his responsibility for the interests of the company, shareholders, and its employees. He was driven by unswerving loyalty to more than two thousand people working on the five plantations.

PB had first made things clear to *Mor* before he spoke to the assembled family.

"Now please listen to me, dear ones," he said at the dinner table. "In my own mind it is just a matter of time before there is fighting in Malaya and Borneo, and serious bloodshed is inevitable. It is going to be no place for women and children. And there's no knowing how far it will spread … perhaps to Burma and India. I have thought a lot about it and, my dear boys, I have been talking with *Mor* about our situation. I am getting you all three out of here.

I am sending you to Australia, where you will be safe and sound until the British finally face the realities, come to grips with the Japs, and get things back on track and under control again throughout the Far East. Australia has to be the safest place to go, as Europe is obviously not an option, even if ships could get safely through the north Atlantic. Allied ships are being sunk by the dozens, and the Germans are on a march across Europe. Nor is India an alternative, because I don't think that country is safe from the Japs either."

Far paused for a moment as he could see that *Mor,* and therefore both of us boys, were struggling to stem the tears.

"You see, my dearest boys, there are times in life when you don't know enough, you can't predict for sure what is going to happen, so you simply can't be confident you're doing the right thing. Whatever the government says to reassure us all, there's no way in which I can tell what's going to happen here in Malaya, nor do I know exactly what *Mor* and you boys will find at the other end, or how she will manage in Australia. All I do know is that the three of you will be safe in Brisbane, Sydney, or Melbourne. I hear that the Australians are responding to this situation with kindness

and generosity, and that refugees are being well treated. But
I don't know more than that. Your safety is the priority, and
I am convinced you are going to be in harm's way if I keep
you here … so that's out of the question. You boys and *Mor*
are off to Ozzie, sink or swim!"

Far's whole life was characterized by momentous decisions made on the
basis of carefully assessed risk. He was bright, pragmatic and usually right;
the family reaped benefit and progress as a result.

~~~~

The image which still leaps out at me, after all these years, is that of Far's
gray silhouette waving his wide-brimmed straw hat at the edge of the dock
in Singapore Harbor, as M/S Boissevain inched away from its berth.
Cascades of water from a leaden monsoon sky engulfed all four of us. Three
of us in trepidation, waving from the ship's top deck, shedding torrents of
tears as if to match the tropical downpour—Far, the only person in sight on
the quay below, signaling his final farewell, hat held high. Although too
young at the time to appreciate the dimensions or implications of what was
happening, I still sense the reeling intensity of that moment's emotions and
the appalling sense of helpless uncertainty. The memory to this day evokes
a shiver and goes to the pit of the stomach. Ever courageous *Mor* simply
could not stem the sobbing. None of us moved until minutes after the dark,
dense curtains of water had completely engulfed the solitary gray figure on
the dock. That moment changed life's direction as we plunged into the
unknown on an uncharted odyssey.

I recall almost nothing of the journey into the Antipodes. The *Boissevain*
made a stop in Batavia, where John first set eyes on eight-year-old Inge-
Marie Nielsen, the girl he was to marry just a decade and a half later in Tokyo,
of all places. *Mor* had arranged to look up Tage Nielsen, whom she and Far
knew from their Danish school days in Horsens. Working for a molasses

trading company, he lived in Batavia—today named Jakarta—with his Dutch wife and two children. The Dutch colonial government was no more alert or better prepared for the Japanese threat than were the Brits in Malaya, and life in Batavia was still complacently normal. Inge-Marie, her younger brother, and her mother were later put under house arrest by the Japs for the duration of the war, and father Tage spent the war in a Japanese prison camp.

The rest of the voyage is but a blur. Family legend has it that Japanese high speed torpedo boats were sighted by passengers as they patrolled the waters of Indonesia or the Dutch East Indies, as they were then known. I was later reported to have called them "speed potato boats."

Arrival in Sydney escapes me completely, but not the long train ride to Melbourne. It was an overnight affair involving a tiresome, sleepy transfer in the dead of night from the initial train from Sydney to another waiting across the border-station's single platform. The explanation for the midnight inconvenience was a change in the gauge of the rail tracks at the boundary between the competing states of New South Wales and Victoria. The two Australian states could apparently agree on very little, and certainly not on railroad gauges. That was my early introduction to ludicrous practices of territorial hubris and protectionism in government, which I was to encounter later in linguistically divided Belgium, South Africa, and pathetically fractured Canada, with its ten parochial provinces—another country divested of national glue to unite it. That Australian idiocy prevailed, prolonging train transfers and billions of dollars of unnecessary waste for decades. To cap it all, the Sydney-to-Melbourne overnight "express" was pretentiously named "The Spirit of Progress." For the governments of New South Wales and Victoria, progress did not extend to standardization of railroad gauges, since that might mean more open markets and competition in interstate commerce.

Dread the thought!

A short spell in a cheap Melbourne hotel did not leave any lasting memory, except that the strange surroundings were never threatening. We were received with open arms. The Aussies were spontaneously and warmly generous without evident plan or coordination by government, extending a welcoming embrace to thousands of European refugees arriving from East Asia. Gregarious *Mor* quickly linked up with three or four other women, all British, who had left Shanghai, Hong Kong and Singapore with their children on various evacuation vessels, ending up for some reason in Melbourne. To this day, I do not know why we or they decided to head for the Victoria State capital.

Together they concocted a plan.

Things in Southeast Asia were getting more ominous by the day, as all-out war with the Japanese became a reality, and a full scale invasion of Malaya loomed. Geelong Grammar, an exceptionally progressive (truly progressive, as opposed to the American political sense of the word) boarding school, inappropriately tagged as the "Eton of Australia," threw its doors open to dozens of boys arriving with refugee families, including John Heilmann. He became the beneficiary of the finest education Australia had to offer, absolutely pro bono for the duration of World War II. The governors of this private school, prompted by its visionary headmaster, James Darling, decided that the young refugees and their families should be guests not only of Australia, but also of Geelong Grammar until the planet's geopolitical convulsions were resolved. Meanwhile, the evacuee women, having hatched their plan, teamed up to rent an old Victorian house on a two-acre plot in the tiny seaside village of Barwon Heads at the mouth of Port Philip Bay, near Geelong and about 60 miles southwest of Melbourne. Here they formed a commune.

Barwon Heads was a peaceful, cozy seaside village, nestled under a beautiful large bluff sheltering it from the Tasman Sea. It was a fisherman's paradise with a tiny harbor and wonderful white beaches nearby, frequented by surfers and vacationing families. In this setting it was difficult to realize that history's most brutal world war was raging across much of the globe.

Mor and *Far* were able to keep erratic communications going via Red Cross letters and occasional cables during the early months of the separation.

As the situation grew ever more threatening, they made a quite specific, preemptive deal to ensure that PB could contact us whenever he got the chance and would know where to find us in case we lost touch. The agreement was that while John went off to board at nearby Geelong Grammar School, *Mor* and I would stay in the Barwon Heads house, come hell or high water. This deal was only to be broken if or when *Mor* knew that *Far* was safely in the hands of the allies, was imprisoned by the Japs, was reported dead or if he actually arrived in Australia. Always pragmatic, PB took a very realistic approach and was able to send one more book of Thomas Cook checks, as he saw the hopes of an allied resolution of the conflict with the Japs dwindle.

The shared property in Barwon Heads did become a veritable commune in which the women distributed responsibilities for housekeeping and generating cash. All of them knew their cash resources were finite, and that they had to do something about it. Otherwise they would run out of funds before too long. A logical division of labor was developed.

The grounds of the property were transformed into a productive horticultural plot, where the women were individually responsible for different crops of fruits, vegetables, flowers and herbs. A garden shed served as a coop and a chicken run was fenced off. Hens and eggs became an important source of both food and income. Chicken prepared in every way became the staple diet: from *a-la-king* to *coq au vin, Bombay-curried, cacciatore*—stir-fried, boiled, sweet and sour, or just plain old roasted chicken. If it wasn't chicken, it was lamb or mutton. Australia was never short of sheep, so when the war impeded exports of lamb and mutton, the glut yielded an extremely inexpensive source of protein. Sheep's brains were a frequent main course, for which I never developed a fondness, despite attempts to disguise them in many presentations. That squishy, smooth texture in the middle, even when they were breaded and deep-fried to a crisp on the outside! Ugh! Tons of beautiful vegetables and fruits were grown for consumption and sale. Fish was a rare treat, although seafood was abundant and reasonably priced at the mouth of Port Philip Bay; it was still too expensive. *Mor* was a handy seamstress, so she was assigned specifically to the production of lambskin gloves, for both men and women, which fetched good prices at the local market and selected shops in the nearby city of Geelong. It was quite clear that Australian generosity and eagerness to give support boosted the income stream of the commune. The Aussies were not only extraordinary hosts, but also extraordinarily loyal and generous customers of the commune, who made sure that any hardship suffered by the refugees in Australia was minimized.

Being so young, living happily with other kids of my age, I was all but oblivious to *Mor's* chronic anxiety and the emotional hardships of the women in the group. I grew physically strong, enjoying a healthy diet of fresh food and the vigorous climate of coastal Victoria, no longer the somewhat sickly little fellow struggling with the heat, dysentery, malaria, or the other tropical disorders encountered back in Malaya. Mor's frantic scanning of all newspaper reports and obsessive attention to radio broadcasts covering developments in Southeast Asia escaped my attention. However, the news in fact deteriorated with every week.

~~~~

The Japanese fooled everybody, especially the complacent British, by landing on the northeastern coast of the Malay Peninsula to invade from the South China Sea. This happened only hours before the Japanese air force shocked the United States and allies by bombing the heart out of Pearl Harbor. The Japs made land among the fishermen's *kampongs* on the gorgeous palm-lined beaches of Kelantan, near Kota Baharu, and then used bicycles to move unchallenged southward in hordes towards Perak, then Kuala Lumpur, and eventually Singapore.

At 4:15 a.m. on December 7, 1941, the Japs struck Singapore with their first nocturnal air raid. The Royal Navy's base was ablaze with all its lights still on. *HMS Repulse* and the *Prince of Wales* supposedly guarding Fortress Singapore with several attendant escort ships were sent to the bottom of the

China Sea or the Malay Straits by Japanese Zero dive bombers, or torpedoed by their submarines causing death and destruction deep into the Indian Ocean. The rest of the Royal Navy's East Asian fleet had fled in shame. Japan's disciplined and well equipped air force (those *papier mache* planes the Teluk Anson blimps had scorned) turned out to be state of the art. They meticulously bombed Singapore's strategic buildings, one by one, before annihilating squadrons of Royal Air Force planes—mostly Brewster Buffaloes—still parked on the tarmac aprons of their Singapore or Jahor airbases. The *Nips* methodically took out Britain's mighty tools of war, her fortifications and her strategic centers of communication and government.

Resistance from the overwhelmed Brits was notoriously pathetic. The official British surrender finally came on January 31, 1942. The Japanese renamed Singapore *Syonan-to*, City of Light, and within a month or two their military police had killed up to 50,000 civilians in the *Sook Ching* purge of ethnic Chinese from Penang to Singapore, claiming they were plotting a revolt against the occupying forces. Thousands of Europeans, mainly British civil servants and troops were locked up in Changi jail at the eastern end of Singapore Island, where the nation state's proud airport now thrives.

So much for Fortress Singapore!

Singapore, the fortified trading hub had been there as the eastern cornerstone of the known world's trade for 800 years, a major port of call on the ancient maritime silk route. Temasek, meaning Sea Town in Javanese Malay, or Singapura (Sanskrit for Lion City) became part of the Sultanate of Johor in the early 16th century. It was burned to the ground in 1613 by marauding Portuguese traders based in Malacca, the smaller rival settlement on the southwestern Malay coast. The British did not really make themselves seriously felt until early in the 19th century when Stamford Raffles and William Farquhar established a trading post for the British East India Company in 1819. At that time, they signed a treaty with the Sultan of Johor to legitimize London's dominant role in the development of what was to become today's flourishing, internationally influential city-state. Singapore was later folded into the British *Straits Settlement* colony, which was administered officially by the government of British India. Halfway through the 19th century the wonderful natural harbor was deepened and named Keppel Harbour; this eventually became the strategic East Asian base for His Majesty's acclaimed Royal Navy.

With the fall of Singapore, communications between Malaya and the Western World fell silent, including of course, those between *Mor* and *Far*. Every line had gone dead, but sparse and spasmodic communication with Europe was strangely still possible via Red Cross dispatches, which were the source of some news snippets regarding the family back home in Denmark.

In the spring of 1940, the Germans had turned their attention to Scandinavia. Sweden had declared neutrality, but the Nazis announced that Norway and Denmark had to be "protected from British attack" and proceeded to occupy Denmark on April 9, 1940, en route to taking Norway. The German fleet grouped in the Baltic and the North Sea while the little Danish navy was ordered by the government not to resist. German paratroopers started dropping into Denmark at 5:30 in the morning. The Danish army of less than 10,000 men was barely mobilized, and the only genuine fighting was limited to the region of northern Slesvig on the German border and skirmishes around Amalienborg, the royal residence when the Germans took Copenhagen. By 9:30 that same morning, the Danish government's surrender process was started. Varying reports of Danish lives lost point to numbers in the hundreds, including police and civil servants. Hitler had secured strategic locations for his airbases along the North Sea coastline of Jutland as well as the supply routes for German imports of essential Swedish steel. Seventy years later, Anders Fogh Rasmussen, former Danish Prime Minister and Secretary General of NATO, succinctly described the Danish government's position and reaction to the invasion as "morally unjustifiable."

Months went by while the evacuee families in Barwon Heads waited in limbo. The broadcasts and news stories became ever more distressing. Nerves were hardly calmed by Canberra's announcement of mandatory blackout disciplines and emergency coastal evacuation plans after reports of

Japanese U-boat sightings off the shores of Queensland, Victoria and New South Wales. There was no news of PB or any of the other women's husbands. *Mor* knew that PB would stay on the job on Jendarata Estate to prepare for the worst until it was no longer safe to do so. That of course worried her all day, every day, and through every night. The news of Singapore's fall told of brutal roundups of Europeans conducted by the Japs throughout Malaya, the men being thrown into the infamous Changi Jail, or sent north as forced labor for the Japanese occupiers, many dying of sheer exhaustion or disease on construction sites of the renowned Siam Railway. Women who had remained in Malaya were interned with their children in special camps around the country, sometimes after weeks of marching from one location to another under the blazing tropical sun, deprived of shelter, food, and water. *Mor* and the other commune women, although spared the marches, were on the other hand tortured by nightmare images of their men on the run, or captured and starving in Changi—or dead.

The Red Cross's erratic overseas communication from Denmark brought distressing news. *Mor* received word from her sister that their mother, or my *mormor* as Danes call their maternal grandmothers, had died of a broken heart. She had lost her husband, my *morfar*, soon after the German occupation. *Mor's* sister with my half-Jewish cousin, Lone, had fled from the Copenhagen Gestapo to Sweden, helped by Danish fishermen who smuggled them (and about 8,000 thousand Jews) across the sound, *Oresund*, and the *Kattegat* to the Swedish coast. Aunt Harriet's Jewish husband, Uncle Aage Schoch, was a senior journalist and one of the founding leaders of the coordinated resistance movement in Denmark. The SS were looking for these families in order to prepare for the *Endlösung*, "the final solution." They caught *Onkel Aage* and locked him up on the attic floor of Gestapo Headquarters in Copenhagen's *Shell House*, which had been commandeered and taken over from the oil company. *Mormor* had thus been left totally isolated and alone in Nazi-occupied Denmark until she simply could take it no longer. After the war, an old friend and nursing colleague told my mother that *Mormor* had actually taken her own life.

At last, one of the Barwon Heads commune women got word that her husband had somehow landed safely in distant Brisbane. That reunited family, so favored by Lady Luck, immediately moved elsewhere. The remaining women could not suppress their jealousy over the good fortune of the couple. There was thinly disguised bitterness in the farewells as the lucky family departed Barwon Heads. Why couldn't they all be that fortunate? But reality had to be faced, and the remaining women buckled up and continued to work well together, so there was never any shortage of food, fuel, or clothing, thanks in part to generous Australian customers who, whenever they could, bought their produce, eggs, and chickens from the commune rather than the local shops. The Aussies stopped at nothing in their efforts to support the *pommies,* as the Australians characterized the Brits suddenly injected into their normally homogeneous Australian community. Other foreign women were also the beneficiaries of this rough and ready kindness.

> "Good on ya, sheila! Bonza greeens and stuff you're producing—they're reeelly dinkum freesh! Same for ya chick'ns 'n eeegs."

> "We're reeely happy to look aahfta ya here in Austrile-ya! Yo're a graaait bunch o' shielas, and we jus' love ya kids, bless'em."

> "Chin up, mite, you'll all be Ow Kai in good time! Thaooze little yella-bellied, slit-oyed baahrstards will be good'n fucked before they knaoo what 'appened to'em! Bluddy Nips! Mark moy words!"

The British military performance throughout East Asia had been criminally inept and pathetic. Vainglorious Singapore of the 1930s, the British government, the British Colonial Service, the Royal Air Force and the Royal Navy were all totally discredited. Their inflated reputations, their frothy pomp and pride popped like soap bubbles along with their pretensions. The western world was stunned. Even the isolationist United States was shocked at the fall of Singapore, but not immediately enough to shake their own isolationist complacency in the face of Japanese aggression in their shared Pacific Ocean. Nor did they react to advances of the Hitler-Mussolini Axis in Europe and North Africa. In fact, prior to Pearl Harbor, Roosevelt had been persuaded by his political advisers to stay clear of a war, which "was a European problem in which America had no part."

With Siam, Malaya, and Burma conceded and India now threatened, the British were way back on their heels. Southeast Asia was in utter turmoil as the Empire of the Rising Sun raped the region, its brutal imperial forces crushing the territory like a steamroller.

Civilized Europe, East and West, was also being steamrollered by Hitler's Huns. Neville Chamberlain, that spineless, pontificating proponent of appeasement, had at last been succeeded by Winston Churchill as Prime Minister of the United Kingdom. The new leadership was the only good news around as the British Isles faced a seemingly inevitable German invasion. The Vichy government in Paris had cuddled up to their Nazi invaders while they, with equal cowardice, courted the Japanese in Indochina. For *Mor* and the family an excruciating wait lay ahead. Thousands of mothers and wives suffered this tortured apprehension and traumatic fear of the unknown in World War II, most of them with extraordinary courage and tenacity. It is a sad inequity that their particularly distinct, yet crucial, role in protecting our western civilization has never been adequately recognized. No decorations or medals for these moms and wives. *Mor* would have deserved a big one. She exhibited a stiff upper lip to match that of any Brit.

If you enjoyed the excerpt, you can buy your copy of *Odyssey Uncharted* at your favorite Internet Retailer.

Lightning Source UK Ltd.
Milton Keynes UK
UKHW041843161019
351750UK00002B/32/P